AMIS & SON

Neil Powell's previous books include *George Crabbe:
An English Life* (2004), *The Language of Jazz* (1997) and
Roy Fuller: Writer and Society (1995), as well as six collections
of poetry, the most recent of which is *A Halfway House* (2004).
He is Co-ordinating Editor of *PN Review* and writes for the
Sunday Telegraph and the *Times Literary Supplement*.
He lives in Suffolk.

Also by Neil Powell

At the Edge

Carpenters of Light

A Season of Calm Weather

True Colours

The Stones on Thorpeness Beach

Roy Fuller: Writer and Society

The Language of Jazz

Selected Poems

George Crabbe: An English Life

A Halfway House

Neil Powell

AMIS & SON

TWO LITERARY GENERATIONS

PAN BOOKS

First published 2008 by Macmillan

First published in paperback 2009 by Pan Books
an imprint of Pan Macmillan Ltd
Pan Macmillan, 20 New Wharf Road, London N1 9RR
Basingstoke and Oxford
Associated companies throughout the world
www.panmacmillan.com

ISBN 978-0-330-44072-1

Typeset by SetSystems Ltd, Saffron Walden, Essex
Printed in the UK by CPI Mackays, Chatham ME5 8TD

B
AMI

For Sargy and Frances Mann

'Not bad for a boy from Norbury, eh?'

Kingsley Amis to Julian Barnes, *c.* 1984

'Hey,' I said. 'Your dad, he's a writer too, isn't he? Bet that made it easier.'

'Oh, sure. It's just like taking over the family pub.'

Martin Amis, *Money*, 1984

Contents

Preface xi

1. THE ANGRY CHILD 1

2. THE JAZZ AGE 23

3. JIM AND THE 1950s 63

4. THE SEA CHANGE 126

5. FOLKS THAT LIVE ON THE HILL 211

6. MARTIN AND THE MODS 257

7. RACHEL AND THE 1970s 293

8. THE STATE OF ENGLAND 325

9. FATHERS AND SONS 358

ACKNOWLEDGEMENTS 377

NOTES 379

SELECT BIBLIOGRAPHY 407

INDEX 413

Preface

Some books begin with questions to which the author already knows the answers; this book began with unanswered ones. I wanted to explore the way in which two novelists of adjacent generations who set out with apparently similar intentions – to write comic or satirical fiction about the way we live now – end up with such disparate results. That these two novelists are father and son adds one kind of special piquancy to the project; that the two generations are also my parents' and mine adds another (my mother was born in the same year as Kingsley Amis; I was born a year before Martin Amis). Wrapped up in this starting-point is a somewhat broader question: how did the experience of becoming a writer in England during the 1940s and 1950s differ from its parallel a generation later, during the 1960s and 1970s? Although I began with some suspicions about which of these two I'd find the more engaging and sympathetic, I didn't reach a settled conclusion until quite near the end.

In fact, my sense of *Amis & Son: Two Literary Generations* altered a good deal as I went along. Another distinction: some books turn out almost exactly as planned, which is a matter of uncanny prescience or stunning luck; others change and evolve, and only an abnormally thick-skinned or dull-brained author will try to prevent them from doing so, since that must entail a refusal to learn from what he's reading and thinking. This book's shape was modified as I worked on it by both internal and external factors, which affected each of my main two subjects; but before I briefly describe these factors, I need to say a word about *names*. The contemporary tendency to call strangers by their first names strikes me as unfortunate – both presumptuous and nuance-destroying – but in this book I've really no choice about chummily referring to father and son as 'Kingsley' and 'Martin': to give each his full name for 400 pages or so would have been unbearably cumbersome for the reader and added several pages more. Family members and one or two close friends are treated similarly, for consistency of tone and to avoid clashes of forename and surname within phrases. The one deliberate inconsistency concerns Philip Larkin, who is 'Philip' throughout his early friendship with Kingsley but who has to become 'Larkin' once Kingsley's son Philip is old enough for possible ambiguities to occur.

Zachary Leader's *The Life of Kingsley Amis* appeared when my own 'Kingsley' chapters were well advanced; I've gratefully used it to correct and add a number of details, all of which are identified and acknowledged in my notes. In fact, Zachary Leader and I had met over a year earlier, talked about our respective books and cheerfully agreed that they were quite distinct sorts of project. His astonishingly comprehensive biography has allowed me to do exactly what I wanted – which is to be much more selective about the life and instead to concentrate on a rather different reading of Kingsley's fiction. I agree with Martin when he says that 'the fit reader, the ideal reader, regards a writer's life as just an interesting extra'. With a dead author, this interesting extra – being closed and complete – may be worth some careful attention for the light it throws on his work, which is also closed and complete. With a living author, the case is quite different. For one thing, both life and work remain in a state of much greater fluidity: our guesses about what may or may not turn out to be significant must be far more provisional. For another, I have a possibly unfashionable understanding of the word 'impertinence', and I believe it's impertinent for the biographer or critic to poke his nose into those aspects of a living author's privacy where his nose is least welcome. Martin's only replies to my several letters have been brief factual answers to a couple of questions; and, although (as people as differently close to him as Elizabeth Jane Howard and Zachary Leader have told me) he's a famous non-correspondent, I think I've deduced that he doesn't want to be more closely associated with this book. I've done my best to respect his wishes as far as personal intrusion is concerned; again, this coincides with my own instincts.

The incompleteness which surrounds the living author has one further shaping consequence that I hadn't at first foreseen. The very recent past is hardly more solid than the present and the future: what a writer publishes next month may drastically alter our view of something he wrote a couple of years ago, while recent biographical background is only likely to be of interest to the gossip-columnist. So I've decided to end the main body of this book in 1995, the year of Kingsley's death, after which Martin's work begins to move off in new and (so far) confusing directions: I glance at these more briefly in my final chapter, 'Fathers and Sons'. That also seems the right place for some more personal reflections which follow from the book which precedes them.

One last point. Publishers and booksellers, journalists and librarians all have an entirely understandable desire to place books in categories which don't necessarily correspond to divisions inside the reader's (or the writer's) head. To call this a 'literary biography' might imply a claim of biographical completeness for which I haven't aimed; 'critical biography' is a bit better, as long as it's remembered that 'criticism' here includes appreciative advocacy; 'study' would be nicely non-committal, were it not for its misleading hint of interminably footnoted and secondary-sourced academia. I actually quite like to think of the books around me as primarily just books, so my hope is that this is a decently interesting book about Kingsley and Martin Amis.

N.P.
May 2007

1. THE ANGRY CHILD

1

Kingsley Amis's earliest childhood home – 16 Buckingham Gardens, Norbury, SW16 – is the right-hand one of a pair, on the corner where the shabby suburban lane widens into a little green. It has dirty white pebbledash walls and hazy windows; outside, there's an unkempt privet hedge and a straggling yellow rose, feebly blooming in early November. The house looks unoccupied; it is certainly unloved, except by the local council, which has affixed a green plaque stating that Sir Kingsley Amis was born here (which he wasn't) and rather curiously insisting that he used the Norbury Library. The adjacent grassed space has a pair of unmatched signs saying 'No Ball Games', as if such were likely or possible, though the sentiment might have pleased Kingsley's father, the keenly prohibitive William Robert Amis. Even if Buckingham Gardens hasn't gone down in the world much since the Amises lived here, it hasn't come up; only one of the houses shows the slightest hint of ownerly gentrification, and it looks out of place. The air carries a strong and unmistakable whiff of curry, which Kingsley mightn't in one sense have minded (it was among the few foods he actually enjoyed), though in another he'd have minded quite a bit: he was no racist, but he strongly disliked the quality of English life being mucked about.

Almost directly opposite No. 16, a short footpath leads through to Norbury Avenue, the wider residential road which runs parallel with the railway line: he'd have heard the trains at home. From here, as from the Amises' subsequent houses in Ena Road and Galpins Road, it's a manageable walk to Norbury Station, gabled like a village primary school, for the train journey which Kingsley and his father shared each morning – he on his way to the City of London School on Victoria Embankment, his father to the offices of Colman's Mustard in Cannon Street; William Amis didn't possess a car, though one or two of his neighbours did, and would surely have asserted that he had no need of one. 'Norbury', wrote Kingsley, 'is not a place. When in the early part of the century the railways started building from London to the southern and south coast towns they put a station down every few miles, on the reasoning of various entrepreneurs that such places would form centres for the new population that would be coming to work in London. This proved correct.'[1] The result was 'Two-up-and-two-down by the hundreds of yards ... and shops along the High Street (or "main road").' He gives a version of this piece of social history to his character Stanley Duke in *Stanley and the Women*: 'Half the parts south of the river were never proper places at all, just collections of assorted buildings filling up gaps and named after railway stations and bus garages.'[2] Supplying a 'potted biography' for a correspondent in 1956, Kingsley expunged Norbury completely and offered this disingenuous alternative: 'Born 1922 in London, just about qualifying as a sound-of-Bow-Bells Cockney.'[3] Yet Norbury *is* a place, of a peculiarly South London sort, with its parade of tall, slightly fussy suburban shops along the A23 London Road and its tree-lined residential 'Avenues', 'Crescents' and 'Gardens'. What it lacks is anything at all in the way of landmarks, either historical or in any other way distinctive: you can see why, growing up there, Kingsley became habituated to indifference towards his external surroundings, a writer whose novels seldom possess more than the shakiest and most grudging sense of place. Nevertheless, as his friend Philip Larkin put it: 'Nothing, like something, happens anywhere.'

2

Kingsley's relatives amply compensated for the lack of eccentricity in his early surroundings: the notably high incidence of crazy old codgers in his fiction is also rooted in his childhood. His paternal grandfather, Joseph James Amis, was 'a jokey, excitable, silly little man'[4] from Norfolk, who until his retirement had been a wholesale glass merchant trading as J. J. Amis & Co.: the business was moderately successful, enabling Joseph and his wife Julia (*née* Spinks) – 'Pater' or 'Dadda' and 'Mater' to the family – to move from Denmark Hill to a house, with the misleadingly literary name of Barchester, in Purley, then still a semi-rural part of Surrey. Dadda was, among other things, a tiresome prankster who on more than one occasion sought to demonstrate the unique quality of his revolutionary line in 'unbreakable' glassware by hurling items into the fireplace where, to no one's surprise but his own, they shattered like exploding grenades; this seems not to have troubled him in the least, even when he performed his unlucky stunt in front of important clients. Perhaps, indeed, his business acumen left something to be desired, for although Purley was a notch or two up from Denmark Hill, and a couple of notches more up from Norbury, Dadda and Mater remained notably parsimonious, seldom entertaining members of the family or anyone else. Kingsley recalled two instances of Mater's legendary meanness: before retiring for the night, she habitually left out two matches, the second in case the first broke, for the maid who lit the gas in the morning; and she would cut up and hang up the grocer's paper bags in the lavatory, causing one unfortunate occupant to 'cut his bottom on the lingering remains of an acid-drop'[5] – an economy also attributed, with identical consequences, to Jenny Bunn's 'hymn-singing grandmother' in *Take a Girl like You*.[6] (According to Kingsley's cousin John, the music critic and broadcaster, at a rare dinner party Mater provided five chops for six diners; but this sounds less like deliberate penny-pinching than the incompetence of an unpractised hostess.) They were an undeniably stingy and quite possibly dislikeable couple. Nevertheless, J. J. Amis could take a certain justifiable pride in his achievements as a self-made man from East Anglia who had survived in difficult times and who, with his wife, had established the Amises as a minor South London dynasty. His somewhat obtuse tenacity and wayward sense of humour would prove to be inheritable family traits.

Dadda and Mater had four children: three sons – William, James and Leslie – and a daughter, Gladys. The parallel careers of William and James, alike in so many ways yet always tilted in the latter's favour, provide one clue to the slightly pinched, disgruntled flavour of life at Buckingham Gardens. Both worked in the City of London, but while William was a clerk – albeit quite an important one, fluent in Spanish and responsible for exporting mustard to South America – earning £500 a year at Colman's, James held a post in the merchant bank of Seligmann Brothers in Austin Friars at a substantially higher salary (reduced after the Wall Street crash, but even then a respectable £800 a year). Both lived in South London, yet James's house in Selsdon Road, West Norwood, was perceptibly sturdier than William's, 'a semi-detached, red-brick affair with a laburnum and a lilac in the front garden, a little lawn at the back with vegetables and a loganberry bush at the bottom'.[7] Both had sons born in the same year, 1922: Kingsley attended undistinguished, long-vanished local schools before following his father and uncles to the City of London School, where he couldn't have remained without winning a scholarship, when he was twelve; his cousin John went, fully paid for, to Dulwich College Preparatory School and then on to Dulwich College itself. During the 1920s, the Norbury Amises took their annual holiday at Pevensey in Sussex; the West Norwood Amises took theirs at Saint-Briac in Brittany. William was a keen sportsman, who played tennis 'well into middle age' and as a cricketer 'actively skippered the local side in his sixties', but James was all this and more: a tireless leisure-time all-rounder, 'occupied by rehearsals for plays, committee meetings, tennis in the summer or gardening or a bonfire. Therefore,' wrote his son John, 'I loved him best. He was fun.'[8] Kingsley said that his father thought himself a failure, and it's easy to see why: he was outflanked by his brother James at every move. Yet John Amis doesn't now remember 'any feeling of social difference between Norbury and West Norwood. We both lived in dreary houses in dreary streets.'[9]

Leslie, however, was another matter: 'the only one of my senior paternal relatives to show me interest or affection',[10] according to Kingsley, who was fond of him. Unlike his brothers, he remained unmarried and went into the family business; consequently, after Dadda's death it fell to him to take care both of J. J. Amis & Co. and of Mater in their respective declining years. Mother and son moved to Warlingham, where Leslie endured a miserable commuter's life, stopping each evening on his way home at a pub near the station to fortify himself for the ordeal ahead. In summer, after supper, he would drive Mater to another pub, where she would remain in the car and drink port; perhaps it was passed through the window to her as if she were the frog in Beatrix Potter. Leslie thought himself homosexual and confided as much to his brother William, though whether he put this hypothesis to the test is unknown. When, however, Mater eventually died, 'a large dreadful hairy-faced creature' aged almost ninety, Leslie took off on a world cruise and discovered a vigorous and previously unsuspected heterosexual self.

Then, having 'fucked every female in sight' for a couple of years, he died. Kingsley claimed that this progress sounded like a story by Somerset Maugham, whereas to anyone else Leslie sounds much more like a character in Kingsley Amis.

So, and for a good reason, does the last of Dadda and Mater's children, Gladys. Mater attempted, at the very last minute, to prevent her daughter's marriage to Ralph Foster, a professor at Harvard. The attempt failed and the Fosters escaped, no doubt gratefully, from South London to Massachusetts, where they had two children (Bobbie and Rosemary) before Ralph died, aged only thirty-six, while watching a baseball match. Kingsley incorporated this story, retaining the names Gladys and Ralph Foster, in *The Old Devils*, with a crisp explanation of Mater's obstructionist motive: 'What was interesting was her reason for being against the American. He was American.'[11] However, he altered Gladys's maiden name to 'Ungoed-Thomas' and turned the incident into an anecdote illustrating the incurable cussedness of the Welsh. Although there was nothing actually Welsh about his family, Kingsley would discover a deep temperamental affinity with Wales and feel Swansea to be the place outside London where he was most at home: the Amis brand of cussedness transplanted well there, as both *That Uncertain Feeling* and *The Old Devils* demonstrate.

Kingsley's mother, Rosa Annie (*née* Lucas), was almost a local. Her father, George, had been a tailor's assistant in Brixton and organist at the Denmark Place Baptist Chapel, which is where she met and, in June 1915, married William Amis; as she had been named after a pair of alcoholic aunts, she preferred to be called Peggy. George Lucas was the only grandparent for whom Kingsley cared: 'He liked and collected books, real books, poetry books, had lined part of a room in his little Camberwell house with them.' Since this was the one instance of literary cultivation in the family, it was properly honoured by the bookish grandson; but George's wife Jemima (*née* Sweetland), who resembled 'one of those horrible little old women dressed in black who used to sit on walls or outside shops on the Continent', had no time for her husband's books. As he read his favourite passages aloud to her, a somewhat misguided occupation, 'she would make faces and gestures at him while his head was lowered to the page'.[12] Kingsley's dislike of her intensified when his hope of inheriting his grandfather's library was thwarted: on his death, she allowed him to choose five volumes, insisting that he wrote 'from his grandfather's collection' on each flyleaf, a gesture which managed to combine meanness and sanctimoniousness in about equal proportions.

There were two other Lucas children, apart from Peggy. George 'had curly hair and was a postman', an occupation which Kingsley suspected was too proletarian to permit social intercourse with his parents (who, not having that much class to be conscious about, were all the more class-conscious). Dora, the younger of the two sisters by five years, had formerly been a professional singer, married to a vanished Arthur Mackness, but later lived with her widowed mother in Lowth Road, Camberwell, where Peggy and Kingsley paid dutiful weekly visits. She was thought to be 'off her head': one recurrent symptom of this, apart from her lack of make-up and generally dowdy appearance, was her obsessional collecting of dead matches which she would then hold beneath the scullery tap for thirty seconds before disposing of them; she also imagined strangers lurking in the tiny flower-filled back garden and suffered from other not very serious neurotic delusions. Eventually, however, she was confined to an institution, where her culinary and organisational skills made her an indispensable helper in the kitchen. It was there that she learnt of her mother's death and all her symptoms of mental illness instantly disappeared. She was formally transferred to the catering staff, a move which proved so successful that at the time of her own death she was about to take over responsibility for catering at one of the major London teaching hospitals. As with Uncle Leslie, her own self-discovery had been dependent on her release from an oppressive parent, a motif which was to recur in her nephew's novels.

3

In this company, William and Peggy seemed not at all odd, just culpably dull. Their relationship had begun and continued in the steadiest possible manner: they were children when they first met at the Baptist Chapel, and their marriage took place while the twenty-six-year-old Able Seaman Amis was on leave from the Royal Naval Air Service at East Fortune in Scotland, where he worked on airship maintenance ('a cushy one, if you like', his son remarked). William –

whose height of 5 foot 8 inches or so was average for his generation and who 'had a decent big nose that caused him, so he said, to be occasionally mistaken for a Jew by Jews'[13] – was thus thirty-three by the time his only child, Kingsley William Amis, was born on 16 April 1922 in a nursing home off Clapham Common: old enough for a naturally cautious and intransigent character to have become immovably staid. His son thought him 'the most English human being I have ever known'. The seven-year delay between his parents' marriage and Kingsley's birth, together with the absence of any siblings, may suggest that one or other parent wasn't keen on sex; that Peggy was reluctant first to undergo and then to repeat the trauma of childbirth; or that they decided their modest means could support only one child. Whatever the reason, being an only child shaped the pressures and emphases of Kingsley's early years: a triangular, dialectical relationship evolved, in which William issued prohibitive edicts and non-negotiable opinions, Peggy interceded with temporising amendments, and Kingsley learned to play the two off against each other until some sort of bearable compromise was eventually reached.

The only child is also, among other things, the angry child – though not always in quite the ways a siblinged observer might suspect. 'An only child is short not so much of allies, of supporters, as of means of dilution and diversion, another body to share the weight of parental care,' wrote Kingsley in 'A Memoir of my Father'. 'This isolation may make him over-ready to defend his interests.'[14] He also carries the entire burden of parental ambitions and is the sole repository of his parents' hopes and fears. Fourteen-year-old Peter Furneaux in *The Riverside Villas Murder* – the first of two boys in Kingsley's novels who share their author's background and chronology – puts it in slightly different terms: 'Being an only child did not mean that you were by yourself too much; on the contrary, you got the whole of your parents reserved for just you instead of divided up into three, say.'[15] Kingsley combined intellectual ambition and arrogance with a generous helping of his father's obstinacy, a mixture guaranteed 'to launch us regularly on one or another conversational collision course, immediately recognised as such by both, indeed by all, parties, but not to be deviated from at any price'.[16]

The great emblematic battleground between father and son was, as it so often is, music. William was fond of music, though it came after cricket and tennis in his enthusiasms; however, his taste –

centred on Gilbert and Sullivan and on Edwardian drawing-room
ballads, which he sang well – was precisely that least likely to appeal
to his son. John Amis remembers Kingsley's musical taste as being
'more advanced' than his own, including the Fourth Symphony of
Vaughan Williams and the Walton Viola Concerto,[17] and this interest
in music seems to have developed along two parallel tracks: as an
aspiring intellectual who reckoned he might teach his father a thing
or two, he favoured Haydn, Mozart and Schubert; meanwhile, as a
young rebel not averse to upsetting him, he was discovering jazz.
William contrived to be equally affronted in either case. 'My father's
catholic distaste', wrote Kingsley, 'ranged from Haydn to Troise and
his Mandoliers, from Benny Goodman to Borodin.' For William,
Sibelius's *The Swan of Tuonela* 'called up successive images of a
small animal in pain and a large animal in pain' while a quite
sophisticated piece of Duke Ellington's suggested 'a lot of savages
dancing round a pot of human remains'.[18] Such calculatedly infuriating comic descriptions will, of course, be very familiar to readers of
Kingsley's novels (the Ellington opinion is shared by Jenny Bunn's
father);[19] as a boy, it was the sheer nuisance value of his father's
obstructive disapproval that he mostly registered. High culture in
general, and serious music in particular, was regarded as suspect and
threatening, something not quite for them: another sort of class
distinction. By contrast, over in West Norwood, Cousin John was
encouraged both to practise the piano and to collect gramophone
records. His parents bought him 'a proper "table-model" gramophone'; he saved up his pocket money for the 'agonising but enthrall-
ing' choice between 'vocal gems from *Turandot*, the overture to *Die
Zauberflöte*, Liszt's *Hungarian Rhapsody No. 2*' and, encouraged by
his younger sister, jazz records too ('Fats Waller fascinated me, so did
Art Tatum . . .').[20] All this music in the home, like John's participation as a pianist in concerts at Dulwich, was a shared family
experience. William Amis must have been appalled as well as envious:
it was one more way in which he seemed to have been outclassed by
his brother.

One might expect two young cousins, of the same age and with
similar tastes in music, who lived not far apart, to have been
continually in and out of each other's houses, comparing notes and
swapping records. In fact, Kingsley and John seldom saw each other
– about once every school holiday is John's estimate. It wasn't that

their backgrounds were too different: they were too painfully adja-cent. They made much of the distance between SW16 and SE27 – 'a one-hour hike' is how Eric Jacobs puts it – but it wouldn't have discouraged two boys who actually wanted to know each other and it would have been no trouble at all on a bicycle. 'Kingsley never invited me to Norbury,' says John. 'His mother (Rosie to us) and my mother didn't get on, so Rosie wasn't going to invite me.'[21] Yet the fact that their respective mothers didn't get on could have been turned from an obstacle into a challenge and an incentive. No, the distance was a social and cultural one, and there isn't a more telling symbol of the way in which Kingsley felt himself shut in a particularly narrow and constrained lower-middle-class box than this. It was his loss. In their respective autobiographical reminiscences – Kingsley's *Memoirs* and John's 'Scenes from Childhood' in *Amiscellany* – each mentions the other precisely once, and only in passing.

It might have been instructive and reassuring if young Kingsley could have met two other exact contemporaries who shared many of his ambitions and frustrations. One, born in Barnsley on 17 July 1922, was Donald Alfred Davie; the other, born in Coventry on 9 August 1922, was Philip Arthur Larkin. Apart from their close-ness in age, the parallels between these three writers are striking: all were only children from essentially non-intellectual middle-class back-grounds (Larkin's sister Kitty, ten years older, was too distant to count: Kingsley would borrow this idea for *You Can't Do Both*); all were educated at grammar schools and went on to Oxbridge, where they at first felt socially ill at ease; all became members of the Movement and contributors to Robert Conquest's anthology *New Lines*. Naturally, the points at which these parallels diverge – and, in Davie's case, rupture irreparably – will in due course prove to be even more interesting.

The extent of Kingsley's boyhood social isolation may seem surprising, given the quite dense suburban texture of Norbury and the network of family connections across South London, but it was common enough among children of his background. When his parents weren't worrying about their own nagging sense of failure and inferiority, they would have been busy making sure that he didn't mix with children who were 'common': his early schools, chosen for their respectability rather than their educational distinction, were designed to reinforce just this buffer. St Hilda's was a shrubbery-

surrounded independent girls' school of the kind which also took
small boys, before they became pubescent and dangerous, in its junior
forms. There he became devoted to his English teacher, Miss Barr, 'a
tall, Eton-cropped figure of improbable elegance', and thus to literature. At Norbury College, a boys' prep school which by the time
Kingsley went there in 1929 had sprouted senior classes, he was first
taught English by the larger of two unrelated Messrs Waller, who
spent most of the time reading aloud books 'about the Great War
("I've copped it in the back, sir") or lethal espionage in Eastern
Europe ("For God's sake shoot me and have done with it")'.[22] It was
better than work, though not quite to young Kingsley's taste. He was
luckier with Mr Waller's younger successor, Mr Ashley, who introduced his charges to *The Merchant of Venice* and the almost contemporary Georgian poets. The school was 'just up the road', so Kingsley
came home to lunch, really only escaping from his domestic cocoon
for lessons.

He later described his 'environment and upbringing' as 'insular
almost to a fault' and 'fiercely non-crazy'.[23] Both his parents were
(from the best of motives) ludicrously overprotective: William wanted
his son to grow into a more successful version of himself, thereby
ensuring that he grew up to be one of the least businesslike men on
the planet; Peggy fretted about his diet, pushing forkful after forkful
into his unwilling mouth at mealtimes, plying him with supposedly
nutritious supplements such as 'Parrish's Chemical Food', and consequently putting him off the enjoyment of food for most of his life.
The truth, of course, is that much of what parents do for their
children will always turn out to be exactly counterproductive – all
the more so, perhaps, if the child decides to be a writer.

4

Every writer is a reader first, with the obvious exception of the
schoolboy who may be required to write before he has had a chance
to read anything much. A 300-word short story by Kingsley Amis
called 'The Sacred Rhino of Uganda' – it concerned an unlucky
hunter, Captain Hartly, who foolishly shot the eponymous animal
and was set upon by its 'native worshippers' – appeared in the school
magazine while its author was still at Norbury College. Fifty years

later, he remembered it well enough to describe its stylistic pitfalls (phrases such as 'Raging and cursing in the blazing heat') to his son Martin,[24] but only an ironist would have called it, as he did in *Memoirs*, 'my first published work of fiction'.[25] Otherwise, reading is what shapes writers, by suggesting the possibilities of the craft as well as its problems, and Kingsley's choice of books during his teenage years was to exert a lifelong influence on him.

Adolescents, he remarked in 1971, categorise works of literature as 'terrific or tripe': 'a boy either gobbles a book up or throws it away',[26] and the factors which prompt one reaction rather than the other are often mysterious. Moreover, there is no neat point of transition at which childish tastes vanish and are instantaneously replaced by grown-up ones; in Kingsley's case, the overlapping incongruities are especially intriguing. When we meet fourteen-year-old Peter Furneaux in *The Riverside Villas Murder*, he is engrossed in an adventure story in the *Wizard*: it is 'the kind of rubbish errand-boys read', according to his father, whom he must placate in order to prevent the comic being added 'to the catalogue of forbidden reading-matter, there to join the works of Aldous Huxley, W. Somerset Maugham and other unhealthy influences'.[27] And when, at the same age, Robin Davies in *You Can't Do Both* sets off to visit his relatives in Wales, he takes with him '*Just William*, *The Island of Dr Moreau*, Durell on algebra, *British Battleships*, a bound volume of *Chums* and, with a low growl of resignation, Bury's *History of Rome*'.[28] However, his older friend Jeremy Carpenter has already lent him W. H. Auden's *Poems* – Robin is puzzled by the references to 'Lawrence, Blake and Homer Lane, once healers in our English land' in XII and more deeply troubled by the phrase in XXX about 'the distortions of ingrown virginity' (can that really mean what he thinks it means?) – while failing to persuade him to borrow a novel by D. H. Lawrence: his parents, who have 'never read a word he's written but they know it's all filth',[29] wouldn't allow it in the house. These juxtapositions are very closely modelled on the author's own experience.

Kingsley was an avid reader of the *Magnet*, each issue of which included a 20,000-word story by 'Frank Richards' (the pen-name of Charles Hamilton) set in a public school called Greyfriars, where the most celebrated and very much the stoutest pupil was Billy Bunter. He continued to enjoy these well into his teens, despite their lack of resemblance to his own or anyone else's actual experience of school.

He also read H. G. Wells, sternly regarding *The War of the Worlds* as not 'grown-up'; on the other hand, G. K. Chesterton's *The Man Who Was Thursday* was 'the first grown-up novel I remember reading outside school', having arrived there 'by the way of the Father Brown stories' and going on to *The Napoleon of Notting Hill*. In *The Riverside Villas Murder*, he slyly shifts this part of his literary taste on to the middle-aged and ultimately admirable Colonel Manton. The scene in which his library is observed by Detective Constable Barrett, whose liking for 'serious stuff like biographies, history and war memoirs' mirrors that of William Amis and of Norbury College's 'Big' Mr Waller, tells us a good deal about the popular reading habits of 1936 (the year in which the novel is set) and about the author himself:

> At first glance, the collection was unprepossessing, the greater part still in their jackets (many of a garish yellow), the visible bindings cheap and often scuffed. The first authors' names Barrett happened to come across were unfamiliar: John Dickson Carr, John Rhode, Anthony Berkeley. Nor were the first titles any help: *The House of the Arrow*, *The Nine Tailors*, *The Incredulity of Father Brown* – fancy someone writing a whole book about a parson's incredulity. Then Barrett caught sight of *The Mysterious Affair at Styles*, by Agatha Christie, and knew where he was: he ought to have guessed the old boy would be a 'tec fan. Interesting, but a little disappointing – what fiction he had time for himself came from real authors like Hugh Walpole or J. B. Priestley. Across the room were a couple of rows of better-bound volumes, but he only had time to glimpse one title – *Medical Jurisprudence* – before Colonel Manton came briskly into the room.[30]

As is often the way with Kingsley's fiction of this vintage, the joker hints and nudges are a shade heavy-handed: the garish yellow jackets might belong to Collins' 'Crime Club', though he probably has in mind the distinctive livery of his own first major publisher, Victor Gollancz; Barrett's misunderstanding of Chesterton's title, which is meant to suggest his literal-mindedness, makes him sound a simpleton. But the points about literary taste are deftly made: the detective novels are approved of, as intelligent entertainment, perfectly appropriate for Colonel Manton's leisure; the slow-witted Constable, by contrast, manages to choose authors who are both middlebrow and dull.

When Kingsley 'gobbled up' *The Man Who Was Thursday* in 1935, he was thirteen years old; later, he would remember Chesterton's death the following year as 'the first total stranger's death that meant anything to me personally'.[31] The book's opening, in which a two poets discuss 'art and anarchism at an open-air party in a romantic setting under an extraordinary sunset', 'caught me by the scruff', he said. It was a lesson he thoroughly absorbed, for his novels invariably open with an obvious grab for the reader's attention, more often than not in the form of a conversation, and his passages of Jamesian elaboration or Proustian introspection occur deep into his books, if at all. He learnt too 'that the extraordinary is, if not the most ordinary thing in the world, as G.K.C. might have put it, then at least almost literally round the corner';[32] and he would also take heed of the flaws in *The Man Who Was Thursday* – the transparent improbabilities, the muddled seasons and the over-telescoped time-scale. It was, in fact, the perfect example of a book which, for the adolescent writer, began in entertainment and ended in instruction.

Like Peter Furneaux and Robin Davies – like all boys in their teens – Kingsley was also irresistibly drawn to anything which might, on grounds of taste or decency, be prohibited by his parents. In his case, this urge was quickened by the fact that William and Peggy were, even by the standards of their time, comically censorious: Kingsley remembered overhearing their next-door neighbour's 'very mild reference to somebody's honeymoon or some such depravity' when he was fourteen, at which his mother 'gave her a fierce (and absurdly visible) shake of the head'.[33] Luckily, there was Uncle Tommy: not an actual uncle but an admirer of Peggy's, whose respectable devotion (he once popped up while the family was holidaying on the North Norfolk coast) posed not the remotest threat to the Amises' marriage. Uncle Tommy, who would present Kingsley with a Mars bar whenever he appeared, subscribed to *John o'London's*, a literary weekly later merged into *Time and Tide*, and owned plenty of books, some of them in the Tauchnitz series which, like the Olympia Press, published works considered too risky by British firms. *Lady Chatterley's Lover* wasn't among them, Kingsley discovered; when he did read it he was disappointed on two counts, finding it insufficiently salacious and disliking Lawrence as a novelist. But Aldous Huxley's *Point Counter Point* was there and, as 'a then almost equally illustrious monument of supposed filth', self-recommending: that, however, supplied 'the greatest literary disappointment I have ever suffered'. It was 'grown-up *in the wrong way*, never getting to the point' and 'about as arousing as the *Magnet*'.[34] Huxley and the *Wizard*, apparently so incompatible in their shared danger of being consigned to 'the catalogue of forbidden reading', had more in common than Peter Furneaux's father could possibly have imagined.

Kingsley's literary tastes, especially in poetry, were further shaped by two masters at the City of London School. The first of these was Mr Marsh, from whom 'you could borrow Auden and MacNeice . . . but I made nothing of them at that time, 1936–37'.[35] His bafflement would certainly have resembled Robin Davies's, yet he must also have felt that these two writers were, like Huxley, insufficiently swift in 'getting to the point'; elements of Auden's prosody, in the more sprawling early poems, would have bothered him too. In this, he differed sharply from his future friend Philip Larkin who, coming across Auden at school, not only read him but was strongly influenced by him. It was a relief for Kingsley when Marsh was succeeded by 'the man who taught me most, about English literature among other things', the Reverend C. J. Ellingham: he was the sort of teacher, more common in the post-war years than in the 1930s (and since then, of course, snuffed out by the National Curriculum), who reckoned that the syllabus could largely take care of itself and instead devoted much of his time to ensuring 'that we did not remain totally ignorant of classical music, painting, and English poetry outside the official courses'.[36] His favourite poet was A. E. Housman. Kingsley 'came to share Mr Ellingham's preference and eventually retain it even in face of Larkin's work', a judgement which goes some way towards explaining why his own poetry differs in tone from the Auden- and Empson-influenced work of his 1950s Movement contemporaries. Not that Mr Ellingham's taste was wholly reliable. For instance, he admired T. E. Lawrence's *Seven Pillars of Wisdom*, a book which Kingsley at the time decided he was 'not well-read or clever enough to appreciate', although he would subsequently come to regard it as 'a piece of pretentious bullshit'.[37]

Many of the adult writer's enduring tastes and habits are already evident here: a preference for direct, lively narrative connected with everyday life and a corresponding suspicion of writing which seems pointlessly inflated or difficult; an interest in genres such as detective and science fiction; and a fondness for intelligible poetry using conventional prosodic structures. But, both before and alongside the stimuli Kingsley received from outside the family, there was one source of literary encouragement at home – his mother. Peggy remained an enthusiastic reader throughout her life, her determinedly middlebrow taste steering as clear of classics as of sensationalism. Her son wrote that 'the names of Norah C. James and Ann Bridge come to mind', now forgotten except by historians of popular fiction but typifying a kind of writing which was enormously popular before social change in general, and television in particular, pushed it aside. This in itself might actually have dampened Kingsley's literary ambitions but, as he said, there were other ways in which she got him started as a writer, such as 'not producing a sibling for me, restricting my choice of companions, having had a father with a literary bent, suggesting on rainy afternoons when I had no book or comic to read – quite innocently and without premeditation, I am sure – that I should do a bit of writing'.[38]

5

William's decision to send his son to the City of London School in 1934 was at once cautious and reckless. He had been a pupil there himself, as had his two brothers, so it was hardly an adventurous choice, but it was risky in the sense that he simply couldn't afford it. The fees of £90 per year, plus travelling and other expenses, added up to almost a quarter of his modest annual salary. He gambled on Kingsley's ability to win a scholarship in his second year and his confidence was, fortunately, justified. Such risk-taking seems as dramatically out of character as the apparent intention to make Kingsley's intellectual development his first priority, but William would also have been driven by more conservative impulses: by his conviction that the son should follow in his father's footsteps and also by his determination not to be utterly outdone by his brother James. Moreover, in choosing the safe familiarity of CLS, he thought he was ensuring that his son, while receiving a proper eduction, didn't get too far above himself. This was a decent school which had been good enough for him and he evidently preferred it – despite the daily commuting by train it entailed – to Whitgift or Trinity, the academically distinguished schools nearby in Croydon.

But CLS had altered since William's day. F. R. Dale, the head-master appointed in 1931, had high academic ambitions for his school. Among his introductions to this end was a system of academic streaming, with an 'A' or express stream enabling bright boys to progress faster and thus allowing them more time in the sixth form to prepare for Oxbridge scholarships (the corollary, that duller pupils would benefit from taking their time, undaunted by the presence of high-flyers, is arguably more questionable). Boys were also grouped into three 'sides' – classical, modern or science – according to preference and ability. Dale seems to have embodied the ideal head-masterly balance of discipline and humanity. As T. B. Williamson, his first Captain of School, recalled: 'Here was a man, we felt, who would stand no nonsense. Within a few months we had revised our opinion on this point. Under this Head there would be little if any nonsense to stand.'[39] His firmness was matched by a fairness which included such startlingly progressive innovations as a school council, called the Boys' Representative Assembly, whose democratically reached decisions he would wherever possible endorse. He may have shrewdly realised that such bodies, if they take themselves seriously, are likely to prove conservative rather than revolutionary in character: for example, it was the Assembly, rather than the headmaster, which proposed the adoption of a notably formal, neo-Etonian school uniform – black coat and striped trousers in winter, jauntily lightened by blazer and boater in summer. Above all, Dale was an outstanding classical scholar: 'To hear him read Greek verse, observing tonic accent, metrical ictus and the run of the meaning all at once, was to be given a distant view of some ideal beauty as well as to marvel at a virtuoso.'[40] He was chosen by the BBC as the finest available reciter of Greek to read Homer aloud on the Third Programme, in the days when such civilised and civilising things were still possible. Kingsley felt for him a 'terrified veneration' and became an enthusiastic member of the classical 'A' stream. This was not precisely the solid grounding for a business career that William had originally envisaged.

In fact, at the City of London School, Kingsley received a very good academic education in a remarkably civilised environment. 'It was an excellent school, not just for the teaching but for the big cross-section you got of the social strata,' he told William Van O'Connor in 1958. 'One of my friends was a Jew from the poor quarter of London's East End; another was the son of a prominent

Church dignitary. But you just didn't know what most boys' fathers were: your status depended on your amiability.'[41] This social and religious diversity was partly due to the generous number of scholarships available to pupils from inner London. After the announcements at morning assembly, but before the Anglican hymns and prayers, the senior Jewish boy would lead from the hall 'the others of his faith, the Roman Catholics and the Dissenters'. As an agnostic from a lapsed Baptist family, Kingsley might have conjured up two reasons for joining them but stayed, partly because he enjoyed the singing. He guessed that around 15 per cent of the pupils were Jewish, yet – apart from the one moment when the Regimental Sergeant Major barked 'What's your religion?' at a boy called Richenberg, at which 'it was as if every Gentile in hearing had turned white' – he remembered 'not a single instance of even the mildest anti-semitism';[42] and this, in a school containing so diverse a range of London adolescents in the 1930s, is a more remarkable achievement than it may at first seem. When the school's official historian, A. E. Douglas-Smith, claimed in 1937 that 'the anti-Semitism of Fascist countries is incomprehensible to boys who have made their life's friendships in the School',[43] he was telling no more than the truth.

CLS was a tolerant place in other ways which suited the self-contradictory nature of young Amis. There was naturally an Officers' Training Corps, but it wasn't compulsory; 'pacifists and other freaks' (as the old rogue coat-trailingly had in it *Memoirs*) could opt out. Kingsley, of course, opted in and thoroughly enjoyed the uniforms, the parades, the summer camps and above all the shooting: he was a first-class shot who seriously thought of joining the army if he failed to become a writer. Games, on the other hand, he mostly loathed and mostly skipped, on the pretext that the school's sports ground was inconveniently situated at Grove Park, and no one greatly bothered about it; but he would have liked to have been better than his 'lazy' right eye allowed him to be at cricket. Once in the sixth form, he could go out to lunch at the Lyons' near Blackfriars Bridge and, while others played football, he would visit the cinema (which he enjoyed) or the theatre (which, apart from Shakespeare, he never grew to love) or write poems, among them a lengthily Eliotic 'Prelude' ('a kind of suburbanite's *Waste Land* tizzied up with bits of Wilde')[44] which found its way into the school magazine. There was also a 'school parliament', for which Kingsley stood as a Communist.

In his short biography of Kipling, a book which slyly discloses a good deal about its author, Kingsley Amis writes of his subject being packed off to the United Services College at Westward Ho! in Devon: 'Rudyard was to be sent to school in earnest. His luck held, in the sense that his early life continued to be quite different from that of any other writer; in the ordinary sense, his luck was out again, at least to begin with.'[45] The first crucial point is that the childhood experiences which shape a future writer may be diametrically opposed to those which are good 'in the ordinary sense'; the second is that Kingsley felt that his own young life had been far too ordinary. The worst that could be said of his childhood at home was that it was dull and mildly oppressive; while CLS was, as schools go, almost infuriatingly civilised and tolerant. As a natural rebel, Kingsley found himself continually presented with targets which were far too soft. Moreover, both the character of CLS itself and its distance from Norbury reinforced the social vacuum which his parents had already created for him. Unlike boys such as Donald Davie and Philip Larkin who went to their local grammar school, he had no throng of school friends in his immediate vicinity, to whose homes he could gratefully escape (with the notable exception of a boy called Billy Mingo, the model for Peter's friend Reg in *The Riverside Villas Murder* and for Bobby Bailey in the poem named after him), and he equally lacked the traumatic formative experiences, the intense friend-ships and enmities, of those who were sent away to board, like Kipling, at peculiar and forbidding public schools. By comparison, his own life seemed so maddeningly *normal*: he was angry about the insufficiency of his causes for anger. This was no way to become a writer.

6

At lunchtime on Friday 1 September 1939, the same day that W. H. Auden sat 'in one of the dives / On Fifty-Second Street' to reflect on the expiring hopes of 'a low dishonest decade', the boys of City of London School assembled in crocodiles, marched to Blackfriars Station and there took the District Line to Ealing Broadway. With an organisational efficiency reminiscent of *Dad's Army*, they were then packed on to a waiting express bound for Taunton since, for reasons of security, no one had actually been told where they were supposed to be going. Arrangements were made to stop the train at Savernake, which was the nearest station to the boys' secret destination, Marlborough. There, the evacuation authorities found themselves coping, two hours earlier than scheduled, not only with a schoolful of stripey-trousered Londoners but also with a separate, unanticipated trainload of mothers with their babies. They had been expecting primary school children.

CLS had agreed its contingency plans for evacuation to Marlborough College a year earlier and was quick to implement them, two days before the declaration of war and also (scarcely less significantly to the schoolmasterly mind) in good time for the start of the new academic year. Marlborough was, astonishingly, able to offer teaching space and catering facilities – provided that the CLS boys lived a topsy-turvy existence which entailed eating while the Marlborough boys were in class and having lessons at lunchtime or after school – but it could hardly be expected to house 500 extra pupils. Nor could anyone else: Kingsley spent several nights in a barn, before being billeted with four other boys in an empty farm labourer's cottage, sharing a tiny room with Leonard Richenberg and supervised by Mr and Mrs Ellingham. There was no electricity or plumbing: the tin bath in the kitchen had to be filled with water heated on the stove; there was an earth closet in the garden. The only heating came from the living-room fire: during the icy winter of 1939–40, it was so cold in Kingsley's and Leonard's bedroom that their urine froze in the chamber-pot. If he had wished for release from the suffocating normality of Norbury, the train to Blackfriars and the long days on Victoria Embankment, his wish had been granted. But he hadn't expected it to be quite like this.

The experience was to change him, though not necessarily in ways which were predictable or permanent. Deprived both of his excuse about inaccessible playing-fields and of his father's counter-productive encouragement, he became, for the first and last time in his life, an active sportsman; he even managed to enjoy rugby and twice played for the school's First XV. For not wholly dissimilar reasons – liberation from his agnostic parents and from his habitual self-consciousness – he took up singing in the chapel choir: 'the apex of non-sensual pleasures',[46] he called it, and Marlborough's tremendous chapel would have supplied some acoustic assistance. Usually indifferent to his surroundings, he found himself observing – and remembering – the rural world around him, so that for years afterwards 'some image of Marlborough' would appear whenever he tried to envisage 'a generic country scene'. He became sociable in a new way, allowing the jokey façade of comic impressions (a knack inherited from his father) to drop in favour of more serious and sustained friendships with contemporaries such as Leonard Richenberg and Saul Rose as well as 'the great Ellingham himself' – a glimpse, in these rather surprising conditions, of the university life to come. Eric Jacobs, writing in 1995, spoke to several of Kingsley's sixth-form co-evacuees, all of whom remembered him as gregarious, popular, something of an intellectual star as well as a subversive comedian; he already did Jim Dixon's faces. But he resisted any temptation to run wild: he was, after all, a prefect and he behaved responsibly. Some CLS pupils, exploiting the lax regime of masters who had no previous experience in looking after 'boarders' of any sort, let alone those scattered in digs throughout the area, took off on minor sprees of petty criminality and sexual adventure. Kingsley didn't. Nor did he form any friendships with Marlborough College boys who, he found, contrived to extend their initial, unsurprising standoffishness almost indefinitely.

Like many clowningly arrogant adolescents – like many boozily sociable and contentious adults – Kingsley was extremely shy. The impersonations and the funny faces; the striking of contradictory attitudes at school; the relaxation into unexpected pleasures when away from home: all signal his personal insecurity and his quite effective strategies to cope with it. But in Kingsley's case the problem went well beyond ordinary youthful shyness and lack of self-confidence. He was already in the grip of deep-rooted phobias. At the age of ten, as a great treat, he had been given a 'five-bob flip' in a De Havilland Dragon Rapide from Croydon Aerodrome; the experience so terrified him that he never flew again. When his parents judged that he was old enough to be left without a babysitter – and he naturally assured them that he was – he would be terrified until their return; he hated being alone in a house for the rest of his life. In due course, his fears multiplied to encompass tube trains and cars (he could drive, but wouldn't), as well as any social occasions, especially dinner parties, where he might find himself trapped. The creativity-producing trauma and distress he detected, with something approaching envy, in Kipling's childhood was not, after all, so entirely absent from his own. And this is one of the keys to his novels: even the big, blustering, sexually predatory characters – Roger Micheldene, Roy Vandervane, Maurice Allington, Jimmie Fane – almost always have a hollow, terrified abyss within them; and when they don't (as, perhaps, Julian Ormerod in *Take a Girl like You* doesn't) they become extraordinary in some way that their author, or his surrogate consciousness within the book, seems to regard with astonished admiration.

With Kingsley, it is always worth considering the possibility that he is most vulnerable when he seems most assured. He was the outstanding Classicist of his year in an academically strong school which, thanks to Dale's headship, had acquired a reputation for excellence in Classics: he could have walked into a major scholarship at Oxford or Cambridge. Instead, he switched to English Literature, for which CLS had until then no teaching provision at this level and in which there were very few scholarships available at Oxbridge – two at each university, he thought. It looks like reckless, arrogant self-confidence, but it is the exact opposite. What if he *failed* to win his major scholarship in Classics or (as Oxonians call it) Greats? On the other hand, should he not succeed in something as quirkily eccentric as English Literature, for which his school-in-exile had no experience in preparing candidates, there would be no shame attached. So, in 1940, he travelled to Cambridge and sat the scholarship examination for St Catharine's College, without success; the successful candidate was a boy from Barnsley called Donald Davie. There was, however, an exhibition – 'a kind of cut-price scholarship'[47] – to be tried for at St John's College, Oxford. Kingsley sat the examination, was awarded the exhibition and, the war having already begun to disrupt the natural cycle of academic years, went up to Oxford in May 1941.

7

'If I had known it, the whole future must have lain all the time along those Berkhamsted streets,'[48] wrote Graham Greene, remembering the Hertfordshire town in which he grew up – and to which, coincidentally, the Amis family moved in the summer of 1940. It was the point at which Kingsley would have left school, had he not stayed on to prepare for his St John's exams, and Peggy was finding Norbury too worryingly near the flight path of German bombers. Greene's sentiment isn't, on the face of things, one which Kingsley might have been expected to share. Yet, in that revealing little book about Kipling, he writes, with what is surely a chime of inward identification: 'The circumstances of his early childhood in fact were uniquely valuable in his growth as a writer; without them, he would have been not only different but diminished.'[49] And in his final novel, *The Biographer's Moustache*, Jimmie Fane – one of those pompously obnoxious creations who thus become so much more effective as a disguise for authorial utterance – tells his biographer: 'Rightly or wrongly, and if I had to choose I should probably plump for rightly, a large and unchangeable part of each one of us is decided by the circumstances of our birth and the environment, to use the word correctly for once, in which we did the first part of our growing up.'[50] However much he liked to scorn the ordinariness of his own early years, Kingsley knew the truth of this. 'It is a sad fate to be the child of the urban or suburban middle classes,' he once remarked.[51] Yet he would come to recognise that there's no denying the complexities of the suburban soul.

2. THE JAZZ AGE

1

In the sly, funny and subtly disingenuous introduction which Philip Larkin wrote for the 1964 reissue of his Oxford-in-wartime novel *Jill* (originally published in 1946), he remembered his first meeting with Kingsley. It was at the start of Trinity Term in 1941. Kingsley had just come up to St John's – arrivals in mid-academic year were commonplace during the war – when Philip's friend Norman Iles, who had bumped into Amis when they were both trying for scholarships at Cambridge, spotted his name on a list in the porter's lodge. He was, said Iles, 'the hell of a good man', before incomprehensibly adding: 'He shoots guns.' Later that afternoon, when they spotted the fair-haired newcomer emerging from a college staircase, Iles 'instantly pointed his right hand at him in the semblance of a pistol and uttered a short coughing bark to signify a shot'. The stranger's reaction was immediate and impressive. 'Clutching his chest in a rictus of agony, he threw one arm up against the archway and began slowly crumpling downwards, fingers scoring the stonework. Just as he was about to collapse on the piled-up laundry ... he righted himself and trotted over to us.' Almost before the introductions were over, Kingsley was producing further effects, such as 'when you're firing in a ravine and the bullet ricochets off a rock'. 'For the first time,' wrote Philip, 'I felt myself in the presence of a talent greater than my own.'[1]

We needn't be fooled by this. The only talents in which he felt awed by Kingsley were those for comic effects and (a little later) apparent success with girls. Then, as Andrew Motion says, 'It was all very well for Kingsley to assure Philip that everyone had "difficulties with girls", but their difficulties were very different: Kingsley had girls; Philip didn't.'[2] When it came to the talent that mattered most, he had nothing to fear. But he seems to have been struck almost at once by the paradox at the heart of their relationship. In some respects they were very alike, in others utterly unalike, yet the unalikeness was so closely wedded to the likeness, as with the indivisible faces of a coin, that the two can seem barely distinguishable. Love, after all, is quite often like that. And, says Martin Amis: 'It was love, unquestionably love, on my father's part.' Philip, he adds, 'felt the same way, or rather he felt the Larkinesque equivalent'.[3] In a letter written some five years after their first meeting – by which time he was back at St John's after war service and Philip was a librarian in Shropshire – Kingsley tried to define the sympathetic understanding at the heart of their friendship: 'I enjoy talking to you more than to anybody else because I never feel I am giving myself away and so can admit to shady, dishonest, crawling, cowardly, brutal, unjust, arrogant, snobbish, lecherous, perverted and generally shameful feelings that I don't want anyone else to know about; but most of all because you are *savagely uninterested in all the things I am uninterested in*.'[4] His recasting of so positive a relationship in ironic and self-deprecating terms is a typical defensive ploy.

Kingsley Amis and Philip Larkin constitute one of English literature's notable double-acts: in this respect, they belong with Wordsworth and Coleridge or Auden and Isherwood. Kingsley half seriously acknowledged as much: 'Well with you as the Auden and me as the Isherwood *des nos jours*, "our society" is doing not so bad,' he told Philip in 1957.[5] All three pairs enjoyed long and intimate friendships which became inextricably entwined with their creative development, and each of these six major writers owed a substantial if unquantifiable portion of his success to his friend. Having so close a relationship with so gifted a contemporary may be the luckiest single thing that can happen to a writer, yet there are disadvantages too: the other's latest book (to say nothing of its advance, its reviews, its sales) may provoke as much irritation as admiration, while posterity's comparisons will usually take the form of finding one writer less significant than his friend – Coleridge, Isherwood and indeed Amis have all at one time or another looked like second fiddles. In Kingsley's case, this was at least partly self-induced by his lifelong tendency to present himself as someone of whom too much shouldn't be expected.

While Philip's recollection of their first meeting focuses on that memorable gun-shooting image, Kingsley's own account of his arrival at Oxford is far more equivocal. In *Memoirs* he was keen to stress the 'impeccably proletarian' style in which he was driven over from (not so very distant) Berkhamsted 'by the family butcher in his battered Morris' as well as the 'nasty little pair of rooms in the top corner of the front quad' which he was assigned on account of his 'comparatively lowly school'.[6] He knew nobody at St John's, but there were 'fewer than a dozen' whom he'd known at school scattered among the other colleges – not such a bad tally for a 'lowly' establishment – and they 'decently threw a sherry party' in Balliol to welcome him. Kingsley, unaccustomed to anything stronger than beer, was notably drunk by the time he staggered back to his own rooms where, shortly afterwards, two canvassing representatives of the Oxford University Conservative Association discovered him slumped in his armchair and nursing a chamber-pot in his lap. It's an amusing enough tale as Kingsley tells it, though the defensive air of blokeishness is typically sly and misleading: his father's reluctance to own a car didn't make him 'proletarian'; CLS, while not in the same league as the major public schools, was far from 'lowly'; and sherry would not have been such a startling novelty to a boy from a middle-class family where social drinking was the norm (his mother was especially fond of gin and tonic). Even his unshared rooms were decent enough for a mid-year arrival in wartime; other parts of the college were being steadily requisitioned by the Ministry of Agriculture. Larkin, when he came up in October 1940, not only travelled by train but found himself having to share rooms with his fellow-Coventrian Noel Hughes. Kingsley was luckier than he cared to admit.

As is often the way with freshmen at university, the random first impressions that Kingsley and Oxford made on each other were to have indelible consequences. His extrovert surface of clowning and mimicry, together with his underlying shyness and insecurity, drew him into a set of friends where he could entertain and be entertained, where high seriousness would always be tempered by irreverence and ribaldry, and where, above all, he would feel comfortable rather than stretched. In one respect, this was enormously damaging, for one might plausibly argue that his prospects of a great career in academia (for which he certainly had the brains) melted away in the moment that he and Norman Iles fired imaginary guns at each other across the quad at St John's. Philip, of course, *was* highly intelligent too; but loneliness and a nagging sense of social inferiority weighed even more heavily on him than on Kingsley, so the chance of becoming the straightish man in a culturally debunking double-act was one to be seized gratefully. Norman Iles, on the other hand, with whom Philip had the doubtful pleasure of sharing tutorials, was solidly and, as it were, sincerely philistine: 'a kind of ideal bad undergraduate, cutting lectures, not delivering essays, doing what he could to undermine the academic outlook by representing the university as a place where charlatans lorded it over ambitious or apathetic noodles, supplementing this image by one of a bad college man, stealing coal or "borrowing" jam (severely rationed) and other consumables out of neighbours' rooms'.[7] It was, thought Kingsley, 'hard to say what he was doing at Oxford at all'. The negative and subversive attitudes which Kingsley and Philip would adopt in a spirit of subversive glee, as the public foil to their more serious private selves, were held by Norman as uncomplicated tenets of belief. This type of character – the sociable oaf, wholly devoid of moral seriousness or any other redeeming features – becomes a recurrent figure in Kingsley's fiction, while John Kemp's roommate in *Jill*, the hopelessly feckless Christopher Warner, also owes a good deal to Norman Iles.

There are two evocative photographs of the Amis–Larkin milieu at St John's, both taken in the college garden on a summer's day in 1942. The first is reproduced in Richard Bradford's *Lucky Him* and described by Larkin in his 1964 preface to *Jill*. It reminded him 'how much our daily exchanges were informed by Kingsley's pantomimes', but 'pantomimes', of various sorts, were the group's common currency. In the photograph, Edward du Cann ('Duke'), later a Conservative cabinet minister, is removing an invisible hand-grenade's safety pin with his teeth, while Wally Widdowson is a thumbs-in-belt 'Russian officer'; David West, as a 'Roumanian officer', is inscrutably 'attempting to represent a contemporary saying that every Roumanian private had a Roumanian officer's lipstick in his knapsack'; Mervyn Brown has just 'shot' the unrelated Philip Brown, who clutches in agony at his heart, replicating the earlier Amis–Iles tableau; Norman Iles and David Williams 'are doing the "first today" routine' with imaginary glasses; while Kingsley himself crouches in front of the group, 'his face contorted to a hideous mask and holding an invisible dagger'.[8] Michael Macnaughton-Smith, Nick Russel and Graham Parkes are also present in unspecified roles; the most notable absentee is Larkin, who was holding the camera. In the second, reproduced in Kingsley's *Memoirs*, the same subjects present their cheerfully respectable selves, a supremely confident-looking hands-in-pockets Edward du Cann foremost. Here the only rakish elements are Philip Brown's open shirt and the cigarette in Kingsley's right hand. And this time Larkin is present, standing at the back, wearing a slightly nervous smile, while Graham Parkes takes over as photographer. These St John's undergraduates were mostly members of 'The Seven', an informal grouping with modest literary pretensions, though primarily dedicated to getting drunk and causing mayhem – the kind of 'incidents last night' that Larkin, in 'Dockery and Son', would recall having to explain to the Dean next morning. Among this group, Kingsley was unquestionably the star comic turn, with a repertoire ranging from comic faces and vocal impressions of dons to an imitation of a motorbike starting up which was sufficiently convincing to leave one owner, who had just parked and walked away from his bike, staring at the apparently self-willed machine in puzzled alarm.

Bruce Montgomery wouldn't have wanted to be in the picture, nor would Alan Ross, even though both had come up to St John's, like Philip, in October 1940. It may seem curious that literary-minded exact contemporaries, sharing a comparatively small college in the thrown-together conditions of wartime, should have remained barely acquainted, but Philip claimed not to have met Bruce until 'almost my last term' while Kingsley, who knew him better, regarded him with some suspicion. Catching sight of him on his first morning in college, he observed – indulging his inferiority complex's pious distaste to its full measure – a man 'with an indefinable and daunting air of maturity . . . a sweep of wavy auburn hair, a silk dressing-gown in some non-primary shade and a walk that looked eccentric and mincing'[9] (actually, according to Alan Ross, the consequence of childhood polio). He wasn't much better fully clothed, favouring 'a fancy-waistcoated, suède-shoed style with cigarette holders and rings'. Like Cousin John and the Marlborough sixth-formers, he inhabited a cultural and social world which Kingsley sensed was a rung or two above his own and about which he would often feel chippily resentful. In fact, he did make one attempt to follow in Bruce's footsteps by joining the college choir (where Montgomery was Organ Scholar), but soon decided that he wasn't up to their standard. Apart from dressing extravagantly and preferring hotel bars to pubs, Bruce Montgomery was a precocious creative polymath: he was already a painter and before he left Oxford had completed the first of several detective novels to be published under the pseudonym Edmund Crispin; under his own name, he was to become a moderately successful composer of film music. He was reading Modern Languages and sharing tutorials with the equally though differently talented Alan Ross, an outstanding cricketer whose time at university was cut short in 1942 by his war service in the Royal Navy. Montgomery's 'modern languages–Playhouse–classical music–Randolph Hotel ambience' (as Larkin called it)[10] and Ross's devoted sportsmanship were both useful strategies for negotiating the curious world of wartime Oxford. Kingsley's and Philip's comparable obsession was jazz.

2

Kingsley and Philip had arrived at jazz via broadly parallel routes, uncritical schoolboy enthusiasm blossoming into informed connoisseurship at university, but in contrasting circumstances. For Kingsley, jazz was a central part of the battleground over which he and his father fought, perfectly symbolising the generational and cultural gulf between them. 'Older people were against it then, an added recommendation,' he recalled, whereas he 'was one of the first British generation to whom jazz was a completely natural thing'.[11] For fourteen-year-old Robin Davies in *You Can't Do Both*, the most memorable element of his revelatory first encounter with Jeremy Carpenter (involving cigarettes, Auden and D. H. Lawrence) is a 1929 record by Louis Armstrong; but Jeremy, unlike Robin, is a wholly fictional character, an invented version of the knowledgeable older friend that the young Kingsley so badly wanted. By contrast, Philip's enthusiasm for jazz was cheerfully encouraged by his surprising father, who even bought him a drum kit, and shared with his close school friend James Ballard Sutton. 'Sitting with a friend in his bedroom that overlooked the family tennis-court,' he wrote in the introduction to *All What Jazz*, 'I watched leaves drift down through long Sunday afternoons as we took it in turn to wind the portable HMV, and those white and coloured Americans, Bubber Miley, Frank Teschmacher, J. C. Higginbotham, spoke immediately to our understanding.'[12] Jazz, he added, was 'something we had found for ourselves, that wasn't taught at school (what a prerequisite that is of nearly everything worthwhile!), and having found it, we made it bear all the enthusiasm usually directed at more established arts.' To that, at any rate, Kingsley could gladly have assented.

At St John's, they not only discovered – and encouraged – each other's enthusiasms but found themselves among other jazz fans. One was Edward du Cann, who usefully possessed a jacket with a large concealed pocket, just the size of a 10-inch record, in which deleted jazz discs might be liberated from Russell's and Acott's in the High (Kingsley borrowed it to steal a rare Sidney Bechet item). Another was Graham Parkes, from whose rooms below du Cann's could be heard records such as Louis Armstrong's 'Bessie Couldn't Help It' which helped to 'cheer him through working on a Greek prose' and so delighted his upstairs neighbour that du Cann would run down to relish Satchmo's 'gurgle of indescribable lasciviousness' in the vocal refrain. For Kingsley and Philip, 'our heroes were the white Chicagoans, Count Basie's band, Bix Beiderbecke, Sidney Bechet, Henry Allen, Muggsy Spanier, Fats Waller, early Armstrong and early Ellington – amazing that there were early bits of them by 1941 – and our heroines Bessie Smith, Billie Holiday, Rosetta Howard ("I'm the queen of everything") and Cleo Brown'.[13] In particular, the two friends converged on a set of musical touchstones – 'the Banks sides', as Kingsley called them in *Memoirs*, by which he meant the records made in 1932 by Billy Banks and his Rhythmmakers, featuring Henry 'Red' Allen, Pee Wee Russell and (on four of them) Fats Waller: 'Banks himself was the singer, a sort of counter-tenor, not very jazzy perhaps by some standards but fascinating to me, especially in the words he sang.'[14] Banks's singing voice was certainly peculiar, so it wasn't wholly unreasonable for Jill Williams, one of Kingsley's Oxford girlfriends, to wonder: 'Billy Banks and Billie Holiday; which is the man and which is the woman who sings like a little girl?'[15] (Banks was, or appeared to be, the latter.) The words, too, were extraordinary: Kingsley recalled the 'awesome surrealism' of 'Spider Crawl', a scarce record he didn't possess, though Philip did; he eventually acquired a copy while in the army, simply so that he could gaze reverently at it, since he had nothing on which to play it. No less odd is 'Mean Old Bed Bug Blues', in which 'Bed bugs bigger than jackass will bite you and stand and grin' before demolishing the 'quart of moonshine' on the bedside chest. In a letter to Philip in 1953, Kingsley chose as an image of intolerable disaster the prospect of finding his 78-rpm copy of 'Mean Old Bed Bug Blues' cracked; it was a disc much prized, too, by Colonel Manton in *The Riverside Villas Murder*.

Pee Wee Russell, says Larkin in his introduction to *Jill*, 'was, *mutatis mutandis*, our Swinburne and our Byron. We bought every record he played on that we could find, and – literally – dreamed about similar items on the American Commodore label.'[16] For him, this enthusiasm remained undimmed as late as 1970, when he nominated an LP reissue of Billy Banks and his Rhythmmakers as his record of the year in the *Daily Telegraph*: 'Allen, Russell, Waller and the rest in a splendid tumult of 'thirties ad-libbing'.[17] Nevertheless, the practised Larkin reader will notice something subtly characteristic there: the merest touch on the brakes in 'splendid tumult' and 'ad-libbing'. It's exactly the note sounded by the distinguished authors of *Jazz on Record*, who say of the Banks sides that they 'are worth having if you like the curried and spiced flavour of the vintage music of that period':[18] they are, in short, engaging curiosities rather than jazz classics. Kingsley and Philip enjoyed their somewhat bizarre exuberance, but they were also responding to elements of cultural transgression and fugitive scarcity. The Banks sides represented a miraculous reconciliation of opposites: populist and unpretentious, yet every bit as arcane as anything favoured by those dreary academics and avant-garde-seeking intellectual snobs whom they so despised and feared.

The attraction for Kingsley of an art which inextricably combined accessible pleasure with fiendish obscurity – rendering it absolutely unplaceable in the spectrum of high and low culture – will be immediately evident, for his entire literary career was founded on just such a premise. Twenty years later, in a review for the *New Statesman* in 1961, he returned to precisely this question:

The mention of jazz raises an interesting dilemma . . . It clearly isn't all high culture, nor, while men like Miles Davis and Thelonious Monk are still active and yet so far from making the Top Twenty, can it be all undifferentiated mass culture. Then perhaps the good bits of it have graduated to a sort of rough and warty high culture, while the bad bits are still hopelessly limed in mass culture. But then we notice that the good bits and the bad bits are all muddled up together on individual records, that the finest modern jazz is riddled with *kitsch* and empty virtuosity, the finest traditional jazz with cliché and rabble-rousing. So we can have three and a half bars of mass culture, followed by seven of high culture, followed by five and a half of mass culture, can we?[19]

Not only does this make an astute point about jazz's pleasingly slippery cultural status; it also applies to the shifting elusive tones and registers, the 'rough and warty high culture' and the populist troughs, of Kingsley's fiction.

But there's a good deal more to be noticed about the youthful Amis–Larkin view of jazz. We may need to remind ourselves that, born in 1922, they were of roughly the same generation as Dizzy Gillespie (born 1917), Thelonious Monk and Charlie Parker (both born 1920), and Miles Davis (born 1926); and that the invention of bebop or, more loosely, 'modern jazz' by these musicians coincided with Kingsley's years at Oxford. Yet, far from embracing the musical innovations of their contemporaries, as students very often do, Kingsley and Philip had already anchored their tastes in the recent past. Although modern British jazz musicians such as George Shearing and 'the seven-year-old Victor Feldman' (an astonishing child prodigy, he was indeed born in 1934) played at the Oxford University Rhythm Club, Kingsley preferred the sessions in a back room at the Victoria Arms, where Philip played straightforward blues and Kingsley 'would sometimes sing, or rather bawl, a series of lyrics culled from records';[20] their performance of the single exception, 'Locksley Hall Blues' (Tennyson–Larkin), must have been worth hearing, just the once. Not only did their choice in jazz confusingly mix high and low culture, obscurity and accessibility, it also managed to be simultaneously subversive and conservative. In doing so, it exactly anticipated the literary aesthetics of the 1950s.

Nor was the deliciously inapposite kidnapping of Tennyson as a blues lyricist an isolated case. Over the fireplace in Kingsley's subsequent New Quad rooms, a large photograph of Pee Wee Russell was captioned with an adapted quatrain from Tennyon's 'To Virgil':

> I salute thee, Pee Wee Russell,
>   I that love thee since my day began,
>   Wielder of the wildest measure
>   Ever moulded by the lips of man.[21]

In fact, Kingsley and Philip continually turned to jazz as a way of making the academic study of English literature less irksome. A long-running joke involved the arrangement of authors' names in the manner of jazz personnel listings and giving them suitable pieces to play. For instance, there was a blues called 'Revaluation' by Bill

Wordsworth and his Hot Six: Wordsworth (tmb), 'Lord' Byron (tpt),
Percy Shelley (sop), Johnny Keats (alto and clt), Sam 'Tea' Coleridge
(pno), Jimmy Hogg (bs), Bob Southey (ds). Later came the splendid
coupling of 'Volpone Drag' and 'Jumpin' at the Mermaid' by Big Ben
Jonson and his Tribesmen (actually Jonson fronting Donne's Meta-
physicals): Big Ben Jonson (tpt and voc), Abe Cowley (clt, alto), Dick
Crashaw (tmb), Harry Vaughan (ten), Jack Donne (pno), Tommy
Carew (gtr), Andy Marvell (bass), George Herbert (ds). Kingsley also
recalled an evidently more kitsch than jazzy 'Café Royal Quintet . . .
with "Baron" Corvo on xylophone'.[22] Those interested in both literature and jazz will find these personnels extremely funny, but even the
unconverted should see what is going on here: a joyful debunking
of academic seriousness combined with an equal and opposite
celebration of some fairly recherché expertise. That would prove a
lifelong habit, too.

3

Reading English in wartime Oxford was a peculiar experience. Students came up at odd times and their courses might be shortened or
interrupted by military service (Kingsley fitted in four terms before
the army claimed him); college premises could be requisitioned for
government use; facilities were restricted, catering was basic, and
almost every trace of pre-war *Brideshead* lavishness had been eradi-
cated. Philip Larkin, making the best of things, thought that the 'lack
of *douceur* was balanced by a lack of *bêtises*' and that 'our perspec-
tives were truer as a result'. Perhaps; but, as he also remarked, 'The
younger dons were mostly on war service, and their elders were too
busy or too remote to establish contact with us.'[23] It didn't help that
his and Kingsley's first tutor at St John's was Gavin Bone, a specialist
in pre-medieval literature, who died of cancer in 1942; he treated
Philip and his tutorial partner, Norman Iles, 'like a pair of village
idiots who might if tried too hard turn nasty'.[24] He probably thought
not much better of Kingsley, who remembered him as 'very nice' and
'very tolerant' but was unenthused by his subject: 'All Old English
and nearly all Middle English works produced hatred and weariness
in everybody who studied them.'[25] Moreover, Old English – which
largely consisted of what Philip memorably called 'ape's bumfodder'

– carried the additional disincentive of lectures by the 'incoherent and often inaudible' J. R. R. Tolkien.

Lecturers, Kingsley later suggested, could be divided into the hard and the soft, like policemen. The former imparted the sort of necessary, if barely intelligible, information which was 'likely to reappear in the relevant parts of the final examination'; the latter more enjoyably but less usefully offered 'civilised discourse with perhaps some critical interpretation and ideas about the past'. Some, like 'the narcotic David Nichol Smith', were simply beyond classification (according to John Wain, he could take half a minute to tell his audience that Pope and Swift were friends). Tolkien was, clearly, granite-hard; while the best of the soft – indeed, 'the best lecturer, in more than one sense, that I have ever heard'[26] – was C. S. Lewis. There was also, and here softness melted into spongey eloquence, Lord David Cecil, of whom Wain originated and Kingsley polished a magnificent parody: 'Laze . . . laze and gentlemen, when we say a man looks like a poet . . . dough mean looks like Chauthah . . . dough mean . . . looks like Dvyden . . . dough mean . . . looks like *Theckthpyum* [or something else barely recognisable as "Shakespeare"] . . . Mean looks like Shelley [pronounced "Thellem" or thereabouts]. Matthew Arnold [then prestissimo] called Shelley beautiful ineffectual angel Matthew Arnold had face [rallentando] like a *horth*. But my subject this morning is not the poet Shelley. Jane . . . Austen . . .'[27]

The scurrilous irreverence with which Kingsley and Philip treated both their subject and its teachers has occasioned some pious disapproval, but this is to misread the spirit both of the times and of the individuals. In a late, retrospective poem, 'Their Oxford', Kingsley rather ingeniously converted disrespect into a species of flattery:

> In my day there were giants on the scene,
> Men big enough to be worth laughing at:
> Coghill and Bowra, Lewis and Tolkien.
> Lost confidence and envy finished that.[28]

As for literature itself: 'Whatever one made of it in private, most people at Oxford, not just Philip, treated literature . . . as a pure commodity, a matter for evasion and fraud, confidence trickery to filch a degree,' wrote Kingsley.[29] That distinction is crucial; for the jokey contempt which may appear to be a denial of seriousness is actually its counterpart and foil. And, of course, more recent literature untainted by inclusion in the syllabus was another matter: it was Philip who 'quickened my interest in or even introduced me to the work of Auden (above all), Isherwood, Betjeman, Anthony Powell, Montherlant (a lonely foreigner) and Henry Green, to *The Rock Pool* (Connolly), *At Swim-Two-Birds* (Flann O'Brien) and *The Senior Commoner* (Julian Hall)'.[30] The list is fascinating in its combination of helpful and unhelpful influences: for instance, Julian Hall's Eton-set *The Senior Commoner*, 'a wonderful marsh-light of a novel', though its understated dryness would prove beneficial to Philip in *A Girl in Winter*, 'was to help to render unpublishable the predecessor of *Lucky Jim*'. On the other hand, Auden, who had so baffled the schoolboy Kingsley, and Betjeman would both become perceptible voices in Kingsley's own poetry; Isherwood helped him to write natural-sounding prose; Anthony Powell taught him the nuances of social comedy. Both Betjeman and Powell became lifelong friends of his.

'You were a nest of singing birds at St John's,' Betjeman told Kingsley in 1978.[31] But, for the time being at least, Philip was not only the more advanced and informed off-syllabus reader but also much the more prolific writer. Before his graduation in 1944, he had completed a hundred and fifty or so surviving poems, as well as the pastiche girls' stories *Trouble at Willow Gables* and *Michaelmas Term at St Brides's*: these two fictions, which many readers would have guessed to be works of lurid adolescent pornography until their eventual publication in 2002, are in fact surprisingly decorous and technically mature (the closest we get to adolescent humour is in minor characters: a school benefactor called Lord Amis, an expelled 'Miss Gollancz' and, surreally, Arthur Waley as a bookmaker). Kingsley's literary development was more leisurely in pace and even more uncertain in direction. For one thing, he was living a more complicated sort of life, taking in areas which Philip viewed with nervousness or hostility. He joined the Communist-affiliated faction of the university Labour Club – Iris Murdoch was Treasurer – and did a stint as editor of the Labour Club's *Bulletin*. Edward du Cann thought that he had 'political steel', but in this he was mistaken. Kingsley could certainly put on a show: he actively recruited members to the party, went to meetings of the People's Convention and (though his older self would disbelievingly choke at the recollection) read

Marx, Lenin and Plekhanov. There are, to be sure, two curious letters
(dated 5 November 1941 and 13 January 1942) to John Russell
Lloyd, a fellow student: in the first, he dourly reports that he has
been 'doing a satisfactory quantity of Party and Russia Today (Party)
work'; in the second, he fires off a series of questions about 'CP
policy'.[32] If these letters seem comical, it is only because they are
among the very few documents in Kingsley's oeuvre to be wholly
devoid of comedy; their particular style of earnestness bears no
resemblance to the barbed wit with which he sharpened his most
serious points. Moreover, Kingsley was and would remain someone
who chose political stances to suit his tastes and prejudices, rather
than the other way round. There was never much purpose, as his
friend Robert Conquest ruefully pointed out, in trying to hold a
political discussion with him.

The Communist Party held two particular attractions: it was an
infuriating snub to his parents' middling liberalism – Kingsley even
attended party meetings at Berkhamsted during vacations, to hammer
the point home – and at Oxford it was a way of mixing with girls,
'not very nice-looking ones, though, most of them'. His upbringing
had effectively insulated him from sexual experience: the lack of a
social milieu near home, the boys' day school at commuting distance
and the men's college had conspired to eliminate easy encounters
with girls. Apart from some adolescent mutual masturbation with
Billy Mingo, his homosexual experience was negligible too, and the
rumoured goings-on among Marlborough public schoolboys merely
added to his sense of exclusion, while at Oxford, the flagrant sexual
deviance of Anthony Blanche had gone the way of other pre-war
pleasures and excesses. The Labour Club, with its helpful if somewhat
joyless left-wing permissiveness about sex, seemed to offer him a
decent chance to lose his virginity; he may well have consoled himself
with the thought, grounded in insecurity rather than in cynicism, that
this way it wouldn't much matter if he made a mess of things. In
Memoirs, Kingsley is uncharacteristically reticent about the event,
preferring instead to transfer a lightly fictionalised account to Robin
Davies in *You Can't Do Both*. Robin, who becomes the Classicist his
author might have been, meets his girl (Barbara Bates) through the
equally unpromising Classical Society but via an identical strategy: a
female member (Patsy Cartland) lets him know that 'any advances he

might make' to a friend of hers will be 'well received' and one or other of them lends him a sexual handbook – in the novel called *Happier Love* by Vanderdecken – for his guidance. But the very idea of anything resembling a textbook was of course anathema to Kingsley, especially as this one came with moralising asides: immoralising asides might have been another matter, more in line with the teachings of Homer Lane, which had filtered through to Kingsley and Philip via Auden and Isherwood (in the novel, it is the helpful though homosexual Jeremy Carpenter who, for not wholly altruistic reasons, recommends Lane to Robin).

Barbara is 'attractive without coming much higher than half-way up Robin's Category 2, that comprising girls it would be jolly nice/ perfectly all right to find yourself in bed with but not worth serious trouble to get them there'; it is only Patsy's disclosure of her availability that sends her 'zooming up into Category 1'.[33] Everything is wrong about this, of course, as Kingsley knows: the novel is merciless in exposing Robin's, and his own, youthful idiocies. Robin's seduction-by-numbers method when Barbara first visits his rooms is only a nominal success: 'an act of sexual intercourse did take place, though not one satisfactory to either Vanderdecken or Robin Davies'.[34] His wham-bam approach on the second occasion, having given up on the moralising Dutchman, is an unmitigated disaster: Barbara walks out, taking *Happier Love* with her, while he is making post-coital tea, and they do not meet again. Robin is left gloomily pondering the possible consequences of the fact that 'sexual inexperience must include contraceptive inexperience'.[35] In this, at least, Kingsley had been better prepared: enlisting the moral support of his friend George Blunden, he summoned up the courage to buy condoms from a chemist's shop. It was a detail Kingsley would remember when his own sons were adolescents.

We can't, obviously, assume that Kingsley's own experience was identical to Robin's; yet this is one of several passages in *You Can't Do Both* which carries a strong sense of retrospective self-examination. The novel doesn't seek to provide excuses or to beg forgiveness, but it does try to understand why the younger self behaved as he did and sometimes, as we shall discover shortly, to make amends by setting the record straight.

4

As Kingsley had rather enjoyed the OTC at school, he wasn't too unhappy about joining the Senior Training Corps at Oxford, apart from the fact that it used up a day and a half each week: he knew he would end up in uniform sooner or later anyway. There was a good deal of drilling, but much compensatory satisfaction to be gained from hearing Sergeant Major Reid bawling out some aristocratic nincompoop from Magdalen or Christ Church. He also undertook signals training, having been advised that the Royal Corps of Signals were 'always in the back' and thus likelier than most to escape with their lives from any real conflict. Unlike Philip Larkin or John Wain or Bruce Montgomery – who were exempt on account, respectively, of their eyes, lungs and legs – Kingsley was A1, 'not even A(X)1 Psychopathic, the enviable distinction of another composer of my acquaintance',[36] despite the lazy eye which had so hampered his performance as a cricketer; and so he was 'hauled off into khaki' in the summer of 1942. In some respects at least, his experience in the school OTC and university STC served him well: 'I looked a goon and a bleeding civvy in uniform, but boy, could I drill a squad.'[37]

In fact, the British Army might have been specifically designed to reinforce Kingsley's complex blend of authoritarianism and anarchy. It seemed to him to resemble the kind of society 'you read about in some science-fiction stories, a world much like our own in general appearance but with some of the rules changed or removed, a logic only partly coinciding with that of our own world, and some unpredictable areas where logic seems missing altogether or to point opposite ways at once'.[38] You could never be quite sure whether its anecdotal oddities recorded actual experience or some higher symbolic truth, and perhaps that didn't matter. Were there, for instance, specially filed and varnished pieces of coal to be placed on top of barrack-room buckets in the Grenadiers at inspection time, thus creating a smooth surface of shiny black crazy paving? Quite possibly; but the essential point was the seamless intersection of high seriousness and absurdity. Lewis Carroll would have understood perfectly; so did Kingsley, and his novels are full of such inscrutable lunacies.

In September 1942, after two months' basic training, he was

posted to the Royal Signals unit for officer cadets at Catterick;
early in 1943, he was commissioned as a second lieutenant. After
this, he set off on the merry-go-round of assignments so beloved
of the services: Salisbury, High Wycombe, back to Catterick for
an advanced wireless course – he ended up with a Q2 rating, the
equivalent of a third-class degree, and 'never touched a wireless set
again' – and then to Headington Hall, Oxford, the future home of
Pergamon Press and its owner, Robert Maxwell ('the sort of thing
that gets called ironical these days'). There, in November 1943, he
joined Second Army HQ Signals and set off on another series of
exercises, dotted across southern England, with codenames such as
Eagle, Goldbraid and Mara. To his superfluous wireless training was
now added the equally redundant 'learning to fight as infantry', as he
(and his characters) recalled in the story 'I Spy Strangers' (1962):

> All present could very well remember the cross-country runs, the
> musketry competitions, the three-day infantry-tactics schemes with
> smoke-bombs and a real barrage, the twelve-mile route-marches
> in respirators which had seemed in retrospect to show such a
> curious power of inverted prophecy when the unit finally com-
> pleted its role in the European theatre of war without having had
> to walk a step or fire a shot.[39]

So, indeed, it would prove. Kingsley finally reached Normandy with
the Second Army Signals at the end of June 1944; in November his
unit was posted to Sonnis in Belgium, but he saw no more of actual
warfare than he did of wirelesses. What may well strike us most
forcefully about this progress is the ridiculous disparity between the
time and expense of training and the use made of it, but Kingsley's
case was by no means an exceptional one. Roy Fuller, called up into
the Royal Navy in April 1941, not only experienced a comparably
protracted and dispersed sequence of training as a radar mechanic
but was then exported by troopship to East Africa, where he did
almost nothing before being very slowly brought home again. And
this suggests a flaw in Kingsley's theory that the Second World War
lacked the poetry of the First because so many of his literary
contemporaries were unfit to fight in it. Even more to the point is the
fact that some of the finest writers who were in the services, such as
Roy Fuller and himself, got nowhere near the war.

What he actually did, between June 1944 and his discharge from the army in October 1945, is well conveyed by the present-tense vignette, in the style of Isherwood's 'Berlin Diary', in *Memoirs*. It begins in an officers' mess, a ponderously furnished Belgian 'bourgeois' drawing-room; outside, there's an aerial-festooned lorry, a Jeep with no exhaust, a hen-house full of looted chickens and, beyond a lilac bush, the officers' latrine. Later, he is at his desk in the signal office, where trays full of 'traffic', or messages in transit, are emptied on to a counter and sorted for onward transmission; there are racks of 'expired traffic', an enormous file meant to show the location of every unit in the army, and a blackboard indicating the functioning status (or not) of lines and equipment; Kingsley himself is favoured with a call from Lord Glenarthur – 'the biggest shit on the entire staff' – who wants a special dispatch rider 'to fetch some urgently needed military object like a parcel of clean washing or a dozen of cognac'.[40] He also described the scene in a startlingly Roy Fullerish poem called 'Belgian Winter':

> From my window stretches the earth, containing wrecks:
> The burrowing tank, the flat grave, the
> Lorry with underside showing, like a dead rabbit.
> The trees that smear all light into a mess;
> World of one tone, stolid with fallen snow.
> Here is the opaque ice, the hum-drum winter,
> The splintered houses suddenly come upon
> Left over from wounds that pierced a different people.[41]

This sort of routine, in which periods of not obviously purposeful activity alternated with spells of lassitude, was relieved by bartering expeditions (white-haired farmers were reckoned the best bet, 'old enough to have served alongside the Tommies in the Great War') and occasionally 'a whole forty-eight hours' leave'. On one of the latter, spent in Brussels, Kingsley shared a room at the officers' club with a Royal Tank Regiment captain called Joe, who was 'all right, by which I most immediately mean that his sole objectives for this operation were drink and women'.[42] Having fully succeeded in both these, Kingsley found himself a few days later troubled by 'an acute itching, accompanied by red spots . . . in an intimate area'. Swiftly identifying scabies, the scholarly-looking medical officer had as little trouble in guessing the cause: 'A forty-eight in Brussels, I presume. People find it hard to keep themselves clean in wartime. Mix with one another more than usual.'[43] While the MO's assistant, Corporal Clough, 'ministered' to Kingsley with 'some pleasant, cooling white stuff and a shaving brush', they spoke of Virginia Woolf and Arnold Bennett; as a civilian, Clough had worked on the books page for a Northern paper. After a week of this treatment, the MO pronounced him fit, adding: 'Try to be a bit choosier next time, eh? I don't want to see you again.' But he did, the following October, in the front quad of St John's, where the erstwhile MO had become the college doctor.

It isn't entirely fanciful to suggest that although Kingsley still thought of himself primarily as a poet (just as Philip thought of himself primarily as a novelist), this sort of incident – with its neatly symmetrical pendants of Clough's previous career and the MO's subsequent one – was formative in making him the kind of novelist he would eventually become; or, to put it slightly differently, while the lack of war experience turned Philip in on himself and towards poetry, Kingsley's army life extended his appreciation of the sheer oddity of human life, the cussedness and contingency of things. In his full-length fiction, the army is mostly a subtext rather than an explicit motif, culminating in the extraordinary retro-futuristic *Russian Hide and Seek* (1980), in which the twenty-first-century Russians-in-England army shares several characteristics with its British predecessor of a hundred years earlier. But he also wrote three short stories closely based on his wartime experiences and collected in *My Enemy's Enemy* (1962). They vividly illustrate Kingsley's unresolved conflict between authority and anarchy, as well as his faltering political idealism.

In 'My Enemy's Enemy', though a good deal of authorial sympathy filters into the shambolic Lieutenant Dalessio (the son of a Welsh–Italian café owner, whose nephew appears in *That Uncertain Feeling*), the Amis-like character is Tom Thurston: he has an Oxford degree, teaches at a minor public school, reads literary magazines and has a 'vaguely scholarly manner and appearance'. Much of the detail comes straight from the Second Army Signals: the 'hanging lampshade, which at its lowest point was no more than five feet from the floor' is borrowed from that Belgian drawing-room; 'Lord Fawcett', who telephones Thurston for an SDR 'to take in the Brigadier's soiled laundry and bring back his clean stuff, plus any wines, spirits and cigars' is clearly the similarly imperious Lord Glenarthur; and Thurston's superior officers share the same infuriatingly middlebrow cultural tastes – '*The Warsaw Concerto*, the Intermezzo from *Cavalleria*

Rusticana, and other sub-classics dear to their hearts'[44] – as Kingsley's actual Colonel. The story turns on a moral dilemma. The Adjutant ensnares Thurston in a plan to get rid of the unsuitable Dalessio by arranging a Colonel's Inspection of his chaotic quarters; Thurston's human duty is to tip off Dalessio, but he has been irritated by a trivial and harmless prank of the latter's and does nothing. In the event, Dalessio is saved by the quiet intervention of Bentham, a regular soldier. He tells Thurston: 'Yes, you could talk about them [the Adjutant and his cronies] till you were black in the face, but when it came to doing something, talking where it would do some good, you kept your mouth shut.'[45] The bluff professional, rather than the thoughtful amateur, has made the correct (which also happens to be the anti-authoritarian) moral response. These interlocking conclusions – that the cautious intellectual may be incapable of right action and that human decency may be concealed beneath the most prosaic exterior – are recurrent ones in Kingsley's work.

The other two stories concern an Amis-like character called Archer. 'Court of Inquiry' is slight, involving the loss of a charging-engine which was obsolete anyway – something that might quite easily have happened to Kingsley, but didn't. 'I Spy Strangers', which Kingsley described to Bill Rukeyser as 'an 18,000-word effort about the British Army and how bloody stupid it is',[46] is more substantial. Its central image is a mock parliament held at an unidentified location, based on the Reinforcement Holding Unit to which he was later posted, after VE Day and in the run-up to the 1945 General Election. The unit's commanding officer, Major Raleigh, is an unreconstructed old-school Conservative whose only cultural ambition is to stage a production of *Journey's End*, which of course includes a heroic namesake of his; he and other senior officers may not be members of the parliament but they are allowed to sit in the visitors' gallery (this parliamentary geography is largely imaginary: the whole thing takes place in a former schoolroom). Notable on the ominously leftish government benches is the Foreign Secretary, Sergeant Hargreaves; while equally passionate on the opposition side is the ultra-right-wing (in favour of enlisting the Nazis to repel the Reds) Sergeant Doll, a great favourite of the Major's. Frank Archer is the Speaker. He tries to be even-handed, although naturally his sympathies are with Hargreaves rather than Doll, and to defend the lively debate to the Major: 'rank doesn't count in there', he tells him. 'Everyone

accepts that.' Everyone, that is, apart from the Major himself, who is
keen to ship Hargreaves off to Burma, by this time the only place to
which he could still be shipped. What is the matter with Hargreaves?
he wants to know. 'That's very simple, sir. He doesn't like the
Army.' Or, more precisely: 'But it isn't being in the Army that gets
him down. It's the Army.'[47] On another level, which precipitates the
story's magnificently extravagant ending, Hargreaves is homosexual
and suspected of an improper relationship with Signalman Ham-
mond; Archer's human good deed – a sort of counterbalance to
Thurston's failure in 'My Enemy's Enemy' – is to ensure that they are
both transferred together. By this time, however, a double catastrophe
has struck Major Raleigh: he has been expelled from the visitors'
gallery, having intervened in the mock parliament and been challenged (by Hargreaves) with the traditional formula 'I spy strangers';
and Labour has won the real General Election. Raleigh's last chance
of sending Archer somewhere unpleasant is thwarted, as Doll explains
to him: 'Well, Mr Archer showed me a letter from the head of his
college in Oxford, the Master I think he called himself. It said they
were arranging his release from the Army and reckoned he'd be out
in good time to go into the college when the term begins, which I
gather is about the 10th of October . . .'[48]

Archer also appears as an Amis-surrogate in 'Who Else Is Rank',
the unpublished fiction he wrote as a kind of Auden–Isherwood
collaboration with his fellow officer E. Frank Coles. In one of his
chapters, Coles lists the reasons why his friend and collaborator was
viewed with such puzzlement, suspicion or hostility by his military
superiors: Archer 'was easily discountenanced which argued ineffi-
ciency, he too readily told the truth and was therefore considered
irresponsible, he was honest in his opinions and this made him
conceited, he unguardedly made intelligent contributions to the
desultory discussions in the mess and was accused of posing, he
was polite and considerate to his inferiors and was therefore unable
to exercise command'. Kingsley was, as so often, hampered by the
betwixt-and-between status of his lower-middle-class background:
neither an Oxonian gentleman with public-school manners and a
lofty contempt for vulgarity nor a straightforwardly down-to-earth
proletarian. No one knew quite what to make of him, a fact he could
turn to his advantage in other circumstances, but not in the army.
'Who Else Is Rank' also provides a lightly fictionalised account of the

affair he had begun in Catterick with a married woman, Elisabeth Simpson, his first adult sexual relationship to be underpinned by genuine emotional involvement. The affair lasted, in the necessarily sporadic circumstances of Kingsley's army postings, for two years. 'My parting with Betty was heart-breaking, because we love each other, or so we say,' he told Philip Larkin, writing from Berkhamsted while on leave in November 1943. 'Her full name is Elisabeth Anne, which I like, and her married name is Simpson, Mrs. E. A. Simpson . . .'[49] As Kingsley evidently knew, she shared these initials with Mrs Ernest Aldrich Simpson, Duchess of Windsor.

It was during this leave that a ludicrous sequence of events almost precipitated a total rift with his father who, having run out of cigarettes, most unwisely decided to search for some in his son's overcoat pocket. But the packet of Player's he cheerfully opened had been used by Kingsley as a not especially safe hiding-place for the condoms left over from his brief stay with Betty. William's subsequent discovery of her marital status was hardly calculated to improve matters; he ruined his case, however, by making unwarranted insinuations about her ('no better than she should be') and by writing his son a pompous 500-word letter packed with moral indignation. There is no reason to doubt the genuineness of his feelings, yet at this distance two equally powerful motives for his anger emerge: frustration that the time had come when he could no longer keep his son on a tight moral rein; and, perhaps, a sort of envy from a man who had led so regular a life and whose own war experience had been even duller than his son's. For Kingsley, the incident represented his achievement of a hard-won independence, and he would always remain grateful to Elisabeth Simpson. It is significant that, although he tended in time to become reticent about both his marriages, he nevertheless retained 'Letter to Elisabeth' as the opening piece in his *Collected Poems*. Love, he recognised, was a kind of education, and it was also the cause of somewhat unguarded optimism:

> At last, love, love has taught me to speak straight,
> To make my body walk without a strut;
> Dearest, on our first anniversary
> Nothing exists now that can go awry.
> The eyes that looked good-bye will look at love
> As from this sleep we know ourselves alive.[50]

After the closure of Second Army HQ on 25 June 1945, Kingsley was transferred to the Reinforcement Holding Unit at Minden in Westphalia, which provided the setting for 'I Spy Strangers': 'Several hundred other British officers with nothing to do were also there, waiting for someone to send them somewhere else and eventually to England.'[51] Kingsley didn't have to wait long. During his disembarkation leave in England in the autumn of 1945 – when he might still have been sent to 'various points east, where the war was over but plenty of disagreeable things remained to be done' – a telegram arrived summoning him to Thirsk, to receive his Class 'B' Release. Louis Armstrong's 'Tight like This' was playing on the radio at that moment. He turned the volume up.

5

Oxford had changed, and so had Kingsley. The pre-war *Brideshead* ambience and the wartime austerity had both given way to something unlike either: a university newly focused (insofar as Oxford could be expected to contemplate such a thing) on the post-war meritocratic future, in which exams, qualifications and jobs were to be taken a little more seriously. 'In 1946–48,' he said, 'it was sometimes as if exams filled the world.'[52] This came as a considerable shock to someone who had imagined 'the tasks of peace' as 'not working, getting drunk and pursuing young women' and had tended to assume that three years of messing about in the army might give him a head start over undergraduates less experienced in these matters. It would have been simpler if he had been surrounded by entirely new faces; but, although most of those who had come up with him – including Philip – had graduated and gone, and others had been sent off to Burma, there were several old friends, including Mervyn Brown and Graham Parkes, who were returning to resume their degrees. There was also John Wain who, with uncanny skill, had fitted in his three years of undergraduate life at St John's in Kingsley's absence, becoming a junior Fellow of the college in 1946 and three years later a lecturer at Reading.

Wain was younger than Kingsley but, with his tweed hat and walking stick, he seemed older: almost donnish, in fact. Born in 1925, he had grown up in the Potteries – Stoke-on-Trent, Newcastle-under-

Lyme – and was thus an example of that recurrent figure in his own and others' novels of the 1950s: the southward-heading grammar-school boy from the North. He and Kingsley initially got on well; and their developing literary styles, in both poetry and prose, seemed to have a good deal in common. Wain, the more ambitious though less talented of the two, was to be instrumental in shaping his friend's career – by persuading him to try for a First, a higher degree and a university lectureship, rather than settle for schoolmastering – and in promoting his early work. They shared a liking for pubs and beer, often meeting for lunch at the Eagle and Child, as well as for jazz; Wain's third novel, *Strike the Father Dead* (1962), is grounded in jazz, as is his long poem 'Music on the Water' in *Letters to Five Artists* (1969). The benefit of hindsight may suggest that they were too jarringly alike, too closely competitive in similar fields, not to fall out eventually. In fact, Kingsley formed his opinion of Wain early on, as he made clear to Philip in a typically error-enriched letter of October 1946:

> Did you know that JBwain is nay a FELLO of John's? Why are you shong your teeth in that way, and screwng up your eyes, and bending forward, and cryng 8 as if in pain? I KNOW WHY. The news fills me with the liveliest horror; *nay*, it isn't that I prize academic stanadards (no offence, old boy), but that he *does*, and he will *go on* beng WORNG about words *more and more* and *lader and lader* and beng MORE THAN EVER convinced he is right when he is WORNG and he will make young chaps thikn about words IN THE WORNG WAY . . .[53]

He supplied a postscript gloss for 'FELLO', which does indeed look like a Latin verb: 'fello–are, v.t. *I suck*, etc. Also in sens. obsc. When are you coming up?' All the same, the instinct which told him not to quarrel with Wain, at least not yet, was a sound one.

Bruce Montgomery had also graduated and gone off to teach at Shrewsbury. More significantly, he was producing detective stories at an alarming rate, under the pseudonym of Edmund Crispin. They were published by Victor Gollancz, whose daughter Diana had been an art student at the Slade when it was evacuated to Oxford during the war; she had become friendly with both Philip (hence the appear-ance of her surname in *Trouble at Willow Gables*) and with Bruce Montgomery. The first Crispin novel, *The Case of the Gilded Fly*, was written during a university vacation and appeared in 1944, very swiftly followed by *The Moving Toyshop* and *Holy Disorders*: the recurring central character in all three books is Professor Gervase Fen, an amateur sleuth in a great if implausible English tradition, who is closely modelled on Montgomery's and Alan Ross's tutor at St John's, W. G. Moore. Sending the first of these to Ross, by then in the navy, Montgomery described it as a 'piece of nonsense', which is about fair. Kingsley thought it 'a rather bad novel, if not something worse' and particularly disliked 'the constant flippancy and facetiousness of the style, an excessive striving after high spirits or their effect'.[54] *The Moving Toyshop* is better, with some enjoyable careering about in and around Oxford although, apart from the gloriously eccentric Fen, the characters are no more interesting than the wooden pieces on a Cluedo board. Of *Holy Disorders*, Kingsley wrote to Philip in February 1946: 'I don't like all those silly literary allusions, and some of the funny bits are funny, but not many, and the blend of fantasy and detective novel isn't done skilfully enough, and there is a lot of pointless facetiousness and sheer bad writing.' Bruce, however, visiting Oxford for the weekend, was 'just as nice as ever'.[55]

As for Philip, he was by now a librarian at Wellington in Shropshire, a dozen miles from Shrewsbury. He and Bruce would meet once a week to talk about their writing and drink too much: Andrew Motion rightly points out that because 'Montgomery's reputation has declined since his death in 1978 . . . the ways in which he helped to form Larkin have disappeared from view'.[56] Their meetings were for a while the high point of Philip's social life, the limits of which he had anticipated in a stanza written at the time of his appointment (in November 1943) though unpublished until the *Early Poems and Juvenilia* appeared in 2005:

> I'm sorry to say that, as life looks today,
>   I'm going to reside out in Wellington,
> Where everyone's rude, and ashamed of a nude,
>   And nobody's heard of Duke Ellington;
> Life, you aren't a god, you're a bloody old sod
>   For giving me such an employment
> 'Cos in such a bad job only pulling my knob
>   Will bring me the slightest enjoyment.[57]

Philip, however, had already learned the knack of transforming his isolation into creativity. He had completed his first novel, *Jill* (1946), the extraordinarily assured portrait of John Kemp, a lonely, fantasising and (apart from a Northern, Lawrentian background which looks palpably grafted on) generally Larkinlike Oxford undergraduate; his second, *A Girl in Winter* (1947), even more ambitiously, tackles the isolation of Katherine Lind, a refugee from an unspecified European country, who ends up in a provincial English city, working in a library. Both books are indebted to the nothing-much-happens style of *The Senior Commoner*. The first is dedicated to James Ballard Sutton (to whom Philip had written, in June 1944: 'There is no one like you for me: since you left I have tried each friend carefully and plumbed them to their depths and found them wanting'),[58] the second to Bruce Montgomery. Kingsley, who in due course dedicated *his* first published novel to Philip, would have been hurt by this: Philip's friendship with Jim went back to their schooldays, so that was understandable, but he certainly regarded himself as a closer friend than Bruce. In fact, he felt about Philip exactly as Philip had felt about Jim Sutton a couple of years earlier: 'There is nobaddy esle but you who contributes as much as I contribute to the total of interest, and who HATES the thigns I HATE as much as I HATE them (who NEVER says things like Just a minute while I look at this car).'[59] He always remained lukewarm in his praise of both books, yet this was partly because, in their patient and inward explorations of loneliness, they achieved something which was beyond his own scope. Philip would later, self-deprecatingly, remark: 'The fault of the novels is that they're about me.'[60]

Jill's publishers, Fortune Press, had already brought out Philip's first book of poems, *The North Ship*, in 1945. This deeply eccentric firm was run single-handedly by R. A. Caton, whose principal interests were tenanted properties in Brighton – where he owned ninety houses with, he claimed, 'not a bathroom between them' – and homosexual and/or flagellant pornography: *Boys in their Ruin*, *Boy Sailors*, *A Brute of a Boy*, *Fourteen: A Diary of the Teens* (by a Boy) and *Chastisement across the Ages* were typical Fortune titles. There was also, rather mysteriously, a poetry list. Caton can hardly have supposed this would add to his firm's profit or its respectability, so it seems inescapable that he must have actually enjoyed publishing it. And, although his authors often suspected that he read not a word of their books, he managed to show remarkable taste: in publishing early collections by, among others, Dylan Thomas, C. Day-Lewis, Gavin Ewart, Roy Fuller, Philip Larkin and Kingsley Amis, he displayed a flair for literary talent-spotting unrivalled at that time even by Faber. What Caton tended not to do was pay. Julian Symons, one of the contributors to *Fortune Anthology*, tartly observed that the publication's initials alone might suffice.

If Kingsley had possessed a quarter of the business sense his father had so earnestly wished him to own, he would have steered well clear of Caton; but, niggled by Bruce's and Philip's success in becoming published authors while he was dutifully passing his days in khaki, he set about assembling a slim volume as soon as he was discharged from the army and in December 1945 submitted *Bright November* to the Fortune Press. Caton accepted it in May 1946 and then went silent: 'And good Master Cayton at the Sign of the Swyngyng Scrotum says nothing to mee at All,' Kingsley complained to Philip on 24 October.[61] By 2 December he was becoming angrier: 'THAT SOD CATON *still* hasn't replied to my letter, through [*sic*] he had it over a fortnight ago.'[62] Four days later, he telephoned Caton and gained some useful if unwelcome insight into the business methods of the Fortune Press:

This morning, *angered* and *discouraged* past endurance I rang up the CRAP FACTORY ('Oh.') the fortune press ('Eh?'). THAT SOD CATON occupied most of the time asking me to tate his miserable books *for nothing*. He REFRAINED FROM APOOG-LISGNI for not writing to me for TWENTY-NINE WEEKS, said I would get the proofs in about a month I DIDN'T BELIEVE HIM, said the book would be out in February I DIDN'T BELIEVE HIM, said would I try to get Oxford bookshops interested in it ISAID pss I SAID I'D HELP AS MUCH AS I COULD, and was POLITE, feeling with HUMILIATION that if I told him I HATED HIM AS MUCH AS I HATE HIM he would have become ANGRY with me and refuse to publish my book. He showed he'd done bugrall by telling me I could put in any more poems I'd got. His pattern phrase was 'Things are so difficult' oh farks work it up yer. Don't you HATT his voice? I do, *So do you*. SO DO I. Oh, and *I* paid TWO SHILLINGS AND FIVEPUNCE to hear him speaking out with it from his mouth.[63]

He sent Caton six new poems and asked him to delete one existing piece; but when galley proofs finally arrived in May 1947 none of these changes had been made. The book eventually appeared in September, some eighteen months after the promised publication date. Kingsley rewarded this dilatoriness by including a cameo part for a character called Caton, with the initials L. S. for 'Lazy Sod', in each of his first six novels.

Bright November, like *The North Ship*, is a false start in the sense that its style and voice are completely at odds with the author's subsequent work. Kingsley was never tempted by 'apocalyptic' excess, nor did he share Philip's transitory admiration for Dylan Thomas, but he had yet to discover the clipped, conversational, ironic tone which was to typify his poetry in the 1950s. Only six pieces from *Bright November* would eventually survive into his *Collected Poems*: three look back on his affair with Elisabeth; two, 'Radar' and 'Belgian Winter', draw on his time in the army; while the sixth, 'Beowulf', glances with surprising affection at the part of English Literature he liked least. In thus apportioning his interests during the mid-1940s, the balance seems about right.

It's tempting to say that Kingsley hadn't found his voice as a writer; but the voice is already there, not only in the poems but in the frequent and often extravagantly funny letters he wrote to Philip. What he had yet to find was the voice's appropriate form. It was fun to bat back and forth chapters of another soft-porn fantasy, *I Would Do Anything for You*, with Philip, but this was at best a kind of limbering up and at worst a waste of time. So, early in 1947, he embarked on a proper novel, the one he claimed was made unpublishable by the influence of Julian Hall's *The Senior Commoner*, and by September had completed it. It was called *The Legacy*, and its most radical, apparently postmodern and indeed Martin Amis-like feature is a central character called Kingsley Amis. This other Kingsley stands to inherit £30,000 provided he marries a girl approved by his brother and joins the family firm; whereas, of course, he wants to be a writer and marry someone else altogether. *The Legacy* thus articulates a dilemma which the real Kingsley had faced since childhood and which confronts many first-generation students from middle-class families: should he settle for a safe job in his parents' world or branch out into the doubtfully respectable, financially precarious literary life? (A similar question nags at Philip in poems such as 'Toads' and 'Toads Revisited'.) The fictional Kingsley takes the money.

The Legacy hung around in Kingsley's life for the next three years. He sent it to Mark Longman of Longmans, Green (then still a general publisher), who returned it in March 1949: 'Log fog Longmans sent the Legacy back, of course, saying it was "altogether too slight".'[64] He thought about asking Erik Kintisch ('a rich young Yid publishing swine with money to burn') to print it privately, but sent it off to Victor Gollancz instead. In May, 'Golly' returned it, commenting with typical publisher's understatement: 'I don't think *The Legacy* quite comes off.'[65] Eventually, he persuaded a publisher's reader, Doreen Marston, whose son Adrian was an Oxford friend, to provide him with a frank, detailed appraisal. She found two major weaknesses: one was excessive 'redundancy' ('the number of times your characters repeat themselves, the number of times they light a cigarette, pour out tea, pass plates of food, etc.'); the other was 'lack of conflict' ('no suspense . . . a great deal of boredom'). There was no point in tinkering with *The Legacy*: 'I do believe it would be a waste of time and of money to try it on any other publisher even through another Agent. My advice to you is to scrap it and to regard it as a useful essay for the future.' He grumbled to Philip that 'Mrs. M.' was 'QUITE RIGHT in about half of what she says, but the rest of the time she's missing the point isn't she?' His self-estimation seems for a moment completely shorn of either bravura or irony: 'An original writer who isn't very much good, that's what I am; I'll never be Joyce or Warwick Deeping, so where do I stand?' He wondered, with some justice, what Mrs Marston would have made of Flann O'Brien's *At Swim-Two-Birds*: 'Try and cut down your sentences and long words . . . there is no real conflict between the hero and Brynsly . . . the Dublin atmosphere is first-rate . . . your work suffers from a lack of narrative and dramatic interest . . .'[66] But he wasn't either Flann O'Brien or James Joyce; nor, for that matter, was he Warwick Deeping.

By then, in any case, the solution to this problem was staring him in the face.

6

One afternoon in January 1946, soon after he had returned to Oxford, Kingsley spotted an extremely attractive blonde girl across the room of the *salon du thé* at Elliston & Cavell's in the Cornmarket.

A mutual acquaintance agreed to pass on his interest in meeting her, although it turned out that he had two rivals: one reading Chemistry, the other PPE. Hilary Bardwell, fearing her expertise in these subjects might be insufficient to sustain the likely conversation, chose to meet the man reading English: she didn't find him strikingly handsome and she disliked his clothes, but at least she'd be able to talk to him. Kingsley guessed her age to be about twenty-one. In fact, Hilly was seventeen, 'and hence not nearly so depraved as I had hoped'.[67]

She was certainly different from his other girlfriends – the occasional pick-ups during his war service and Oxford acquaintances such as Gillian Williams – and from Elisabeth Simpson: if Kingsley had regarded his relationship with Elisabeth partly as a learning experience, his relationship with Hilly would, he thought, be more like a teaching experience. She had been born at Kingston upon Thames in 1929, the fifth and youngest child of Leonard Bardwell, who worked for the Ministry of Agriculture, and his wife Margery. Hilly was educated at Bedales, a 'progressive' school in Hampshire, but evacuated in wartime to Dr Williams's School for Young Ladies in North Wales, from which, understandably perhaps, she ran away. She returned to Bedales, though left at the age of fifteen without academic qualifications – by which time her father had retired and moved to Harwell, ten miles south of Oxford – and took a job in Bracknell at a kennels run by two lesbians (a detail which couldn't fail to entrance Kingsley and Philip: 'Me: "Did they lezz with each other or with other people?" – geuss Who I maent eh you old Bugar I know my sort').[68] After the war, she enrolled at the Ruskin School of Drawing and Fine Art, though she soon gave up her course to become their 'head model': Kingsley interpreted as meaning their 'best model' until he discovered that in fact she modelled her head, not her body. But when in March she was persuaded to take off her clothes in the service of art, which was more than she had so far done for him, she sought and received his grudging approval. 'I'm sorry to have to tell you this,' he wrote to Philip, 'but it's a man who's doing the painting.'[69]

In its early stages, the relationship was largely shaped by their mutual and distinctly competitive interest in jazz. Indeed, Hilly's ownership of records by Cleo Brown and by Red Nichols and his Five Pennies very nearly compensated for her disappointing lack of depravity: 'So I am prepared to carry on until I get some records or fin bocqs find that she won't sell. *BUT NO LONGER THAN THAT*.'[70] Within days, she was driving a hard bargain, parting with Hoagy Carmichael's 'Georgia on my Mind' for the substantial sum of 7s 6d, 'the price of a front and rear cycle lamp';[71] Kingsley may have consoled himself with the thought that she could now travel more safely to him in the hours of darkness. When Taphouse's, the music shop in Cornmarket, had a sale of second-hand but mint-conition deletions, Hilly got there first, greeting Kingsley with a copy of the Joe Venuti–Eddie Lang 'After You've Gone' / 'Farewell Blues' under her arm. This common ground – together with Hilly's humour, straightforwardness and lack of pretension – was one reason why, in the early months of 1946, they got on so well as chums rather than lovers, a point not always fully appreciated: both Eric Jacobs[72] and Humphrey Carpenter[73] alight on a phrase from Kingsley's letter to Philip of 18 March ('Hilary was stupider and more boring than ever') without seeing that this refers not to Hilary Bardwell but to Hilary Morris, a male student at St John's.

There *was* a bone of contention, of course, and it was the inevitable one. In mid-May, Kingsley wearily noted that he and Hilly had been 'arguing for the past week about sleeping in the same bed as each other'. 'First she said no, and I said she would have to say yes,' he told Philip, 'then she said yes, and I said I had forced her into it and what she meant was no, then she said no, and I feel hurt and angry and disappointed and am trying to make her say yes, and there for the moment the matter rests.'[74] Patrick Standish and Jenny Bunn were to go through precisely this sort of negotiation in *Take a Girl like You*. However, ten days later, Kingsley could report with evident satisfaction that 'Hilary has yielded.'[75] Throughout this period, he had been somewhat incongruously dispensing tactical and, a little later, contraceptive advice to Philip on how he should conduct his affair with Ruth Bowman. The fact that both Kingsley and Philip had embarked on relationships with girls who might still have been at school (Ruth was, to start with) suggests two things about them, one obvious, the other less so: clearly, this was a strategy for translating the fantasy world of Willow Gables into reality; but what it more interestingly reveals is their continuing sense of insecurity, their nervousness about emotional relationships with equals, elders and betters which needn't apply to their juniors. Apart from that, they both happened to be in love.

Or were they? Kingsley, at least, had a difficult lesson to learn that August, when he went on holiday to France with Hilly and their physicist friend Christopher Tosswill as decoy or mock-chaperon. Apart from worrying that they might be 'THROWN OUT of this hotel for IMMORALITY', he was 'starting to think that Miss Hilly and myself have been seng quite enough of each other, and I want to get my life to myself again'.[76] Things hadn't improved by 7 September: 'Miss Hilly and I have not been getting on quite so well of late: at the moment she wants me to pock her more than I want to pock her, and I am starting to think that Sir tea er tea has more or less the same effect on a young chap as fruss tray shun. There is the same wanting to be by oneself, and the same not wanting to take trouble to be nice, and the same feeling that one has let onseelf down, and the same feeling that one has been caught in an unpleasant and ineluctable conspiracy.'[77] Two interconnected discoveries – that he could have too much of the woman he loved and that she in turn might actually make demands on him – seem to have taken Kingsley by surprise. More broadly, they signalled the deep fault-line in his personality: as an only child and as a writer, he was predisposed to solitude and impatient with other people; yet he continually needed company and was terrified when alone, as well as being hopelessly incapable of looking after himself in practical terms. (It didn't help, either, that they were stuck with Tosswill who, Hilly thought, 'talks too much like a BADLY-WRITTEN BOOK'.)[78]

When they returned home, their relationship once again became intermittent and, consequently, improved. 'This', Kingsley recalled, 'was the era when the tones of Bunny Berigan's record of "I Can't Get Started" seemed to come floating out of every window between Beaumont Street and Wellington Square,'[79] and when Philip questioned the accuracy of this recollection, in 1982, he remained adamant: 'No you fool it *was* ICGS in 1946 coming from every other window in St John St & Wellington Sq. Hilly confirms.'[80] It was the era, too, of midday meals at a 'British Restaurant' (shepherd's pie and rice pudding cost 1s 3d) and an evening omelette at the Stowaway, otherwise known as the 'Chinese', although (as Kingsley's alter ego Robin Davies says), 'it had never been known to serve any food even distantly associated with that land'.[81] And it was the era during which Hilly proved her mettle by being rejected as 'not readily hypnotisable' by a hypnotist and 'by washing her hair and her smalls

in the Randolph and, much to my trepidation, in the bath-house at
St John's'.[82] At Easter, Kingsley moved out of his rooms at college
and into digs at 19 St John Street, which he shared with two Welshmen and 'an extravagantly handsome Lothario type' who smuggled
girls into his bedsitter; the landlady, Miss Butler, regarded all four
of them as 'gentlemen'. He and Hilly stayed, chastely, with the Amis
parents in Berkhamsted and, less chastely, with the Bardwells at
Abbey Timbers, Harwell; they went off to London, supposedly to
visit Kingsley's army friend Frank Coles for a weekend, but in fact
to the Morton Hotel in Bloomsbury. Over the next year or so, Kingsley was as devotedly faithful to Hilly as he would ever be – rather
uncharacteristically turning down other sexual opportunities on moral
grounds – and as early as February 1947 Bruce Montgomery, having
bought them dinner at White's, urged him to marry her. But nothing
was further from Kingsley's plans: he couldn't yet contemplate that
sort of emotional or financial commitment, and he certainly didn't
want children. Hadn't Cyril Connolly listed the pram in the hallway
among his enemies of promise?

Kingsley graduated with First-Class Honours in December 1947
– the wartime distortions of the academic year hadn't yet entirely
disappeared – and immediately embarked, as John Wain suggested,
on his BLitt. He tried to profess astonishment at his First, especially
the alpha for his Chaucer paper, but he shouldn't have been surprised
and neither should we – for his comments on literature, not least the
satirical and scurrilous ones, had always been underpinned by a sharp
critical intelligence. Unluckily, his allocated supervisor was Lord
David Cecil, who seemed disinclined to supervise anything at all;
after a term and a half had passed without any contact between them,
Kingsley decided to go in search of him at New College. This caused
much amusement at the porters' lodge, as if he had asked for the
Shah of Persia: 'Oh no, sir. Lord David? Oh, you'd have to get up
very early in the morning to get hold of him. Oh dear, oh dear. Lord
David in college, well I never did.'[83] The only solution was to switch
supervisors. Kingsley approached F. W. Bateson of Corpus Christi
and found that this would be a simple enough procedure, merely
requiring Cecil's signature on the appropriate form – which, of
course, posed precisely the same problem of actually finding the man.
Almost immediately, he spotted him outside Blackwell's and intro-

duced himself as 'one of your B.Litt. people'. 'Oh, how awful!' Cecil
replied. 'I'd quite forgotten.' Back at New College, the form was
produced and completed without difficulty. Kingsley thought that
Cecil probably had a drawful of them, labelled '*Forms for fucking
fools who are fed up with me just pocketing my fee and want a
serious supervisor*'.[84] Having accomplished this, he and Bateson
'cobbled up' a thesis topic which seemed likely to sustain the interest
of them both: 'English Non-Dramatic Poetry 1850–1900 and the
Victorian Reading Public'. It ought to have been rather good.

But he had something else on his mind before the end of 1947, as
he told Philip on 6 December: 'Hilly and I are making a man at the
moment which is worrying me rather, but not as much as it might
because we have assembled a lot of chemicals which are inimical to
the continued retention of the fertilised ovum.'[85] This proved ineffec-
tive, for by 27 December he had arranged to take Hilly 'up to London
to see the nasty man, and he is going to give her an injection of a
substance derived from the interior of a cow, which we hope will
cease her Mary Shelley activities'; should this also fail, there was the
last resort of 'a surgical operation, costing £100'.[86] During the first
week of January, they stayed (genuinely, this time) with Frank Coles
and then with Gillian Williams while they tried to organise an
abortion – the doctor was 'Central European and very agreeable and
reassuring'[87] – and borrow the money to pay for it from, successively,
Christopher Tosswill, Nick Russel and another, otherwise unidentified, acquaintance whose name was Lightfoot. At this point, Hilly
went back to Harwell, while Kingsley returned to Coles's flat so that
he could sort out the financial and practical details. Fortunately, he
also consulted Coles's friend Hugh Price, a 'real doctor', who enlight-
ened him about the probable and possible consequences of the
Central European doctor's 'sheer butchery'. The following morning,
he revisited the abortionist in an attempt to improve matters, for
instance by ensuring that Hilly would have a proper period of
convalescence, but Hugh Price told him that the new arrangement
was hardly better than the old one.

And so: 'I went down to Abbey Timbers and told Hilly all this
and, as I had expected, she agreed that it would be best to get
married.'[88] As romantic proposals go, it must have scored poorly, but
it was a better idea than he realised at the time or would always

appreciate in the future. His view of marriage, as expressed in his letter to Philip of 12 January 1948, is a mixture of unsentimental common sense and startlingly immature self-deception:

> As regards the impending marriage, it's hard not to look upon it as a *faute de mieux*, though this feeling is decreasing slightly. I don't want a filthy baby, but Hilly is so overjoyed by the prospect that it seems unkind not to allow it, and since I'm determined to keep Hilly and she would never be happy for any length of time without a baby, having one sooner or later seems inevitable. Since I enjoy living with Hilly better than I enjoy living anywhere else, it's difficult to believe that I shan't enjoy living with her all the time, especially since it'll mean in addition that I shall be able to do as I like, eat the food I like, and stop worrying about not being able to ejaculate when I want to. As against this, I shall have to 'find somewhere to live', and eventually spend money on a *pram* and *furniture*, and have to nurse the baby, but can foresee myself not minding these things as much as I have minded other things in my life, and this time I shall be getting things in return. Also Hilly has £3 a week of her own *for life* [this wasn't in fact the case], which makes me feel happier. I should be glad to have your unprejudiced opinion on this situation. I don't want you to think (anymore than I want to think) that it will mean our association had become less intimate. You know of course what Hilly's opinion of you is (you bastard). I imagine we shall be living in Oxford for some time yet. I'd like to see you very soon.[89]

There's nervousness and bluster as well as selfishness here. Kingsley would never much care for babies and he was as truly terrified by the domestic practicalities of marriage as he was grateful for the prospect of being looked after. As for the prediction that he would enjoy living with Hilly all the time, he chooses to forget that he had already tried this in France and not liked it much. He frankly acknowledges (by attempting to discount) the possibility that marriage might compromise or diminish the most intimate of all his friendships and in this rather unusual sense promises the continuance of an emotional *ménage à trois*. The marriage took place at the registry office in Oxford on 21 January. Nick Russel was there and so, thanks to Peggy's diplomatic efforts, were both sets of parents. The registrar was 'a Hitchcock fat character with bursting eyes and lips like wizened Paris sausages . . . We only had two sentences each to repeat after him, and then there was nothing to do but signing and paying money.'[90] Afterwards, there was tea at the Randolph, and in the evening Russel took Kingsley and Hilly out to dinner at the George. A few days later, the couple moved into a 'rather small and very expensive' flat at 14 Norham Road: it was Hilly, naturally, who supplied 'crockery and cutlery and pots and pans and a carpet-sweeper and bed-linen and between two and three hundred pounds'. Kingsley ironically signed off a letter to Philip in his newly earned style – 'My wife and I send our best wishes' – before reverting to his usual form of valediction: 'Rather sudden wasnt it bum.'[91] Reconciling those two selves wouldn't be easy.

Kingsley says nothing about Hilly's pregnancy and the circumstances of their marriage in *Memoirs* and the account in his letters to Philip is notably restrained; the version which rings truest emotionally is in *You Can't Do Both*. Much of the detail is fictional: the abortionist is transplanted to Cardiff; the money is borrowed from Robin's elder brother; and his father has already died (the preceding illness enables Kingsley to establish the 'straight' Dr Wells, based on Hugh Price, as a character earlier on). But the dismayingly plausible Dr Beck, who 'spoke almost without accent but pronounced unstressed syllables more precisely than a native speaker would have done',[92] is a brilliantly judged version of the Central European abortionist: there is hardly a hint of the grotesque and only a deft understatement of his motives ('the tortured sincerity of a man who knows that whatever happens his money is safe').[93] Equally striking is the generous spirit in which Robin's mother receives the news of her son's sudden and imminent marriage to Nancy Bennett: 'Well, for what it's worth I give the two of you my blessing. The three of you. I can't help feeling pleased about that.'[94] Nancy's parents are less understanding and attend the marriage ceremony only after Mrs Davies's personal intervention; in reality, it was Peggy who had to reconcile her husband to the situation as well as persuading Hilly's parents not to boycott the ceremony. Helped by the long perspective of *You Can't Do Both*, Kingsley could at last acknowledge how much he owed to his mother.

7

'The trouble with marriage, my dear little fellow,' Kingsley wrote to Philip on 9 February, 'is not that you are too much on your own with your wife, but that you are too much alone with your mother-in-law, and your father, and your father-in-law, and your mother, and your mother's friends, and your father-in-law's friends, and your father's friends, and your mother-in-law's friends.'[95] We have heard precisely this note before, in Kingsley's – or rather Peter Furneaux's – complaint about his childhood: 'Being an only child did not mean that you were by yourself too much; on the contrary, you got the whole of your parents reserved for just you instead of divided up into three, say.'[96] In each case, it was the wrong kind of attention. One consequence of marriage was that his own parents felt they should come to Oxford, bearing gifts and helpful intentions: 'They are nice parents, but I don't seem to find what they find interesting interesting, nor do they me, if your pursue me.'[97] It was no better when he visited them at Berkhamsted soon afterwards: 'My parents suffer from being bad at being nice to people they like, and I am bad at "respecting" them in the way they enjoy, so things were rather difficult some of the time.'[98]

Nevertheless, they didn't begin to compete with the family into which he had married, for in his father-in-law, Leonard Bardwell or 'Daddy B', he had scored a bullseye. From the moment he makes his first tiny appearance in Kingsley's letters to Philip, as early as 13 May 1946, Daddy B – 'an extraordinary old man like a music-loving lavatory attendant'[99] – is quite clearly a character in search of a novel. When Kingsley visited Abbey Timbers in July that year, he not only made a frightening discovery about his future father-in-law – 'And the father does folk dancing (polk dancing? pock dancing? fock dancing?)' – but also met Hilly's brothers, one of whom wore '*sandals* and *saffron* trousers, and No Socks, and a *green* shirt, and plays the *recorder* (yes) and likes Tudor music'.[100] Once married to Hilly, Kingsley soon became incensed by Daddy B's table manners, his conversational digressions, his linguistic hobbyhorses and his misplaced pedantry ('when I am corrected from what is right to what is wrong, I become angry in my brain').[101] In the middle of January

1949, he glimpsed his means of retaliation: 'I have jotted down a few notes for my next book about Daddy B; I don't see how I can avoid doing him in fiction if I am to refrain from stabbing him under the fifth rib in fact. I have been thinking of a kind of me-and-the-Bardwells theme for it all, ending with me poking one of Hilly's brothers' wife as a revenge on them all.'[102] Both strands of this – Professor Welch, the fictional equivalent of Daddy B, and Jim Dixon, the central character who steals Welch's arty son Bertrand's girlfriend – were indeed to appear in his 'next book'. In the meantime, Daddy B became a major player in the comic narrative of Kingsley's letters to Philip, prompting spasms of upper-case rage:

> The best news from here for a long time is that old Bardwell was taking part in some lunatic folk-fandango in which the men swung a lot of staves about and ducked and jumped over them (SILLY OLD DIPPY OLD SOPPY OLD DAPPY OLD POTTY OLD FOOLS) – you know the kind of thing. Well, old B's opposite number swung his stick at the wrong time, or old B mistimed it or something: anyways, the upshot is that old B takes *one hell of a crack on the brain-box*, and is *laid out for some time*, and *suffers a lot of pain*, and *has to be treated for shock*. NOW THAT'S FUCKING GOOD EH?[103]

A few weeks later, he was almost equally delighted to report that the recorder-playing son, William Bardwell, had '*given himself the shits by his own filthy French cooking*',[104] just as would happen to Neddy Welch's other son, Michel, in *Lucky Jim*.

Philip had moved in the summer of 1946 from Wellington to a sub-librarian's post at University College, Leicester – the former asylum and future setting for Malcolm Bradbury's *Eating People is Wrong* – where Kingsley visited him in March 1948; Philip had digs in Dixon Drive, with 'a landlady who resembled a battered old squirrel and a dough-faced physicist co-lodger'. On the Saturday morning, Kingsley found himself parked for a while in the college's senior common room: 'I looked round a couple of times and said to myself, "Christ, somebody ought to do something with this."'[105] That 'something' was, of course, *Lucky Jim*, which has the small provincial university college, the shared digs and the name Dixon, together with a recognisable portrait of Philip's English-lecturer colleague Monica Jones. Kingsley himself, for reasons which are both plausible and canny, liked to suggest that his visit to Leicester was indeed the novel's primary source. But by the time he came to write *Lucky Jim* he was teaching at a small university college, where for his first couple of months he lived in shared digs; the features of the book which seemed to derive from his visit to Philip had all been echoed by his own experience, although Leicester came to play a useful strategic part in his protestations that the book wasn't about Swansea. (Many readers, perhaps taking their cue from Professor Welch's surname, remain convinced that it is, despite the absence of Welsh characters and the location's obviously greater proximity to London.) The main aspect of *Lucky Jim* which couldn't have come from this experience – and which provides the novel's comic mainspring – was based on the Bardwell family. He ought to have been grateful to them.

The Amises knew that their flat in Norham Road would soon be too small to accommodate Kingsley, Hilly and the 'baybay', so in May 1948 they moved to Marriner's Cottage, Newland Street, Eynsham, just outside Oxford. It was the first time Kingsley had properly *noticed* the place in which he lived, and it was the only one of his homes which he would remember with unqualified affection. The cottage had 'a stone-flagged passage from front to rear and a walled garden with rambling roses, hollyhocks, a walnut tree and the best gooseberries I have ever tasted';[106] the 'small, dapper, but dignified ginger cat called Winkie' from Norham Road was soon joined by a dog, Mandy, and some evenings 'a hedgehog came visiting'; the village pub, with a real parrot in it, was part of the same short terrace. Human visitors to Marriner's Cottage included Philip Larkin and Ruth Bowman; Kingsley's first post-war tutor, J. B. Leishman; and John Postgate, physicist, trumpeter and future jazz critic for the *Gramophone*. To the one party the Amises were able to give came 'Ken Tynan ... with some of his train'; Kingsley's *Oxford Poetry* co-editor James Michie and his blonde girlfriend; Arthur Boyars, the editor of *Mandrake*; 'Randolph comics like Niko the Greek, Randolph wits like Stanley Parker'; sundry jazz musicians; and 'groupies associated with the Playhouse, the Experimental Theatre Club, the *Cherwell* – along they all came'.[107] Though not quite in the Gatsby league, it was a starry enough gathering for Eynsham: the closest, Kingsley thought, he ever got to 'glittering'.

And there was fatherhood. On the morning of 15 August, in the

Radcliffe Maternity Home, Hilly gave birth to Philip Nicol Amis: he had 'very fair hair and a conical head (it will not stay conical, they said), and a face like that of an ageing railway porter', wrote the proud father to the baby's godfather. 'I don't know what this business is supposed to make you feel; I seem just the same as before.' However, he added: 'Hilly is very happy and glad, as I am, to have something to name after you.'[108] Five days later, he was able to report: 'The shape and arrangement of his face seems more usual than formerly. If I can continue to regard it as a pet too stupid to do tricks, except involuntary and nasty ones, I think I shall be able to get on with it all right.'[109] As, of course, he did; by 25 August, while sparing Philip none of the colourful details of his ten-day-old godson's evacuations, he had to admit feeling 'much more kindly towards him than I thought I should; of course I know "your own is different" OOTZZSCH, but he seems an inoffensive and almost apologetic little boy, with a face only about half as ugly as I expected'.[110] Given the well-established tone of Kingsley's letters to Philip, this translates into something approaching adoration.

In retrospect, Kingsley could view the year-and-a-bit he and Hilly spent at Marriner's Cottage as idyllic. So it mostly was, apart from the visitations of Daddy B – who turned up unannounced, '*spoiling everything by his presence* and *not realising it* and *doddering about and missing his bus*'[111] – and Hilly's brother-in-law Roger Partington: Kingsley swiftly transformed him into an absent-minded, accident-prone honorary Bardwell called 'Old Rodge', while admitting 'how much funnier than RGP is our conception of old Rodge', a remark which applies to many of the characters in his letters. But there were three indications, symptoms of the life to come, that this generally pleasant existence couldn't last for ever. One was that, with Hilly safely distant from Oxford and either pregnant or nursing a baby, Kingsley almost immediately embarked on a series of casual relationships, including one with a fifteen-year-old schoolgirl, 'very pretty and amusing, and like a little startled horse,'[112] whom he met each morning on her way to school. Secondly, by the beginning of 1949, Hilly was pregnant again: their second son, Martin Louis Amis, born on 25 August, was 'Blond (frup) as P, less horrifying in appearance'.[113] And thirdly, to support this growing family, Kingsley would have to get a job. His BLitt thesis was far from completion but, having finished the coursework element of his higher degree, it would be perfectly feasible for him to take on a university lectureship from October 1949. He put in applications to Birmingham, Bristol, Durham, Liverpool, London, Manchester and even Prague. He made arrangements to leave Marriner's Cottage – 'There was no farewell moment, though of all places I have ever lived in, this deserved one'[114] – and decamp temporarily to Abbey Timbers; Hilly, Philip and Martin would have to stay there, or with his own parents, while he started work and found somewhere to live. He was interviewed everywhere – twice for Prague – but they all turned him down. At the start of October, he was parked at Harwell with his family, without a home of his own and without a job.

3. JIM AND THE 1950s

1

Quite what the University College of Swansea thought it was doing in October 1949, interviewing candidates for a lectureship in English to start work the following week, is anyone's guess. The vacancy was created by the appointment of Bernard Blackstone to a chair at Istanbul, but he can hardly have left without notice. Kingsley, when summoned to attend, was flat on his back at Abbey Timbers, suffering from 'Vincent's infection, or trench mouth, with minor streptococcal variants and suspected diphtheria'.[1] He couldn't come to Wales on the Friday, he told them, but would the following Tuesday do? Swansea replied, with what he would soon come to recognise and admire as a peculiarly Welsh sort of humour, that Tuesday would be perfectly all right with them, although they expected to have made their decision on the preceding Saturday. His doctor sternly announced that he wouldn't 'hear of my going' on Friday unescorted; but, since the likeliest person to accompany him was Daddy B, he went on his own anyway. It was the last university vacancy in English to be filled that academic year, and Kingsley got the job.

If, as Hamlet supposed, there's a divinity that shapes our ends, it had a waggish disposition about it when it sent Kingsley off to South Wales. Hitherto, he'd imagined Wales as 'a rugger ground with Cader Idris on one side and a spoil-heap on the other, populated by dirty pit-miners who only stopped singing "All Through the Night" to bawl "Look you to goodness whateffer" at one another, and subjected to continuous rain'.[2] Yet he had, after all, landed in exactly the sort of milieu – a small university college in a town well away from London – which he'd glimpsed on that visit to Leicester three years earlier: it would contribute obliquely to *Lucky Jim*, directly to *That Uncertain Feeling* and then spasmodically to much of his work, culminating in the most deliriously Welsh of all his novels, *The Old Devils*. Beyond this, Swansea simply suited his temperament: the college was less intimidating than a major university, more likely to appreciate his clowning seriousness; while the wider social context provided a pageant of mostly genial human absurdity. For his first couple of months there, he was in digs with 'an eccentric Irish Latinist in his thirties called Willie Smyth and a landlady who had waved hair, kept a spaniel called Sandy and was the sort of woman who could not be dissuaded from drawing the sitting-room curtains to stop the sun putting the fire out'.[3] This is unmistakably the world of *Lucky Jim*, *That Uncertain Feeling* and *Take a Girl like You*; but it is also, and in one sense just as appropriately, the world of Mrs Ogmore-Pritchard, the landlady in *Under Milk Wood*: 'And before you let the sun in, mind it wipes its shoes.'[4] For the first time in his life, Kingsley found himself noticing other people who were not family, friends or fellow students; and they in return, being nosey and Welsh, wanted to know a good deal about him.

The English Department at Swansea was tiny – at first consisting of Professor W. D. Thomas, Isabel Westcott, James 'Jo' Bartley, David Sims and himself – and this increased his workload: a class, whatever its size, is still a class; a lecture still a lecture; and teachers in small departments can't confine themselves to their special subjects. He also suffered from the handicap of all beginners in academia: he had no stock of old lecture notes to fall back on, so everything had to be prepared afresh and, although academic expectations were lower than at Oxbridge, the amount of reading and preparation required to produce six new lectures each week was staggering. Because he had experienced, or endured, such widely varying standards of lecturing at Oxford, he was determined to emulate the best rather than the worst of them: his own style owed much to that of C. S. Lewis, from whom he borrowed the useful trick of reading out important but hard-to-find quotations at dictation speed. He could be more abrasively critical than was wholly to the taste of the amiable though bland Professor Thomas, but his students were delighted by him. He told Larkin that his lecture on the first morning of the spring term in 1950 was to be on Oscar Wilde and the Aesthetic Movement of the 1890s: '"Wilde united the qualities of silliness and high intelligence in a degree unparalleled except in Keats" – yes, I'm going to say that.'[5] This combination of critical intelligence and iconoclastic wit is the voice of quite another Movement.

By this time, in fact well before Christmas, Hilly had visited and found them a proper home of sorts: 'a ground-floor flat in an ill-built house' at 82 Vivian Road, Sketty. Though this was an improvement, it was a close thing: 'Although deaf-landlady bum and bad-food bum and ration-book bum were bad where I was, bottle-mixing bum and coal-cellar bum and up-early bum and washing-up bum are bad where I am. But not as bad as the former things that were bad.'[6] Indeed, as described by Kingsley, it sounds like a location from a novel by John Wain, John Braine or Alan Sillitoe, or from one of those films – *Saturday Night and Sunday Morning, A Taste of Honey, This Sporting Life* – which so exactly captured the texture of provincial British life in the decade or so after the war: it was approached via 'good hefty steps punctuated by right-angle bends for the twin pram to be lugged up to the front door'; Martin, now aged four months, 'slept in a drawer'; the airing-cupboard 'was a tea-chest lined with towels and warmed with hot-water bottles'; and the Baby Belling cooker, as was almost traditional with such appliances, 'gave you shocks when you tried to fry bacon on it'.[7] In the early months of 1950, the family shared a house near by (at 11 Haslemere Road, Sketty) with David Sims, Kingsley's closest friend in the department and in Swansea; then they moved to the Mumbles Road, where the first of their two flats was 'part of a derelict shop with an outside sink fed by successive kettles' – there is in *Memoirs* a photograph of Philip and Martin cheerfully bathing in it. Several aspects of the Amises' Swansea flat-life inform *That Uncertain Feeling* and the related short story, 'Moral Fibre'; but the 'much-shared bathroom with a quivering geyser if you could stand it' from Mumbles Road would have to wait until *Take a Girl like You*, where Dick Thompson so unsuccessfully attempts to show Jenny Bunn how the fearsome machine actually works, or doesn't.

In 1949, an assistant lecturer's salary was about £300: not much, even by the standards of the day, for a man with a wife and two young children, especially if the man was as clueless about money as Kingsley. For some time, Hilly added to the family income by spending her evenings washing up in the Tivoli cinema's café, while Kingsley stayed at home babysitting and writing tomorrow's lecture; she'd collect some leftovers 'for her Alsatian' and, with luck, her tips might buy a bottle of beer on her way home, to go with the Alsatian's supper. During the summer vacation of 1950, Kingsley and David Sims took on the marking of one paper – some 800 scripts – of the Joint Welsh Board's school certificate exam, retreating to David's mother's cottage at New Tredegar to work nine-hour stints with only the prospect of a Guinness in the local to keep them going; he found this sustained exposure to his future students' literary talents deeply dispiriting. Then, in 1951, Hilly inherited a legacy of £2,400 and, as Kingsley put it, 'the world was changed'. This was enough for them to buy a house 'within a stone's throw of that Cwmdonkin Drive that Dylan Thomas was Rimbaud of' – 24 The Grove in the Uplands district of Swansea – as well as a car, a fridge and a washing machine. And, above all, he now had a room in which to write. It was a modest space, big enough to contain just a table and a chair and a typewriter, and with an undistractingly dull outlook on to the blank wall of the house next door. Nevertheless, its existence had two important, interconnected consequences. One was that it enabled Kingsley to absent himself, as he would do for the rest of his life, from anything connected with domestic chores or organisation. The other was more momentous still: 'I sat down and started writing *Lucky Jim*.'[8]

2

If only it could have been that simple. In reality, *Lucky Jim* was a tortuous book to get right, and its final shape owed much to its dedicatee, Philip Larkin. The draft material which Kingsley had brought with him to Swansea sprang from two as yet irreconciled impulses: the need to 'do something' with the provincial university theme he had spotted in Leicester, perhaps with a central character based on his librarian friend; and the no less urgent need to revenge himself in fiction on his tiresome father-in-law and other assorted Bardwell relations. But as the book provisionally called *Dixon and Christine* grew, it became increasingly diffuse and unfocused; it was Larkin who eventually went through it, rigorously excising irrelevant material until, like *Jill* and *A Girl in Winter*, it consisted of a single-strand narrative. 'He decimated the characters that, in carried-away style, I had poured into the tale without care for the plot: local magnate Sir George Wettling, cricket-loving Philip Orchard, vivacious American visitor Teddy Wilson. He helped me to make a proper start.'[9] To that extent, *Lucky Jim* is the novel Larkin himself might have written if only he'd been more interested in other people.

The nature and extent of Larkin's influence on the book can be
accurately tracked through Kingsley's letters to him. When he first
mentions it by name, as *Dixon and Christine*, on 22 March 1950, it's
to report that he has written 'a few more pages'[10] which he wants to
show his friend, who is about to visit Swansea; on 12 June, he hopes
to snatch a few days, between the end of term and the start of Higher
Certificate exam marking, to 'work on *Dixon and Christine*, which I
haven't touched since you were here';[11] by 10 August (despite all the
marking and some depressing summer-school teaching) he has 'done
about 10,000 words' and reached an interestingly right-and-wrong
interim judgement: 'I don't think it's as good or so verbally funny as
The legacy, but it may be more publishable and perhaps some of the
things that happen are funnier.'[12] He seems not to have made much
progress for the rest of the year, during which he suffered two
unrelated discouragements, as academic and as novelist: his BLitt
thesis was turned down on viva (by a quirk of ill luck, the internal
examiner was Lord David Cecil), and Doreen Marston delivered her
damning verdict on *The Legacy*. But at least his financial problems
were about to be alleviated by Hilly's inheritance; and he had taken
more notice of Mrs Marston's advice than even she might have
expected. That these two considerations were closely linked is clear
from his letter of 8 January 1951: 'When I get my nice new grey
typewriter and a room to myself I shall start writing *Dixon & Xtine*,
cutting out a lot of redundancy, inserting stacks of conflict, strength-
ening my female characterisation, grammaticising my writing, and
whacking away with the old funniness. I am quite serous, though,
about the first 2 things, and quite keen to get started.'[13]

He was indeed 'quite serous' and, unusually, prepared to seek and
take advice (whether it came from Philip Larkin or Doreen Marston)
because he was working in the dark. *Dixon and Christine* was turning into a book defined not by its likeness but by its unlikeness to
other novels: Kingsley's letters to Philip are full of references to the
novelists whom he didn't want to resemble, including Evelyn Waugh
and (for the time being) Anthony Powell; while the writers he *did*
admire, such as Graham Greene or Christopher Isherwood, tended
to be working in areas (too foreign, too queer) which weren't quite
his own. He was still a literary apprentice without a clear sense of his
literary master; there was one, of course, but this chronologically
distant figure wouldn't be clearly identified until Kingsley's third

novel, *I Like It Here*. Meanwhile, his progress was spasmodic. On 12 June 1951, as the long vacation began, he could report that he had 'started on *Dixon and Chr* again; I shall opt for dipsomania if no one takes it'; he still felt that it was 'not as funny as *The legacy*, but is I hope more solid'.[14] But the summer brought other distractions: 'Life here would be all right if I had more *time* – the house keeps filling with self-invited craps – and more *energy*; honestly old boy without a word of a lie three pages of *Dixon* and I'm licked for the day,' he grumbled on 15 July,[15] having yet to discover that three pages might be a decent daily output for a novelist.

When, in the spring of 1952, he thought he had finished *Dixon and Christine*, he sent it off to Michael Joseph, who had expressed a politely conventional interest in seeing anything Kingsley might write after *The Legacy*. He was desperate to get into print. 'I know you think I'm a bit funny about printer's ink, and that the important thing is to write well,' he told Philip; but he wanted 'to think of myself as a writer, not entirely (I like to think) for motives of vanity, and that the one characteristic shared by all writers is that what they write is printed down for people who want to read it to read it, even if nobody does read it, d'you see'.[16] There were good reasons for this urgency: he was envious both of Larkin's publishing head start and of John Wain's successful self-promotion; and he would be thirty – which must have seemed terribly old to a 'young' author with only a Fortune Press book of poems to his name – in less than a fortnight. Two months later, Michael Joseph returned *Dixon and Christine*, 'rejected I suppose by a pal of John Wain's'; it wasn't right yet.

Meanwhile, the first of the annual PEN anthologies – *New Poems 1952*, edited by Clifford Dyment, Roy Fuller and Montagu Summer, and containing poems by Kingsley – was published in May. He went to the launch party with the mixed feelings familiar to most writers, 'in case there's anybody there I can impress with my genius or virile member, and even though I know there won't be I shall still kick myself when in the future people send my poems back'.[17] He knew he'd regret wasting the fare from Swansea 'just for 2 hours of talk' and, with a glumly resigned humour which Jim Dixon might have appreciated, saw himself 'stagger retching from the coach, trying to tell myself I've saved half the rail fare, into a gloomy room full of Richard Church and Paul Dehn, everybody knowing everybody else and those who know who I am impregnably persuaded that I'm

Welsh'. In the event, the party went better than that: Kingsley evidently enjoyed meeting 'John Lehmann, false and smiling, Roy Fuller, nice and doggish and looking like an ageing subaltern in the Indian army, Alan Ross, the cricket king, now caricaturing an Italianate Elizabethan, Ronald Bottrall, an emaciated clown'; he also met for the first time Robert Conquest, who 'recited a very long sequel to *Eskimo Nell*' to him just before he left.[18] Kingsley was more accomplished in the black art of literary schmoozing than he cared to admit. But the real significance for him of *New Poems 1952* lay, thus far unsuspected, in his contributor's note, where he guilelessly confessed that he was working on a novel.

Kingsley now turned to Philip – who, having completed two novels with apparent ease, was unaccountably having trouble with his third – for help with *Dixon and Christine*; almost at once, he was prompted to rethink quite fundamental aspects of the book. 'About D and C: I'm jolly glad you're taking such a decent interest in the thing: *don't let it slip*. We should be able to fudge up something good between us,' he wrote on 24 July, suggesting, even if ironically, the newly collaborative nature of the enterprise.[19] 'My feeling at the moment is that your "D should sod up the romantic business entirely" is the most acute criticism,' he added, though this idea would be reversed again by the time the book was finished, since Dixon pretty much ends up with 'The fame and the girl and the money / All at one sitting'. Both the state of flux and the extent of Kingsley's proposed overhaul of *Dixon and Christine* that summer are clear from his letters. On 11 August, he told Philip:

> I've thought of no more real ideas for *D&C* . . . I think, perhaps, the title had better be changed into *The man of feeling*; D. has more to feel about than he had before, and the Xtine business had better be concealed I suppose for as long as we can until she appears anyway. I think that while I feel I've come near hitting the bell with the provenance of J G-S, I am out on a) the introduction of Catchpole b) how Xtine finds out about Bert & Vic. No doubt you'll have looked into all that.[20]

There's a nice implication here, in which affection is tinged with imperiousness, that the librarianish Larkin is the one to be 'looking into' things. But Kingsley's next letter, on 8 September, is even more remarkable both for the range of ideas (some retained, some dropped)

thrown up by this creative partnership and as evidence of the author
thinking through possibilities at the very moment of writing to his
friend. Consequently, it is worth quoting at some length:

As regards D&C: *the library*: Dixon can be collecting griff for a
contribution of Welch's to a folk-dance conference or a lecture on
arts and crafts in eighteenth-century Hamberton; needn't be anything to do with his book. Still, thanks for the tip.

the lecture: I see what you mean about this, though it would
be awfully difficult to do. I could have a shot at it, anyway, and
you could decide whether it should go in; it's an optional scene as
regards the plot, story, etc. He'd have to be drunk, I think.

the job: agreed. The grammar-school touch is a winner.

Betrand's pass: yes. Would it do to make Carol deduce from
watching D&C at the sherry party that they are deliberately
avoiding each other – sort of looking at each other and then
looking quickly away when their glance is returned? And then
Carol asks Christine what's up? Would that do? The poke-invite
could be placed anywhere off-stage. The snag is that this deprives
us of the excuse for keeping Christine upstairs with her headache
when Dixon pays his abortive visit. Well I suppose she could
appear and go off with them. But that means 6 in the car. Unless
Mrs Welch doesn't 'feel like going'. Or neither Bert nor Chr are
going. But it would be nice if they did; they could be going off to
dinner with the Goldsmiths, where B. could deliver his poke-invite
& Carol could have a chance to watch things & start liking
Christine. Then Mrs W must stay behind, say to receive some lute-
player from Sweden who is expected. The placing in the car would
then be Christine next to Welch in the driver's seat, and at the
back Bertrand–Dixon–Veronica. Yes I think Mrs Welch is waiting
for Ole. 'Ole ole ole ole Moses keep her sweet to me' Dixon sang
under his breath in imitation of a dance record he had once heard.

Medievalism: yes; then we could make Welch fond of children's
art and Mrs Welch the anglo cathoclic fascist, eternally engaged
in arguments with Welch over the significance etc. of children.

Further notes: Do you agree about the black decade?

Do you agree about making G-S a new lover for Carol?

About the successive-days point: I think a lot of it *has* got to
be crowded up for reasons of motivation; e.g. the hotel tea mustn't
take place too long after the ball – they wouldn't want to wait;

and the whole of the 2nd part (from summer ball on) must take place in the confines of Christine's stay at the Welches, and she has got a job to go to after all. Eh?

I think the best thing about Veronica's name would be to change it to Margaret Jones; then I could enjoy cutting at Margaret Ashbury as well as at Monica. You can tell Monica that I'm cutting at some frightful Welch girl, and I'll tell Margaret that I'm cutting at some frightful Leicester girl. How would that do? It's a common enough sort of name, God knows.

Would it be asking too much to ask you to skim quickly through the typescript, making marginal indications of anything that displeases you? ('Bad style', 'damp squib', bad bit of dialogue & so on, to prevent me using them again.)[21]

The sustained seriousness of tone and the absence (apart from the unremarked 'cathoclic') of Kingsley's characteristic typos with their attendant frivolities are as notable as the density of detail: it's very clear that he means business. And it's equally clear that Philip's suggested changes were all of a literary-critical sort, with one exception: the naming of the character eventually called Margaret Peel was a matter of far greater sensitivity than Kingsley's brash jollity implies. Monica's full name was Margaret Monica Beale Jones, so 'Margaret Jones' plainly wouldn't do.

By early November, he had 're-begun *The feeling* [i.e. *The Man of Feeling*]': 'The trouble is there are so many "threads" (Margaret (she has reverted to Peel, by the way), Welch, Johns, Atkinson, Michie, Caton, Bertrand, Christine, Carol) that the reader will expect someone to be murdered any chapetr fartr chapter bo po now – probably Dixon.'[22] This 'trouble' would be overcome simply by making everything else in the novel plainly subservient to Dixon's shambling progress through it. Rather to Kingsley's surprise, his work on the book had been assisted by the recent presence of his father-in-law: 'As a matter of fact, it was his visit that made me get on with *Feeling* at last. Over the sound of his certifiable baaing to the children my typewriter tapped out sternly "They made a silly mistake, though . . ." and the artist had once more found the point of release for his trauma.'[23] It was the closest he'd yet come to acknowledging the crucial role Leonard Bardwell had played in the book's evolution.

Then, in the first week of December, he received a letter which not only spurred him on to complete his novel but completely altered his literary career. The sender was Hilary Rubinstein, who had been at Merton College, Oxford, in the late 1940s, when Kingsley returned to complete his degree; they had known each other slightly. Now he was working as an editor for his uncle, Victor Gollancz. There were, of course, other pre-existing Gollancz connections: his daughter Diana had met Kingsley at Oxford; Bruce Montgomery was published by him; and he had turned down *The Legacy*. But the twenty-six-year-old Rubinstein, brought into the firm as an editorial new broom, read Kingsley's contributor's note in *New Poems 1952* and wondered whether he might see the novel mentioned there. 'I shall be very glad to send you my novel when the time comes,' Kingsley replied, adding with carefully crafted modesty: 'It would never make an author's or a publisher's fortune, but I think it is quite funny; that, at any rate, is its aim.'[24] The agent Rubinstein would later become might have advised caution, questioning whether Gollancz was the right list for Kingsley and instead suggesting that they should try the book with Chatto or Faber or Secker. But Kingsley, understandably enough, showed no such hesitation: for the first time in his life, he was within sight of having a proper publisher.

All he needed was a finished book. On New Year's Day 1953, he told Philip that he was up to page 150 of *Dixon*, which had temporarily regained its old title, and that he had 'made up very good words for the Beethoven piano concerto theme that Dixon sings to himself';[25] a fortnight later, he had reached page 185. 'Some bits', he admitted, 'are boring me terribly, particularly the Margaret/Veronica bits.' He thought the bogus letter to Johns was 'the only good part of the chapter. It is a threatening letter from the mythical boyfriend of a typist in Johns's office: "you lay of yuong Marleen" – you know the kind of thing. I quite laugh at it.'[26] All this, however, was still the penultimate draft: in February, he started again from the beginning. By 3 March, *Dixon* was 'up to p. 95 of the final, to-send-off version', and at this point two crucial changes occurred. Firstly, Philip's role as collaborator, critic and 'inner audience' came to an end: 'It wouldn't be any use giving it to you to look at again, except for your entertainment, because the bloody thing will just cease to exist if it gets any more structural tinkering.' And secondly, the novel, although Kingsley still called it *Dixon* at the start of his letter, had acquired a new identity:

To tell you a little more about it: things that I think you will like are: the madrigal-singing, the Welch tune ('you *bloody* old fool'), the phone-interview with Dixon as the reporter, the Johns letter, Bill Atkinson, Welch and the revolving door, the Principal, and the faces . . . I've called it *Lucky Jim* now, to emphasise the luck theme – epigraph Oh, lucky Jim, How I envy him *bis*. Bertrand is as *à la* [Christopher] Tosswill as you could stand now, I hope. I'm afraid you are very much the ideal reader of the thing and chaps like you don't grow on trees, course not.[27]

Kingsley completed this final draft on 30 March: 'Well, my old bandolero, I have just this moment finished my last task on that Dickson thing, so that it is all ready to send to a lot of men who don't know a good thing when they see one . . .' It consisted of 349 quarto pages, which he calculated was 'about 87,000 words, which is a lot'. And he was adamant that this was to be his last revision: 'The only thing I feel with any certainty about the finsi quinsi finished draft is that it is the finished draft; no, or almost no, bugger is going to make me do anything to it ever again.'[28]

Lucky Jim seemed to attract luck almost from the moment that Kingsley sent it off to Rubinstein on 15 April, a delay as likely to have been caused by lack of money for stamps (cash flow in the Amis household had swiftly reverted to its pre-legacy state) as by nervous indecision. The next day, his thirty-first birthday, he learned that 'the BBC (Wain Division)' had accepted an extract of 2,000 words – the scene in which Jim sets fire to his bed while staying at Professor Welch's house – to open John Wain's new Third Programme series *First Reading* on 26 April. *First Reading* was the successor to John Lehmann's earlier anthology series *New Soundings*, and Wain's brief was specifically to identify and promote the new generation of writers whom Lehmann had overlooked: as a plug for a novel which wouldn't be published until January 1954, the *Lucky Jim* excerpt was of limited commercial value, but it was a wonderful way of concentrating editorial minds at 14 Henrietta Street. These minds were well disposed towards the book in any case: for Rubinstein, it was precisely the kind of title he had been hired to acquire – 'I think it is a really brilliant book and got more fun out of it than anything else I have read for a long time'[29] – and the firm's senior reader, J. R. Evans, agreed with him. Only V.G. himself had reservations: in finding the novel 'vulgar and anti-cultural', he anticipated exactly the terms in which a minority of reviewers would damn it; but he had sense enough to see that he ought to back Rubinstein's judgement. He did, however, intervene in the publication schedule: Kingsley had hoped that *Lucky Jim* would appear in the traditionally strong autumn season; Gollancz held it back until the new year, on the basis that a first novel from an unknown author would receive more attention at a quieter time. He was right.

Meanwhile, Rubinstein was working hard on *Lucky Jim*'s behalf. Initially, he had some doubts about the title (but liked *Dixon and Christine* even less) and some worries about libel; with magnificent disingenuousness, Kingsley assured him that while Professor Welch was 'based slightly on my father-in-law (between ourselves)', 'Bertrand Welch, Margaret Peel and Carol Goldsmith are as fictitious as any fictional characters ever are, I should imagine.'[30] He sent proof copies to – and received pre-publication puffs from – C. P. Snow, Harry Hoff (the novelist William Cooper, author of *Scenes from Provincial Life*), John Lehmann and J. D. Scott, the literary editor of the *Spectator*; he fixed up an article, complete with author photograph, in *Vogue*; and he sold the American rights to Doubleday for $2,500. 'I've long admired old Cooper,' Kingsley told Rubinstein on 3 July, 'and should very much like to meet him and Snow.'[31] They met briefly at Hoff's shortly afterwards and again, in more relaxed pubby company, soon after the book's publication. Snow's puff, used on the dust-jacket, described *Lucky Jim* as 'humorous, self-mocking, hopeful and endearing. For promise and achievement combined, it is the best first novel I have read in the last two years.'[32] This struck the right balance of generosity without fulsomeness, though the last phrase seems curiously specific, as if Snow remembered having read a much better first novel exactly twenty-five months earlier.

As for the American rights, Kingsley's main concern was to liberate some of the dollars due to him as soon as possible or, better still, to find a way in which Doubleday could open an account on his behalf at a New York jazz record shop so that he could be paid in rare and otherwise unobtainable jazz discs; Rubinstein had to tell him that would be illegal, though he did contrive to release some of Gollancz's advance on publication as well as a portion of the Doubleday money. Apart from being short of money, Kingsley had two other causes for disappointment as *Lucky Jim* made its way towards publication. 'I feel a bit let down now that *Jim* is finished and accepted,' he admitted to Philip on 26 May. 'In a way it makes me want to *stop writing*, like a man who's satisfied with one seduction because he's proved he can do it and wanted reassurance, not pleasure.' The only reliable cure for this condition is to start work on another book, but he worried that he was already running out of backgrounds: 'I won't do Oxford, the Ormy is more or less out of the question – I didn't do any fighting and I've forgotten what I did do – which leaves only bourgeois life in Swansea, and that's really *too boring* to do.'³³ In fact, he began *That Uncertain Feeling*, about bourgeois life in a place very like Swansea, almost immediately; by November, he could assure Rubinstein that the book was 'coming on' and that he was up to page 154.

His other disappointment was one he would never quite get over: Gollancz's tactical delay meant that John Wain's *Hurry on Down*, published by Secker and Warburg that autumn, would be out before *Lucky Jim*. He had several reasons to be grateful to Wain, who at Oxford had saved him from a life of schoolmastering; then he had given *Lucky Jim* pride of place in *First Reading*; and now he was arranging for the School of Art at Reading to publish Kingsley's new collection of poems, *A Frame of Mind*, as the second in a limited-edition series (Wain's own *Mixed Feelings* had been the first). None of this made him any more likeable, however, nor did it diminish Kingsley's growing conviction that as a writer Wain wasn't any good: of Wain's second novel, *Living in the Present* (1955), he memorably told Philip that it wasn't 'so much a bad a book . . . no, *LITP* goes further than that in not *seeming to be by a writer*'.³⁴ The fact that *Hurry on Down* had attracted a substantially greater advance from Secker than *Lucky Jim* from the notoriously parsimonious Gollancz only made matters worse. Kingsley's, as he cheerfully told Wain when they met during the summer, was £100. 'Oh,' Wain replied, 'I'm getting two hundred and fifty for mine. You see – mine isn't Joe Soap's first novel.'³⁵ A month or so later, Kingsley delightedly discovered that his own 'combined English and American advances' amounted to 'nearly twice John's – ho ho'.³⁶ But this was small consolation for having had his thunder stolen and for the mistaken assumptions that readers and reviewers would continue to make about the chronological sequence of the two books. In January 1958, for instance, he had to write an understandably tetchy riposte to the anonymous *TLS* reviewer of *I Like It Here*, pointing out that he 'first became acquainted with Mr Wain's *Hurry on Down*, and its "rescue-by-millionaire theme," soon after its publication in August, 1953',[37] whereas his 'own novel *Lucky Jim*, complete with "rescue-by-million-aire theme," was accepted for publication in April, 1953'. Wain, for his part, would always remain keen to exploit his accidental tactical advantage. A quarter of a century later, in a retrospective introduction to *Hurry on Down* from which he contrived to omit all mention of Amis and Larkin, Wain claimed that 'if there was a "movement" at all . . . I cannot be accused of tagging along behind it. I might even be credited – or blamed, if you will – for having *started* it.'[38]

3

There was, or there soon would be, a Movement with a capital M, and John Wain could justly claim to have been one of its instigators; but this had little to do with *Hurry on Down*. His essay on the poetry of William Empson, 'Ambiguous Gifts', which aptly appeared as the last item in the final issue of *Penguin New Writing* (1950), was far more influential in shaping the literary practices of his generation. This was essentially an appreciation of Empson as an already neglected poet, in whom Wain detected the Donne-like metaphysical-ity which would become a key feature of the Movement, but it was also, in its concluding attack on the lazy romanticism of the 1940s, a call to arms. 'For', wrote Wain, 'the plain fact is that many of the reputations which to-day occupy the poetic limelight are such as would crumble immediately if poetry such as Empson's, with its passion, logic, and formal beauty, were to become widely known'; if Empson's poems were to be 'read and pondered, and their lessons heeded', it would be 'a sad day for many of our punch-drunk random "romantic" scribblers'.[39] The new decade could hardly have presented its credentials more clearly. If no one seemed to take much notice, this was because the writers who would answer Wain's call were either still largely unpublished or (as with Larkin) had yet to publish their most characteristic work. In this context, *Hurry on Down* was a less important book than Wain liked to think.

It can't be denied that there are striking similarities between *Hurry on Down* and *Lucky Jim*. Like Kingsley, Wain began writing his novel in 1949, in his first year as a junior lecturer in English at a non-Oxbridge university and in the third year of a precarious (though in his case childless) marriage. One odd consequence of the gap between the novels' conception and their eventual publication is that both books, though their tone and approach so clearly belong to the new decade, are rooted in a social and political landscape which was rapidly vanishing by the time they appeared; the same is true of John Braine's *Room at the Top*, completed in 1953 but not published until 1957. Wain's hero, Charles Lumley, is a recent graduate of an unsettled, characteristically post-war sort, as is Jim Dixon; and the novel concerns Charles's picaresque progress towards a rather sudden, well-paid job in London, which is also Jim's destiny. Charles is emphatically from the North of England; Jim is from Lancashire, though so unemphatically that most readers fail to notice. And here the similarities begin to give way to the even more significant differences: for Kingsley – even though he would find himself lumped together with John Wain (from Stoke-on-Trent), John Braine (from Bradford) and even Alan Sillitoe (from Nottingham) – was ineradicably from suburban South London; Jim Dixon's Lancastrian background is as arbitrary and unconvincing as the Lawrentian baggage with which Larkin, for similar reasons of attempted distancing, saddles John Kemp in *Jill*. Whereas Wain, Braine and Sillitoe were Northerners drawn, as was commonly the case, towards the more affluent and cultured South, in Kingsley this magnetism was exactly reversed: he was a Londoner who fled to the provinces and who wouldn't write a novel which was substantially set in London until *I Want It Now* in 1968. This crucially affects his – and, through him, Jim Dixon's – whole approach to experience. Jim is almost entirely without ambition: his one pressing concern is somehow to avoid being sacked at the end of the academic year, and the fact that this turns out not to matter after all depends entirely on his extraordinary luck. By contrast, the heroes of Wain's, Braine's and Sillitoe's first novels – Charles Lumley in *Hurry on Down*, Joe Lampton in *Room at the Top* and Arthur Seaton in *Saturday Night and Sunday Morning* – are actively seeking to alter their condition, though Charles's desire for reinvention is so unfocused that it at first takes him dramatically downhill. Jim Dixon wouldn't have been able to make the slightest sense of him.

Kingsley, writing in November to John Wain (who was in Switzer-

land, recuperating from tuberculosis), did his best to sound positive
about *Hurry on Down* and failed: 'I thoroughly enjoyed *Hurry on
Down* and read it whenever I had a free moment till I'd finished it. It
is very funny in parts and does succeed above all in getting across a
grotesque and twisted view of life . . . which is the main point as far
as I'm concerned.' His 'only complaint' was that 'a few parts are
over-written'.[40] He would find more to complain about in his letters
to Philip and in his *Memoirs*. But he did conclude his letter to Wain
with arguably his funniest – and surely his most prescient – spoof
jazz personnel:

> It occurs to me to try an old gag – more for my amusement than
> yours, I imagine:

> JACK WAIN AND THE PROVINCIAL ALL-STARS
> Wain (tpt; voc) directing Phil Larkin (clt), 'King' Amis (tmb),
> Don Davie (alto), Al Alvarez (pno), Tommy Gunn (gtr),
> George 'Pops' Fraser (bs), Wally Robson (ds).[41]

The Movement is usually, and correctly, said to have come into being
on 1 October 1954, when the *Spectator* published J. D. Scott's
anonymous literary lead article 'In the Movement'; but it was
invented in all but name by Kingsley in this letter of 6 November
1953. 'Provincial All-Stars' wouldn't, at least for a while, have been
a bad alternative title; 'Tommy Gunn' on guitar is especially felici-
tous, incidentally, given that the world had yet to hear of Elvis
Presley or of Thom Gunn's poem 'Elvis Presley' (ideally, Kingsley
should have added the blues singer Bessie Jennings as well as Big
Bob Conquest on some suitably large wind instrument). Jack Winn
– rather than Jack Wain – was an obscure, probably pseudonymous
bandleader of the late 1920s: a 78 of 'Melancholy' by Jack Winn's
Dallas Dandies (who were most likely Johnny Dodds and his Black
Bottom Stompers, featuring Louis Armstrong and Earl Hines) was
among the jazz records owned by Hilly which had especially endeared
her to Kingsley in 1946.

The word 'provincial' had been bouncing about in literary debate
that autumn, in an excited though not terribly useful way, after G. S.
Fraser used it in the *New Statesman* on 1 August: there, defending
First Reading, he remarked in passing that many of the programme's
contributors were 'young dons, and often young dons in provincial

universities'. Though this seems little more than a statement of the obvious, it infuriated a number of self-consciously metropolitan literary figures, who unluckily included Stephen Spender (co-editor of *Encounter*, launched in October 1953) and John Lehmann (editor of the *London Magazine*, which appeared from February 1954). The irony, of course, is that Spender and Lehmann, whose literary tastes had developed during the 1930s, had far more in common with Amis, Larkin and Wain than with the neo-romantic writers of the intervening generation. As it was, the two major new literary monthlies of the 1950s initially set themselves against the very writers they might have been expected to champion. But factionalism, always a feature of literary life, had been given a special impetus by the perceived need to discover a new movement to go with the somewhat wishful 'new Elizabethan Age' inaugurated by the coronation of Queen Elizabeth II in June. Meanwhile, the fact that some of the emerging Movement writers, particularly Thom Gunn, did indeed have appropriate interests in and affinities with Elizabethan literature went largely unnoticed.

On 30 October, in *Truth*, George Scott proposed his own far more inclusive list of the decade's significant new writers: A. Alvarez, Kingsley Amis, Arthur Boyars, Charles Causley, Hugo Charteris, Hilary Corke, Donald Davie, Iain Fletcher, G. S. Fraser, W. S. Graham, Thom Gunn, Thomas Hinde, Elizabeth Jennings, Iain Scott-Kilvert, Francis King, James Kirkup, Philip Larkin, Derek Lindsay, Mairi MacInnes, Jean Morris, John Raymond, W. W. Robson, Paul Scott, Richard Sleight, Sydney Goodsir Smith, Desmond Stewart, Frank Tuohy, John Wain. Some, inevitably, failed to establish lasting reputations, but those who did become well known are a notably diverse bunch, among whom the Movement poets remain dominant: of the nine contributors to Robert Conquest's 1956 anthology *New Lines*, no fewer than six – Amis, Davie, Gunn, Jennings, Larkin and Wain – are already on Scott's list. This was partly because the decade's new poets happened to emerge sooner than its novelists: in the autumn of 1953, Kingsley was still known mainly as a poet with a novel forthcoming, while the enormously significant first novels of both William Golding and Iris Murdoch were to appear later in 1954.

Lucky Jim was published on 25 January 1954, just over a week after the birth of Sally Myfanwy, the Amises' third and last child, on 17 January, an event reported to Philip by Kingsley in his characteristic style: 'The baby is quite hefty and looks no worse than might be expected. Rather better, really.'[42] Larkin responded almost immediately with 'Born Yesterday': 'Sodding good and touching was the poem, moving me a great deal as poem and as friendship-assertion,' wrote Kingsley, adding that 'it's about the nicest thing anyone could do for any new-born child'.[43] At the same time as he was celebrating the birth of his daughter, however, he was fulminating over the appointment of a new head of department at Swansea, in succession to the retiring Professor W. D. Thomas: only two candidates had been interviewed, the 'pleasant and intelligent' John Holloway – Fellow of All Souls, published poet and critic, future *New Lines* contributor and author of *The Story of the Night* – and the 'ugly and pompous' James Kinsley, who 'was hated by everyone at Aberystwyth, smokes a pipe and is a Scottish Methodist lay-preacher'. Philip would 'have no difficulty in guessing which one got the job'.[44] Meanwhile, Kingsley had also become embroiled in a splendid row which was brewing in the pages of the *Spectator*, where since November he had been a regular reviewer; the literary editor J. D. Scott and his deputy Anthony Hartley were keen to promote the 'Provincial All-Stars'. On 8 January, Hartley used the pretext of reviewing Edith Sitwell's *Gardeners and Astronomers* as a springboard for some thoughts on 'the present divided state of poetry': clearly favouring the line from Eliot through the poets of the 1930s such as Auden and Empson to the 'University Wits (Kingsley Amis and Donald Davie, for example)' over 'Neo-Symbolists' such as Sitwell, he found her work over-allusive and congested, illustrating 'the consequences of letting the imagery rip'. Sitwell replied in a fine fury, defending her own allusiveness and adding: 'I shall, no doubt, be told that little Mr Tomkins (or whatever his name may be), this week's new great poet, does not incorporate in his work phrases from the past, giving them a twist, and importing new meaning.'[45]

This opportunity was one Kingsley couldn't resist. On 29 January, in the very week of *Lucky Jim*'s publication, the *Spectator* carried the following letter:

> Sir, – As last week's new great poet, I was very glad to see the letter from a Doctor Sitwell telling Mr. Anthony Hartley that it's okay for great poets to copy bits out of dead writers. The lady is wrong, though, if she thinks I never copy bits out of dead writers

like she does. Here is a bit out of one of my poems, which I
haven't managed to get published yet:

> What noise is that? How, now, what hath befallen?
> I'll tell the news; here comes the general.
> Tomorrow – out of joint – the pity of it –
>   Ripeness is all.

Do you get the way I've twisted the meanings there? I'd like to see
Mr. Anthony Hartley having the cheek to teach, not only Doctor
Sitwell and that Donne man, but me and William Shakespeare
how to write.

    Personally, I think the sap of a tree is more like Double
Diamond than peridots and beryls but if Doctor Sitwell likes to
say it's like peridots and beryls then that's quite okay by me. It
just shows how we great poets differ. – Yours faithfully,

LITTLE MR. TOMKINS
[Name and address supplied][46]

It was a lovely childish squib, supplemented the following week by
an anxious little note which purported to come from Peridot and
Beryl themselves, and there the matter might have ended, had not
Sitwell herself reappeared on 19 February with a riposte which was
tactically more brilliant than she may have guessed. 'I cannot be
expected to waste my time in arguing with anonymous semi-literates,'
she said, before rather unexpectedly concluding: 'Mr Hartley and I
have at least one thing in common. I gather that he admires the work
of Mr Kingsley Amis. I have not, as yet, read Mr Amis's poetry, but I
have read his most remarkable, most distinguished first novel *Lucky
Jim* with enthusiastic admiration.'[47] This left Kingsley with the ticklish problem of 'how to make decent amends to old ES for being
Little Mr. Tomkins'. After much agonising, he wrote to the *Spectator*:
'A writer at the outset of his career can rarely hope for such generous
praise as that contained in the last paragraph of Dr. Sitwell's letter. I
am sincerely grateful to her. At the same time I feel I should point
out that I myself am "Little Mr. Tomkins".'[48] But Edith Sitwell
wasn't going to allow him to get off so lightly. She invited him to
lunch.

    Although Kingsley would subsequently refer to her as 'the old bag' and provide Philip with a suitably disrespectful account of this occasion (which took place in June), comparing it to 'lunching with a kindly maiden aunt who wants to show you she's interested in all that writing you're doing',[49] it was Sitwell who had the last laugh. Kingsley thanked her afterwards in a letter of irreproachable courtesy, sounding like a chastened schoolboy. She had neatly demonstrated the tactical advantage possessed by literary grandees such as herself over the Tomkinses: a capacity to be generously if rather pompously inclusive, whereas Amis and Larkin seemed altogether too keen to hammer on about what they didn't like and wouldn't admire. In fact, the improbable collision of Edith Sitwell and Kingsley Amis may suggest that the fault-line running through English writing in the early 1950s was less a matter of ideology, social class or literary style than of manners. And this indeed was the basis on which many of those who disliked *Lucky Jim* attacked the book and its author: over the next few years, *Jim* and Jim and Kingsley would find themselves interchangeably described as vulgar, uncouth or philistine by readers who had been needled by the book's air of compulsive disrespect (it was typical of Daddy B, Kingsley thought, to have formed his first impression from Julian Maclaren-Ross's *Sunday Times* review, 'High Jinks and Dirty Work', which took just this line). But the novel has a double layer of ambiguity, or perhaps simply of bluff: Jim Dixon needn't sincerely hold all the values he seems to assert; and Kingsley Amis needn't share them. It can be read as the work of a conservative satirist, a 'Peter Simple'. Edith Sitwell presumably read it this way and Somerset Maugham certainly did. *Lucky Jim* won the Somerset Maugham Award for first novels in 1955; as the prize money had to be spent on foreign travel, Kingsley at first planned to write 'a long-short on Dixon's experiences on the Continong'.[50] Some time after he returned, he wrote a fulsome letter of thanks to his benefactor and received a friendly reply, which Maugham reworked into a 'Books of the Year' piece for the *Sunday Times*. In it, Maugham saw the 'ominous significance' of this 'remarkable novel', which he took to be a keenly observed and brilliantly described depiction of 'the white-collar proletariat': 'They have no manners, and are woefully unable to deal with any social predicament. Their idea of a celebration is to go to a public house and drink six beers. They are mean, malicious and envious ... Charity, kindliness, generosity, are qualities which they hold in contempt. They are scum.'[51]

Maugham had trapped Kingsley even more effectively than Sitwell. Much of what he said about *Lucky Jim* (and there was more) was shrewdly to the point: it simply won't do to dismiss it all as a 'farrago of misreadings and prejudices', as Harry Ritchie does in his painstaking though oddly uncomprehending *Success Stories*. Kingsley must have viewed with reluctant admiration the way in which Maugham had selected one aspect of the book's multiple viewpoint and honed it into a single polemical perspective, a technique which would later become known as 'being economical with the truth'. For Maugham's remarks are not merely an uncannily parodic version of some of Kingsley's own later utterances: their underlying concerns already formed an implicit strand in his early thinking. He may have found himself, like Jim Dixon, living in the provinces and teaching at a small university college, but while he was working on *Lucky Jim* it had become perfectly clear that – for *part* of him, for one of the contradictory components which made up Kingsley Amis – this was a terrible mistake. 'You know what I should like to see?' he asked Philip, rhetorically, on 13 January 1953:

> I should like to see *a bit of life*. Almost *any sort*. Drinking, or sex, or fine talk, especially (I don't know why I should pick *that*) *that*. I don't want to talk about the unemployment at Llanelly, or the next meeting of the Gower Riding Society, or Dylan Thomas, or how many of the Finals class we shall be able to push through, especially *not* that.[52]

Soon after *Lucky Jim* was published, as the first amazing wave of fame and fanmail swept over him, he even contemplated an escape route very similar to Jim's: 'I *may* find myself with a job in London in a year or so, which would please me mightily. The higher journalism, it would be.' Jim Dixon intends to leave behind the provincial world of 'the white-collar proletariat', which Maugham so detested, when he opts unequivocally for metropolitan culture, security and respectability. That is why he is 'lucky'.

4

The most contentious two words in *Lucky Jim* are 'filthy Mozart'. Jim overhears Professor Welch singing in his bathroom: 'The piece was recognisable to Dixon as some skein of untiring facetiousness by filthy Mozart.'[53] On that pair of words, on what they do or don't imply, rests the whole argument about the alleged anti-cultural, anti-intellectual philistinism of Jim Dixon, the novel and its author. Counsel for the defence must first point out a possible mitigation in the text itself – if Dixon so loathes Mozart it's unlikely that he would instantly recognise the piece – and then produce two items of irrefutable-looking supporting evidence. One is the letter to Philip, written while Kingsley was working on his first draft (he was 'up to p. 94') on 15 July 1951:

> I have just bought 3 more Mozart piano concertos and some other longhaired stuff which would all be a bit beyond you I fear. As regards your stricures pricures strictures YOUFFOOL on divine Mozart. Your trouble is you've been brought up on things like the minuet from the Serenade in D and Iner Cliner, WHICH ALL THE BOOLDY SAM ARE A BOLODY SIGHT BETTER THAN YOU THINK YOUFFOOL, and in addition your musical appreciation unquote seems to have stuck at the basic ego level. The trouble with Mozart is really his intolerable pessimism, his loading of the ordinary allegro with more blisteringly tragic content than it'll stand IM PERFECTLY SEROUS YOUFF Anyway, go into a gramophone shop and play to yourself the first side of the D minor pno concerto, or the slow movement of the C maj one (K. 467) and see if you can go on thinking what you do YOUFFFFFOOL.[54]

The point about Mozart and pessimism is not only acute in itself but neatly reflects back on its author, for Kingsley too can load an 'ordinary allegro' with 'blisteringly tragic content' on occasion; and it's notable that he returns with such gusto (as he would continue to do) to the cultural battleground of his childhood.

The second item is the essay 'Real and Made-up People' (1973). Here Kingsley starts by proposing the 'plain distinction between action based on what the writer has made up and that based on what has actually happened to him';[55] he suggests that the second kind of fiction belongs characteristically to the twentieth century, that D. H. Lawrence was more or less to blame for inventing it, and that he himself writes novels of the first kind. Although he concedes that 'All my heroes, and other principal figures, have a great deal of me in them,' he is at particular pains to scotch, once and for all, the notion that he and Jim Dixon are interchangeable, and he provides examples of the 'distancing' he placed between author and character: 'he must not come from anywhere near London, teach English, be married, admire Mozart, be much too law-abiding – or cowardly – to appear drunk on the lecture platform or hijack a professor's taxi, as in my own case'.[56] Perhaps this looks 'plain' enough, but it immediately creates problems of its own. For one thing, if Kingsley and Jim are to be regarded as in crucial respects antithetical, we are well on the way to Maugham's reading of *Lucky Jim*. Alternatively, it may rather look as if the distancing differences have been introduced for no other purpose than to mask deeper similarities. A few months later, Kingsley returned to the same point in an interview with Clive James: 'In fact I enjoy madrigals. The idea that you can only guy things you hate is of course false. You can guy things you like. "Filthy Mozart", for example.'[57] The important word is 'only'; the implication is that the reader can't be quite sure how the author regards the subjects he satirises. The novelist (lucky him) can have it both ways.

This is what liberates *Lucky Jim* and lends the book its airy lightness, its comic zest, yet it also explains one's lurking sense of an evasive hollow at its heart. It's a novel which, while presenting a frank and open appearance, carefully refuses to say just what it means. In fact, Kingsley supplies a clue to his intentions, in the most obvious yet least regarded place, the epigraph:

> Oh, Lucky Jim,
> How I envy him.
> Oh, Lucky Jim,
> How I envy him.
>
> *Old Song*

If 'I' here stands for the author – and why else quote it? – then we need to ask what precisely he envies about Jim. As he hints in 'Real and Made-up People', he envies Jim's recklessness; yet he also envies both the cause and the consequence of this recklessness, Jim's unmarried state and his ability to chuck his provincial university job in favour of an altogether more stimulating metropolitan life (even though his own marriage and university teaching career would last for another decade). The fact that Jim is enviable is the novel's non-negotiable starting point.

Enviable, yes, but admirable? It isn't difficult to identify Jim

Dixon's least likeable characteristics: he's cavalier and thoughtless in his treatment of others as well as being lazy and incompetent in his work; he's also, and overwhelmingly, the house guest from hell. His attitude to Professor Welch and his dreadful family will strike most readers as both funny and forgivable (all the more so, given our knowledge of their Bardwellian originals). The difficulties that are likely to arise stem from his treatment of Margaret – and here our awareness of her resemblance to Monica Jones makes matters worse rather than better. To the question 'Is Christine favoured simply because she is sexy, attractive and available, whereas Margaret is plain, neurotic and badly dressed?', Kingsley might have offered two answers. The first would have been something like: 'Too right, you flat-faced pullet, of course she bloody well is.' The second: 'No, Margaret is rejected because she is manipulative, emotionally dishonest and dangerous.' There's absolutely no question of either/or here: you can't have one Kingsley without the other. But his clear authorial awareness of the problem is signalled by the parachuting-in of Catchpole to shore up the latter, and more respectable, position. Catchpole is the least convincing character in the book, partly because he arrives so late in it but mainly because we have no sense of him as anything other than the moral vindication for Jim's ditching of Margaret.

The question of Jim's attitude to his work is also more troublesome and complex than it at first appears. It's easy to sympathise with his predicament: to the pressures of being a junior lecturer in a small university college, with which Kingsley was all too familiar, are added the crowning fictional burden of a professor who closely resembles Daddy B. (It seems safe to assume that, had Professor Thomas shared this resemblance, Kingsley would have lasted no longer in his job than Jim.) But Jim, in the moments when he sounds most like his creator, crystallises the problem which rattles about in the Amis–Larkin correspondence and, in the view of unsympathetic readers, diminishes the work of both writers: he is too smug about his own ignorance and too scornful of others' learning. Quite early in the book, he is contemplating his dangerously bright and annoyingly male student Michie, named after James Michie, Kingsley's Oxford contemporary and one of his many subsequent *bêtes noires*: 'Michie knew a lot, or seemed to, which was as bad. One of the things he knew, or seemed to, was what scholasticism was. Dixon read, heard, and even used the word a dozen times a day without knowing, though he seemed to.'[58] On one level this is funny, and blushingly familiar to anyone who has taught under pressure; on another, it implies that Dixon is simply not much good. 'Haven't you noticed', he asks a few pages later, 'how we all specialize in what we hate most?'[59] To which his university colleague and fellow-lodger Beesley, instead of pointing out that this is nonsense, merely puffs at his pipe and gets up to go. Jim Dixon is, of course, a medieval historian, and Kingsley had acquired a powerful dislike of medieval literature at Oxford; but the transference is illogical, especially given that Kingsley now spent much of his time teaching literature which he *did* enjoy. When Jim finally and magnificently disgraces himself, in his drunken public lecture, the result is a comic scene of great brilliance; yet it is also one which entirely vindicates the ludicrous Professor Welch's lack of confidence in him. If Jim is lucky to escape, Welch is lucky to be rid of him.

Naturally, the novel – written in the third person but from Jim's point of view – seeks to minimise our sympathy for Welch; much of its comedy derives from the limitations and misapprehensions of Jim's perspective, the fact that his satirical observation of other people is unmatched by any real understanding of them. He realises this: 'Dixon fell silent again, reflecting, not for the first time, that he knew nothing whatsoever about other people or their lives.'[60] It's a stance which both liberates and limits the range of *Lucky Jim*. It makes Jim Dixon more likeable and forgivable than the evidence against him would reasonably allow. But, of course, one characteristic of luck is that it needn't be fully earned.

5

While Kingsley could truthfully insist that Jim wasn't an autobiographical character, he was in almost every respect a response to his author's own circumstances: marriage, in-laws, job, location – 'that deadly provincial background' – and the rumbling, unfocused discontent which all of these prompted. In this sense, he was emphatically an individual rather than a representative or a symbol or a type. Walter Allen, however, in a *New Statesman* review which he subsequently incorporated into *Tradition and Dream*, saw Jim as a new sort of fictional hero, 'the intellectual tough, or the tough intellectual', and wondered where he had come from: 'The Services, certainly, helped to make him; but George Orwell, Dr Leavis and the Logical Positivists – or, rather, the attitudes these represent – all contributed to his genesis.'[61] Allen thought that he had first arrived 'as the central character of Mr John Wain's novel *Hurry on Down*': thus Jim took his reluctant place alongside Charles Lumley as an early example of the 'Angry Young Man'.

Allen's suggestion was a shrewd but ultimately a misleading one, for *Lucky Jim* might be more interestingly compared with the work of two other emergent novelists of the 1950s, on both of whom Kingsley would soon write in the *Spectator*. One was Iris Murdoch, whose *Under the Net* he reviewed enthusiastically on 11 June 1954: it was 'a winner, a thoroughly accomplished first novel',[62] he declared, with the slightly comical benevolence of one who only the other day had been hearing this sort of thing said of his own work. He could scarcely have commented on the odd affinities between their books, starting with the merely coincidental fact that the two anti-heroes, Jim Dixon and Jake Donaghue, share the same initials: coincidental but not irrelevant, since those chummily shortened first names in which the letter 'J' is so prolific (Joe had already featured in *Scenes from Provincial Life* and would reappear in *Room at the Top*) say a good deal about the characters and the way in which their authors regard them. By calling their young men Joe, Jim and Jake, rather than Sebastian and Charles (Wain made a tactical error there), post-war novelists instantly signalled that there was nothing remotely *dorée* about this *jeunesse*. Jake, like Jim, is an *accidental* sort of man; what happens to him tends to happen by chance, or luck, rather than as a result of ambition or premeditation. His world, though unlike Jim's, is nevertheless one which Jim would have recognised; he would certainly have enjoyed that memorable London pub crawl. Then there is Hugo Belfounder who, although a prototype for subsequent Murdochian manipulators and not (at least yet) at all Amisian, stands in an oblique-above relation to the central character which Kingsley would subsequently explore, starting with Julian Ormerod in *Take a Girl like You*. And the comic–picaresque light-footedness of both Amis's and Murdoch's first novels stands in sharp contrast to the driven underlying earnestness of more authentic 'angries' such as John Osborne, John Braine or Alan Sillitoe. Kingsley identified and did his best to accommodate the philosophical undertow, the 'shade of Wittgenstein' and the 'apparition of M. Sartre', in *Under the Net*; the only part he disliked was the Parisian section, as if the combination of philosophy and abroad were really too much for him.

When, two years later, he reviewed Angus Wilson's *Anglo-Saxon Attitudes*, he reacted very differently. The book has obvious points of contact with *Lucky Jim*: it's a contemporary social comedy; it moves in and out of academia (though at a more elevated level than *Jim*, since the central character, Gerald Middleton, is a professor rather than a junior lecturer); and it introduces a rich cast of grotesque and ludicrous minor characters (here the social polarities are reversed: Wilson's unforgettably named Vin Salad, for instance, is a waiter rather than a professor's son). Kingsley's analysis of the novel's failure is so compelling that it's hard to imagine ever re-reading *Anglo-Saxon Attitudes* with pleasure, but it is also self-revelatory: he sees exactly what has gone wrong for Wilson because he has so nearly been there himself. For instance, his chief complaint about Gerald concerns his inertness; by the end of the book he has achieved 'modest enough victories' but 'the sad thing about them is that they just happen', a judgement which comes close to rebounding on Jim Dixon. He feels that the characteristic Anglo-Saxon attitudes of 'Priggishness, righteous discomfort, goat-voiced didacticism' aren't sufficiently deflated and implies that the author himself may be tainted by them; and he notes that, when it comes to the major female characters (Inge Middleton and Elvira Portway), Wilson 'writes them down or writes them off, passes superficial judgements about them *in propria persona*, tells us lies about them in a curiously off-hand and bored, almost angry way'.[63] Here the review almost becomes self-instruction, a series of memoranda to himself about pitfalls to avoid. Kingsley mentions priggishness more than once, yet he also observes, while describing the various groups of characters, 'The third group is the expected little posse of pansies, one of whom has a Dickensian grandmother and another a reciprocated interest in the chief historian's younger son,'[64] which is a prize-winningly priggish sentence even for 1956 (when, incidentally, that nastily placed 'expected' might well have been actionable). He tries for generosity in his conclusion – and would sound more convincingly generous in his *Spectator* review of Wilson's *A Bit off the Map and Other Stories* the following year – but the feeling of distaste is unmistakable.

There were warning signs in these two reviews, both in the specific aspects of each book which Kingsley found unpalatable and in the more general point that Wilson never would be and Murdoch would soon cease to be Kingsley's kind of novelist. He had even less in common with slightly younger writers such as Braine, Sillitoe and Colin Wilson. The novelist whom he read with most pleasure, despite some early reservations, was Anthony Powell ('I would rather read Mr Powell than any other English novelist now writing').[65] However, the book which above all affected his own work in the 1950s, and perhaps later, was William Cooper's *Scenes from Provincial Life*. Reviewing the Penguin reissue, together with the first publication of its disappointing sequel *Scenes from Married Life*, in 1961, Kingsley recalled: 'What impressed me most about Mr Cooper's book was that Joe Lunn, its hero, was just like me (and just like, I imagine, tens of thousands of other young men all over these islands).'[66] There are echoes of Joe Lunn – his mixture of innocence and unshockability, his sexual readiness and his appearance of straightforwardness – in each of the central young men in Kingsley's first four novels: Jim Dixon, John Lewis, Garnet Bowen and Patrick Standish. They also represent the four professions which Kingsley might reasonably have contemplated after Oxford: lecturer, librarian, freelance writer and schoolmaster, the last of which is also Joe Lunn's. But Cooper's novel was to prove influential at an even deeper level. *Scenes from Provincial Life* is an almost ridiculously underwritten book: its wilful naivety of style actually grows, at tremendous risk, into a convincing first-person voice: although a literary man who has published three novels, Joe is also a physics teacher in a grammar school and it's in this persona that he writes. Kingsley, with his ingrained distrust of 'writerly' novelists from Virginia Woolf to *Brideshead*-vintage Evelyn Waugh, was seduced by this unmannered tone. Although he would always be a more careful and finished writer than Cooper's Joe Lunn, his wariness of literary style as something footling, precious and a bit pansyish was to remain. He would have felt that this guarded him from pretentious excess, but it was a mixed blessing, and it owed more to his residual sense of lower-middle-class inferiority than to any clear artistic principle.

The novel which Kingsley had started before *Lucky Jim* was published, *That Uncertain Feeling*, might equally well have been called – had the title been available – *Scenes from Provincial Life*. In one essential respect, it's a book very like *Lucky Jim*: an utterly conventional novel of a sort Jane Austen would have recognised, in which the central character undergoes a modest yet life-changing experience within the scope of a local community, constructed as a personal narrative punctuated by a few big social scenes. That, after all, is exactly what happens in *Emma*. But *That Uncertain Feeling* differed crucially from *Lucky Jim* in the method and timing of its composition: the book was written fast and to an (unmet) deadline, and it shows. Gollancz rashly announced it long before it was completed or delivered. On 1 October 1954, Kingsley wrote to Hilary Rubinstein that his 'guilt-feelings' had been 'exacerbated to scream-ing-pitch' by seeing it listed among the Autumn and Winter Books in the *New Statesman*.[67] On 18 October, he reported that he had 'done 15,000 words, perhaps more, of the final draft', but this clearly wasn't going to be an autumn or winter book. In fact, he delivered it early in the new year and it was published in August 1955.

Although *That Uncertain Feeling* was well received – there was a perceptible feeling of relief that this wasn't the traditionally disastrous second novel – it's a book which mercilessly exposes Kingsley's limitations at the time. It opens with a clutch of allusive jokes about his deposed 'inner reader', Philip: the narrator, John Lewis, is a librarian who has a 'long thin body', whose hair is 'just beginning to go' and whose patience is tried beyond endurance by dim-witted borrowers, just as Larkin's had been in Shropshire. But all this is swiftly cancelled by greater dissimilarities: the action is set in the fictional South Wales town of Aberdarcy, where Lewis is married and soon to embark on an unlikely relationship with Elizabeth Gruffydd-Williams. By the end of the novel, marital peace will have been restored between John and his wife Jean, who shares some character-istics (and domestic arrangements) with Hilly, who is also the book's dedicatee. This sense of an implicit transition from Philip to Hilly is neither accidental nor quite convincing.

The plot of *That Uncertain Feeling* is preposterous. Mrs Gruffydd-Williams appears in the library, in search of a book about costumes for an amateur dramatic production, and introduces herself to John with a ringing double entendre: 'I'd really been hoping to find someone here who might be prepared to help me out personally.'[68] In due course, he will oblige, but in the meantime it becomes clear that she can also help him out, since her husband happens to chair the Libraries Committee which will decide on John's promotion. The proffered quid pro quo, and John's ultimate rejection of the deal, is the book's moral linchpin: 'What *I* didn't realise at the time of writing, so how could he, was that he was scared, and wanted out.'[69] On the way there, we accompany John on a series of excursions with Elizabeth and her cronies: to a country pub, where an unhandbraked car almost slides into a river (oddly anticipating the scene in Iris Murdoch's *The Sandcastle* where the car actually does so, and sinks); to a dance hall, where the unexpected intervention of a neighbour prevents John from being beaten up (Elizabeth, warningly, seems rather to relish rough trade); to an appalling sub-Dylan Thomas play, followed by an appropriately farcical adventure at the Gruffydd-Williams's home; and finally to a beach party, which precipitates their only sexual encounter and a melodramatic night-time traffic accident, incredibly resolved by the arrival of Elizabeth's husband who happens to be driving in the opposite direction. Of course, the reader will tolerate almost any number of implausibilities in plotting, as long as he is fully engaged in other ways. The problem here is that Kingsley is out of his depth. He, like John Lewis, thinks of the Gruffydd-Williams set as 'that upper-class crowd', although Philip Larkin's phrase 'a cut-price crowd' would be nearer the mark. Their fatuous vulgarity and nouveau-riche provincialism are very far from 'upper class', but the Amis–Lewis viewpoint – one of fairly unsubtle early 1950s left-wingery – doesn't easily perceive this; they are insufficiently imagined or inhabited as characters. One crucial consequence is that Elizabeth's pursuit of John fails to ring true. In both his first two novels, Kingsley seems to make the unwarranted assumption that men mostly notable for their clowning ineptitude will prove irresistible to rich women (his abandonment of this notion is among the reasons why *Take a Girl like You* is so vastly superior to them).

Nevertheless, *That Uncertain Feeling* works well enough as an entertainment until quite near the end. Indeed, as Harry Ritchie says, 'Most of the criticisms were directed at the ending, where Lewis renounces his socialite temptress and is reconciled to the virtues of his lower-middle-class home and hearth.'[70] The problem is a little more complicated than that. After the post-beach-party fiasco, John returns home to find his wife in the unwelcome company of Probert, the dreadful Welsh poet; there is a predictable falling-out, after which John wanders the streets until he bumps into his downstairs neighbour Ken Davies, drunk and incapable. They escort each other home, where John earns the gratitude of Ken's tiresome mother for the first and only time in the book. Just before they arrive there, John reflects:

> I thought how much I liked him, as he stood there in his mucked-up finery, not inquiring why I had these or any cigarettes on me, not wondering how I'd happened to be out at this time, not thinking there was anything odd about anything, not, above all, knowing or caring anything whatsoever about Elizabeth or Gruffydd-Williams or Whetsone or Theo James or Probert or Gloriana or Stan Johns or Margot Johns or the dentist or the dentist's mistress or Bill Evans.[71]

This is, among other things, warm-hearted nonsense: the idea of the literate librarian and the amiably stupid Ken remaining soulmates in the cold light of day is absurd. Yet Amis uses the encounter to prompt not just transitory benevolence but a life-changing decision. Once home, with his wife and children safely asleep, John has his modest moment of epiphany:

> Since I seemed to have piloted myself into the position of being immoral and moral at the same time, the thing was to keep trying not to be immoral, and then to keep trying might turn into a habit. I was always, at least until I reached the climacteric, going to get pulled two ways, and keeping the pull from going the wrong way, or trying to, would have to take the place, for me, of stability and consistency.[72]

These two sentences, more than any others in the book, explain the dedication; for this is Kingsley's resolution and apology to Hilly as much as it is John's to Jean.

There the book might have ended, with a closing gesture which is undeniably admirable despite its wobbly foundations. But it doesn't. The final chapter takes us forward a further year: John has resigned his librarian's post to work in the sales office at a colliery and moved back, with his family, to the mining village where he grew up. Here they are happily settled among genuine Welsh people who, despite their amusing idiosyncrasies and pretensions, have nothing in common with the Gruffydd-Williams set. Yet, in solving one moral dilemma, this creates another. Of course John is right to reject posturing duplicity in favour of honest stability; but is it right, or even sensible, for a graduate librarian to work in a colliery or to assume that this is the only alternative to his former life? Unlike Jim, John isn't offered the luxury of an escape to London; instead, he accepts a life of diminished expectations, a species of *trahison des clercs*. The matter is of importance in two ways which early readers of *That Uncertain Feeling* couldn't have foreseen. The whole question of the art–life balance – how far can or should we compromise our cultural and intellectual selves in the pursuit of apparent happiness? – is one which would haunt Kingsley throughout his literary career, resurfacing as a major theme as late as *The Russian Girl* (1992) and *The Biographer's Moustache* (1995). And John's problems of an emotional involvement with someone of a more elevated social background than his own, with the necessity of finding a strategy for return when things go wrong, would find their echo, much later on, in Kingsley's own life.

6

Since their memorable first encounter at the 1952 PEN anthology party, Kingsley and Robert Conquest had become close friends. In some respects, they were strikingly unalike: Conquest, five years older, was during the early 1950s a Foreign Office diplomat whose international interests contrasted very sharply with Kingsley's settled distaste for 'abroad'; he was to become a leading authority on Soviet Russia and at the time of writing he remains, in his ninetieth year, Senior Research Fellow at the Hoover Institution in Stanford, California. Kingsley would later draw on Conquest's Kremlinology in *The Anti-Death League*, *Russian Hide and Seek* and *The Russian Girl*. For the time being, their common ground concerned sex, science fiction and poetry.

Cheerfully recalling their friendship in *Memoirs*, Kingsley tends to dwell on the first of these. Conquest, he notes, was 'a generous and discreet flat-lender and of great usefulness to me in my unregenerate days',[73] a piece of archness which roughly translates as this: Kingsley would borrow his Eaton Place flat for assignations during his career as a serial adulterer, while Conquest would help out in auxiliary ways, by (for instance) despatching letters concerning Kingsley's Swansea adventures with a London postmark, instead of a give-away local one. 'Have been seeing a bit of your pal Bob Conquest recently,' Kingsley told D. J. Enright in February 1955. 'They very kindly let me use their house as a base when I come to London'[74] – which was another way of putting it. On one notable occasion, as Kingsley opened the flat door, the absent Conquest's taped voice commented, 'Lucky sod,' a reference to Kingsley's poem 'Nothing to Fear', which opens: 'All fixed: arrival at the flat / Lent by a friend, whose note says *Lucky sod* . . .'[75] 'No one else I know', says Kingsley in *Memoirs*, 'would ever have dreamt of going to that trouble,'[76] not perhaps an unambiguous compliment; it certainly seems an odd application of Foreign Office technical expertise. But it characterised the practical-joking, bawdy-limerick-writing side of Conquest's personality, which Kingsley relished and shared.

This sort of thing hasn't really worn well; nor, for different reasons, has the interest in science fiction which resulted in the Amis–Conquest-edited series of *Spectrum* anthologies, as well as Kingsley's 1958 Princeton lectures and their subsequent publication as *New Maps of Hell*. By contrast, Conquest's most significant literary role in the mid-1950s, as editor of the anthology *New Lines*, goes entirely unmentioned by Kingsley in *Memoirs* and by Eric Jacobs in his biography; even Zachary Leader gives it only a glancing mention in his enormous *Life of Kingsley Amis*. *New Lines* had its origin in a group of poems called *Reflections on Landscapes*, which Conquest submitted for the Festival of Britain Poetry Competition: the winning entries were collected in a Penguin anthology.[77] D. J. Enright wrote a favourable review; an exchange of letters and a visit followed; and this provided the impetus for both *New Lines* and Enright's *Poets of the 1950s*. Initially, Conquest saw his book as anti-Movement, a term he then associated with Alvarez, but he deleted 'a paragraph critical of the "movement"' from his introduction 'because it was a bit into Wain, and even Kingsley'.[78] Kingsley became involved with the project a year or two later: Conquest, who had assembled his list of proposed contributors by the beginning of 1955, consulted his friend about four possible additions. On 23 January, Kingsley gave his verdicts. Gordon Wharton and Mairi MacInnes were both 'P.P.P.', which stood for 'pretty piss poor'; Philip Oakes suffered from 'a kind of smugness perhaps, that I find rather off-putting'; only L. D. (afterwards Laurence) Lerner struck him as 'pretty good and well worth encouraging'. A '5th chap, old Holloway', he thought, 'stands slightly above Lerner'.[79]

In the event, John Holloway's work was to be included in *New Lines*, although Laurence Lerner's wasn't; however, Kingsley's instinct in choosing the two writers closest to the prevailing academic–ironic tone of the anthology had been a sound one.

New Lines was published by Macmillan in August 1956. The contributors, in order of their appearance, were Elizabeth Jennings, John Holloway, Philip Larkin, Thom Gunn, Kingsley Amis, D. J. Enright, Donald Davie, Robert Conquest and John Wain. Conquest's Introduction, though calmly and almost austerely written, was unsparing about the 'collapse of public taste' in the 1940s and 'the sort of corruption which has affected the general attitude to poetry in the last decade'. 'Poets', he continued, 'were encouraged to produce diffuse and sentimental verbiage, or hollow technical pirouettes: praise even went to writers whose verse seemed to have been put together from the snippets in the "Towards More Picturesque Speech" page of the *Reader's Digest*.'[80] He was a little more wary when it came to defining the characteristics of *his* group of poets – 'What they do have in common is perhaps, at its lowest, little more than a negative determination to avoid bad principles'[81] – and he remains true to that engaging modesty, now describing *New Lines* as 'a collection of poets I liked, regardless of politics or sex or any such. As I, and I think they, saw it, it was a batch that was neither too wet nor too dry.'[82] The main participants would haggle over their coherence (or not) as a group for years, sometimes pointing to geographical separation or lack of personal acquaintance as illogical 'reasons' why the *New Lines* poets – the Movement poets – couldn't have much in common. It was Donald Davie who put this matter straight, in typically acerbic terms, when in 1959 he wrote of 'the . . . craven defensiveness which led us when we were challenged or flattered or simply interviewed, to pretend that the Movement didn't exist, that it was an invention of journalists, that we had never noticed how Larkin and Gunn and Amis had something in common, or that, if we had noticed, it didn't interest or excite us'.[83] A few years later, in his 'Postscript' to the 1967 reprint of *Purity of Diction in English Verse* (1952), Davie could see this in a more equable light:

> One of my pleasant memories is of Kingsley Amis, when we met for the first time, telling me how he had come across *Purity of Diction in English Verse* in Swansea Public Library, and had read

it with enthusiasm. What pleased me was that Amis had liked the book, not in his capacity of university teacher (as he then was), but from the point of view of himself as poet. For it was thus that I had written the book: not in the first place as a teaching-manual, nor as foundation-stone of my own career in universities (though it has usefully performed both these functions), but principally so as to understand what I had been doing, or trying to do, in the poems I had been writing. Under a thin disguise the book was, as it still is, a manifesto.

All this was at a time when Amis and I and one or two others discovered that we had been moving, each by his own route, upon a common point of view as regards the writing of poems. That point of intersection, or an area of agreement around it, came to be called The Movement, and under that title has earned itself a footnote in the literary histories, being considerably blown up in the process. I like to think that if the group of us had ever cohered enough to subscribe to a common manifesto, it might have been *Purity of Diction in English Verse*.[84]

Though there were other equally plausible critical foundations for the Movement – such as the work of Yvor Winters, then little known in England, but with whom Gunn was by 1956 working in California – Davie's suggestion isn't wholly ludicrous. The vital point, of course, is that the Movement, which was increasingly a poetic rather than a looser literary grouping, was largely defined by technique and style; and in this sense it had a logical coherence which the Angry Young Men – a vague and often inaccurate description of attitudes rather than literary procedures, externally bestowed by journalists – couldn't hope to attain.

At the time Conquest was assembling *New Lines*, Kingsley had other reasons to refocus on his own poetry. One was the lack of a new novel to begin after he had finished *That Uncertain Feeling*; he had the germ of *Take a Girl like You* but knew, wisely, that he wasn't ready to write this yet. Another was a letter from the young independent publisher Peter Owen, asking whether he had sufficient poems for a new collection. Kingsley thought Peter Owen 'a pretty shaggy kind of concern' and asked Conquest whether he would have 'a sort of private and unofficial word' with Alan Maclean at Macmillan about his 'chances of getting a book published by Macmillan, or at any rate accepted, by the end of the year, say?'[85] In fact, hearing of this proposal was enough to persuade Hilary Rubinstein at Gollancz – not normally keen on poetry but anxious to retain their successful novelist – to publish *A Case of Samples* in 1956.

Although *New Lines* presented Kingsley's poetry in a sympathetic context to a wide audience, it also marked the downward turning-point of his poetic career. The nine poems by which he is represented exhibit several of his characteristic strengths. It was a shrewd move to open with 'Masters', an exploration of his recurrent power–authority theme which moves towards a paradox reminiscent of Gunn, who immediately precedes him in the book: 'By yielding mastery the will is freed, / For it is by surrender that we live . . .';[86] the subject recurs in the maddening riddle, based on the parade-ground game of 'O'Grady says . . .', 'The Voice of Authority'.[87] At the centre of the selection is the piece which would become his best-known poem, 'Something Nasty in the Bookshop' (otherwise, 'A Bookshop Idyll'), with its celebrated distinction between male and female poets: men, says Kingsley, write poems called 'Landscape near Parma', 'The Double Vortex', 'Rilke and Buddha', while women prefer 'I Remember You', 'Love is my Creed', 'Poem for J.'. This, he suggests, is why women are much more agreeable human beings (though lesser poets?) than men:

> Should poets bicycle-pump the human heart
> > Or squash it flat?
> Man's love is of man's life a thing apart;
> > Girls aren't like that.
>
> We men have got love well weighed up; our stuff
> > Can get by without it.
> Women don't seem to think that's good enough;
> > They write about it.
>
> And the awful way their poems lay them open
> > Just doesn't strike them.
> Women are really much nicer than men:
> > No wonder we like them.[88]

In a typical attempt to have it both ways, he manages to present the supposed inability of men to write love poems as a sort of blessed limitation; sceptics might note that his own conduct at the time certainly displayed some adeptness in keeping 'love' and 'life' conveniently apart. The poem is followed by the equally deflationary 'Here is Where', which might have been a riposte to Philip's 'Here' (except that the Larkin poem wasn't completed until October 1961). 'The country, to townies, / Is hardly more than nice,'[89] he writes, reminding us that the only time he really noticed it was at Marlborough. The remark, though quite funny in its context, has a reflexive–defensive edge to it, a recognition both pugnacious and disappointed that as a descriptive writer he isn't much good.

And this is half the problem. Despite the commonsensical manifesto of *New Lines*, Kingsley's poems continually veer from observation into rambling abstraction – as in the long opening stanza of 'Against Romanticism', where the last seven lines don't contain a single concrete noun. The other half of the problem is that his poetic ear is faulty: effective enough when held in check by tight ballad metres and constant wordplay, but hopelessly slack elsewhere, with little feeling for verbal music and a weakness for misplaced metrical stress. Kingsley's poems come in the middle of *New Lines*, where he is immediately preceded by Larkin and Gunn. A thoughtful reader going though the book sequentially (if anyone ever does that with an anthology) could have seen 'Church Going' as a centrally defining poem in Larkin, 'On the Move' in Gunn. But in Amis? The big poem never appears. At last it had been established beyond doubt which of Kingsley and Philip was the novelist and which the poet.

7

'Kingsley sets out for Portugal this week, on the Maugham money, for three months,' Philip Larkin told his friend Patsy Murphy on 18 June 1955. He had a nice sense of this adventure's creative improbability: 'A travel book may result, like a space-thriller by John Hewitt, a verse play by Mickey Spillane, or a good poem by A. Alvarez. Hilly's with him, of course!'[90] On 28 March, Kingsley had learned from Hilary Rubinstein that *Lucky Jim* had won the Somerset Maugham Award, administered by the Society of Authors: the prize money had to be spent, then as now, on at least three months' 'travel or residence abroad'. He gamely assured Rubinstein that it was 'wonderful news', adding: 'I look forward to writing a long-short on Dixon's experiences on the Continong.'[91] To Philip, on the same day, he wrote with markedly less enthusiasm: 'Honestly, don't tell Hilly, who I shall be taking with me, but the whole prospect fills me with alarm and depression ... What a sodding *waste of time* it'll all be.'[92]

It would be easy to read the first response as a polite fiction and the second as unvarnished truth, but Kingsley was more complicated than that. However much he may have denigrated the idea, the likelihood of some new experience kick-starting his third novel held strong attractions; now that he had 'done' Swansea in *That Uncertain Feeling*, it was more or less a necessity. His 'alarm and depression' sprang from deep-seated insecurities: his refusal, going back to child-hood, to fly; his reluctance, going back to the army, to drive (Hilly would have to do that); his inextinguishable nervousness about not being quite good enough and making a fool of himself. Moreover, the potentially disastrous notion of 'Lucky Jim Abroad' – which might have led Kingsley into a string of terrible sequels, of which 'Lucky Jim in America' would surely have been the next – was also more complex than it sounds. For a long time, Kingsley toyed with the idea of Gore-Urquhart, whose secretary Dixon becomes at the end of *Lucky Jim*, sending him off to Portugal, where he would meet the actual Kingsley Amis; a vestige of this survives in *I Like It Here* as Garnet Bowen's mission in search of Wulfstan Strether. He recorded absurd events for possible use in precisely those terms: 'One of the things that will happen to Dixon when he comes to Portugal on behalf of Gore-Urquhart is a ride on the back of a motor-bike after dark, in a high wind, part of the way in very fast traffic through Estoril, with a Portuguese on front *practising his English* turning his head to say "Would you like to take a cerp of cerffee later? Do you like Portuguese cerffee or is it too strerng?"'[93] (This too would survive into *I Like It Here*.) What is more interesting, however, is that Kingsley should have contemplated so unconventional a form: he had once before tried to use a self-named alter ego in his unpublished novel *The Legacy*, but this genre-bending proposal would have been even bolder. Although the idea of a self-exiled, lightly fictionalised 'Kingsley Amis' owes something to 'Herr Issyvoo' in Christopher Isherwood's Berlin books, the collision with Dixon, a fictional char-acter from another book, belongs equally to a tradition of experimen-tal comic fiction – from *Tristram Shandy* to *At Swim-Two-Birds* –

which had always appealed to Kingsley; and this tradition, rooted in the eighteenth century, supplies the subversive, surreal voice which continually disrupts the surface realism of his fiction and baffles readers who can't hear it.

Nothing was to come of 'Jim Abroad', not least because Kingsley was deeply wary of the travel-book element in his mixed genre. With impeccable timing, he published a hostile review of Laurie Lee's *A Rose for Winter* and Peter Mayne's *The Narrow Smile* in the *Spectator* on 17 June. Lee, he thought, indulged to the full the travel-writer's tendency to be charmed and delighted by behaviour which at home he would recognise as intolerable and to present this in an ineptly 'poetic' style; *A Rose for Winter* was a 'vulgar and sensational little book'. The following week, the veteran critic John Davenport sprang to Lee's defence, cunningly surmising that Kingsley had never visited Spain – 'Mr Amis seems to be unfamiliar with Spain; or did he once perhaps make a brisk Anglican survey from a bus?'[94] – and wondering whether it would be 'an impertinence to hope that the talented winner of the Somerset Maugham Award may gain some tolerance from his coming experience of furrin parts? Who knows, perhaps he will bring back a travel-book with him?'[95] Next, Conquest weighed in as well, on Kingsley's side, particularly supporting his attack on ' "poetic" prose'. Then on 8 July, Kingsley himself, writing belatedly from Portugal (the *Spectator* was 'more difficult to obtain in the cold, tasteless urbanism of western civilisation's Nordic sector'), assured Davenport that he was 'not grumpy about furrin parts, only about people being silly about them, and that the furrin part I'm in now seems good-oh so far'.[96] This genial debate had raised two related issues, which Kingsley summed up in a letter addressed from 'Estoril and so on, Portugal' to Robert Conquest:

> To finish off this Lee business (Christ, it'll look bad in our published letters: LEE, Lawrie, 232–264) – I think the 2 classes (a) chaps who think abroad is mystically fine (b) chaps who think L.L. & D[ylan] T[homas] are 'true poets' overlap quite a lot in practice, hard perhaps to distinguish, but after much consideration I will admit that it *is* a worse failure in *taste* etc to esteem L.L. & D.T. than to be one of (a).[97]

Clearly, it would now be tricky for Kingsley to write anything resembling a travel book (and especially not a 'poetic' one). What he would have to write was an anti-travel anti-novel: the traveller's book against travel, the novelist's against fiction.

Portugal obliged with a handsome provision of raw material. The Amises were to be 'paying guests with an English business type about a dozen miles from Lisbon and near the sea'; this, Kingsley thought, ought to protect them 'from the worst excesses of those filthy Portuguese greaseballs'. The 'English business type' was J. G. 'Billy' Barley, an Anglo-Portuguese translator employed by friends of the Swansea businessman John Aeron-Thomas, whose wife Margaret was David Sims's former girlfriend and the model for the social worker Mair Webster in 'Moral Fibre'. Philip Larkin, temporarily reinstated in the role of 'inner reader', was to be 'the recipient of My Portuguese Journal, and in return for this fabulous privilege I expect to be given access to it whenever I may so desire'.[98] This 'journal' opened with a parody of Isherwood, as does *I Like It Here*, where experience and fiction run more closely in parallel than in any of Kingsley's other novels. His anxiety over the huge number of things which might go wrong with the actual journey appeared to be confirmed when Billy Barley failed to meet them at the dock; he turned up an hour later. Otherwise, Kingsley's first impressions were almost disappointingly favourable: 'Actually, considering this is abroad, and so one can't do what one likes to do, this isn't a bad place.'[99] For Philip he supplied a detailed account of the food (edible) and drink (plentiful), although 'the house is very small, SMALLER THAN WE WERE LED TO BELIEVE, and there are a hell of a lot of lfi sfi flies'.[100] In fact, Barley had spent much of the previous month constructing partition walls to produce the necessary number of rooms in his modest single-storey house. Conquest received a brisker summary: 'Yes, Portugal is where I am. Quite all right "considering it's abroad", as I always say. Wonderful hot days. Food a bit oily but v. palatable. Drink abundant. Women so fine that I have cultivated an efficient protective armour of nursing the baby, playing with the boys etc. and now hardly notice all the fine skins, imposing gaits, enormous busts etc.'[101]

This qualified optimism didn't last. The house seemed to shrink still further; it certainly became dirtier and smellier. The flies were augmented by fleas. Barley's Portuguese wife ('an amiable half-wit') proved incapable of producing food which 'a yelling Sally' could eat, while Barley himself seemed slippery in the financial matters which had never been Kingsley's strong point. By the end of July, relief had arrived, accompanied by a secondary raft of comic characters: a 'nice and pretty amusing' Swansea couple called Brown, whom Kingsley knew from the university, arrived on holiday and 'their company did us a lot of good'.[102] Better still, the Browns introduced them to the Tyrrells, who proposed that the Amises should have free use of their chalet at Monchique in the Algarve when it became vacant at the end of August. In the meantime they 'offered to fix us up in a *pensão* (or *pension*) not far from the chalet', at greater comfort and less cost than their accommodation at the Barleys'. This hadn't been improved by the arrival of Billy's mother-in-law who, he warned Kingsley, 'has fainting fits, falls over, has to be helped to chairs, flies into rages, takes dislikes to people, etc'. The Tyrrells, he added, were 'well worthy of fictional transcription': she was 'a Goanese lady with whitening hair who talks all the time, but often says good things, like "Hurrawlnd" (her husband's name is Harold) "Meezda Emmess's glarz is ampty. Ornder another of thawz mwontles (bottles) off vine. The rad"'; he, from Belfast, was given to public performances of 'very long, very clean and quite funny stories that typically involve mimicry of some kind' and other party pieces, such as imitating 'four different people reciting *The Charge of the Light Brigade*'.[103]

Monchique turned out to be 'much more abroad, this place, than any of the other abroad places we have struck'. Kingsley tried very hard not to enjoy it too much, but in the instalment of his 'Portuguese Journal' of 22 August he starts to sound dangerously like one of those despised travel writers:

> Anyway, we spent three days in a nice *pensão* and then came up here. There are a lot of donkeys and mules hereabouts, and Philip has regular rides on one of the former. Everybody wears black and carries an open black umbrella. They stare all the time, of course, but not always with hostility. Next door there is a mad-woman who peeps at you and has tried to steal stuff left out at night. Tyrrell got her jailed recently for this, but she's out again now. Grapes grow profusely in the garden. There is a W.C. – the only one for some miles – but all water has to be pumped. I usually do this at the start of the day, after breakfast, while the water to wash me is getting warm. Then most of the morning I write letters to friends, or work at my new novel. At noon, I smoke a cigarette and drink a couple of glasses of wine ... then after a salad lunch and getting drunk on the wine I drink some of

the local firewater: *medronha*, made from a thing like a strawberry on a tree which grows in these parts. But you don't want to know about that, do you? Then I have a rest or go to the beach. Lots of pretty kids there. There's one in particular who helps look after some orphans with a young friend of hers. It's rather sweet to see the way they behave together; so affectionate. The prettier one seems to have taken quite a fancy to me . . . Then we come home and I get drunk again, then I *light the pressure lamps* (aaoh! aoh! aooh! argh, sxxt, farks!), we eat and I drink more, then we retire to our hard but flealess couches – it seems the little creatures referred to were endemic to the Barley household, LIKE FILTHY BASTARDY AND MEANESS . . .[104]

It isn't Laurie Lee, to be sure, but it's a newly relaxed and observant version of Kingsley. Interestingly, too, the pattern he sketches here is a holiday version of his later freelance writer's day. One thing he was learning from 'abroad' was that there might eventually be life after lecturing.

Those Portuguese locations and the people encountered there will sound familiar to readers of *I Like It Here*, who might suppose the novel to have been written more or less concurrently with the events on which it is based; but that wasn't the case. It would take almost two years for Kingsley to ditch irrevocably the Dixon–Amis plot by recognising that they were more or less the same character: 'Garnet Bowen, an English Welshman, does both Amis and Dixon.'[105] During these two years, a good deal had happened to impede his progress, quite apart from the publication of *New Lines* and *A Case of Samples*. This was partly to do with the company he kept – in particular, that of George Gale, then a *Daily Express* journalist and subsequently editor of the *Spectator*, at whose Gower Street office Kingsley met him in 1955. Gale was a pugnacious right-wing prankster, recalled with enormous affection in *Memoirs*, and as efficient a leader-astray to Kingsley as Julian Ormerod is to Patrick Standish in *Take a Girl like You*. In April 1956, the Amises moved to 53 Glanmor Road, Uplands, 'an infinitely more palatial house' with a study 'as big as a real room'.[106] It was a better place to work, certainly, but also to entertain, often in an extravagantly boozy style: 'People came to stay: Powells, Gales, Kilmartins, Karl Millers, Henry Fairlies.'[107] In September, the Amises took a fortnight's holiday, with their friends Mavis and Geoff Nicholson, at Pramousquier, near Cavalière, in the South of France: Kingsley, in his usual grudging anti-abroad style, conceded that 'it would be wrong to pretend I'm not enjoying myself'.[108] That autumn, he embarked on an affair with a rugby widow, whom he visited on Saturday afternoons when Swansea were playing at home and her husband safely at the match; he also acted as judge for the local heat of the Mazda Queen of Light Competition, an extra-curricular activity which did nothing to improve his deteriorating relationship with Professor Kinsley, whom he mildly described to Philip as a 'Filthy fat Scotch Burns-worshipping Dryden editing recently-moustached scheming mean schoolboy of hell'.[109] Despite these richly assorted distractions, he continued to 'bash on' at his novel and by 16 October had written 10,000 words of it.

That week, however, Kingsley learned not only that Hilly had been having an affair with Henry Fairlie – the *Spectator* columnist and friend of Conquest and Gale, who had visited them at Swansea in June – but that she was in love with him and wanted a divorce. It might be tempting to say (as Kingsley knew perfectly well) that it served him right. He, of course, would have argued that his own extramarital activities hadn't actually been marriage- or family-threatening. Now, he told Philip on 22 October, his marriage had 'about one chance in four of surviving'. 'If I do get a divorce,' he continued, 'it means presumably that the children, about whom I feel strongly, will accompany their mother to their new home.' He re-emphasised the point with self-lacerating brutality: 'Having one's wife fucked is one thing; having her taken away from you, plus your children, is another, I find. And old Henry, though a most charming lad, is a rather emotional and unreliable one, really, and not quite the kind of chap one wants to see *in loco parentis* to one's kids, supposing one wants to see anyone.'[110] He would have been all too aware of the ways in which 'charming' and 'unreliable' rebounded on his own personal conduct. To Fairlie, who wrote to propose a face-to-face meeting, he replied on 1 November, declining the suggestion with great dignity and restraint. He didn't doubt that Hilly and Fairlie were in love. 'But it remains true that you are having an affair, and the situation of an affair – absence, partings, reunions, letters, phone-calls, guilt, grief – sharpens and heightens such feelings of love until people are prepared to act foolishly and cruelly upon them.'[111] There is some painful self-knowledge in this, while the fact that it sounds

exactly like the synopsis of a novel is, curiously, an index of its
seriousness: of life attaining to the gravitas of art. These 'agonising'
circumstances would be aggravated by the fact that Fairlie was – as
Kingsley coolly but frankly informed him – 'selfish and ruthless'
and 'excitable to the point of instability'; 'and so when Hilly tells
me that you are prepared to leave not only Lisette but Simon and
Charlotte too [his wife and children] in order to go to Hilly, I take
this as an indication of the depth of your love, yes, but far more as
a sign of the irresponsibility and greed of which you are capable'.
He doubted whether Fairlie possessed the 'patience, resolution, calm,
self-restraint' to sustain a 'second marriage, founded on the unhappiness (in varying degrees) of seven other people'.[112]

Kingsley was right to refuse a meeting – at which things would
doubtless have been said in a far less measured way, with unforesee-
able consequences – and he was right in his assessment of Henry
Fairlie, who a few days later spent a night in Brixton for failing to
appear before a bankruptcy court and who, according to Memoirs,
was subsequently 'denied these shores on pain of arrest for fraud for
many years before his death in early 1990'.[113] By 20 November he
could tell Philip that 'the Hen–Hil stuff has quietened down a lot'
and that his 'marriage now has the odds heavily on its side'[114] – and
yet, two days after that, abruptly cancelling a trip to a Humphrey
Lyttelton concert in Hull, he explained that he would have been
'a miserable companion' for a surprising reason: 'Getting up after a
count of nine (as Wain would say) I have been felled again for the
time being: my young lady whom I was rather attached to (not the
rugby enthusiast's wife) has just decided to give me up.'[115] The
surprise is a double one: partly that Kingsley should have been
pursuing his own lesser – or at any rate less committed – infidelities
quite so close to the Fairlie debacle, but mainly that he shouldn't
have regarded a weekend listening to jazz with Philip as a welcome
respite. Thereafter, the marriage continued to mend: on 6 December
he wrote that he had 'more or less got my wife back (no Henry for 6
months; resumption of marital relations; much increased cordiality . . .)'[116] and by 19 February 1957 the 'Hilly business' was 'much
better now than for a long time, before even the Henry business
began'.[117]

One simple reason why Kingsley's and Hilly's marriage was not
only repaired but strengthened was that they had other things to

worry about. On the very day in October that Kingsley had first written to Philip about the Fairlie affair, their daughter Sally had fallen and fractured her skull, 'involving vomiting, convulsions, coma, 999, ambulance, casualty ward and the rest of the caper';[118] she spent several weeks in hospital but seemed to make a full recovery. A few months later, in March 1957, while Sally was staying with her grandparents in Berkhamsted, Peggy Amis fell in her bedroom and died immediately from a stroke; since William had left for work, the three-year-old Sally was left alone with her grandmother's body until he returned. For Kingsley, the shock of his mother's death was muffled by the turbulence of his own life and by the practical problems of moving his father – and much of his parents' furniture – into the house at Swansea. In all these circumstances, I Like It Here understandably made slower progress than That Uncertain Feeling had done.

The book was completed in August 1957, serialised in Punch during the autumn and published by Gollancz in January 1958. Kingsley thought it was 'by common consent my worst novel';[119] that was in 1973 (after The Green Man and before one or two other rivals for that honour), yet the consent has remained fairly common. It is, however, nonsense. I Like It Here is certainly a slight book, but to condemn it on that basis is to confuse quality with quantity; and although it suffers from one major flaw (a group of inadequately imagined characters), this is equally and more damagingly true of That Uncertain Feeling. By way of compensation, I Like It Here includes some of the funniest and one of the most serious moments in Kingsley's early fiction, as well as marking an important transitional stage in his development as a novelist.

I Like It Here is dedicated to Philip, Martin and Sally – none of whom was yet old enough to enjoy it, although they had surely earned this symbolic gesture of gratitude – but its 'inner reader' is, once again, Philip's godfather: this accounts for the profusion of in-jokes, some of which would have remained incomprehensible to ordinary readers until the publication of the Letters in 1999, scattered through the early chapters. The opening exchange (' "Owen?" the telegraph boy asked. "Garret Owen?" "More or less," Garnet Bowen told him . . .')[120] parodies Isherwood, echoing the first lines of Prater Violet (' "Mr Isherwood?" "Speaking." "Mr Christopher Isherwood?" "That's me" '),[121] and the whole book will flirt with the tone of his lightly fictionalised Berlin travel journals. Bowen immediately embarks on a series of linguistic and literary frolics identical to those in the Amis–Larkin correspondence: for instance, he silences Frank Sinatra 'in mid-phoneme' ('"When you did that to me I knew somehow th—" You tell us how, a part of Bowen's mind recommended . . .');[122] he reflects on his recent lecture on French writers whom he calls 'Mowl-roe and Mont-along';[123] he picks up 'the new Graham Greene' which, 'like most of the old Graham Greenes, was about abroad';[124] and, a little later, he remembers talking about Greene to an audience of foreign students, who questioned him not only on 'Grim-Grin' but more bafflingly on 'Edge-Crown' (although prepared for 'Ifflen-Voff, Zumzit-Mum and Shem Shoice', 'Edge-Crown' baffled him, the explanation 'Sickies of sickingdom' not helping much, until finally decoded as *The Keys of the Kingdom* by A. J. Cronin).[125] Abroad, for Bowen, is a place filled with 'policemen, waiters, beggars, hotel clerks, drunks, madwomen, Customs officers, porters, ferry supervisors, car-park attendants and persons who had perforce to be asked the way to the nearest lavatory'[126] and he anticipates the practical difficulties of his forthcoming trip to Portugal in terms which, though funny enough in themselves, extravagantly expand Kingsley's habitual valediction in letters to his friend:

> Currency bum, Bowen thought to himself when she had gone. Allowance for self, wife, three children and car bum. Arrangements for drafts on foreign banks bum. Steamer tickets bum. Return vouchers bum. Car documents bum. Redirection of correspondence *by landlord* bum. Permission from Secretary of Extra-Mural Studies to absent self from end-of-session Tutors' and Lecturers' Discussion and Planning Meeting bum. Passport bum. Passport photograph bum. Visa bum.[127]

In a neat continuation of the joke, a mis-spaced telegram from his mother-in-law, delivered as Bowen and his family embark at Southampton, urges him to 'KEEP PHOTOGRAPHAL BUM'. The kinship between Bowen bum and Amis bum couldn't be closer.

Garnet Bowen is more serious about politics, and hence more confused about politics, than either Jim Dixon, who scarcely considers the matter, or that identikit post-war lefty John Lewis: he reflects the conflict of old allegiances and new friends in his creator, who in 1957 could simultaneously publish a Fabian Society pamphlet,

Socialism and the Intellectuals, and write regularly for the *Spectator*, cheerfully mixing with the likes of Conquest and Gale. Kingsley's year of marital crisis, 1956, had also been the year in which simple political faith ceased to work for him: Suez showed the Conservative government in a predictably appalling light – and prompted him to join a student-organised street protest in Swansea – but who, after the Soviet invasion of Hungary, could retain an uncomplicated belief in the ideals of the left? Writing to Victor Gollancz in December 1957, in a letter which begins by furiously berating him for postponing publication of *I Like It Here* until the following January, Kingsley turned his fire on the political historian Stephen King-Hall's naively benign assumptions about a putative Soviet takeover of England in his anti-military, anti-nuclear *Defence in the Nuclear Age*: 'The Russians wouldn't behave as he thinks: they would take what loot they wanted, set up their bases and leave the population to rot. And they would simply suppress the B.B.C. and the Press, not to mention shooting half a million chaps out of hand.'[128] This scenario was to resurface over twenty years later, in *Russian Hide and Seek*, but matters of liberty and oppression, and their far from predictable correlations with left and right in politics, are already troubling Garnet Bowen. When his Rubinstein-like publisher friend Bennie Hyman proposes the Portugal trip, his first reaction is: 'What about that filthy Fascist government?'[129] But his Portuguese host, the not greatly disguised C. J. C. (or 'Titus') Oates, is eloquent in praise of 'this chap Salazar', who 'has got hospitals and clinics and convalescent homes going, and schools and orphanages . . . the Portuguese have every reason to be grateful to Salazar'.[130] This in turn is countered by Gomes, who appears from nowhere at the Bowens' café table, for the specific purpose of describing the corrupt state of 'this wonderful country where I have the honour to be a citizen'.[131] Gomes is more convincing, and less comical, than Oates; yet the very fact that political ideology is now to be questioned and discussed, rather than simply taken for granted, is a huge advance on early Amis.

The most serious point of all, in this surprisingly bookish novel, is a literary one. Bowen's secret mission in Portugal is to track down the elderly and reclusive novelist Wulfstan Strether, who has lately delivered an enormous novel called *One Word More* to Hyman's firm, and to determine somehow whether or not the man is an impostor (his name, incidentally, provides a fair indication of what

Amis wants us to think of him: Wulfstan, an early medieval Arch-
bishop of York, was a prize author of 'ape's bumfodder'; while
Lambert Strether, the central character in Henry James's *The Ambassadors*, has long been regarded by ungrateful students as among the
most tedious characters in literature). This part of the plot is ridiculous, while Strether and his circle – which includes a blackmailer, a
temptress and a psychopathic chauffeur – are barely realised as
characters at all. Nevertheless, Strether serves an important purpose,
which is to convey Bowen to Lisbon and place him in front of Henry
Fielding's tomb:

> Bowen thought about Fielding. Perhaps it was worth dying in
> your forties if two hundred years later you were the only non-
> contemporary novelist who could be read with unaffected and
> whole-hearted interest, the only one who never had to be apolo-
> gized for or excused on grounds of changing taste. And how
> enviable to live in the world of his novels, where duty was plain,
> evil arose out of malevolence and a starving wayfarer could be
> invited indoors without fear. Did that make it a simplified world?
> Perhaps, but that hardly mattered beside the existence of a moral
> seriousness that could be made apparent without the aid of
> evangelical puffing and blowing.[132]

This is a remarkable paragraph, and a finely written one. It is, in
several respects, the key to Kingsley Amis's first four novels. Fielding,
of course, is their shaping spirit; and the tendency of Kingsley's young
male heroes – Jim, John, Garnet, Patrick – to stagger through a
sequence of comic misfortunes, before somehow turning out all right
in the end, is just what happens to Joseph Andrews or Tom Jones.
Moreover, Fielding's pursuit of 'moral seriousness' without 'evangel-
ical puffing and blowing' is clearly shared by Kingsley, while to be
'read with unaffected and whole-hearted interest' two hundred years
later is not only a magnificent achievement but an honourable
ambition.

8

'Well,' said Christopher Isherwood to W. H. Auden, as they boarded
the boat train at Waterloo in January 1939, on the first stage of their

journey to New York, 'we're off again.' 'Goody,' Auden replied.[133]
Something of the sort may have passed between Kingsley and the
three other male Amises – his father and his two sons – who, early in
September 1958, set off for New York aboard the *Queen Elizabeth*;
Hilly and Sally, who was recovering from a minor operation, were
to follow a week later. Since his Portuguese summer, this English
provincial novelist with his horror of 'abroad' had become something
of a seasoned traveller, holidaying in France, lecturing in Denmark,
and now embarking on a year's Visiting Fellowship in Creative
Writing at Princeton. He wouldn't fly, of course. 'I think this deprivation has weakened and impaired my understanding of the contemporary world,' he admitted.[134] Had he overcome this aversion, he
might have turned into a quite different sort of globe-trotting celebrity
writer – a species he came, necessarily and perhaps defensively, to
dislike a good deal.

The preliminaries and the formalities of travel had, as usual, been
designed specifically to irritate him: applying for his Fulbright Travelling Grant in May, he complained to Larkin about the form-filling
('Mr., Mrs. or Miss. Then – Sex. How many female Mr's and male
Misses do they get? Good mind to put "Yes" for Sex'),[135] photographs (four copies) and medical examination. Two months later, he
still hadn't got over 'Filling in my ARSEHOLING forms for those
BLAZING CRAPS at the Fulbright Foundation', even though the
problems had now been resolved; Garnet Bowen, he reckoned, should
'have been sent to U.S.A., not to the republic of Protugal'.[136] (Meanwhile, his novel in progress, provisionally called *Song of the Wanderer*, was 'pleasing me and interesting me greatly' but looked as
though it might be the length of *War and Peace*.) He was altogether
'rather panicky about the Yank trip': unconfident about teaching
'Creadive Wriding' and perhaps doubting whether it should be taught
at all; bothered about the high cost of renting a house in Princeton;
above all, 'afraid of hating it so much over there I feel I must come
back by about Bonfire Night'.[137]

He'd underestimated the power of magic, a commodity which had
been in rather short supply in his life and fiction to date; but magic
was what awaited the traveller who arrived in New York from the
grey England of 1958: 'by the time we sailed out into the dusk past
the marvellously foreign-looking building-fronts of that area ...
and among the wondrous multi-coloured lights of the New Jersey

Turnpike, at that time utterly unparalleled at home – by then I knew
that the lefties, European and American alike, were all liars and this
was my second country and always would be'.[138] Though coloured
by hindsight, the point remains valid: there was no going back to the
viewpoint of Jim or John.

The Amises had rented a house, in 'the best posh-rural American
style', at 271 Edgerstoune Road, Princeton, from Murray Kempston,
a New York journalist who was spending a year in Italy. Kingsley
couldn't believe their luck: the place was 'alive with neighbours,
helping with the children, finding plumbers, schools, maids, mechan-
ics, cars, talking about Europe, which they were all constantly
visiting, inviting one to cocktails and to brunch'; best of all, he
quickly found that 'Swansea or even London' were mere beginners
compared with Princeton when it came to 'the art or custom of
drinking' (even his professor, R. P. Blackmur, the hugely distinguished
'New Critic', was a 'shifter of enough bourbon for two quite thirsty
men'). There was a maid called May, 'a stout middle-aged black
woman', who was amiable enough but stole their sweaters and had
to go, though not before she had magnificently chauffered Kingsley
to his first day at his office in the Firestone Library in her pink
Cadillac. The Firestone, late-nineteenth-century Gothic, was a building that at least tried to look like a university, and it proved to
contain not only 'books that in a manner new to me the librarians
tried to help you find as fast as possible' but the room in which
Kingsley was to teach Creative Writing. All he needed now was some
outstanding students; and these Princeton could supply.

Kingsley had vaguely imagined lecturing to a class, to whom he
would have to impart varieties of wisdom that neither he nor anyone
else was likely to possess, so he was relieved to find that his dozen or
so students came to him one by one, to go over material that they
had earlier handed in. He didn't much care for the solitary poet, who
may have been startled to discover that his work ought to conform
to the sound Movement principle of clarity for the reader, nor for the
solitary playwright, even though his play was actually performed.
All the rest wrote prose fiction, much of it so good that Kingsley
remembered it over thirty years later, when he wrote *Memoirs*. Apart
from this, his other regular obligation was to teach a weekly seminar
which, unluckily for him, included as a prescribed text 'The Aspern
Papers' by Henry James, which he later described as 'the only work

of his I have ever read through to its conclusion',[139] although this wasn't strictly true: on 12 June 1950, he'd told Larkin that he'd read 'The Bostonians, by you-know-who'.[140] James – like Jane Austen or Virginia Woolf – remained one of those strange Amisian blind spots, where chirpy iconoclasm shades into baffling philistinism and which ultimately diminish Kingsley as a literary figure.

From February onwards, Kingsley was to be one of four contributors to a series of two dozen open lectures called, slightly misleadingly, the Christian Gauss Seminars in Criticism. His intention, a perfectly respectable one in view of Princeton's distance from Wales, was to recycle material from the course on eighteenth-century literary theory which he taught at Swansea; but the first lecturer, Dwight Macdonald, was speaking on ' "mass culture", then a new phrase', which set a rather different tone for the series. Kingsley knew and liked Macdonald, while thinking him 'a bit of an old ass' and 'just the chap to fall for the kind of popular social anthropology that was starting to become all the rage in the States just then, other champions being Ashley Montagu, Marshall McLuhan and Vance Packard'.[141] It was, however, Blackmur who, over one of their regular lunches at La Hyère (where Kingsley would invariably consume a dozen large clams and two bottles of Foreign Guinness), suggested that he might take science fiction as his subject, 'an unexpected and enterprising choice for 1958'. Kingsley's own SF collection was, of course, in Swansea, so he had to take an empty suitcase into New York and fill it with paperbacks and magazines as source material for the six lectures subsequently published as New Maps of Hell. He managed somehow to sidestep the huge intellectual inconsistency this entailed. He already felt wary about the growing academic interest in popular cultural forms, such as jazz, and he viewed Macdonald's chosen subject of 'mass culture' with suspicion. Weren't his Princeton lectures on science fiction an instance of exactly the same phenomenon? Well, he acknowledged, 'both jazz and science fiction have in the last dozen years begun to attract the attention of the cultural diagnostician, or trend-hound, who becomes interested in them not for or as themselves, but for the light they can be made to throw on some other thing'.[142] Although Kingsley wanted to imply that he wasn't a bit like that, it naturally proved impossible to discuss science fiction at lecture-course length without some cultural diagnosis, trend-spotting and light-throwing 'on some other thing'. Anyway, he'd found an enjoyable method of fulfilling his terms of appointment, and the lectures were a great success.

To supplement his stipend from Princeton – a necessity, if he was to cope with the hefty rent for 271 Edgerstoune Road and the expenses of a most unWelsh lifestyle – Kingsley took to the road, or sometimes the rail, to lecture at a variety of mainly north-eastern campuses on 'Problems of the Comic Novelist'. Since the lecture was identical in every case, and the audiences were sufficiently civil to eschew heckling or hostile questioning, he remembered the venues for their incidental eccentricities: the parodically English couple who put him and Hilly up in Philadelphia; the Henry Moore statue he kicked (and was silently rebuked by an Oxonian porter for kicking) at Vassar College; the Dry Martini handed to him even before he had taken off his overcoat at Yale; and the awfulness of Champaign-Urbana redeemed, after a lunch where 'I was at the very apex of my form', by the overhearing one faculty wife ask another, 'How much do you think there is in national characteristics? Have you ever met a *reserved* Englishman?'[143] Somewhat to his own surprise, Kingsley was a natural on the lecture circuit.

Food, drink and hospitality helped a great deal; never before had England seemed so ungenerous and unfriendly. Sometimes, hospitality could take on aspects which a more susceptible man, or a more sober one, might have found overwhelming. For instance, Kingsley's first social visit to New York began with several of Gene Lichtenstein's large bourbons even before the four-in-the-afternoon start of *Esquire*'s twenty-first-birthday party (Lichtenstein was the magazine's deputy literary editor), carried on through a sequence of other parties, and ended at the Five Spot, where Sonny Rollins was playing. At this point, belatedly realising that he ought to have got back to Princeton, he was offered a bed at Lichtenstein's apartment in the Bowery. Not any old bed, however: Auden's bed, its usual occupant being in Vienna. But even that wasn't all: 'In the sitting-room of this modest establishment I took down from the shelves a copy of Crabbe's poems, rationing myself to just one sample. "To Wystan," somebody had written on the fly-leaf. "We must love one another AND die. Cyril." Connolly, I assumed resignedly, as I made for the indeed empty bed.'[144] Richard Bradford thinks Kingsley is implying that Auden 'had an affair with Cyril Connolly',[145] whereas of course Connolly was simply pointing out the illogicality of the line 'We must love one another or die' in 'September 1, 1939', an emendation accepted by Auden before he withdrew the poem altogether.[146] Had his musical sympathies been slightly different, Kingsley might have reflected that coming across Crabbe's poems in America had sent another Englishman home to compose *Peter Grimes* and found the Aldeburgh Festival.

At the home of his American agent, Alan Collins, Kingsley met and immediately took to Elizabeth Bowen; at Cyrilly Abels's, he met and was less impressed by Carson McCullers. A literary occasion of a different and much odder sort was the debate on 'Is There a Beat Generation?', held at the Young Men's Hebrew Association in New York; here, Kingsley found himself sharing a platform with James Wechsler of the *New York Post*, the social anthropologist Ashley Montagu, and Jack Kerouac. Each opening speech was meant to last ten minutes, but Kerouac's went on for over a hour, 'mentioning Popeye, Laurel and Hardy and Humphrey Bogart as ancestral Beats and eulogising his friend Allen Ginsberg, whose raucous *Howl* had appeared in 1956'; Kingsley judged that in the end his side 'won the argument (argument?) but lost the performance'.[147] It was a piquant instance of the transatlantic misapprehension that the Beats must have something in common with the Angry Young Men, of whom Kingsley was in any case at best a semi-detached representative; but the AYM were no closer to sharing the moral and social anarchy of the Beats than the Beats were to embracing Movement ideals of rational intelligibility and disciplined poetic form. The following year, Gene Feldman and Max Gartenberg edited an anthology called *Protest*, in which Kingsley and John Wain rubbed (or politely declined to rub) shoulders with Ginsberg and William Burroughs. There were plenty of places in which English and American writing touched and overlapped, but this was emphatically not one of them.

Fifteen years after the early, baseball-watching death of Professor Ralph Foster, Kingsley's aunt Gladys had remarried and settled in Washington. Her second husband, Virgil A. Case, was a 'flamboyant grey-haired figure in overalls and a baseball cap or sailor's cap', tattooed from head to foot and possessing a 'rumpus room with its dartboard, ping-pong table, pump air-rifle with target',[148] all of which proved irresistible to Philip and Martin when they visited him. He was indeed a deeply improbable brother-in-law for Kingsley's father, but in practice they seemed to get on – prompting the unfulfilled hope that William might decide to settle with them in Washington – and Kingsley himself also took to the solid, proletarian, unintellectual warmth of his Uncle Virg.

In a letter to Larkin written soon after his return to England in July 1959 (and notably unapologetic about not having written a word to him during the preceding year), Kingsley summed up his Princeton experience: 'for the first half of my time there I was boozing and working harder than I have ever done since the Army ... for the second half I was boozing and fucking harder than at any time at all. On the second count I found myself at it practically full-time.'[149] He makes it sound too easy – carefree, responsibility-free – but neither half was quite that simple. As far as working was concerned, he was a star performer: affable and enthusiastic, with learning lightly worn and a refreshingly open approach to popular forms of literature. Yet, as some colleagues and students at Swansea had already discovered, this too often entailed a contempt for received opinions, an avoidance of difficult material, an infectious intellectual laziness. One of his best Princeton students, Mark Rose, finding it subsequently impossible to work with the intellectually challenging Blackmur, came to realise that Kingsley had been 'a closer off as well as an opener up'.[150] As for the fucking, Kingsley would leave behind him a trail of emotional wreckage: among his many affairs was one with Jean McAndrew while Hilly, not to be outdone, was not only involved but seriously in love with Jean's husband John. Hilly, indeed, realised that 'you couldn't possibly carry on like that without having a terrible fall and causing an awful lot of misery to a lot of people'.[151] The McAndrews' daughter Megan told Zachary Leader: 'It was a completely lost year in my parents' lives. They had this great failure of rectitude. They all shed inhibitions for a year and everybody encouraged everybody else to do it.'[152] That's all the more damning for being quietly put, and it's also strikingly reminiscent of something in one of the relatively few American literary novels Kingsley actually liked, The Great Gatsby: 'It was all very careless and confused. They were careless people, Tom and Daisy – they smashed up things and creatures and then retreated ... and let other people clear up the mess they had made ...'[153] That, more or less, was what Kingsley did at Princeton.

What he hadn't done, as his academic year in America drew to its close, was write: he 'had seven pages of my current novel and four poems to show for the whole of my nine- or ten-month stay'.[154] That was one reason why he turned down the offer of two more years at Princeton; then there was the matter of the children's education, the friends he'd left behind and in some cases curiously neglected, the approach of middle age. Kingsley was thirty-seven, which he decided was 'just too old to set about becoming an American': 'just too old', like 'just too late' in Larkin's 'Annus Mirabilis', was becoming something of a mantra for these writers whose youth had been so complicated by wartime and its aftermath. He'd have to settle for turning into one fat Englishman instead.

9

The novel with which Kingsley made so little progress in Princeton was the one he'd begun in 1955, before *I Like It Here*; it was called at first *Song of the Wanderer* and eventually *Take a Girl like You*. On his return to England, however, he set to work with unusual diligence and was able to deliver this, his longest book so far, to Gollancz at the end of April 1960. He was, he told Violet and Anthony Powell a month later, 'bogged down' by 'penury, for one thing, which is connected with another thing, my having to finish the novel I started in 1955 or bust – the connection is via the fact that writing the novel meant I had to stop doing all that criticising in the papers that used to bring me in so much money'.[155] Like most Amisian adventures, the year in Princeton had proved more expensive than he'd anticipated; while, back in Swansea, his reputation as a writer and his distinction as a Visiting Fellow cut no ice at all with Professor Kinsley. After a decade of service to the English Department, Kingsley hadn't yet been offered promotion to Senior Lecturer, nor would he be; so cutting back on reviewing for a year meant surviving – with Hilly, three children and an enhanced taste for good living to support – on a provincial lecturer's basic salary. At least his father was no longer in residence: bored with Swansea, William had returned to London where, following something of an Amis family tradition, he embarked on a late second life and acquired a succession of 'lady friends', to one of whom he would inconsiderately leave all his property.

Take a Girl like You marks a huge advance on Kingsley's earlier novels, in three particular respects. Much the most important of these is the character of Jenny Bunn, the first woman in his fiction to be given a narrative voice in the chapters which she dominates: having to see things from a woman's point of view wasn't easy for him. Jenny is at once an absolutely mid-twentieth-century figure and an eighteenth-century one: Clarissa Harlowe to Patrick Standish's Robert Lovelace, perhaps, except that – as we know from *I Like It Here* – Kingsley's special admiration was not for Richardson but for Fielding. And indeed, as she stands on the brink of the permissive 1960s, Jenny's guarding of her virginity seems almost as anachronistic (and to Patrick as tiresome) as Joseph Andrews's guarding of his. Yet the brilliant paradox of Fielding's Joseph is precisely that, while we are invited to find his moral posture comically absurd, he himself is very far from ridiculous; and this balance, learned from Fielding, is what Kingsley achieves with Jenny. The point is clear from the moment that Jenny arrives in the nameless home-counties town at the very start of the book. She has plenty of qualifications for being vulnerable and ineffectual – she's young, inexperienced, among strangers, far from home, embarking on her first job as a primary school teacher – yet she possesses unmistakable authority: almost everyone in the novel, even serial philanderers such as Julian Ormerod and his bumbling apprentice Patrick, is in awe of her. Moreover, she possesses the unassailable strength (although at times she regards it as a weakness) of moral transparency in a world where those who most immediately surround her – Dick and Martha Thompson, Anna le Page – are not quite what they seem to be. Patrick will get his way with her, but only by cheating; consequently, although her 'old Bible-class ideas have certainly taken a knocking', Jenny's moral integrity is undiminished and her moral authority over him is enhanced.

Patrick, of course, is the second advance. The distance between Kingsley's three preceding heroes and their author had been clearly signalled by Jim's free-floating, job-quitting irresponsibility, John's emphatic working-class Welshness and Garnet's tangled involvement with the publishing business. Patrick, by contrast, is explicitly flagged up as an alter ego: he shares Kingsley's South London background; he is a Classicist, as Kingsley almost was in the sixth form, and a public schoolmaster, as Kingsley had intended to be after Oxford; and he is as immoderately fond of women and alcohol as his creator. Naturally, there are strategic differences: for instance, Patrick drives a Morgan-like pre-war sports car, vaguely called a '110' and part-owned by his long-suffering but tedious flatmate Graham McClintock – a chemistry teacher modelled on the physicist Christopher Tosswill, who had so memorably bored Kingsley and Hilly when they holidayed together in 1946. Above all, Patrick is unmarried. This is indeed a strategy, for it enables him to behave as badly as Kingsley had been behaving during his marriage to Hilly, though just a bit more forgivably; it must have surely struck Kingsley that the married version of Patrick he knew so well would appear utterly indefensible in print. In loading his hero with his own least admirable characteristics, he took a substantial risk; for unless the reader feels some liking for Patrick the novel will collapse into a facile morality tale in which the bad man ravishes the virtuous woman. It has to be more complex than that, so Patrick is given a full dose of Kingsley's engaging verbal fluency and wit – we become, with Jenny, his captive audience – as well as an otherwise irrelevant moment of Good Samaritanish redemption. This occurs on the Saturday afternoon when Patrick has packed Graham off to the Test Match at Lord's (where it rains), so that he has the flat to himself for his prearranged seduction of Jenny. Jenny fails to appear; but Sheila Torkington, the headmaster's sexually voracious daughter, does unexpectedly arrive. Patrick is by this time drunk and, although he delivers a self-parodying moral lecture, he is in no state to resist Sheila's advances. Shortly afterwards, he learns that she is pregnant, not by him but by his 'puny shag' of a sixth-form student Horace Charlton, and needs his help: he efficiently arranges, and pays for, an abortion. This clearly cuts two ways. In one sense, Patrick is buying his way out of the trouble Sheila could potentially cause him and, given the date of the novel, the very fact that he knows how to sort out this problem isn't exactly a ringing moral endorsement of him; but, more importantly, it testifies to a redemptive generosity of spirit which – in view of what will happen later that night – he badly needs to display. Even here, Patrick is closely echoing Kingsley's own experience of the abortion he so nearly arranged for Hilly just before their marriage. And with this proximity comes a new seriousness.

For the third respect in which *Take a Girl like You* differs from its predecessors is this: although it's a very funny book – much funnier, in its dark and abrasive way, than anything Kingsley had previously written – it isn't exactly a 'comic novel'. The burdens of personal unhappiness carried by the main characters are too great for that.

Even Jenny, virginal and vulnerable as she at first appears, is given a surprisingly oppressive past: relations, such as the grocery-bag-recycling grandmother, who share the least agreeable characteristics of Kingsley's own family; a no-nonsense northern father who terrifies even Patrick; and an ex-boyfriend called Fred, with whom she had been in love, whose desertion hurt her into toughness. Meanwhile, the apparently debonair Patrick's visitations by Kingsley's deepest fears and phobias ratchet up the novel's seriousness (and the ambition of the writing) to an extent previously glimpsed only at Fielding's tomb in *I Like It Here*. The point is worth illustrating. Here, early in the book, Patrick has just agreed to produce next term's school play – an idea, and an opportunity, subsequently neglected – and is reflecting on how work, which he thinks he dislikes, constantly ambushes him, so that at his death he expects to 'find St Peter at the Pearly Gates looking at his watch and saying: "Oh, Standish, you're just in time to ref that Colts match with Lucifer's" ':

> While he was picturing this, his heart vibrated in the way it had recently started to do and he had the familiar, but never at other times imaginable, feeling of being outside himself, as if his brain had suddenly frozen, become a fixed camera, while his body continued to breathe and walk and turn its head about in a simulacrum of attention. Terror made him catch his breath; pins and needles surged in his fingers; he stopped and looked up at the sky, but that was worse and he shifted his gaze to an evergreen shrub in a raised oval bed nearby. Some configuration of the leaves under the slight breeze formed, as he watched, a shifting face in profile, the eye blinking with idiotic humour, the mouth gaping as if in the painful enunciation of heavy and foreign syllables. He shut his eyes. Then it passed and he was only retrospectively frightened, soon not even that. Just nerves, he said to himself. Nothing to do with dying.[156]

One rather crude way of suggesting why this passage is so remarkable would be to say that it seems closer to those 1950s novelists whom Kingsley *doesn't* much resemble – Golding, perhaps, or Murdoch – than to early Amis; yet that is indeed crude, because the passage actually digs more deeply than usual into the authentic Kingsley, unfiltered and unironised. So does this, from much later in the book, when Patrick has fled from Lord Edgerstoune's unwelcome description of the forthcoming attractions of old age:

> Almost immediately afterwards he found an outside door and left the house. He did not want to see Lord Edgerstoune for a while or ever again be told anything by him. It was very dark, and he stumbled several times before coming to a level stretch of grass. A couple of hundred yards away, down what he sensed as a slope, the wind was rising in some trees. Nearby there was a strip of illumination from an upper window. Shivering, he went and stood in this, so that he could see parts of himself. After a moment he heard a mumble of voices above his head, followed by a man's laughter: Julian's. This at once calmed him. On the edge of the lighted patch there was a long flower-bed running off into the darkness, with some begonias or azaleas or whatever the hell they were. Patrick went over and stooped down by them.[157]

After Patrick has talked to the flowers ('How are you getting on? Plenty of nitrates and Christ knows what?') he thinks about Jenny and invokes a trusted formula: 'I'm sorry, I know I'm a bastard, but I'm trying not to be.' He recognises, and so do we, that this isn't good enough: it's the agnostic's just-in-case attempt at prayer. But we also know that the terror of darkness, the need to 'see parts of himself' as if from that fixed camera of his brain, is real and deadly serious.

The way in which *Take a Girl like You* moves seamlessly from introspective seriousness to incisive comedy and back again is unsurpassed in Kingsley's fiction. At one level, it's an extraordinarily simple book: Jenny, during her first date with Patrick, reflects that 'two people could not go on all the evening just repeating (chap) *I like you and* and (girl) *I like you but*',[158] yet that is exactly what they go on repeating for most of the novel's 320 pages. It is peppered with the expected range of in-jokes – the familial ones and Tosswill-based character already noted, as well as the aristocrat named after Kingsley's Princeton base and an unpleasant pub landlord after Anthony Crosland – but these are now decorative rather than structural. The book is held together by a range of properly imagined minor characters, among whom Dick and Martha Thompson, whose marriage is raddled with every kind of unsuccess, and Anna le Page are particular triumphs: in the earlier novels, a lesbian from Guernsey masquerading as a Frenchwoman could only have been the subject of ribald humour, yet here she is deftly handled and the moment of her self-unmasking is oddly touching. Some readers are less happy about Julian Ormerod: if he seems over the top, however, it's because over-the-topness *is* his character. He is like one of those predictably scene-stealing turns in Dickens, whose appearances are delightful precisely because they so faithfully reaffirm our expectations, although the point at which, en route to their dirty weekend in London, he cheerfully tells Patrick about his career as an international serial bigamist – 'Think I'm right in saying I'm only unmarried in Mexico'[159] – may be one excess too many.

Take a Girl like You wasn't universally admired on its appearance in September 1960: an especially hostile *TLS* reviewer thought it 'a very nasty book . . . the worst novel ever written by a man who can write a novel as well as Mr Amis'.[160] But that judgement was based on a misreading: in the end, it is Jenny's book, not Patrick's, just as it is Hilly's rather than Kingsley's. If it is in part an apologia for male behaviour which Patrick and Kingsley know to be unforgivable, it is for just that reason a tribute to female resilience and generosity. Writing about his favourites among his own characters, Kingsley once said that he would enjoy 'a drink (no more, thank you) with Patrick Standish of *Take a Girl like You*',[161] and one sees what he meant: likeable chap, but trouble. All the same, it remained the novel of which he was fondest among his own books. 'I have a soft spot for *Take a Girl like You* myself,' he told a correspondent in 1984, adding: 'It is the only book of mine I have ever contemplated writing a sequel to.'[162] To another admirer, two years later, he wrote: 'It is easier to tell you my favourite book, which is *Take a Girl like You*.'[163]

10

Take a Girl like You completes a quartet of novels which – with their irreverent young heroes, contemporary settings and sharp social comedy – would come to represent an enduring image of Britain (and of Britons abroad) during the 1950s; and in seeming to be part both of the Angry Young Men and of the Movement, Kingsley himself could pass for a representative figure of the time. Even before the publication of *I Like It Here*, the Marxist historian Arnold Kettle commented: 'Kingsley Amis is as much a part of the world of 1957 as television, rock 'n' roll and the FA Cup.'[164] It's a beguiling idea, not least because we instinctively like to see our writers as a major part of the cultural mainstream, yet it's in a crucial sense misleading: for, even if his fame rivalled theirs, 'television, rock 'n' roll and the FA Cup' held almost no interest for Kingsley and don't figure at all significantly in his first four novels. If television is mentioned, it's simply as something switched on or off rather than in terms of specific programmes (Jenny Bunn has a vague hankering for it); and there's no sign of football. The heroes tend to share their author's tastes in popular culture – liking jazz, for instance, and loathing Sinatra – but this was, after all, the decade of Bill Haley, Elvis Presley and, in England, Tommy Steele, a rather different sort of young hero on whom Colin MacInnes had written with sympathy and perception; and it was MacInnes, in his London trilogy of 1957–60 (*City of Spades, Absolute Beginners, Mr Love and Justice*) who demonstrated exactly how to capture this zeitgeist in fiction. The world MacInnes brought into print – of coffee bars, skiffle, drug-dealing, petty crime and urban racial tension – barely registered a blip on Kingsley's radar. Had the supposedly Angry Young Man really been a youngish fogey all along?

As with culture, so – in the inescapable pairing of the time – with society. For all their subversive energy, Kingsley's first four novels are constrictingly middle-class in their range: his one attempt to embrace the aristocracy (Lord Edgerstoune in *Take a Girl like You*) is parodic and lightly sketched, while the closest we get to sustained working-class characterisation is the neighbouring Davies family who live, all too symbolically, downstairs in *That Uncertain Feeling*. In view of Kingsley's often stated dislike of Bloomsbury and its alleged affectations, it's ironic that even E. M. Forster should have done better on this count, with Leonard and Jackie in *Howards End*; but Kingsley's parents, like Stephen Spender's, had kept him from children who were rough, and they would always be remote to him. In his first four published novels, he worked cautiously within the limits of his own experience; the most securely realised characters all belong either to the lower middle class from which he had emerged or to the professional middle class into which he had grown. When *Lucky Jim* appeared in 1954, this was hardly an issue: the heroes of *Scenes from Provincial Life* and *Hurry on Down* shared similar backgrounds. But

by the time *Take a Girl like You* was published in 1960, the landscape
of English fiction had become populated by working-class heroes: Joe
Lampton in John Braine's *Room at the Top* (1957); Arthur Seaton in
Alan Sillitoe's *Saturday Night and Sunday Morning* (1958) and Smith
in *The Loneliness of the Long-Distance Runner* (1959); Vic Brown in
Stan Barstow's *A Kind of Loving* (1960); Arthur Machin in David
Storey's *This Sporting Life* (1960). Unlike Kingsley's academic and
literary professionals, they are, respectively, a council clerk, a factory
hand, a Borstal boy, an engineering office worker and a professional
rugby footballer (not the public school sort, either). Even Jenny
Bunn's rite of passage looks relatively placid beside Jane Graham's in
Lynn Reid Banks's *The L-Shaped Room* (1960).

Apart from Braine, whose first book hadn't appeared until he was
thirty-five, these writers were several years younger than Kingsley.
What, meanwhile, had happened to those he regarded as his true
literary contemporaries? Philip Larkin had stopped writing fiction
altogether, while the best that could be said of John Wain was that
The Contenders (1958) was more successful than *Living in the
Present* had been. But the two significant novelists whose debuts
had appeared in the same year as *Lucky Jim*, William Golding and
Iris Murdoch, posed other problems. Golding, like Kingsley, had
published three more novels by the end of the decade, all of them
linguistically rich and startlingly unlike each other: *The Inheritors*
(1955), *Pincher Martin* (1956) and *Free Fall* (1959). In his *Spectator*
review of *Pincher Martin*, Kingsley found admiration easier to summon than enjoyment: he hoped Golding would 'forgive me if I ask
him to turn his gifts of originality, of intransigence, and above all of
passion, to the world in which we have to live'.[165] Murdoch, whose
Under the Net had so delighted him, had also produced a further
three books: *The Flight from the Enchanter* (1955), *The Sandcastle*
(1958) and, arguably her masterpiece, *The Bell* (1958). Writing to
Philip in April 1956, Kingsley described 'the new Murdoch' as 'very
unreal', before elaborating: 'The characters all seem abnormal, somehow. Any moment I expect to come across one of them singing the
only song he knows, or turning out to have been a dwarf all along
... The decade's most overrated writer?' After wondering whether
that mightn't, after all, be 'Lizzie Jennings', he added: 'God this letter
is going to be a treat for our biographers, eh?'[166] It's less a treat,
perhaps, than a somewhat mournful confirmation of Kingsley's self-

imposed limits. Golding and Murdoch were taking their novels in directions where he couldn't follow and which he defensively seemed to resent. Meanwhile, youngsters like Sillitoe, Barstow and Storey were busy pinching the Angry Young Men's clothes.

None of this need affect one's estimate of *Lucky Jim*, *That Uncertain Feeling*, *I Like It Here* and *Take a Girl like You*. What it does affect is Kingsley's relationship with his times. At the end of the 1950s, even as he finished his most ambitious and successful novel so far, he was in a rut. He had several habits to break: he must stop writing fiction which, however obliquely, featured versions of Kingsley and Hilly; he must break out of his restrictive middle-class English milieu; and he must lose his overdependence on undergraduate Kingsley–Philip humour. What he can't have imagined, as the new decade began, was that reinventing his creative world was also going to involve reinventing his life.

4. THE SEA CHANGE

1

'Isn't it a scream about Kingsley, a scream of laughter or rage as the case may be?' wrote Larkin to Monica Jones on 2 March 1961. 'Queer college to have done it, though – all historians.'[1] 'It' was the decision of Peterhouse, Cambridge, to appoint Kingsley as its first Fellow and Director of Studies in English, from that year's Michaelmas Term onwards. Larkin, despite his reputation for reclusiveness, had held posts at three universities – Leicester, Belfast and Hull – and been involved in academic committees; he had a far more nuanced grasp of university politics than his friend. And his sense that Kingsley and Cambridge made an unlikely match was to be abundantly justified.

The appointment had been brokered by George Gale, a graduate of the college, and his historian friends Michael Oakeshott and Brian Wormald, who both held fellowships there. It was Wormald who put Kingsley's name forward to the Master, Herbert Butterfield, and the other Fellows: their response was mixed, slightly puzzled, but cautiously approving. When, five years later, Angus Wilson was appointed to a professorship at the University of East Anglia, the idea of a creative writer holding a senior teaching appointment at an English university became ineradicably established; in 1961, however, it was a bizarre novelty, especially for so conservative an institution as Peterhouse. Kingsley, moreover, had actually spent a year *teaching* creative writing, an unthinkable occupation, at Princeton; apart from that, his academic career consisted of a single junior appointment, held for a decade without promotion, at a university college in South Wales. His publications, other than the ludicrously off-syllabus *New Maps from Hell*, were anything but academic, and even his novels weren't universally admired at Cambridge. F. R. Leavis was famously to describe him as a pornographer, while Graham Hough, the influential critic and Fellow of Darwin College, was said to have remarked: 'Fellow like that shouldn't be here.'[2] A candidate more readily comprehensible to Peterhouse would have turned that thesis on nineteenth-century poetry into a higher degree and a scholarly book, instead of messing about with fiction.

Cambridge wasn't Oxford, though Kingsley at first thought it might be, nor was it Swansea. Donald Davie subsequently pointed out, in an essay called 'The Varsity Match', that 'for the last fifty years each new generation of English poets, as the "generations" were subsequently to be understood and talked about by journalistic commentators, was formed or fomented or dreamed up by lively undergraduates at Oxford':[3] Auden and Spender; Sidney Keyes and Drummond Allison; Amis, Larkin and Wain; John Fuller and Ian Hamilton. Cambridge, though every bit as distinguished in literary studies, had a rather different tradition of launching creative writers, several of whom – Isherwood in his generation, Davie and Gunn in theirs – gratefully climbed aboard bandwagons whose journeys had begun in Oxford. It is, furthermore, bathed in an East Anglian intellectual light which may strike those unused to it as steely and chilly. That is unlike Oxford; and it is even less like Swansea, which Kingsley would always regret having left, where the university was cushioned by homeliness and conviviality:

> The scene is the Bryn-y-Mor pub near the old hospital, and Jack Thomas the landlord, the only man I have ever met with a real quiff (curl plastered down on forehead), is doling out the snacks and bottles of Double Diamond. It is Thursday lunchtime, with a late lecture at 2.30. Around me are local tradespeople, the fellows from the estate agent's and the garage, Jo Bartley, David Sims, Willie Smyth, one or two others. Later I will be taking the first-year Honours through 'Thyrsis', fourteen or fifteen of them at the most. All is peace. Often I wish I had never left, but that is meaningless, like all such wishes, because everything in that picture has disappeared.[4]

John Lewis's after-work pub in 'Aberdarcy' has a similarly eclectic mix of customers: 'an occasional grocer or butcher in his Yacht Club blazer and lavender trousers, a publican or two in subfusc accompanied by an ignorant doctor or two in sportive checks, the odd golfing-jacketed cinema-manager, café-owner or fish-shop proprietor . . .'.[5] Cambridge would be rather different.

The Amises temporarily rented the Mill House at West Wratting before moving to 9 Madingley Road, a 'rather posh'[6] house, since demolished, close to Churchill College on the main road out of the city towards St Neots. That defensive phrase 'rather posh', coming as late as *Memoirs*, says a good deal about Kingsley and about the stickiness of his relationship with Cambridge: his particular bundle of fears, insecurities and prejudices made him simultaneously eager for recognition and wary of its material consequences. He might have quite enjoyed the 'posh' if he hadn't always the derisive sense that it was getting a bit above itself and a bit above him; he had clearly kept in his head that dubiously wondering Swanseaism, 'Now *there's* posh.' (A version of it turns up in *The Old Devils*, too.)[7] Almost everything he disliked about Cambridge was connected with its perceived poshness. Although he got on well enough with his own 'polite and reasonably productive' students, he found the drunken and pretentious foibles of former public schoolboys hard to take, wistfully recalling the more straightforward excuse-making of Mr Cadwallader in Swansea: 'Sorry, Mr Amis, but I left my essay on *King Lear* on the bus, see, coming down from Fforestfach.'[8] In fact, he decided that Cambridge was 'intellectually, socially and in every other way, markedly inferior to Swansea'.[9] He especially detested High Table dinners, not so much at Peterhouse – 'an oasis in Cambridge of good nature and common sense' – as at other, bigger colleges. He'd always hated being trapped socially and preferred pubs to dinner parties, to which High Table added grotesque refinements of its own: formal dress, but no women; Latin toasts and other convoluted ceremonies; above all, stultifying and (for hours) inescapable company. He remembered a particular occasion on which the first thirty minutes of a dinner were entirely occupied by his neighbours discussing the fine art they'd been buying, until one turned to him, saying, 'And what is *your* particular, er, line of country in this, er?' To which Kingsley replied: 'I'm afraid I don't go in for any of that kind of thing.'

> The other man said, 'H'm' – not a vocable in common use, but he used it. Then he said, 'I think that's a dreadful thing to say.' I went on keeping quiet for some time after that, wishing, for perhaps the hundredth time since arriving in Cambridge, that I were back in the Bryn-y-Mor with David, Jo and old Willie Smyth, or, less familiarly, that I had a ticket for Australia in my pocket.[10]

Cambridge, he found, was corrupted not only by such instances of ludicrous snobbery and intolerable bad manners but also, on more modest occasions, by 'a mode of social behaviour that narrowed and formalised and stiffened ordinary intercourse'.[11]

Though there's a good deal of sense in this, Kingsley's perspective is inevitably skewed. Quite apart from his temperamental antipathies to Cambridge, he was probably wrong about Oxford; for he had known Oxford in wartime and in the immediately post-war years, when it was somewhat unlike itself, and he had known it only as a student, not as a don. Had he gone back there in 1961, he mightn't have found it much more likeable than Cambridge: we should remember the unhappiness of Auden's return to live at Christ Church in 1972, another striking instance of mismatched hopes and expectations between an established writer and an ancient university. Kingsley, of course, was younger and a university teacher, so to that extent he should have been better prepared. He wasn't: 'I'm not sure I shall be able to take Cantab, actually. Like Oxford only full of shits you don't know instead of shits you do.'[12] But something else rankled, a shade mysteriously, about Cambridge: the relative lack of 'original and well-grounded talk about English literature', amid the endless discussion of academic administration, 'intra-Faculty discord and personal quarrels', whereas at Swansea 'a not necessarily very profound remark about Traherne or Tennyson would come up now and then'.[13] This is mysterious because it suggests that he simply wasn't looking in the right places; and one place he might have looked was Gonville and Caius College or, failing that, a house on the corner of Long Road and Trumpington Road, either of which might have contained Donald Davie. They could certainly have talked about Traherne or Tennyson.

The failure of the Amis–Davie relationship to prosper is something worse than a missed opportunity: they were sufficiently distinctive in temperament and as writers to have been mutually beneficial influences in a way that Kingsley and Philip, sharing an undergraduate past and a private language, could never be. At the same time, their backgrounds had run in parallel: Davie, having won a scholarship to Cambridge, interrupted his first degree to serve in the Royal Navy, stayed on to read for a higher degree, then taught at Trinity College, Dublin, before returning to Cambridge in 1958; Kingsley, having won a scholarship to Oxford, interrupted his first degree to serve in the army, stayed on to read for a higher degree, then taught at Swansea before coming to Cambridge in 1961. They were founder members of the Movement, principal contributors to *New Lines*, and both would have figured on any intelligent shortlist of the most influential literary figures in post-war England. Davie too was finding the Cambridge of the early 1960s an unsympathetic place. 'About this time,' he writes in *These the Companions*, 'I began to think that my habits of thought and feeling were so alien to those of my countrymen that my future, if I had one, would have to be spent out of England altogether.'[14] This was just when Kingsley was so improbably wishing he had a ticket to Australia in his pocket or was perhaps following Robert Graves to lead a freelancer's life in Majorca.

Davie remembered Kingsley phoning him, one morning in 1961, to say that he was there for the day and to ask whether they might meet for lunch. They did: 'He pumped me about what it was like to teach English in Cambridge, and I was eloquently jaundiced about it . . . only to have to back-pedal, lamely and unconvincingly, when he revealed that that very day he had accepted an invitation from Peterhouse to move there.' He welcomed Kingsley's appointment and supported him when things began to go wrong: it was Davie – together with John Holloway, passed over for the Chair at Swansea in 1954 and now at Queens', another contributor to *New Lines* with whom Kingsley might have enjoyed sympathetic literary conversation – who formally protested when Leavis announced that Peterhouse could no longer be taken seriously, having appointed a pornographer to a fellowship. Recalling this in his own memoirs, Davie adds:

> On the contrary of course he is and always has been a very severe moralist, as one sees from his shocked repudiation of both Philip Roth and Vladimir Nabokov. On the other hand he is a master of comic caprice – a perfectly legitimate and entertaining garment for the moralist to appear in, but one that Cambridge has never been able to account for and acknowledge.[15]

Those two sentences are, a little unexpectedly in their context, among the most acute ever written about Kingsley. Moreover, Davie remained remarkably warm in his estimate both of the man and of his work: 'Kingsley I liked and have always liked, as I like him still; and in fact, if our relations have always been slightly constrained, it's because there is no British writer among my contemporaries whom I have admired more, and the consciousness of that is a little embarrassing to both of us.'

Kingsley's recollection of Davie at Cambridge was shorter and, alas, a good deal less generous: 'All I can remember of Donald Davie of Caius is his accusing me, accurately enough, of thinking him square (though I thought and think him better things besides).'[16] That is all. But when we put the two memoirs side by side, it must surely strike us that neither man is being quite candid. Davie knew that their constraint wasn't wholly due to his excessive admiration; and Kingsley recalled a good deal more about Davie than he cared to let on. There were good reasons for a lack of intuitive rapport: Kingsley's musical enthusiasms meant nothing at all to the tone-deaf Davie who, unswervingly loyal to his wife Doreen, wasn't likely to be impressed by Kingsley's sexual adventuring. The real trouble was more bluntly that Kingsley thought Davie a prig (a charge he wryly acknowledged in *These the Companions* and in various poems) and, later, a madman.[17] Yet what of that? Kingsley too had, as he put it, 'a peep round the twist'. Their failure to develop a close literary friendship is one of those incalculable losses which can be assessed only in dangerous terms of 'What if?' So it must suffice to say that a transfusion of 'comic caprice' in one direction and of intellectual rigour in the other could have greatly strengthened the weakest aspects of each writer's work.

George Steiner, at Churchill College, was more predictably incompatible with Kingsley. Steiner's hybrid American–European background, unfathomable accent, prodigious multilingualism and confident expertise in assorted literatures were all bound to grate on someone so instinctively wary of foreignness; but it was his inattention, as a dinner-party host, to his guests' wine glasses that really did for him. Similarly, although the novelist Andrew Sinclair might have been just about forgiven for writing unreadable books and being a dull dinner guest (his wife was pretty), turning up in a pub without his wallet and expecting Kingsley to pay for everything was the last straw. There's clearly a pattern in these fallings-out, often triggered by events which wouldn't have troubled a happier man or a more confident one: his unconquerable lack of self-confidence is surely the reason why Kingsley remained both so nervous of high-powered intellectuals and so sensitive to perceived, usually drink-related slights.

The natural corollary is that when he did get on with someone, he got on famously, as he did with Larkin and Conquest and Gale – and with Robert Graves. Their friendship had begun in quintessentially Gravesian style: Kingsley had written to him in October 1954, following an article in *Punch* in which the famously industrious Graves joked about authors 'who somehow manage to reduce output to ten words a day (which means a novel of average length every two years)'. This, Kingsley noted, 'will only give you a 7,300-word novel, which is a good deal under average length even these days', adding: 'Must stop now and write my word for the day. I plan to bring out a *conte* every 20 years.'[18] Graves, of course, was delighted: it was exactly the kind of point he'd have made himself. And this gave Kingsley his excuse to write a proper fan letter, 'saying what I've often wanted to say: that for my money you're the best poet now writing in English, if you'll pardon the expression'.[19] They later met for lunch in Oxford, where Graves (with Kingsley among his sponsors) had been elected Professor of Poetry, when he delivered the Creweian Oration in June 1962. Consequently, when the American magazine *Show* commissioned a profile of Graves from Kingsley that summer, he – though still no great traveller – was happy to accept.

The Amises arrived in Majorca on 12 August, staying at the Posada, the guest house on Graves's estate at Deyá, until 21 August. Graves found Kingsley a 'very sane, very decent' man with 'a generous heart, and a sense of vocation'; Richard Perceval Graves also charmingly records that 'the two men made marmalade, while singing comic songs to the tune of "The Internationale" ',[20] something one can't quite imagine Kingsley doing with Philip, who enjoyed what he took to be comic songs but would have baulked at marmalade-making. Kingsley for his part was delighted by his host's constantly modulating moods and range of conversation, his devotion and practicality as a gardener, his insistence on writing with a steel nib and real ink. Nevertheless, Graves had learned to guard a reserve of privacy from his summer visitors, even from so sympathetic an interviewer as Kingsley: 'Amis was not shown the rough steps up to the little shepherd's hut which Graves planned to use when writing his poems and letters.'[21] When Kingsley returned to England, he wrote an unusually full and heartfelt letter of thanks to Graves and his family for 'a marvellous week. To itemise everything you did for us would involve a full diary of what we did. We recall and discuss it ceaselessly.' He also said that he had been 'fired by your example to attempt an 8 a.m. start to the writing day'.[22] What had so powerfully caught his imagination was the example of a writer who was in a crucial sense very like himself – a professional who could move easily between poetry, journalism and a variety of prose books – and the resulting conviction that he must try the full-time literary life. Why not, indeed, leave England and move to this Mediterranean island with its friendly inhabitants and affordably excellent food and wine? The seed sown in Portugal had blossomed in Majorca.

2

There's a curious holiday snap, taken on an Adriatic beach in July 1963, while the Amises were attending a science-fiction film festival at Trieste. It shows a slumbering, sunbathing Kingsley, on whose back Hilly has written in lipstick: '1 FAT ENGLISHMAN. I FUCK ANYTHING.' The last three words were understandably angry but by then untrue: his latest and most serious affair had focused his interest as never before. The first three words are the title of the novel he was finishing that summer.

As had been the case with *Take a Girl like You*, *One Fat Englishman* was a long time in the writing, all the more surprisingly in view of its modest length. The book is several different and not wholly compatible things. It is, firstly, the result of his year at Princeton in 1958–9, the novel which in slightly different circumstances might have become 'Lucky Jim in America'; and it retains traces of that unwritten novel for, beneath his fat and obnoxious exterior, Roger Micheldene still has a good deal of Jim, and of his author, lurking inside him. Secondly, it is Kingsley's reaction to Cambridge, in its largely undiscriminating hostility towards academics and their institutions. Thirdly, it is the book in which he tries decisively to abandon the pattern of his first four novels: it breaks new ground not only in style and location but also in its central character – a man we are quite plainly meant to dislike, at least to start with, even though we find ourselves collusively sharing his point of view. And fourthly, it is a novel which eventually falters and changes direction, as if it had prematurely run out of steam, or venom, or whatever else was driving it.

An unexpectedly reckless and abrasive comic note is struck in the opening pages, where we're introduced to an American university called Budweiser and a philologist named Ernst Bang: it's a calculated coarsening of tone, briefly as disorientating as if Kingsley had put Whitbread College and Professor Fart into one of his English novels. Our guide through this world in which literary and academic life overlap and corrosively react with each other is Roger Micheldene, the Englishman of the title, who (thanks to Kingsley's habitual fogginess about business matters) seems to be a sort of roving talent scout for a literary publisher: unlikely that such a firm should employ such a person; unlikelier still that such a person should be him. Micheldene is grossly overweight, insatiably lecherous, hideously greedy in his appetites for food and drink as well as for sex – not so much the antithesis of Kingsley as a Hogarthian amplification of him. He is also partly based on the future Labour cabinet minister Anthony Crosland, whom Kingsley met in America and heartily disliked. It was Crosland (identified by Kingsley merely as 'a promising young Labour politician') who, encountering a student from Texas who happened to be studying the *Aeneid*, replied, 'Really. Ha, ha, I must say I find the notion of an Easterner working on Virgil interesting; a West Coaster working on Virgil would be amusing, but a TEXAN . . . it's simply GROTESQUE.'[23] This vivid instance of the wrong kind of Englishman in America – offensively patronising in a manner Kingsley recognised as uncomfortably close to his own under provocation – informs one aspect of Micheldene. Perhaps the book's best joke (a joke *on* him, since he's entirely humourless) concerns a game of charades, in which actions are performed in the manner of an adverb to be guessed at: when it's his turn to guess, incorrectly venturing 'Effeminately', 'Haughtily' and 'Efficiently', the right answer turns out to be 'Britishly'. He doesn't get it, of course. Near the end of the novel, the horrible young writer Irving Macher, suddenly gifted with his author's insight, has to explain to him: 'I sometimes got the impression that you think some of the people in this country don't like you because you're British. That isn't so . . . It isn't your nationality we don't like, it's you.'[24]

The trouble with *One Fat Englishman* is that most of the other characters are nearly as repulsive as Micheldene. Macher, for example, is a reworking of Probert from *That Uncertain Feeling*: a minimally talented yet devotedly writerly writer. He has completed a novel called *Blinkie Heaven*, in which the main characters are blind: there is a 'blinkie joke-shop' ('blind seeing-eye dogs, cups for nickels with a sign saying *Take One*, dark glasses with offensive slogans painted on them') and a club called the Blind Spot, with spectacularly ugly strippers. Even Micheldene recognises that this is sick and (consequently) a potential bestseller, one of many occasions when the reader can't help agreeing with him. Despite ending his chummily personal bedtime prayers with the heartfelt request 'And whatever you do see to it that Irving Macher's novel is no good,'[25] he discovers to his distress that the book isn't wholly illiterate, though he consoles himself with the deprivations which acceptance by his firm would entail: 'Stinginess over advertising space and with proof copies, caution about the size of the first impression would ensure a sale of at least 10,000 fewer copies than most rivals could manage.'[26] It's an unsubtle sideswipe at Victor Gollancz, and *One Fat Englishman* was indeed the penultimate novel of Kingsley's to be published by him. Macher leads Micheldene a merry dance, in particular by removing his notes for a lecture at Budweiser and substituting a comic which appears to belong to the Bangs' annoyingly precocious seven-year-old son, Arthur. The lecture never takes place, Micheldene sulkily refusing to extemporise, but the occasion inevitably recalls the fiasco of Dixon's lecture at the end of *Lucky Jim* and further encourages our unwilling identification with him. Macher, indeed, seems to assume a kind of internal authorship within the novel, pulling Micheldene's strings, yet he insists his intention is the exact opposite. He says he wants to allow Micheldene an unfamiliar degree of freedom: 'My role – in your life, that is – is to give you chances of behaving naturally, that's to say not in prefabricated sections, not out of some shooting script but off the cuff . . . I'm your unsteadying influence, the flint in the road that gives your car a flat. No mission about it.'[27] Saki would have called this an 'unrest cure'.

Micheldene's literary motivations – they include an attempt to retrieve the manuscript of his brother-in-law's unpublishable *Perne in a Gyre* and his accidental discovery of Swinburne's flagellant notebook – are flimsy and absurd: what really drives him is his repeatedly frustrated pursuit of Helene Bang. Chief among the frustrations is her intolerable son Arthur, who beats Micheldene at Scrabble by using American spellings – countering his protest, 'But this is a bloody American dictionary,' with 'This is bloody America'[28] – and eventually prompts the thoroughly Larkinesque reflection: 'It was no wonder that people were so horrible when they started life as children.'[29] He has to make do instead with Mollie, wife of the literary agent Strode Atkins, who on close acquaintance turns out to possess 'a complexion that appeared to have been left out in a violent hailstorm for ten years'.[30] Her only recommendation is her availability: she supplies a picnic and a scene of alfresco love-making, during which the couple find themselves being watched by tortoises or (this being America) turtles – a circumstance experienced, according to Jacobs,[31] by Kingsley himself.

Particularly in the second half of the book, Kingsley often seems uncharacteristically interested in background rather than foreground, taking characters on unnecessary excursions: a party on an island, a New York jazz club. In fact, he had written in June 1962 to his former Princeton student William Rukeyser, now researching for a higher degree at Cambridge, with a shopping list of enquiries: he wanted to know what Micheldene 'would notice in Greenwich-Village-type surroundings at night – both in the street and in a bar or two – and in the morning'; he also needed a 'description of modest but not squalid apartment in this or nearby area', as well as something 'about $50,000-a-year house and grounds located anywhere between 30 and 60 miles from Manhattan' and 'material for 3 or 4 scenes set in the undergraduate portions of a university like Princeton or Yale'.[32] A year later, nearing the end of the book, he refined his questions into six numbered points including '1. R's cab-ride from Penn Station to the Village' and '2. Environs, entrance hall etc of prosperous but not plutocratic apartment building in Village'.[33] 'I've only used a small proportion but was able to pick just what I needed,' Kingsley told Rukeyser, after he finished the novel in August.[34] This imbalance between briskly treated characters and carefully observed locations adds to the book's curious flavour.

Yet much the oddest aspect of *One Fat Englishman* is the modulation of tone towards the end. Micheldene is, throughout the novel, a more ambivalent character than some critics seem to recognise: reprehensible, certainly, but sometimes voicing opinions – about, for instance, awkward or ugly American usages – with which we might sneakingly agree. What he consistently lacks is any sense of humour and any subtlety of human feeling. Nevertheless, as his homeward-bound ship leaves the harbour, and just before he discovers that he is to share the voyage with Strode Atkins, he experiences an emotion which seems quite out of character:

> Then he wanted very much to cry and started to do so. This was
> unusual for him when sober and he tried to work out why he was
> doing it. It was obviously a lot to do with Helene, but he had said
> good-bye to her and to plenty of other girls in the past without
> even considering crying. What was so special?[35]

What was so special had happened not so much to Roger Micheldene as to Kingsley Amis. The book is dedicated 'To Jane'.

3

If the Amises had visited Majorca a little earlier in the summer of 1962, Kingsley wouldn't have been at home to receive and eagerly accept an invitation to take part in a symposium on 'Sex in Literature', sponsored by the *Sunday Telegraph*, which was to be held at the Cheltenham Literary Festival in October. The other participants were to be Carson McCullers, Joseph Heller and Romain Gary, with Donald MacLachlan, editor of the *Sunday Telegraph*, in the chair; the Festival Director for that year, Elizabeth Jane Howard, thought that four people on the platform would be enough, but the *Telegraph* added Kingsley without consulting her – initially to her considerable annoyance. Kingsley was usually better at declining such proposals than at accepting them, but he thought there might be some fun to be got out of the symposium's subject; besides, he had briefly met Jane Howard on a couple of occasions and liked the idea of meeting her again.

The symposium itself, held in Cheltenham Town Hall, wasn't a huge success, unimproved by MacLachlan's weak chairmanship and by McCullers being both seriously ill and extremely drunk. Later, Jane remembered Kingsley stating his dislike of 'hairy-chested' sex in novels, while Kingsley recalled Heller's reply to a member of the audience who wondered, rather interestingly, why many fictional characters find sex burdensome. 'They had a hell of a good time in my book,' he said.[36] If those were the high points, they were unspectacular ones. After the symposium and a late dinner, Kingsley and Hilly returned to the house Jane had rented, where they were to stay

the night. When Hilly retired to bed, Kingsley wanted to carry on
drinking and Jane kept him company: 'We talked and talked until
four a.m.,' she says, 'about our work, our lives, our marriages and
each other.'[37] Kingsley told Jacobs that he 'sort of threw a pass at
Jane which was sort of accepted'.[38] By the time they parted next
morning, they had exchanged phone numbers and agreed to meet
in London. Hilly recognised the signs of an incipient affair, but she
couldn't have guessed that this one would end her marriage.

Elizabeth Jane Howard was born in London in March 1923, a
year after Kingsley. Her paternal grandfather ran a successful timber
business, Howard Brothers, which her father David joined after
serving as a major in the First World War; her mother Katherine
spent a year dancing with Diaghilev's Ballets Russes, while her
maternal grandfather was the composer Sir Arthur Somervell. Her
parents' marriage in 1921 thus symbolised the sometimes stormy
alliance of middle-class business prosperity and cultured eccentricity
which figures in so many of her novels. The family had a town house
in Kensington and a country house in Sussex, and Jane was mostly
educated at home by a governess; nevertheless, the Howards were not
quite as well off as these facts suggest. Jane was sent away to study
domestic science: she lasted only two terms before enrolling at the
London Mask Theatre School. It was as an attractive if not over-
employed young actress that she met the naturalist and painter Peter
Scott, whom she married in 1942, when he was thirty-two and she
nineteen. The marriage was a disaster – each was captivated by the
other's glamour without remotely understanding what lay behind it
– and the couple separated in 1947. Jane, according to Scott's
biographer Elspeth Huxley, 'walked out of No. 8 Edwardes Square
with £20, a suitcase containing her half-written novel and some of
her smart New York clothes'.[39] It wouldn't be the last time she (in her
own word for it) 'bolted'.

The half-written novel was *The Beautiful Visit* (1950); it was
followed during the next decade by *The Long View* (1956) and
The Sea Change (1959). Meanwhile, Jane was living the typically
precarious life of the literary freelancer: working as a publisher's
reader and editor, reviewing and broadcasting. In 1959, rather to
her own subsequent puzzlement, she married an Australian called
Jim Douglas-Henry, but they had separated before she encountered
Kingsley in Cheltenham in 1962. By this time, she was working

on her fourth novel, *After Julius* (1965). Although Jane was thus a book behind Kingsley in simple terms of productivity, one might plausibly argue that her first four novels are more ambitious and varied than his: if her reputation was the lesser of the two, this was partly because the English literary novel in the 1950s remained dominated, despite the success of Iris Murdoch, by male writers (Kingsley himself would point to the undervaluation of Elizabeth Taylor, who 'never received her due as one of the best English novelists of the century').[40] But there was also another reason why her fiction may have seemed slightly out of tune with the rough-and-ready social realism of the zeitgeist: this involved the tricky business of social class and of the voice that went with it.

Kingsley had registered this during their first evening in Cheltenham. He told Jane how he'd modified his own speech from South London to literate Oxonian, and she asked him how he'd originally spoken. 'Like this,' he replied, reassuming the accent of Norbury before adding: 'I'm not posh – like you.'[41] Jane denied it. She wasn't, and isn't, exactly 'posh': merely an inhabitant of a different region in that varied terrain called the English middle class. But there it was, the fatal word 'posh' again; and if Kingsley and Jane hadn't fallen in love with an intensity neither of them had previously experienced, 'posh' might have rung an alarm bell even then. In some respects, SW16 and W8 remained a world apart.

After Cheltenham, Jane spent a recuperative week in France with two gay friends; on returning, she agreed to meet Kingsley on the geographically and morally neutral ground of a large pub in Leicester Square. Before even ordering a drink, he said: 'I have to tell you something.' He told her that he'd 'booked a room in a nearby hotel. He knew it was presumptuous, but he'd done it anyway and he needed to know at once how I felt about that. If I didn't want to spend the night with him, he must cancel the room or it wouldn't be fair on the hotel. I spent the night with him.'[42] Jane saw in this an admirable honesty and straightforwardness, as well as a genuine concern about inconveniencing the hotel; and she was partly right. What she didn't see was the terror of lower-middle-class insecurity: the importance of doing the right thing and the unquenchable sense that it was so much worse to upset those in mundane authority (such as hotel managers), who played by the rules, than wives and lovers and friends who didn't, necessarily. She hadn't yet met Kingsley's demons; she would never understand them. The hotel, incidentally, supplies the 'stair of marble' in a 'A Point of Logic', the beautifully spare and very Gravesian love poem which Kingsley wrote immediately afterwards.[43]

For much of the following year, Kingsley and Jane behaved like a pair of guiltily besotted teenagers, meeting in bars or restaurants and borrowing the amenable Robert Conquest's flat or the Belsize Park house of Tom Maschler, Jane's publisher at Jonathan Cape. Cambridge proved at last to have two advantages over Swansea: it was closer to London, and Kingsley's room at Peterhouse was a more secure place to write letters and take phone calls. The letters he wrote to her are extraordinary: in the past, Kingsley's intimacy had always been signalled by frantic, allusive jokiness; yet his letters to Jane are both ecstatic and almost completely unironic (nevertheless, it needs to be borne in mind that, because of the circumstances of their meeting in Oxford, the opportunity for Kingsley to write this sort of letter to Hilly simply didn't arise). The tone is so unguarded, so vulnerably unlike anything else we can read of Kingsley's, that we may feel a touch of unease that these letters should be in the public domain at all. On 21 November 1962, after reporting with eery prescience on a none-too-successful 'anti-drink effort', he writes: 'I can't forget how beautiful you are. I love your *gaze*. I remember particularly (and always will) that sudden eye-to-eye moment in the restaurant. I'm very proud of you.'[44] On 8 January 1963:

> I adored it. I adore you. You get more beautiful all the time. I can't stop thinking about you. Every other woman I see reminds me of you – to her disadvantage. I love and enjoy everything about you. I love your clothes and the way you do your hair and I do feel awed by you as I said at lunch. I can't wait to see you. I do love you. Not just sexual friends any more – though that too. I admire and trust you. I knew it would be wonderful but I had no idea it would be as wonderful as this. Got to go now. Ring you tomorrow. I love you.[45]

And, four days later, in words which seem almost to belong in a love poem by Graves: 'Never so awed as by Thursday. It was like a dream except that I don't dream so vividly. Never been so knocked over by love.'[46] He did in fact enclose with this letter a newly written love poem, 'An Attempt at Time-Travel', although the casual reader may not recognise it as such: it describes an imaginary scene in a horse-drawn open carriage, where a ten-year-old boy is 'defeated' by a silent nine-year-old girl, 'In azure satin blue-trimmed'; her father is driving, wearing a 'festive' brown bowler hat, chatting and laughing over his shoulder, while her grandfather shares the carriage with the two children. At the end, Kingsley wonders how the boy and girl might react to each other as adults; the key is in the one-year gap in their ages, mirroring his and Jane's.[47]

Being in love changed, or seemed to change, Kingsley. Though no longer allergic to 'abroad' – he was, after all, still intending to rent a house on Majorca and live there with Hilly and the children – he would become with Jane a very different sort of traveller; and it was the accidents of travel which were to precipitate the end of his first marriage. The night before the Amises left to attend the science-fiction conference in July 1963 was, he told Jane, 'the worst I've ever spent – a scene that started as soon as I got home and didn't end until 6.30 the next morning';[48] since he and Hilly were due to be collected by taxi at 6.40, this was an inauspicious start to the trip. Once they arrived in Trieste – in the company of Brian Aldiss, Harry Harrison and their respective wives – things seemed easier to Kingsley. Hilly, however, wrote her own terse comment in lipstick on his back. She had, more or less, tolerated his affairs until now; and, until now, he had at least made some attempt at discretion. However, soon after their return from Trieste, he was due to set off on holiday to Spain with Jane, and he was no longer making any secret of the fact; indeed, he seems to have imagined that he and the family would thereafter cheerfully move to the house they had rented in Soller, Majorca, and all would be forgiven. To Jane he wrote that he was looking forward to their Spanish adventure 'like schoolboy going on holiday (as well as sailor going on leave, etc.)'.[49] But love can make us clumsy in our dealings with all but the loved one, and it was a spectacular miscalculation to set off on the morning of Hilly's birthday, 21 July, leaving behind a present which she suspected had been chosen by Jane. He had no idea that he and Hilly had spent their last married night together.

Anxious to vanish into the 'cut-price crowd', Kingsley and Jane went to Sitges, where the local tourist agency found them a comfortable studio flat in a quiet street. They were encumbered with a huge amount of luggage, including two typewriters, for this was to be a working holiday: Kingsley was finishing *One Fat Englishman* – so

tightly against his deadline that a representative from Gollancz had
to meet him at Barcelona Airport to collect the typescript – while
Jane was midway through *After Julius*. Kingsley had never before
lived and worked in such close physical and emotional proximity
with another writer; moreover, although Jane knew his work, he was
still, after almost a year of their relationship, totally unacquainted
with hers. So for two days he sat on the beach reading *The Sea
Change*. 'The second evening, he shut the book and said, "That's a
very good novel indeed. I am *so* relieved. I was afraid you wouldn't
be any good." '50 It was the right book for him to have read at that
moment.

They decided to put their mutual confidence in each other's literary
ability to the test in the most practical way, by each writing a portion
of the other's novel. The results are fascinating. Jane's pages of *One
Fat Englishman*51 – they are part of the dreadful post-island party,
just after Joe Derlanger has drunkenly smashed up his car – blend
almost seamlessly into Kingsley's; the main clue to their authorship is
a slightly more adjectival style (would Kingsley have written 'Someone was standing in the *shadowed* porch when he entered it'?). But
Kingsley's pages of *After Julius*52 are more easily identifiable, simply
because his prose style, though sparser, is more eccentric: there are
typically lopsided parentheses, matily bluff asides ('no mean feat
considering her other manual commitments'), quirks such as the use
of 'plus' as a conjunction and an absence of commas where we might
expect them. Nevertheless, according to Jane, the only reader to
identify both pieces of impersonation was her brother Colin. Thereafter, she says, she and Kingsley enjoyed 'an extremely healthy
working relationship, trying to do completely different things'.53

The holiday, originally planned as three weeks, extended to well
over a month, while Hilly in Cambridge was left to make all the
practical arrangements for the move to Majorca – exactly as had
been the case with the move from Eynsham to Swansea fourteen
years earlier. But, in the last week of August, Kingsley's and Jane's
agreeable routine of writing, eating, drinking and making love
was abruptly interrupted: they were in bed one afternoon when
there was a knock at the door which Jane, supposing it to be the
laundry, answered in her dressing-gown. She discovered instead a
large reporter, a stringer for the *Daily Express*, who swiftly wedged
his enormous foot in the door and demanded an interview. 'He was

far too horrible to be rendered accurately in any work of realistic fiction,' said Kingsley. 'He was an Australian, you see.'[54] The only thing to do was to get dressed and give him his interview outside, without letting the rest of him follow his foot into the flat. Kingsley told Bill Rukeyser that the interview 'consisted of me telling him a lot about my book and saying "no comment" and "that's my business" to everything else'. When the reporter had left, he contacted George Gale at the *Express* to see whether the story could be suppressed; despite this, an item appeared in the paper's 'William Hickey' gossip column. Kingsley half expected a throng of reporters to besiege them afterwards, but none turned up, slightly to his disappointment: a pair of eloping novelists in their early forties were mildly interesting, but not as interesting as all that.

When Kingsley returned to Cambridge in the first week of September, he found an empty house: Hilly and the children had left for Majorca in August, without leaving so much as a note. The unstated assumption was that Kingsley would follow in his own good time; yet she knew that he was incapable of travelling alone, and he could hardly bring Jane along. He caught the next train back to London and – now that their cover had been blown – to Jane's flat in Blomfield Road, Maida Vale: he was in this sense an unusually portable person, having no interest in bulky possessions such as furniture and owning only clothes, books, records and, more transitorily, booze. But if that summer marked the start of his full-time relationship with Jane, it marked the end of a good deal more: his marriage to Hilly, his career as a university teacher, his intimate friendship with Philip; his father had died in April; the end of his professional relationship with Gollancz had been indirectly hastened, too. All these had become interdependent to an extent he can't have appreciated at the time. For instance, his affair with Jane had given him the confidence not to resign from Peterhouse (that decision had been taken already) but to say very publicly how much he detested Cambridge. And this in turn affronted Philip who, on hearing the news at the end of 1962, wrote to Conquest: 'I think it wd have more graceful of K. to glide out of Cambridge without all this public posturing. If he made a mistake in thinking he could write there that's his fault, not anyone else's: no need to put them in the wrong.' It was a fair point. Philip added, reasonably enough, given the information available to him at the time: 'I can't imagine Majorca will be any better. Whose flat will he borrow there? Who'll he screw?'[55] By September, the first question had become irrelevant and the second had answered itself.

Philip never really took to Jane, though he had sufficient tact not to say so: she was an emotional rival and a literary one, in the simple sense that Kingsley now had someone closer at hand with whom he could discuss the problems of his own writing and the vexatious absurdities of almost everyone else's. That, at least, is one way of reading both the diminished frequency and the forced informality of the Amis–Larkin letters from 1962 onwards. Yet, on another level, Philip felt quite gladly disburdened: he sensed more sharply than Kingsley that the tone of their friendship might no longer be appropriate for distinguished authors in middle age; he was genuinely irritated by what he saw as Kingsley's compounded folly in first accepting the Cambridge post and then leaving it with such bad grace; and he was concerned for Hilly and the children, one of whom was his godson. Love blinded Kingsley to the long-lasting repercussions of his actions, just as it did to the problematic differences between him and Jane: her superiority in his over-sensitive perception of social class which, because it didn't matter to her, was all the more niggling to him; her rather *Homes and Gardens*ish concern with the quality of her immediate surroundings (the crowning irony of this would come a decade later when, as part of a long-running campaign, the fabric firm Sanderson furnished a room and photographed them in it, with the strapline 'Very Kingsley Amis, Very Sanderson'); her intuitive political conservatism, essentially inherited from her upbringing and so unlike that of a disappointed lefty such as Kingsley. These ultimately unbridgeable differences were at first part of the attraction. He was, improbably enough, in the emotional condition of Shakespeare's Miranda when she exclaims, 'O brave new world / That has such people in 't!'; and there was no Prospero nearby to mutter, warningly, ''Tis new to thee.'

They almost immediately left Jane's flat in Maida Vale – she shared it with her brother Colin, with whom Kingsley in fact got on perfectly well, but there was also still the possibility of Jim Douglas-Henry turning up – and moved temporarily to Basil Mansions in Knightsbridge. There they were disturbed, while reading in bed one mid-November evening towards midnight, by a knock at the door: it was, Jane remembers, 'a flat where all the rooms led off a long

passage with the front door at one end', and when she had got up to
see who Kingsley had or hadn't admitted (the Australian reporter was
still on their minds), she found him 'walking back from it followed
by two blond-headed boys. "This is Philip and this is Martin," he
said, "and this is Jane".'[56] Hilly had simply put them on a plane,
which landed late, and given them an address to find. Jane cooked
bacon and eggs for them – the right move, both practically and
tactically – and then left them to eat and talk to their father while she
made up beds for them. No one involved seems to have foreseen, let
alone imagined, this inevitable moment which would crucially alter
the dynamics of all their relationships. Kingsley's qualities as a father
were made of the same self-contradictory compound – affectionate-
neglectful–impatient–indulgent – that characterised most of his behaviour towards others. Jane, who had been estranged from her daughter
Nicola Scott, had honest doubts about her maternal competence and
now found herself ironically cast in the role of wicked stepmother.
As for the boys, they of course wanted to be with their mother *and*
with their father; although this was confusing and upsetting for them,
it put them, as they soon realised, in a powerful bargaining position
with Kingsley, who could never again treat them as children. Being
teenagers in London in 1963 counted for a good deal, too.

Before returning to school at Palma, the boys stayed for a week
which turned out to be memorable for quite another reason. On the
evening of 22 November, George Gale came to dinner but, before
they had even begun their meal, the phone rang. Kingsley took the
call, which was from Quentin Crewe, and then passed on his news to
the astonished company: President John F. Kennedy had been assas-
sinated in Dallas, Texas. (Gale left at once, unfed, to return to his
office at the *Express*.) A few weeks later, Sally visited too, bringing
with her a younger and less resentful curiosity. By this time, Kingsley
and Jane had moved back to Blomfield Road: Colin's presence turned
out to be not only agreeable but an enormous asset, alleviating
Kingsley's terror of being alone in a house whenever Jane was
elsewhere. Nevertheless, the flat soon proved too small for their
increasingly complicated lives, and in June 1964 Jane bought a ten-
year lease on an Edwardian villa at 108 Maida Vale; while this was
being made habitable – a process which was to take six months –
they decamped first to the house in Soller, now vacated by Hilly and
the children. 'This is the most heavenly *spoilt* little Spanish town, full

of wine and olives and *retch-fetching* laughter from the peasants and *Huns* and *Frogs*,' Kingsley told Larkin, expressing somewhat qualified approval. 'And a divine artists' colony at Deyá (sitting at that great human being Graves's feet).'[57] When their lease on that house ran out, they moved on to the utterly anonymous Molins Hotel at Pollensa, where Jane was still finishing *After Julius* while Kingsley worked between drinks ('large gins, which are about four times the size of an English double') on an assortment of potboiling enterprises. Meanwhile, Hilly and the children, having returned from Majorca, moved first to a flat in Ovington Gardens, Chelsea; next, to a rented house in the Fulham Road; and then to Wivenhoe, Essex, where she bought a house, paid for by Kingsley, and met her second husband, David Shackleton Bailey. Sally was sent to boarding school, while the boys spent their weeks at Maida Vale, going (or not going) to school in London, and their weekends in Essex. Jane had been divorced from Jim Douglas-Henry in May 1964; Kingsley and Hilly's divorce followed a year later; and on 29 June 1965 Kingsley and Jane were married at Marylebone Town Hall. After two years of being shaken up and redistributed, the human components seemed to have settled into some sort of tolerable accommodation with themselves and each other.

4

Peter Evans once memorably suggested that 'Swinging London', and thus by implication the cluster of phenomena we'd come to know as the 'Sixties', 'most probably began at precisely 11.3 a.m. on the morning of March 22 1963 – when John Dennis Profumo, Secretary of State for War, rose in the House of Commons to lie about his association with Christine Keeler'.[58] Philip Larkin, in that famous though not particularly good poem 'Annus Mirabilis', which sacrifices everything to its joke, would write: 'Sexual intercourse began / In nineteen sixty-three . . .'[59] That autumn, the Harold Macmillan era, which had conversely come to feel like the embodiment of the 'Fifties', ended when he was replaced as Prime Minister by Sir Alec Douglas-Home; meanwhile, in Dallas . . . Kingsley had neatly synchronised his own year of endings and new beginnings with those of the greater world: an age of uncertainty had arrived, and it wasn't about to go away. When, a year later, at the General Election of October 1964, Douglas-Home was ousted (just) by Harold Wilson, Kingsley wrote to Bill Rukeyser: 'It's a pity that power-crazed, pipe-smoking creep has got into No. 10, but a substantially greater relief that that twitching upper-class buffoon is out of it.'[60] This is the voice not of the lefty he had once been nor of the committed Conservative he would become; it is the voice of the provisional, shifting 1960s.

One of the key ingredients of the time was its implicit challenge to the notion of high culture. Kingsley, of course, had been doing this for years: negatively, in his irreverent disparagement of supposedly great writers such as Dryden or Keats; positively, in his lectures on science fiction and his co-editorship of the *Spectrum* SF anthologies. Yet his first five novels, despite their subversive humour, all have central characters who are professionally involved with literary or academic life; no one would have been surprised to discover that their author was a university lecturer. Now, suddenly, he wasn't: this simultaneously gave him a new sense of freedom in his writing and obliged him to make a living from it. In 1965 he published two of his potboilers, *The James Bond Dossier* and – a project co-authored with Robert Conquest which had been hanging about for several years – *The Egyptologists*; and these were swiftly followed by his sixth 'proper' novel, *The Anti-Death League* (1966). *The James Bond Dossier*, which began as a 5,000-word essay and grew to modest book length, was partly designed to affront the intellectual and moral snobs he had gratefully left behind in Cambridge: 'As a recently retired university teacher, I can't help being slightly drawn to any form of writing which (like science fiction) reaches no part of its audience through compulsion,' he wrote in his Preface. 'One volunteer is worth ten pressed men.'[61] He was following the example of his friend Robert Graves, a cheerfully prolific turner-out of potboilers who had an enviable eight-foot shelf of his own books above his writing desk. Certainly, to write something (or about something) almost completely worthless can be an oddly liberating experience for the serious author. It can also help to pay the bills.

For all that, *The James Bond Dossier* is an impossible book to excuse. You don't have to be a Cambridge don to see that a novelist with a major reputation needs to be choosy about the fellow-novelists whose work he endorses. Kingsley knew this perfectly well, which is why his enjoyment of Bond is qualified by weasly formulae such as

'I like reading about you and me as much as the next man does, but not all the time.'[62] That provides a hint of distance, but it isn't nearly enough. Kingsley fails to grasp – and therefore can't argue and defend the opposite case – the very real possibility that Ian Fleming might be a bad and pernicious author: for example, his bland dismissal in an appendix of the Bond novels' strand of pornographic sadism is breathtaking in its naivety. Then there is the matter of simple literary misjudgement: after all, it would have been perfectly possible for him to have written a book-length study of a novelist he admired and whose morally simplified world is transformed by intelligence, humanity, wit and linguistic brilliance – Henry Fielding. That he chose instead to write about Fleming confirms things which we may already suspect about Kingsley: about his frightened denial of the complexities of good and evil, his avoidance of novels which he feared might turn out to be too difficult for him (his reluctance to read James or Faulkner, for instance) and his lifelong recourse to the easy escapism of popular cultural forms with their uncomplicated heroes and villains. The only way to read the Bond books without nausea, for anyone who can tolerate Fleming's wretchedly vacuous prose, is to retreat to the comics and Saturday matinees of childhood and, in Kingsley's case, to re-enter the suburban soul of Norbury, SW16. The best parts of *The James Bond Dossier* are some nicely ironic footnotes, especially the one in which he tries to imagine how Bond might have thought about England if he were, improbably, 'a keen Labour Party man of the sort that goes canvassing': '*His mind drifted into a world of soccer pitches and recreation grounds and Trade Union leaders, of Walsall, of the demonstrators being photographed with guitars across their knees in Trafalgar Square, of the pansies blooming outside Transport House* ... It can't be done.'[63] Otherwise, *The James Bond Dossier* is best forgotten.

So, for different reasons, is *The Egyptologists*. Kingsley had first mentioned this to Larkin as long ago as 30 July 1958, describing it as one of Conquest's 'forthcoming two novels' and adding that it sounded 'as if it would be quite good if someone other than Bob were doing it'.[64] Someone other than Bob did do it. On 31 December 1963, having settled into his freelance life with Jane at Blomfield Road, he told Larkin, evidently in the spirit of a new year's resolution: 'When I've finished my critical appraisal of Ian Fleming I've undertaken to revise Bob's Egyptology novel for him.' He foresaw practical difficulties arising from interminable discussions with his co-author, but added: 'Still, it's for money.'[65] It was: Richard Attenborough paid £25,000 for the film rights, although the film was never made. Kingsley's main difficulty, however, would not be with Conquest but with Victor Gollancz: for not only was the Bond book to be published by Cape, who had been Fleming's publishers, but Conquest had sold *The Egyptologists* to them as well. The idea of two books with Amis's name on them appearing from a major rival was almost more than Gollancz could stand. 'I cannot help feeling rather uneasy,' he told Kingsley on 1 October 1964, 'for the appearance of the James Bond book by yourself alone under a Cape imprint, followed by a second book, with your name on it, under the same imprint – both coming out before another book by you under my imprint – is bound to cause widespread comment . . .' Gollancz worried, rightly, that people would ask: 'Is Kingsley Amis leaving Gollancz for Cape?'[66] Kingsley's loyalty had started to falter when Hilary Rubinstein, apparently forced out by his uncle, left the firm in 1963, but he found Victor Gollancz himself 'an engaging rogue' and enjoyed the paradox of someone who was at once 'a monster of egotism, vanity and self-delusion' and 'entirely capable of disinterested generosity both moral and monetary, genuine warmth of heart and readiness to go to endless trouble on behalf of those he valued'.[67] He finished working on the book that month, in Majorca, and delivered it to Tom Maschler at Cape in early December.

The Egyptologists is what Graham Greene would have called an 'entertainment' rather than a novel. It concerns the adventures and misadventures of the all-male Metropolitan Egyptological Society, an organisation whose members' interest in their subject takes its cue from Shakespeare's Antony: 'The beds i' the east are soft . . .' Each chapter carries an epigraph from *Antony and Cleopatra* and the book is aptly dedicated to Charmian, who was in fact Conquest's sister. The society's meetings and excursions are occasions for organised marital infidelity, although wives are occasionally invited to open evenings at which the Egyptological content is impenetrably tedious and the sherry intentionally undrinkable. The twin dangers of this jape are that it will be accidentally infiltrated by someone actually interested in Egyptology and that one of the wives (who, of course, can get up to anything in the absence of their husbands) will find herself coincidentally involved with one of the other erring

Egyptologists. The book is written with enormous gusto and contains scenes of nocturnal careering about in London which come close to parodying Iris Murdoch's *Under the Net*; yet it's hard not to feel that the whole joke is too slight to be sustained at this length. It's a novel that wants to be a short story.

Both *The James Bond Dossier* and *The Egyptologists* were evasions. The pressing, problematical question was: what ought the English novelist to be doing after 'the tranquillised fifties'? Some, like John Braine or David Storey, followed their early successes with books which widened the original territory yet remained, in tone and technique, recognisably sequels. But some more considerable writers seemed to share a dissatisfaction with the staple diet of 80,000-word contemporary social comedies, and Kingsley was among them: 'I don't want to do documentary realism any more,' he told an interviewer in March 1963. 'In England one is supposed to be a writer about Britain in the '50s and '60s. I don't want to write that kind of book.'[68] Angus Wilson's *The Old Men at the Zoo* (1961) was set in the then near future; his next two novels, *Late Call* (1964) and *No Laughing Matter* (1967), reached back almost to the beginning of the twentieth century. William Golding had never been precisely a social realist, but in *The Spire* (1964) he produced a medieval allegory in modern prose. And although most of Iris Murdoch's novels of the 1960s purported to be set in contemporary England, their worlds had elements of strangeness or remoteness which would have greatly puzzled Jim Dixon, Patrick Standish and – as his comments on her in letters and reviews suggest – Kingsley Amis. His solution to the dilemma, a more Murdochian one than he'd have liked to admit, was to write a novel in which the action, although it takes place in an English here and now, bears almost no resemblance to what most readers would have understood by 'real life'.

The Anti-Death League is a confused and a confusing book. Its opening suggests that Kingsley had deliberately unlearned everything he knew about novel-writing. The title of its first section, 'The Edge of a Node', though conceivably inviting to a science-fiction reader, is likely to seem jarringly rebarbative to anyone else. The opening paragraphs introduce two nameless groups of characters – 'A girl and an older woman' and 'three uniformed men' – who are discovered in a starkly underdescribed setting: 'a metalled pathway', 'a strip of grass', 'a large high building', 'a pointed turret', 'a tower-like structure supported by stone pillars'. The writing is curiously flat and unatmospheric, and when the first two characters open their mouths they speak a bad identikit English. 'What's happening?' the girl asks, and the woman replies, 'That's just the old cat. He's spotted something under the tower, there I expect.'[69] After a page of this, the reader will be chilly with alienation: yet, in its bleak way, this is a prose almost as experimental as that of the modernists whom Kingsley so distrusted.

Though the characters soon acquire names (rather arbitrary-seeming ones), the understated sense of menace persists and intensifies. The three army officers find the tower – it is simply a water-tower designed to match the mysterious building nearby – 'a bit sinister' and are almost immediately cowed by a low-flying aircraft which is 'like the passing of the shadow of death'.[70] The painter Sargy Mann, noting that Kingsley's novels contain 'more good visual stuff than he's given credit for' because 'he knows how to make something vital happen inside your head', points out that the image of the plane's shadow is 'powerful because it's so sparing'.[71] Then the soldiers' path broadens into a circle with an ornamental pond, in the middle of which is a grotesque stone creature. By this time, the youngest of them, James Churchill, has to all intents and purposes instantaneously fallen in love with the younger of the two women, Catharine Casement, though not a word has passed between them. She, we learn, is the survivor of two disastrous marriages and now a patient about to be released from the mental hospital (which is what the 'large high building' is), while the officers are visiting a hospitalised alcoholic colleague, Max Hunter. But other discoveries and questions crowd in. Why is one of the officers a padre and another an Indian? What is the significance of Fawkes, the NCO on guard duty outside Hunter's ward? Who is the mysterious Captain Leonard who put him there? And will (as is already hinted) Dr Best, who apparently runs the hospital, turn out to be a lunatic in charge of the asylum, the first of several barking-mad psychiatrists in Kingsley's later novels?

The book is driven by equal and opposite forces, like Yeats's gyres, and these are no less than death and life. On one side is the military plot, set in a nearby base which incongruously combines memories of Kingsley's army days with the jargon of espionage borrowed from the world of James Bond. Everything about it is a double bluff: Brian Leonard, the man whom Colonel White mildly describes as 'our spy-catcher',[72] is, to borrow one of Jenny Bunn's favourite expressions, a stooge; the grotesque 'Operation Apollo' depends precisely on its secrets being infiltrated and leaked to the enemy, who will thus be so demoralised that the operation itself becomes unnecessary; and the 'Anti-Death League' itself is similarly self-cancelling. (There *are* deaths, to be sure, but they are random and accidental: an unnamed army motorycle courier, Corporal Fawkes, Captain Ayscue's dog and – most bizzarely – the character modelled on Kingsley's first publisher who has cameos in all his early novels, L. S. Caton.) Death isn't so much defeated as made to look slightly ridiculous. Life, on the other hand, flourishes via the love plot: this is centred on the novel's third main location, the home of Lady Lucy Hazell, who runs a kind of salon at which she provides conveyor-belt sexual favours for the army officers and who is also the protectress of Catharine Casement, who has a room in her house. It's Lucy who arranges Catharine's therapeutic, getting-to-meet-people pub job, where James Churchill can plausibly re-encounter her; but both are to be symbolically tested – she by operable cancer, he by a nervous breakdown – before *amor vincit omnia*. That, after all, was what Kingsley believed at the time.

Each of his earlier novels has a recognisable centre of gravity: one character who resembles the author in significant respects. *The Anti-Death League* is much more diffuse. James Churchill has a good deal in common with Kingsley, as Catharine has with Jane, and this explains the quite new tone of their love scenes:

He felt the sheet on his back and the sheet under his forearms and knees and toes.

'I love you,' she said.

'I love you.'

'I know.'

'That's nice as "I love you" really, isn't it? As nice a thing to say and to have someone say to you as well. Nearly as nice, anyway.'

'Have you loved anyone before?' she asked.

'No. Only been fond of people.'

'I've loved other people. Is that all right? You don't mind?'

'There's nothing about you or that you've ever done that I could ever mind.'[73]

The benign effects of being properly in love spread out beyond the loved one: seized by an urge to give poor Brian Leonard a birthday present, Churchill 'jumped now to the conclusion that there must be less love than there ought to be in a world where so many people went on being nasty to and bored by one another. How many people had the good-nature to love everybody without loving somebody first?'[74] Near the end of the novel, when the twin terrors of Catharine's possibly imminent death and the horror of Operation Apollo cause him to go AWOL at Lucy's, he tells Ayscue why he had to leave the camp and take to Catharine's bed: 'There was nowhere else I wanted to be. I couldn't think of anywhere else I could be. But it's just as bad. There isn't anywhere to be.'[75] This – the last sentence especially – is the authentic voice of depression, and only a depressive could have written it.

Churchill has Kingsley's new capacity for love and his old susceptibility to despair, but Max Hunter possesses other characteristics of his author ('Hunter' was Kingsley's pseudonym in many of his letters to Jane during the year before Hilly left him). Most obviously, he is a recovering alcoholic: while Kingsley was working on the book he was trying hard – though in the end unsuccessfully – to reduce his intake of alcohol, which both he and Jane saw as a long-term threat to his health and their relationship. He is also ferociously anti-religious: speaking of Willie Ayscue, the padre, he remarks, in that familiar Amisian vein of borderline-offensive wit, 'Always suspect somebody who goes down on his knees in front of an instrument of torture, even if it is an out-of-date one.'[76] Less obviously like his author, Max is gay: the absurd Dr Best repeatedly tries to diagnose him as a 'repressed homosexual', the joke being that there's nothing at all repressed about his homosexuality, though at one point he wonders whether he mightn't be a 'repressed heterosexual'. He is the most sympathetic gay character in Kingsley's fiction, rivalled only by Colonel Manton in *The Riverside Villas Murder* – a further instance, perhaps, of love spreading into general benignity but also a more specific acknowledgement of friendship, for he shares his sexuality with Jane's brother Colin, the dedicatee of *The Anti-Death League*.

One slightly problematical consequence of Kingsley having divided himself between two characters – and given unmistakably Amis-like utterances to several others – is that the novel's viewpoint is more blurry and unstable than in his earlier books. There are also signs of carelessness in writing and construction. During the scene in which four officers and Dr Best meet in Lucy's sitting-room, Kingsley simply fades up a pair of conversing characters while others are left dangling inaudibly until their intervention is required (what are Ayscue, Ross-Donaldson and Dr Best doing while Hunter and Leonard are talking?),[77] an effect he greatly disliked when it occurred in television drama.[78] Elsewhere, the corrupting influence of Bond becomes comically obtrusive, as when a card table, tankards and 'a metal cylinder about the size of an eight-inch naval shell' are produced from a jeep in the middle of a field exercise: 'The cylinder turned out to be a thermos container and to have in it a very well chilled magnum of Krug 1955.'[79] The military plot itself can only be resolved by the arrival of a helicoptered-in *deus ex machina*, Jagger, who shares Julian Ormerod's parodic RAF-speak but doesn't have the developed larger-than-life personality to go with it. Yet, for all its faults, *The Anti-Death League* just about earns the indulgence traditionally granted to a writer risking a new departure.

It certainly needed some indulgence from Victor Gollancz. Having already tried his patience over the two books with Cape (he seems not to have owned up to a third, the pseudonymous *Book of Bond* by 'Lt. Col. William ("Bill") Tanner'), Kingsley now demanded a glossy, fully illustrated Cape-style jacket for *The Anti-Death League*, although the standard Gollancz livery still consisted of unlaminated yellow paper; with notable tactlessness, he even proposed a designer, Raymond Hawkey. Hawkey was design editor at the *Observer* and did paperback covers for Penguin, but the example of his work Kingsley chose to cite was 'Len Deighton's *Horse under Water*, which thereupon sold 80,000 in the first 2 days (which the book's merits, and its author's standing, would hardly have done unassisted)',[80] published by Cape – to whom, through Jane and Tom Maschler, he was now evidently so close that he had access to other authors' sales figures. Gollancz, agreeing to Kingsley's demands, must have wondered how much longer this sort of thing could go on. In fact, the matter resolved itself in the most non-negotiable of ways: Victor Gollancz died in February 1967, whereupon Kingsley wrote briskly to his daughter, Livia, to say that 'sadly, my loyalty is at an end, and I am off'.[81]

5

After their marriage, a party at Cape's in Bedford Square and a dinner at Prunier's, Kingsley and Jane spent a brief honeymoon at the Hotel Metropole in Brighton. In a typically affectionate note to Hilly on 4 July 1965 (signed, as usual, 'Love, Binks'), he reported: 'It was okay in Brighton really, only there wasn't much sun, and it was hard to find anybody else there under 65.'[82] It was by some distance the least adventurous of their travels over the next few years. In September they were holidaying with their Princeton friends Mike and Mary Keeley in Greece, which Kingsley needed as a location for his own James Bond novel, *Colonel Sun* (published in 1968 under the pseudonym Robert Markham). In January 1966, they sailed to Jamaica, to stay with Bobby and Dolly Burns, the daughter of Lord Duveen; she would, by way of thanks, be transformed into Lady Baldock in *I Want It Now* (1968). Kingsley disliked the mixture of 'rather horrible rich white people' (Dolly Burns pre-eminent among them) and 'rather miserable resentful black people': 'My old left-wing, or just humanitarian, feelings came back with a rush,' he wrote.[83] That summer, the Amises were again with the Keeleys in Greece, which would also figure in *I Want It Now*. In October 1966 they visited a Czechoslovakia still eighteen months away from its Prague Spring: a demoralising experience, for it was clear to both of them that the apparent freedoms available to Czech writers were still underpinned by justified fears of state surveillance. Here Kingsley's 'old left-wing' feelings promptly evaporated again, only to reappear the following autumn in Tennessee, where he had been appointed to a visiting professorship at Vanderbilt University, Nashville, for a semester.

Yet although he shifted his increasingly portly self around these places with a fair show of goodwill, Jane couldn't really turn him into a traveller. His letters home – to Colin Howard and the boys at Maida Vale – make his priorities pretty clear: 'Not much more than an hour later I was sitting half pissed in the Trinidad Hilton, eating Columbus Mangrove Root Oyster Cocktail – bloody good – and drinking Foreign Guinness, which as you know is to me the prince of beers. Then we had Native Caribbean Pork Stew and I had more Guinness.' It was Foreign Guinness which had accompanied his

Princeton oysters, too. 'Finally we lurched back on board and in due course bingo'd and champagned our way up to Kingston.'[84] When called upon to show the conscientious admiration of the true traveller, however, he seems to disappoint himself almost as much as he is disappointed by the places he observes: Delphi, for instance, is 'massively, authentically unimpressive', 'a heap of rubble'.[85] This is due partly to his overdeveloped instinct for bullshit-detection and partly to a simple absence of any real aesthetic sense, which would pose an increasing problem in his later writing where, as we shall see, the comic exuberance of youth declines to leave a vacuum unfilled by the consolations of good taste which often come with age. Meanwhile, the paradoxes of his politics, which to many English readers seem perfectly comprehensible if not inescapable, puzzled and wrong-footed his foreign hosts. In Prague, he was known primarily as the author of *Lucky Jim* (its Czech translation was the first to appear of any of his novels in Eastern Europe) and was expected to be an angry young lefty, thoroughly committed to socialist values; in Nashville, there was a more up-to-date though no less misleading assumption that he had turned into a virulent right-winger. Consequently, in both places he was presented with assumptions and points of view with which he was expected to sympathise but which instead deeply offended him. There is, of course, no pleasing a contrarian.

He had been persuaded to accept the Nashville appointment by Russell Fraser, whom he'd met at Princeton and who was now in charge of the English Department at Vanderbilt. Fraser assured him that Nashville wasn't how Kingsley imagined it, 'the home of lynchings and all that, of a particularly horrible popular music . . . and of all those Southern writers',[86] and that, moreover, you never met another Englishman there, so he'd be safe from re-encounters with the likes of Tony Crosland. (As it happened, he *did* meet another Englishman there, another Labour MP: Ivor Richard, who was speaking about Britain's new closeness to Europe. At the end of his speech, the chairman, 'displaying the modest pride of a provincial zoo official who reveals its possession of not one but *two* Arabian oryxes',[87] called on Kingsley to add a few words: Richard and Kingsley fell out over Europe and America, and fell back in while getting drunk afterwards.) He and Jane sailed on the last voyage of the old *Queen Mary*, going first to Princeton before heading south, complicatedly and by train, to find themselves in a place that with its burger joints and gas stations resembled a television mock-up of a typical American town although it reminded Jane, no less damningly, of the Edgware Road in London. They rented a single-storey house at 3627 Valley Vista Road from Edgar and Ivar-Lou Duncan; she was a 'Scandinavian-American lady . . . of parsimonious bent' who attempted to charge Kingsley for using her husband's typewriter. As she handed over the house, she said of the black maid who was standing there: 'You'll have to give her something at Christmas. Just something cheap and gaudy – anything will do.'[88] The cellar was full of decaying foodstuffs and exploding jars of pickles; the attics were crammed with the owner's belongings; the cooker, fridge and television broke down almost immediately. As the sultry autumn gave way to a snowy winter, the place could only be kept warm by burning, or attempting to burn, logs so damp that they had to be partly dried on the radiators first; a snarling mastiff next door tried to get at Kingsley every day as he fetched them in from the woodshed. The best things about the house were the squirrels in the surrounding trees and the chipmunk who visited a windowsill in the evening for a saucer of milk.

Of his six months in Nashville, Kingsley later wrote: 'I would put it (that period) second only to my army service as the one in my life I would least soon relive.' His account of it in *Memoirs* has been subsequently challenged, most significantly by Walter Sullivan, the professor whose sabbatical leave he was covering, to whom Kingsley attributed the words: 'I can't find it in my heart to give a negro [pron. nigra] or a Jew an A.'[89] If, as seems likely, Sullivan didn't utter them, it is equally likely that someone else did. And indeed, given the patchy reliability of Kingsley's memory, his pages on Nashville are best regarded as a series of representative anecdotes, not to be too firmly attached to specific individuals. *Someone* made that remark, just as someone hectored Kingsley about 'all these coloured people yawl letting in' in England; someone else expressed horrified astonishment at 'Surr Laurence Oh-livyay' as Othello being made to 'look like a black mayun'; and someone else again (a female student) explained that black doctors and lawyers were only to be found in the North because '*here* we know how to keep them in their place'.[90] When he asked about black students at the university, Kingsley was told: 'Oh, certainly. He's called Mr Moore.' This, he said, wasn't a joke; and although there were actually some fifty black students, that isn't much of a joke either. Far from being not as Kingsley would have imagined it, as Russell Fraser had rashly promised, Nashville was turning out all too predictably. 'One can forgive a lefty here,' he told Conquest, 'in that "conservative" opinion is so shitty.'[91] Even an expedition to the Jack Daniel's whiskey distillery at Lynchburg, the sort of occasion Kingsley couldn't help enjoying, was both disappointing and disconcerting. Instead of a boardroom lunch with plenty of rare-vintage liquor, he and Fraser were entertained to a frugal, teetotal meal at Madam Bobo's Boarding House – Moore County being 'dry' – before an audience with the chairman, who cheerfully told them how a couple of careless 'nigras', trimming trees near the revered statue of Jack Daniel, had once chipped the brim of his hat. 'Well, when Mr Motlow [the then proprietor] heard about that it made him real mad – of course, he was in his wheelchair by then. Anyhow, he had them nigras in and he opened his desk drawer and he took out his six-shooter and he emptied it right on the spot and them nigras wasn't seen in Moore County no more.'[92] When was this? Kingsley wondered. 1911? 1923? No, 1952.

Nevertheless, his students were 'about the best I have ever taught'. His course was on the Modern British Novel, and among the writers he discussed were John le Carré, Len Deighton, Ian Fleming, William Golding, Graham Greene, Iris Murdoch, Anthony Powell and Evelyn Waugh. At the end of it he took a vote to discover which of the novels the hundred or so students had liked best: the clear winner was *Decline and Fall*, as it had been when he taught a broadly similar course at Swansea in 1959–60. *Decline and Fall* is an attractive book for which Kingsley was no doubt a persuasive advocate, yet the nature of the course itself and the result of the vote raise a couple of awkward questions which can't be avoided. The first is about exclusions. Waugh's novel was published as long ago as 1928; so, if the course was going to stretch back to the 1920s, shouldn't it have included E. M. Forster, D. H. Lawrence, Virginia Woolf, Christopher Isherwood? The second is about inclusions. What are Le Carré, Deighton and Fleming doing there? And the answer to both questions is more or less the same, or one answer follows from the other. To teach a course specifically on a popular literary form – science fiction at Princeton – is one thing; to include popular authors in an academic course on the Modern British Novel is quite another. On the one hand Kingsley was following what looks like a laudable instinct to

concentrate on books he found genuinely enjoyable, opening doors
to kinds of literature usually excluded from academic consideration.
But on the other he was selling his subject short and, even more
damagingly, closing doors on the challenging and the new. Some of
his students realised this, sensing that his emphasis on simple literary
pleasure, like his boozy affability, might be a symptom of laziness or
evasion. He knew, he had always known, that he wasn't quite good
enough; now, fame and success had enabled him to turn being not
quite good enough into a public persona. His growing intellectual
complacency is reflected, too, in his occasional writings: during the
early 1950s, he'd been a regular reviewer of the latest literary fiction;
by the late 1960s, he was more likely to be found writing on detective
novels or science fiction or films or drink. Yet these were also the
years when, at least partly spurred on by guilt, he became most
vociferous about falling standards in higher education, typically
berating the editor of the *Observer* in April 1965: 'Perhaps only you
could have published a whole article on university failures that laid
no weight on the almost inevitable cause of failure: *insufficient ability*,
or, alternatively, *excessive stupidity*.'[93] He had never been stupid, but
he could be indolent; and that is another way to fail.

When they eventually escaped from Nashville towards the end of
January, Kingsley and Jane travelled to Mexico, once again to join
their friends the Keeleys, before spending February in San Miguel
de Allende, visiting the science-fiction writer Mack Reynolds and
completing their respective novels *I Want It Now* and *Something
in Disguise*. Kingsley's book, which draws heavily on his travels in
Greece and America, is in Zachary Leader's phrase a 'Sleeping Beauty
novel', like *The Anti-Death League*; it was also his first proper – sole-
authored, non-pseudonymous – novel for Tom Maschler at Cape,
a different sort of publisher with whom he had a different sort of
relationship, closer and blokier than his somewhat guarded dealings
with the old rogue Gollancz. A well-disposed reader could hardly fail
to find *I Want It Now* among the most entertaining of Kingsley's
books, and it contains some corrosively funny set pieces: Vassilikós's
luncheon-party; Lady Baldock's disrupted Thanksgiving dinner; the
final televised confrontation between herself and Ronnie. Yet this
shouldn't obscure the considerable problems it presents.

The central premise is as preposterous as it is simple. A shit called
Ronnie Appleyard is transformed by love into something approaching

a saint; meanwhile, Simona Quick, a surly and frigid rich girl, learns to become a passionate, devoted girlfriend (and, as the book ends, wife): *amor vincit omnia* once again. Unfortunately, the most convincing aspect of Ronnie is his shittiness and there's nothing convincing about Simona, or Simon as she calls herself, least of all her falling for a grasping and uncouth television presenter. Ronnie's initial attitude towards Simon, a hard one for the reader to eradicate, is clear from their first meeting, when she rhetorically asks him: 'Do you think I'm out of my mind?'

> On the whole Ronnie did, but he did not want to antagonize the girl. Yet. The time would come for an elephant's dose of antagonizing, or whatever else might be needed in order to get her out of his bed, flat and life. That, however, was looking a couple of hours ahead.[94]

It seems questionable whether anything much short of brain surgery could change a man who thinks like this into the decent, honourable fellow who has Lord Baldock's blessing to marry his stepdaughter two hundred pages later; it's certainly doubtful whether anyone quite as vapid as Simon could do the trick, although sleeping beauties are obviously meant to be sleepy. Ronnie's feelings about Simon alter when he learns that she probably has money, and by the time he discovers that she probably hasn't (it's safely locked up in a trust) these new feelings have perplexingly become irreversible.

The book is about money at least as much as it's about love; the 'It' that's wanted 'Now' is wealth as well as sex. Ronnie, who is poorer than seems likely for a television chat-show presenter even in 1968, shares his author's prickly dislike of people who are better off or otherwise more privileged than he is. Encountering a complete stranger with an 'upper-class honk' (who turns out to be Lord Upshot) on the steamer to Malakos, Ronnie immediately goes on the offensive: 'He was short on the one attribute certain to win the immediate respect of the rich – i.e. being rich – and must therefore obtrude deterrents against being buggered about.'[95] The flaw in his strategy of despising and attacking the rich is that it prevents him from imagining what they might really be like individually; since we share his point of view in the novel, it therefore becomes inevitable that all the wealthy people in it, of whom there are an inordinate number, will be mean, stupid, dislikeable and if possible burdened with ridiculous names. Though funny, generalisation continually works against characterisation: 'He had never found anything about the rich half as sweet as their constant Stilton-paring: 50 centimes in the cloakroom saucer at the Tour d'Argent after a 2,000 franc dinner-party, the telephone in the guest bedroom available for incoming calls only.'[96] There are variations according to nationality. A rich Greek is likely to be schemingly, vindictively stingy and comically given to speaking of himself as one of the 'Ritz people'. A rich Southern American will be a loud-mouthed racist imported from Kingsley's time at Vanderbilt and be called something like Student Mansfield (he had actually met someone in Nashville called Tupper Saucy and regretted that the names weren't the other way round). Although the Greek Vassilikós and the American George Parrot eventually behave generously towards Ronnie, their generosity is qualified by being essentially the product of malice towards Lady Baldock. The televised debate in which Lady Baldock is joined by Vassilikós and Ronnie, among others, to discuss 'The Rich' is bound to result in her satisfactory demolition, yet Ronnie's contributions are problematical in the same way as Roger Micheldene's benign thoughts at the end of One Fat Englishman: when he says, 'If you're rich, you can afford to abandon reason, justice and good manners whenever you feel like it,'[97] we can't help recalling how often he has been irrational, bad-mannered or both during the novel.

I Want It Now is the first of Kingsley's own-name books to feel like the work of a professional hack rather than a vocational author. There are even moments when he seems to forget which sort of novel he's writing: Lady Baldock's Greek-island retreat, approached via 'a winding staircase of white stone that apparently extended several hundred feet above their heads', at the top of which she is discovered 'standing not on a crag but at the end of a terrace and near a large boomerang-shaped swimming-pool',[98] is a setting more appropriate to James Bond. And the prose itself is heavily dependent on formulae which become overfamiliar: artful tautologies ('Ronnie recognised that being nervous of being nervous must be an unusually trouble-some form of being nervous. You had to stop it before you could stop it')[99] or trademark stock phrases such as 'Ronnie wished that they had not done that . . .'[100] and 'As Juliette Baldock drew Hamer away, Ronnie mentally supplied what they could just go and do.'[101] Compared with the much more subtly nuanced and carefully written

Take a Girl like You – another novel about a manipulative man and
a vulnerable young woman – *I Want It Now* represents a worryingly
steep decline.

6

Kingsley and Jane returned to London in March 1968. Colin, who
had been charged with the task of looking after the house and (when
they were there) the boys, had in the meantime enlisted the help of a
painter friend, Sargy Mann, who was only too happy to exchange his
bedsit in Fitzrovia for the comparative luxury of Maida Vale. The
boys were setting off in the directions which would shape their own
careers: Philip, who had huffily moved out after a row over drugs but
kept turning up on a scooter, would study painting at Camberwell
School of Art, where Sargy taught; Martin, whose school truancies
had been replaced by a year of uncharacteristically intensive work at
Sussex Tutors in Brighton, had just won an exhibition to read English
at Exeter College, Oxford. On the evening that Kingsley and Jane
arrived back, Sargy cooked them all a special meal and then said he'd
better be off. 'Do you have to go?' asked Kingsley. 'Don't go,' said
Jane. He didn't: he remained with the household for the next eight
years, until he married Frances Carey, a fellow painter and former
student, in 1976.

At 108 Maida Vale, Sargy remembers, Kingsley and Jane were
'ecstatically happy, apart from the problems with the children'.[102]
Nevertheless, although the household was expanding, the house
wasn't; moreover, Jane's lease was a short one. Kingsley, of course,
was usually oblivious to such matters, but he had a vague, unexpected
wish to live in the country: they even contemplated a property in
Somerset, to be near Anthony and Violet Powell. It was Jane who
saw a late-Georgian, eight-bedroomed house at Hadley Common,
near Barnet, advertised for auction in *Country Life* and thought they
should look at it. Martin, Colin and Sargy went with them: all of
them were delighted, and Kingsley's modest requirements – it must
contain a large study where he could surround himself with bottles
and books (in that order) and it must be within walking distance of
the Northern Line – were met. Larkin thought they were mad:
Kingsley, when they met for lunch in May, 'babbled of £50,000

houses in Barnet – this must be the saying of Crazy Jane, mustn't it? Poor bugger.'[103] Clearly, it was a project which would tax their resources, both financially and in terms of actually running the place, but they managed to secure it for £48,000, almost £10,000 less than the maximum advised by their accountant. At this point, however, the mortgage fell through, the accountant swiftly took himself off on holiday and they turned (via Tom Maschler) to Anton Felton, an accountant specialising in author's affairs, who found them a mortgage and looked after their financial affairs thereafter. But even he couldn't disguise the fact that things were going to be tricky. They moved into Lemmons – resurrecting the house's old name – on 28 November 1968. 'This is a bloody great mansion, in the depths of the country though only 15 miles from the centre, and with lots of room for you to come and spend the night,' Kingsley reported to Larkin the following spring, perhaps not entirely allaying his fears. 'Let us know. You get on the Northern Line to High Barnet, see, and then we pick you up at the station. Do try.'[104]

Either as a response to their financial pressures or as a way of avoiding more practical chores, Kingsley was pushing ahead rapidly with another potboiler, *The Green Man* (1969). I've already borrowed Graham Greene's term 'entertainment' to refer to works lighter than literary novels, because it makes no concessions about quality: *Brighton Rock* is an 'entertainment', and that's quite good enough for me. Kingsley preferred 'genre fiction', as he made clear when rebuking Julian Symons for describing thrillers and spy stories as 'sensational literature' in 1972: 'Genre fiction is a phrase harder to get one's tongue around, but I find it more accurate.'[105] Over the next few years, Kingsley would attempt a number of such works, including a ghost story, a detective story and two 'alternate world' novels (a sort of science fiction from which the science has been extracted). Other writers have reached for pseudonyms on these occasions – C. Day Lewis as Nicholas Blake, J. I. M. Stewart as Michael Innes, Julian Barnes as Dan Kavanagh – but Kingsley, like Graham Greene with his 'entertainments', published these books under his own name.

The Green Man is a book full of ill omens. In it, Kingsley deals with many of the less desirable aspects of living in Hertfordshire almost before he had set foot in it; he also manages to imply several of the ways in which he would eventually come to find domestic and social life with Jane irksome. To do this, he invents a first-person narrator, a slightly older, alcoholic version of himself called Maurice Allington, who is the landlord of a reputedly haunted coaching inn further north in the county (he habitually refers to his pub, with a pompous ambiguity that serves Kingsley's purpose well, as 'my house'); he sees ghosts when drunk but this, as we and he discover, is partly because there are ghosts to be seen. Allington's prejudices and weaknesses – and his unAmisian belief in the supernatural – are perhaps intended to be sufficiently ludicrous to distance him from his author; but, as with Roger Micheldene, the strategy is unconvincing.

If novels were houses, a surveyor could point to terrible structural faults here. One, the most central defect possible in a first-person narrative, is the unattractive character and inconsistent tone of the narrator himself; but there are unforgivable carelessnesses at almost every level. *The Green Man* opens with a spoof guidebook description of the eponymous inn: this is effective enough, and the list of celebrity recommenders who happen to be among the Amises' acquaintances – 'Bernard Levin; Lord Norwich; John Dankworth; Harry Harrison; Wynford Vaughan-Thomas; Dennis Brogan; Brian W. Aldiss; and many others'[106] – is the first (and last) really good joke in the novel. Kingsley's uncertainty about what kind of fiction this is to be is immediately evident. He takes trouble establishing his fictional village, Fareham, in a precise authenticating location: he tells us where it is in relation to the A10 and the A505; to Stevenage, Royston and Baldock, the nearest town; even to the actual village of Sandon and the tiny hamlet of Mill End. He also says, impossibly, that it is eight miles from the M1; he means the A1(M) but doesn't know the difference. Ignoring that single false lead, you could locate the inn (except that it isn't there) on an Ordnance Survey map. And that, no doubt, is what the author did, for there is no sense of a physical reality to the pub or the village and when Kingsley guesses at the detail of these places – as when he sends Maurice off to various non-existent facilities in Baldock – he gets it wrong. There is also a good deal of driving around this unimagined locality, including an implausible account of a traffic accident which can only have been reconstructed from a stunt in a film or television programme, visualised through the eyes of a non-driver.

Allington is a mass of unassimilated contradictions, though not in the useful sense which results in a complex or enigmatic character. Almost every drinker at some time wonders what it would be like to run a pub, and Allington seems to be the product of some such daydream: he does almost no work, drinks a bottle of Scotch a day, seldom eats properly (he hates food) and deviously talks customers through the menu, 'pushing the rather boring salmon and some incipiently elderly pork'.[107] A country hotelier at once so idle and so prone to recommend his worst food would be bankrupt within months. On the other hand, like many an Amis fantasy-figure, he manages to remain irresistible to women: he has quite recently married his second (and much younger) wife, Joyce; he has extra-marital affairs, to which staff bring champagne, in one of the hotel bedrooms; within hours of his father's death on the premises, he accomplishes the alfresco seduction of the certifying doctor's wife, Diana; and, on the day of his father's funeral, Joyce and Diana join him in a threesome before going off together. Interwoven with this tomfoolery is an arbitrary and stereotypical ghost story: unravelling the associated documents, which are written in a conveniently Mummerset form of Olde Englishe, takes Allington to nearby Cambridge, of which university he is so distinguished an alumnus that senior academics, including one called Duerinckx-Williams, greet him warmly and college archives open at once to his bidding. Kingsley is here presumably attempting to suggest the silliness of Cambridge (Oxford would have been another matter), but the notion of Allington as in any sense learned or scholarly is absurd. A still more peculiar instance of unchecked authorial prejudice is to come, in the supposedly comic portrait of the local Rector, the Reverend Tom Rodney Sonnenschein. He is a compendium of easy targets: trendily progressive in his theology, flamboyantly gay and, worst of all, 'sort of hooked on Benjie': Allington's derisory survey of his Rector's living room is accompanied by 'An invisible singer with a bad head-cold . . . doing his best to reach some unreasonably high notes among a lot of orchestral fuss'.[108] The reader will identify the allusions to Britten and Pears.

All this makes for a bad novel; but it also points to a more worrying puzzle. Why did Kingsley – by then in his late forties, a successful writer in the early years of his second marriage – still feel so threatened by passing fashion, by homosexuality and even by mainstream high culture that he felt impelled to score such cheap points? The sexual sneers may have something to do with his joshing of Colin Howard; and Britten, of course, rather conveniently combined homosexuality with the high cultural ambition which so often rattled Kingsley. But by 1969 Britten was scarcely avant-garde (it's as if Jane Austen had been affronted by the music of Handel); and in any case his cousin John points out that 'K admired Britten, certainly the Rimbaud poems of *Les Illuminations*'.[109] The pseudo-philistinism which in his younger days could be passed off as a subversive running joke was becoming settled and corrosive, while the tedious preoccupation with excessive drinking, a minor irritation in his earlier books, had grown into a major obstruction. There's also a more interesting preoccupation with the nature of death, including a passage – 'It's a pretty arresting thought, not being anything, not being anywhere, and yet the world still being here'[110] – which is directly echoed in Larkin's poem 'The Old Fools' (1973). Otherwise, the best that can be said of *The Green Man* is that writing it may have been a way for Kingsley to alert himself to problems he needed to confront. Whether or not the physician could heal himself was another matter entirely.

In fact, by the time *The Green Man* appeared, Kingsley was drinking as much as Allington. The quantity was only part of the problem, which was more a matter of what and where. He was by now writing regularly on the subject for the *Daily Telegraph Magazine* (the articles formed the basis of *On Drink* in 1972), which justified a good deal of 'research'; and, as visitors gratefully noted, there was always an abundant supply of the stuff at Lemmons. The main focus of his enthusiasm and expertise was not real ale, which at least would have got him out of the house, nor even fine wine, but spirit-based concoctions: a 1974 photograph of him in his study – a room which, as he later said, contained 'almost as many bottles as books'[111] – shows the bottles more conveniently within reach than the books. Concoctions apart, *On Drink* displays a good deal of cheerful ignorance: he is 'not much of a wine man'[112] and, as for beer, he thinks there is such a thing as 'a decent Worthington or Double Diamond'[113] and that it comes in a can; his opinion of white Burgundies ('Whatever I may have said elsewhere') is, incidentally, the opposite of Allington's.[114] Midway between pubbable youth and clubbable age, he had become a quite different sort of drinker, and *On Drink* provides an explanation: 'I should single out one stress (or strain) as distinctly more burdensome, and also more widespread, than most: sudden confrontation with complete or comparative strangers in circumstances requiring a show of relaxation and amiability – an experience that I, for one, never look forward to without misgiving, even though I nearly always turn out to enjoy it in the event.'[115] It's a long way from the easy camaraderie of a Swansea pub.

Lemmons, rather than Jane, was the trouble. Though a house itself can hardly take the blame for the lives it shelters – except in the ominously prescient case of Allington's 'house' – Kingsley must have seen that, in committing himself to this one, he was voluntarily submitting to precisely the sort of social existence with which he was least at ease: a life of weekend guests and dinner parties. He had, of course, fallen in love with and married Jane partly because of the ways in which she was so unlike him: her skilled interest in cooking, gardening and interior design, and her fondness for foreign travel, seemed to promise a new, different and better quality of life. She, from the start, had seen this as part of her mission. 'Perhaps you might enjoy *more* of your life through me,' she had written to him in February 1963. 'I mean collect aspects, add more bits to it.'[116] From Jane's point of view, Lemmons was part of this project; but both she and, less forgivably, Kingsley himself had underestimated the extent to which his apparent indifference to surroundings was a mask. He may have been reluctant to appreciate places, but he certainly noticed the aspects of them he didn't like. And he had no conception of the practicalities involved in running a place the size of Lemmons. Bruce Montgomery, when he visited in November 1969, reported to Larkin that 'Jane's aim of gracious living seems to be being militated against by an almost total lack of servants.' There was in fact a 'wonderful' housekeeper, Lily Uniacke, who lived in the mews cottage, as well as a part-time gardener and 'a very genteel person who ironed shirts twice a week'.[117] 'Kingsley simply doesn't *realise*,' Jane told Montgomery.[118] He never would. Despite its comforts, Lemmons embodied a world to which he vaguely aspired but into which he would never fit.

This rumbling, unfocused domestic discontent, combined with a study full of bottles, seemed to reinforce a number of changes in Kingsley. Always capable of rudeness, he became ruder, 'pissing on' close friends as well as unsuspecting strangers. He had always held strong opinions, sometimes self-contradictory ones, but around the time of the move to Lemmons he became spectacularly opinionated, firing off articles and letters to the press on a variety of topics – often those on which his own views were in a state of angry turmoil. The old lefty and the new Conservative were constantly in dispute with each other. In 'Why Lucky Jim Turned Right' (published in the *Sunday Telegraph* on 2 July 1967) he had declared: 'I am not a Tory, nor pro-Tory (who could be pro *this* Tory Party?), nor Right-wing, nor of the Right, but of the Centre, equally opposed to all forms of authoritarianism.'[119] Communism, he added in a letter to the paper published on 25 July, 'is a threat to us, and to freedom everywhere. What about getting our priorities straight?'[120] Just over a year later, in a lengthy reply to Goronwy Rees's unsigned 'Column' in the September 1968 issue of *Encounter*, he explained his 'dislikes of the Lefty and the Labour party as it is now' ('The Lefty is an intellectually disreputable and morally desensitised person . . .') and his qualified support for Edward Heath and Enoch Powell who, 'among others of their party, represent what I want rather better than any of the array on the Government benches, excluding Mr Powell's emotionalism about immigration'.[121] In November, he wrote to *The Times*, opposing the candidature of Yevgeny Yevtushenko, whom he had liked when they met in Cambridge seven years earlier, as Oxford Professor of Poetry, listing the ways in which Yevtushenko had in the meantime become (as a statement by the students whom he had addressed in Mexico put it) 'a tool of the Soviet Government in exchange for being allowed to publish your poems'.[122]

Then there was Vietnam. When Ian Hamilton collected the views of writers for his symposium 'Poets on the Vietnam War' in *the Review* (April 1968), Kingsley's view was robustly pro-American but, again, qualified: 'American policy in Vietnam, as far as its aims go, has my whole-hearted support, on the simple grounds that Communist aggression must be resisted. As regards American methods there is, of course, room for argument. I would oppose the use of napalm, a weapon that damages the image of its user out of all proportion to its effectiveness.' He even suggested that 'British policy should go further in its support for America. The sending of even a token force would be an important reassurance to her.'[123] It took Paul Johnson, who was some way behind Kingsley in his progress from left to right, to describe this in the *New Statesman* as 'unqualified' support for American policy and to prompt a deservedly stinging riposte: 'Perhaps you really can't see the difference between "unqualified" and "unequivocally" . . . They certainly start off the same, and they both have that "qu" thing in the middle.'[124] It's interesting that the misuse of language troubled him as much as the misrepresentation of his views.

For language – and in particular its devaluation by fashionable movements in education and culture – had become and would remain a major preoccupation which was to endure until the posthumous publication of *The King's English* in 1997. His much quoted and even more misquoted remarks on the then proposed expansion of university education and the effect this might have on the intellectual ability of undergraduates had appeared in an article for *Encounter* in 1960: 'You cannot *decide* to have more good ones. All you can decide is to have more. And more will mean worse.'[125] By 1968, which Stephen Spender called 'the year of the young rebels', it was perfectly clear to him that his prophecy had been fulfilled. This was the year in which students at a number of British universities, taking their cue from events in Paris, staged a series of protests: sit-ins and walk-outs might be triggered by almost anything from the conduct of the Vietnam War to the quality of refectory food. The noisiest and most disruptive student unrest occurred at the new University of Essex where Donald Davie, continuing to fulfil his accidental role of living Kingsley's parallel life, had been appointed Professor of English and Pro-Vice-Chancellor; in the face of the 1968 protests (and the collusion of some members of the academic staff in them), he resigned and accepted a chair at Stanford, California. Another response to the sense of crisis not only in universities but in education generally came from C. B. Cox and A. E. Dyson, editors of the *Critical Quarterly* and its offshoot targeted at schoolteachers and sixth-formers, *Critical Survey*. They proposed to devote the March 1969 issue of *Critical Survey* to a 'Black Paper on Education', and in September 1968 Brian Cox wrote to Kingsley, inviting him to contribute: the result was 'Pernicious Participation', the first of several articles (the later ones written with Robert Conquest) in what became a series of 'Black Papers'. The editors, says Cox, 'were taken aback by the extent of anger and agreement from who replied, and when the pamphlet appeared by the press view that we must be a tightly-knit group'. Just as with the Movement, however, they were no such thing: 'I don't think I met Kingsley until the first press conference for the first Black Paper at Brown's Hotel.'[126]

'A student,' Kingsley's article begins, 'being (if anything) engaged in the acquiring of knowledge, is not in a position to decide which bits of knowledge it is best for him to acquire, or how his performance in the acquisition of knowledge can most properly be assessed, or who is qualified to help him in this activity.'[127] One might think this piece of common sense a bit rich, coming from someone who at university had so enthusiastically endorsed his friend Larkin's dismissal of great literary works as 'ape's bumfodder'; but in 'Pernicious Participation' Kingsley attempts to resolve this conflict and, in doing so, significantly shifts his ground. With robust belt-and-braces logic, he argues that he had been 'an unusually well-trained' undergraduate, thanks to 'excellent and intensive fifth- and sixth-form teaching', whereas 'all but a very few of today's students are even less qualified to judge of these matters than I was at their age'; *despite this*, he would have made terrible and irrevocable mistakes if he had been allowed to pick and choose his own university syllabus. Precisely because he was a student, he 'had no way of knowing then what a close study of Spenser, Milton and Wordsworth, pre-eminently but not exclusively, would reveal to me', though he still can't 'pretend I am glad to have studied *Beowulf*'. In other words, because there's no way of telling what a reader will gain from a text except in retrospect, it's good for students to study books which they think they may not (and actually may not) enjoy reading at the time.

Though this seems incontestably true, it's a long way from seminars on science fiction or a modern novel course which includes James Bond (and there's little doubt that Kingsley the contrarian, if suddenly placed in an ultra-conservative university environment, would have swiftly reassumed his populist hat). He has, however, two more related points to make in 'Pernicious Participation'. One, in a long parenthesis, is a just assault on the concept of 'relevance': 'The student who is himself looking for relevance is looking for vocational training, a harmless desire in itself, though anti-academic and therefore not to be indulged at a university; the teacher who wants to import it is an enemy of culture.' The other questions the motives behind student participation, demands for which 'conceal, or do not conceal, a simple desire to have less studying to do, less of everything that relates in any way to studying'.[128] These are both bullseyes: Kingsley, who had left university teaching five years earlier, might on this evidence have been welcomed back with fanfares by his more sensible former colleagues. Instead, he was busy exploring the topic of trendily disaffected youth, and of the adults who disastrously indulge it, in a new novel: *Girl, 20*.

7

Girl, 20 (1971) is a proper novel. It isn't an entertainment or a genre piece; and it mostly concerns, in the slippery terms of Kingsley's 1973 essay, made-up people (with some cameo appearances by real people). It also has a satisfactorily anecdotal origin, which Kingsley recounted on more than one occasion – in, as it happens, 'Real and Made-up People'[129] and, the following year, in his conversation with Clive James. The germ of the book, he told James,

> emerged one day when I was in Tottenham Court Road trying to get a taxi. A taxi swept past a small brown man and stopped for me. I thought, wouldn't it be funny if I said to the driver, 'You racialist'. Wait a second: not me, another man. And it would be better if there was a cock-hungry girl with him at the time, who wouldn't like him doing it – who wanted him to climb into that cab and shut up. Which leads you to a man of liberal sentiments who needs a young and awful girl. Which makes him a trendy Lefty.[130]

This is Sir Roy Vandervane, the eminent composer, conductor and violinist whose disastrous affair with Sylvia, the eponymous Girl, 20 ('Well, between ourselves, Duggers, it's actually Girl, 17'),[131] forms one of the novel's main strands. He is the best sort of made-up character, with the right mixture of authorial distance and sympathy, and with teasing hints of real people well removed from his occupation, his politics, or both: Christopher Hitchens sees A. J. Ayer as 'the obvious model', while alert readers may also detect traces of Jane's cousin Peregrine Worsthorne, who stayed with the Amises at Maida Vale during his own marital difficulties, in some of Vandervane's mannerisms. He needs a counterbalance, a mouthpiece for authorial views with a different sort of distance, and is given one in Douglas Yandell, a sympathetic younger music critic – the young fogey is artfully set against the old trendy – who writes for a stingy right-wing newspaper editor called Harold Meers, recognisably based on the Conservative MP Harold Soref (the largest of the 'real' cameos; elsewhere we glimpse Robert Conquest leaving his club). Halfway through the book, in a moment of queasy coincidence, Vandervane's girlfriend Sylvia is discovered to be the daughter of Yandell's editor Meers: this discovery allows the plot to tick over, rather as the magical appearance of Jagger does in *The Anti-Death League*, but the plot really isn't the central point of either book.

Girl, 20 is, rather surprisingly, the first of Kingsley's novels to be set entirely in and around London although, apart from one strikingly non-domestic scene, it doesn't venture south of the river (that vulnerable proximity to childhood home was to come in his next book). Douglas Yandell lives, mostly alone but with visitations from a woman called Vivienne, in a flat in Maida Vale; Sir Roy Vandervane, his second wife Kitty, his three children (two by his previous marriage) and a black factotum called Gilbert Alexander all live just north of London in a house which is exactly like Lemmons. This risky device of using settings so close to those of his own present and recent past actually works to distance the characters who inhabit them. Roy Vandervane is, like Maurice Allington, a terrible warning of some of the things Kingsley might have become: he's a terrific drinker, of course, but also a dedicated lecher of a different sort. His pursuit, in every sense, of all that is trendy and youthful has led him to compose a disastrous pop crossover piece called *Elevations 9*, in homage to the Beatles' *Revolution 9* (and we know well enough what Kingsley thought of *them*: 'Oh fuck the Beatles, I'd like to push my bum into John L's face for forty-eight hours or so, as a protest against all the war and violence in the world');[132] he is to perform it in concert with a group called Pigs Out. Douglas, the novel's reliable though ineffectual moral voice, finds the piece detestable and its motivation transparent: 'All I think you're really trying to do is arse-creep youth.'[133] There is also a deeper moral problem: Roy's dedicated interest in girls, twentyish, is creating a life of sustained misery for Kitty, who bears a number of minor resemblances to Jane. Nevertheless, one of the strengths of *Girl, 20* lies in its thwarting of easy correspondences. Kingsley, in comparison with his conduct during his first marriage, was only unfaithful to Jane once or twice and was in any case beginning to go off sex altogether: hence, partly, the novel's adoption of the far less sexually driven Douglas as its narrator. When Roy, appalled, realises that for Douglas music may be more important than sex, the latter replies: 'I think it may well be.

I think I'd rather be a monk in a world with music than a full-time stallion in a world without it.'[134] An unexpected twist on this idea was to form the basis of *The Alteration*, published five years later.

It's Douglas's position that the author silently endorses here, and it confirms a shift in his point of view: the younger Kingsley would have been more likely to cast his vote for sex, reckoning that high art could take care of itself. This is part of the novel's coded self-reproach. In the same conversation, Douglas goes on to accuse Roy of 'helping to bring that very important stuff, music, into disrepute'. Substitute 'literature' for 'music' and you have exactly the charge which the science-fiction anthologies, the Bond books and the 'genre' novels suggest might have been brought against Kingsley. This isn't an isolated example. Persuaded to give an interview to Harold Meers's newspaper, Roy Vandervane's neglected son Chris precisely echoes what Kingsley's neglected son Philip thought about his father: 'He's always let us do exactly as we like, and we liked that until we realized it was all just less trouble for him. We don't get on much with our stepmother, but you can't really blame her.'[135] (The difference is that Philip did blame his stepmother.) Another kind of self-reproach, or at least a rueful retrospect, comes in details which reach further back into Kingsley's past. When Kitty confronts Sylvia in an attempt to save her marriage, she uses the same terms Kingsley had employed to Henry Fairlie in 1956 in order to save his to Hilly: 'I've nothing to fight with, no bribe to offer. I can only ask you to realize the unhappiness you'll be bringing four people who've never hurt you.'[136] And when Douglas unwillingly attends (and sabotages) the Pigs Out concert, his private reactions to the noise are, delightfully, reminiscent of Kingsley's father's when forced to endure jazz.

Although *Girl, 20* seems to end on a note of unrelieved bleakness – with Roy's daughter Penny, now on heroin, mindlessly insisting: 'We're all free now'[137] – the impression it leaves isn't wholly pessimistic. This is partly because it is among the most successful of Kingsley's middle-period books, tightly organised and well written, with some vintage verbal humour: especially Roy's habit of collapsing word endings (at one point he says that the words 'high tea' suggest to him 'Ham and Russian salad and sweep pickle and tim peaches and plung cake')[138] and Sylvia's murderous emphasis on certain syllables containing the vowel 'a' ('I can't *stuhnd* all these put-ons').[139]

Sargy Mann, whose suggestion of 'vogka' for Roy came just too late,
says that contributing to Kingsley's novels was 'one of the joys of
living in the ménage': 'One was always trying to think of things that
would make him laugh, storing up instances of some Lefty crappiness
that he might not have noticed.'[140] Colin Howard, too, supplied some
notable Kingsleyisms, such as 'uncontrollably rich'. And Jane remembers a vein of Kingsley's verbal humour which couldn't so readily
find its way into print, his habit of deliberately mispronouncing
words, especially names of foods he thought fancy or pretentious:
'minestrone', stressed and rhymed as in 'telephone', or 'pipérade',
made to sound like an assault by plumbers.[141]

The novel's pessimism is further mitigated because Douglas's
moral sanity, however ineffectual it may finally prove, is surprisingly
refreshing in being given to one of the *younger* characters. Unlike
Roy's up-to-the-minute *trahison des clercs*, Douglas's values seem
about twenty years out of date: they are, indeed, those of George
Garner in Roy Fuller's *The Second Curtain* (1953). Garner, a freelance editor and writer rather than a freelance music critic, spends
part of his morning browsing through the records in Harridge's and
the art books in Zwemmer's before heading for 'the pub on the
corner of St Martin's Court' where he orders a pint of mild; after an
afternoon's work at a publishers, he looks forward to the prospect of
'two Mozart piano concertos at the Wigmore Hall'.[142] Douglas, after
a morning recording at the BBC, decides to 'go along to the George
and have a pint of bitter and a round of cheese-and-pickle and a
round of ham with too much mustard. Then, at the flat, the new
Walter Klein of K.415 and K.467.'[143] The two days share similar
rhythms and are punctuated by identical consolations. Both men,
alone and dejected at the ends of their respective novels, nevertheless
possess rich inner cultural and imaginative lives that are unavailable
to apparently cleverer, more successful characters; love has failed
them, but not the redemptive power of art. It's a state which Kingsley
seems to endorse, almost with a touch of envy.

He was nearing fifty as he finished *Girl, 20* and had started to feel
older than his years. Like Larkin, he wrote a fiftieth-birthday poem
to himself, but whereas Larkin's 'The View' is crisply sardonic in that
characteristic way which simultaneously voices and expunges self-
pity, Kingsley's 'Ode to Me'[144] is a sad, straggling affair. Nevertheless,
there are other and better poems which reflect his preoccupations at

this time; closest to the themes of *Girl, 20*, though dating from a year or so earlier, are a matching-bookend pair based on a famous line by Walter de la Mare. The one called 'Lovely', the second of the two in the *Collected Poems*, begins, 'Look thy last on all things lovely / Every hour, an old shag said . . .', which seems a bit unfair on a poet who died as recently as 1956. On the contrary, says Kingsley, the approach of death isn't at all the moment for such contemplation:

> The best time to see things lovely
>   Is in youth's primordial bliss,
> Which is also when you rather
>   Go for old shags talking piss.[145]

There it is again: the note of self-reproach and regret, acknowledging both the vanished pleasures of youth and the author's own steady transformation into an old shag talking piss (and here the balance is managed with Larkinesque precision). The other poem, 'Shitty', opens with a catalogue of Sir Roy Vandervane's enthusiasms:

> Look thy last on all things shitty
>   While thou'rt at it: soccer stars,
> Soccer crowds, bedizened bushheads
>   Jerking over their guitars,
>
> German tourists, plastic roses,
>   Face of Mao and face of Ché,
> Women wearing curtains, blankets,
>   Beckett at the ICA . . .[146]

But again there's a twist: even these hateful things are 'a sight more lovely / Than the screens around your bed'. And that's true too, as Gloucester says.

Still more interesting, not least because they possess a delicacy of tone and cadence rare in Kingsley's superficially boisterous verse, are two poems in loosely loping three-stress lines: 'Wasted' and the untitled, unfinished 'Things tell less and less . . .' 'Wasted',[147] written at the same time as *Girl, 20*, picks up the motifs of retrospect and regret: its opening scene, with 'the whole family' gathered on a winter evening around 'the dismal grate / Where rain-soaked logs / Bubbled, hissed and steamed', looks back to Swansea (Nashville also had a

cold winter and non-inflammable logs, but not the entire family).
After the others have gone to bed, Kingsley remains downstairs; and
the wood starts 'to flame / In clear rose and violet' – a recollection
not only of an actual scene but of that flickering violet flame in
Coleridge's 'Frost at Midnight', where the writer is identically placed
by the fireside. This is an old flame in more than one sense, in its
conjuring up of Hilly; on one of their Greek holidays in the late
1960s, Kingsley had told Mike Keeley that 'there wasn't a day that
went by that he didn't think of Hilly'.[148] It's unusual for Kingsley to
be quite so subtly allusive, but the final four lines, separated by a
stanza break, spring an even greater surprise:

> Why should that memory cling
> Now the children are all grown up,
> And the house – a different house –
> Is warm at any season?

The allusion here – in tone, metre and imagery – is to a writer
Kingsley didn't claim greatly to admire: Robert Lowell. The particular
Lowell poem he seems to be recalling also describes a memory of a
former house and a lost wife; and it is, of course, called 'The Old
Flame'.[149]

'Things tell less and less . . .' remained unpublished until 2004,
when it appeared in the *TLS*.[150] Zachary Leader may well be correct
in thinking that it belongs to the late 1970s or early 1980s; nevertheless, 'Wasted' is the collected poem of Kingsley's it most resembles
both formally and in its air of retrospective melancholy.

> Things tell less and less:
> The news impersonal
> And from afar; no book
> Worth wrenching off the shelf.
> Liquor brings dizziness
> And food discomfort; all
> Music sounds thin and tired,
> And what picture could earn a look?
> The self drowses in the self
> Beyond hope of a visitor.
> Desire and those desired
> Fade, and no matter:

Memories in decay
Annihilate the day.

There once was an answer:
Up at the stroke of seven,
A turn round the garden
(Breathing deep and slow),
Then work, never mind what,
How small, provided that
It serves another's good

But once is long ago
And, tell me, how could
Such an answer be less than wrong,
Be right all along?

Vain echoes, desist

The poem is puzzling in all sorts of ways. Several of its qualities are uncharacteristic: its cadences and its quietly glum recital of dissatisfactions might easily pass for late Larkin. The speaker seems elderly: on that score, it could date from Kingsley's last years. On the other hand, the consolations listed as unavailable in the opening lines are those enjoyed by Douglas Yandell in *Girl, 20*, while its evocation of depression's blindingly negative phase is very close to a moment in an *earlier* novel: James Churchill's terrible perception that 'There isn't anywhere to be' in *The Anti-Death League*. Bearing that in mind, we might wonder whether or not Kingsley is writing *in propria persona* here. Did any picture ever 'earn a look' from him? Did he ever get up at seven and take 'A turn round the garden'? Perhaps the poem invents a fictional character as speaker to disclose truths too painful to be stated by an authorial first person, exactly as happens in the novels; the central truth clearly concerns his loss of savour for life and his recognition that this may now be beyond recapture.

These poems and *Girl, 20* go a long way towards accounting for *The Riverside Villas Murder* (1973), the most obviously attractive of Kingsley's 'entertainments'. Yet, as with several of his middle and later fictions, the narrative surface is just that – a top layer masking other patterns – and it is precisely because this seems to be the most conventional of all his books that it is arguably the most audacious. Writing an orthodox-looking detective story enabled him to explore the world of his own childhood in fiction for the first time: none of his previous novels had been set in the hinterland of South London and Surrey or in the 1930s, let alone both at once. *The Riverside Villas Murder* pretends to concern itself with providing a trail of clues, many of them false, from which the reader is challenged to deduce the murderer's identity before the not altogether astonishing truth is disclosed by the author. But it is more deeply about the journey towards adulthood of its fourteen-year-old hero, Peter Furneaux, who shares Kingsley's age, background and education (City of London School becomes, transparently, Blackfriars Grammar). To this extent, and above all in the sympathy with which it treats the tiresome foibles of Peter's father, it develops the themes of memory and regret into an attempt at restitution.

Yet the process is wilfully complicated, clues gleefully scrambled. Although the relationship between Peter and his father owes a great deal to that between Kingsley and *his* father in 1936, there are intentional anomalies: for instance, William Amis's talent for impersonations, inherited by his son, is shifted sideways to Mr Langdon, a neighbour whom we are meant to regard (perhaps because his wife doesn't care for his boy-throttling imitation of Peter Lorre) as a murder suspect. Both fathers had relatively uneventful wartime careers, but Peter's has invented a heroic excuse for his injured arm, which conveniently prevents him from driving the car that he, like William, couldn't afford anyway. When the more prosaic truth emerges at the end of the book, it prompts a scene of mutual reconciliation:

> 'You mind about it, Dad, but I don't. The way I look at it, you're so unconceited that you tell me some things that are very damaging to your pride, and you don't like telling them, but you're so undishonest that you tell them because they're true, not because you want me to know, and that must be because you want me to know you. I think that makes you a good father.'
>
> Captain Furneaux, still looking out of the window, drew in his breath slowly and deeply, like a diver getting ready to go off the top board, then let it out all at once. 'And you're the best son . . .'[151]

No such moment of emotional bonding occurred between William and his fourteen-year-old son. This, after all, is the sort of exchange sons wish had taken place when it's too late: as Kingsley wrote in 'In Memoriam W.R.A.', 'I'm sorry you had to die / To make me sorry / You're not here now.'[152] Yet there was another reason for this untypically sentimental scene: the recognition, which also surfaces in *The Green Man* and *Girl, 20*, that he hadn't been a good father to his own sons. For Kingsley, at fifty, writing about fathers and sons couldn't help implicating him in both roles: in bestowing posthumous forgiveness on his own father, he was also seeking forgiveness for himself.

It isn't simply the sentimentality of Peter's reconciliation with his father which makes it less than convincing, but the absence of any suggestion that Captain Furneaux is likely to change his irritating ways. These include not only the William-Amis-like disapproval of all Peter's (and Kingsley's) musical interests, from Mozart to jazz, but a prurient–puritanical distaste for anything sexual: 'As part of his undeclared, unremitting, and quite unavailing war on Peter's baser nature, Captain Furneaux had decreed that he should never lock that [bathroom] door "in case somebody wanted something" (the shaving-mirror? the soap-rack?), and had been known to come stealing upstairs at times like this to check that his wish was observed.'[153] To facilitate Peter's journey from comparative innocence to precocious experience, Kingsley supplies him with three mentors. With the first, his 'particular friend' Reg, he indulges in three essential forbidden pleasures – cigarettes, dance-band records and mutual masturbation – while Reg's mother goes off to fetch her husband from the station. (He would prefer to be indulging himself with his annoyingly aloof fifteen-year-old neighbour Daphne, whom he pursues according to his schoolfriend Forester's 'Code of Dishonour'.) Also among the neighbours, however, is the ambiguous Mrs Trevelyan: 'definitely not a girl. What she was it was less easy to be categorical about. She was not a woman . . .'[154] This self-contradictory motif is at first misunderstood by Peter who, although aware that his looks have prompted 'strange men, encountered on the train to and from school or while waiting for it, to take an undue interest in him',[155] nevertheless misreads her interest in him: ' "Good Lord," said Peter, laughing. "You're awfully, I don't know, it sounds silly, but you're awfully wise." '[156] In Chapter V, she advises Peter, 'Don't grow up too fast';[157] sixty pages later, in Chapter IX, she seduces him: 'I'll do everything. And you're to let me do everything. Oh, Peter, you're so nice.'[158] Peter seems remarkably unfussed by this, given that he is the fourteen-year-old son of prim suburban parents in the 1930s; although juxtapositions of childishness and adulthood are characteristic of adolescence, it's hardly an ordinary experience. Like the father–son reconciliation, it has the air of an event Kingsley wished had happened to him.

Peter's third and in some respects even more intriguing mentor is Colonel Manton, the officer in charge of the murder investigation. Manton's most glaring eccentricity, unlikely even in the more relaxed procedural world of the time, is that he works from his splendid home, where lavish refreshments are provided by his housekeeper, Mrs Ellington, whom he dislikes but continues to employ solely on account of her name – for he is a jazz fan. He is indeed so detached from anything resembling a police station that he might almost be an amateur detective, like Bruce Montgomery's Gervase Fen. Manton is fifty, the same age as his author; his army background, with a higher rank than Peter's father, is another signal of authorial sympathy, as of course is the jazz; and so, curiously, is his homosexuality, a device Kingsley had already used to similar effect with Max Hunter in *The Anti-Death League*. This, together with his peculiarly freelance mode of operation, stamps him as an outsider, which is a useful thing for an authorial character to be: his sexuality is the subject of whispered hints among the other characters ('You don't want to have nothing to do with him, not you,' Mr Hodgson warns Peter),[159] but this merely serves to increase our suspicions of them. When Peter is entertained to tea by Manton on the day following his eventful tea with Mrs Trevelyan, it crosses his mind 'that to be seduced on successive afternoons by a solicitor's wife and a retired Army officer would be a stupendous double first . . .'.[160] Nothing of the sort happens, of course. Instead, Manton does something which emphatically demonstrates that at this point Kingsley's sympathy is with the colonel rather than with the fourteen-year-old boy. He plays Peter Billy Banks's 'Mean Old Bed Bug Blues':

Coming in at the same time as one or two other instruments, a man sang in a high voice,
'Something was moaning in the corner – I tried my best to see,'

then, as if by no means satisfied with his first attempt, sang it again, ending that part with what sounded like,

'*It was the mother bed-bug praying to the good Lord for some more to eat.*'

What followed departed a little further from reason, though it was reassurance of a kind to hear someone who must have been Waller shouting vaguely but cordially in the background. A tenor sax with a bad cold and more singing led to a peevish, acid trumpet that rounded off the disc.

'I see you're not impressed.'

'Not very, sir, no, I'm sorry.'[161]

For Kingsley thus to donate his favourite jazz record to Colonel Manton is a mark of rare esteem; conversely, Peter's failure to appreciate it is a mark of his immaturity. 'You know,' Manton tells Peter shortly afterwards, 'that noise is about a quarter of my life.' Kingsley probably could have said about as much. Larkin certainly would have done. Jane never cared for jazz.

Manton represents a different version of Douglas Yandell's lonely integrity: both of them value other things – art, if you like – more highly than sex. Manton may as a gesture of thanks slip Peter a generous fiver in his car, a detail to be replicated in *You Can't Do Both*, but he poses no moral threat. And he knows Peter knows this: 'I now know you know what I am, or what I used to be ... But friendship between us has become impossible, I'm afraid. It's the sort of penalty one pays for – well, for existing, really.'[162] That may be sad; yet it's far less sad, and far less ridiculous, than turning into a lecherous ass like Sir Roy Vandervane. *The Riverside Villas Murder*, written in the very house allotted to Vandervane in *Girl, 20*, is above all a book about homesickness for the modest virtues of a South London childhood and a vanished pre-war world. It wasn't to be Kingsley's last fictional word on the matter.

What, finally, of the plot which purports to be the novel's engine? It works in an apparently conventional way: a row of suspects is lined up; a dim policeman gets it all wrong, a smart but unorthodox one gets it right. I suspect Kingsley had in mind George Orwell's 1946 essay 'Decline of the English Murder' and one sentence in particular: 'The murderer should be a little man of the professional class – a dentist or a solicitor, say – living an intensely respectable life somewhere in the suburbs, and preferably in a semi-detached house.'[163] This is in every respect true of the red herrings he supplies, before eventually revealing the murderer's identity and allowing her to choose the natural justice of suicide rather than the formal justice of the hangman. The form has in fact been riotously subverted and the denouement is preposterous. But that wasn't really the point.

8

'We'll both have to work at things. I'll certainly try,' Kingsley wrote to Jane, who was on holiday in Tuscany, in August 1973.[164] He had, at least for the time being, given up any pretence of enjoying foreign travel, preferring to stay at home as long as adequate arrangements were made for him to be kept fed and watered. Life at Lemmons was proving difficult in a variety of ways: 'we've got a species of commune going, with relations and people living in', he told Clive James,[165] a remark with more ironic bite than seemed obvious at the time. The 'relations' were Colin, Martin (until the end of 1971 and after that at weekends), Sally (sporadically from 1970) and Jane's mother Kit, who arrived from her house in Tunbridge Wells in 1970 and remained until her death five years later. The 'people' included Sargy Mann, Lily Uniacke and a succession of weekend or more-than-weekend guests – notably Cecil Day-Lewis, who moved into a ground-floor room at Lemmons during his final illness, tended by Tessa Craig, who had originally been employed to look after Kit; his wife, Jill Balcon, had a bedroom above, while their children Tamasin and Daniel were also frequent visitors. It was Jane's idea that Day-Lewis should do this while Balcon was filming nearby at Elstree, but it brought out the considerate best in Kingsley too. He at last coaxed Larkin into paying a visit, after telling him that 'poor old Cecil D-L is very ill, dying, in fact, and he will stay with us here until he dies'.[166] This was both appreciated by Day-Lewis and instrumental in reforging something like the old Kingsley–Philip relationship. 'By the living God, cully, that was a fine old time, as far as I remember,' Kingsley wrote to him afterwards. 'We did do nothing else from about 7 but play records, didn't we? Didn't we?'[167] Day-Lewis recorded his gratitude to the household in a gentle, moving poem called 'At Lemmons', dedicated to

'Jane, Kingsley, Colin and Sargy with much love'; he died there on 22 May 1972.

In 'At Lemmons', Day-Lewis wrote of 'the calm a loved house breeds'. This wasn't simply politeness: the 'commune' both masked and exacerbated the tensions within the marriage. Although it meant that there were almost always interesting people about, it also presented Jane with an exhausting burden of domestic organisation, unshared by Kingsley; she *needed* the holidays that he refused to take. She remembers 'feeling constantly tired during those eight years . . . Kingsley being unable to drive, and having absolutely nothing to do with our finances, meant I was a part-time secretary and chauffeur, as well as getting in food, cooking it and clearing it up.' There would, she adds, 'quite often be twelve or more round the table'.[168] Running Lemmons was a full-time job, hardly a compatible occupation for a full-time writer. She published only one novel during the Lemmons years: *Odd Girl Out* (1972), which, like Kingsley's *Girl, 20*, uses the house as setting; Kingsley's influence is detectable in the comic writing and in a graceful allusion to the lines 'Women are really much nicer than men: / No wonder we like them' from his poem 'A Bookshop Idyll'.[169] Her most Amisian novel, *Getting It Right*, owes its local jokiness to this period – its central character, Gavin, is a hairdresser who naturally lives in New Barnet – but didn't appear until 1982.

Meanwhile, Kingsley was writing prolifically. Jane still says, with real admiration, that she has never known anyone to work like him, an ability made all the more remarkable by the amount of drink he was taking on board. Although he was useless in practical and domestic ways, he might with some justice have pointed to his role as principle breadwinner: '*I just prod at the sodding keyboard, more and more every month, running like buggery to stay somewhere near the same place,*' he grumbled to Larkin.[170] After *The Riverside Villas Murder*, he next wrote two very short novels: *Ending Up* (1974) and *The Crime of the Century*, which was published as a serial in the *Sunday Times* in 1975 though not in book form until 1987. *Ending Up* has only five main characters and a single location, as he explained to Dale Salwak while he was working on it in the spring of 1973:

> The setting remains in and around Tuppenny-hapenny Cottage throughout. By the end, all five are dead through a series of

> mishaps. . . One thing the book isn't going to be is a serious, in-depth study of old age. It's about five particular people who wouldn't be behaving as they do if they weren't old.[171]

He was understandably anxious to distance Tuppenny-hapenny Cottage and its five ill-assorted inhabitants from the 'commune' at Lemmons: 'Nobody in the book is anything like any of them, by the way. But the idea occurred, what would this sort of arrangement be like if one had a pack of characters who were all about 20 years older?'[172] Exactly as with *The Green Man*, he moves his setting geographically up a bit, this time to the Hertfordshire–Cambridgeshire border near Newmarket. Nevertheless, elements of Lemmons inevitably find their way in: Bernard Bastable shares some astringent opinions with Kit Howard, while the bedridden, daily-visited George Zeyer had been partly suggested by Cecil Day-Lewis. When, on the very first page, Bernard questions his sister Adela's frugal housekeeping habits, she explains that inflation is making them poorer and adds: 'If you took the slightest interest in the affairs of the household, you wouldn't have to be told that.'[173] Such remarks can't have been unknown at Lemmons. Later, Bernard fails to understand what Adela can possibly mean by a 'rather essential job' (she is preparing to receive guests for lunch): ' "Oh honestly . . . Shopping and cooking and seeing to all the—" "I *see*," said Bernard, in wonder and yet in ready acceptance.'[174] This also looks very like an exchange between Jane and Kingsley.

In other respects, however, Adela certainly doesn't resemble Jane at all. She has never married nor found love: 'This she explained to herself as the result of her extreme ugliness. She was a bulky, top-heavy woman with a red complexion, hair that had always been thin, and broad lips.'[175] If that tone seems startling, it's because it belongs to eighteenth-century fiction rather than to twentieth: this is the way Fielding treats Mrs Slipslop. The effect is both appropriate – Tupenny-hapenny Cottage stands aside from late-twentieth-century life in a way which in different circumstances might be enviable – and unsettling. Fielding's fictional world is morally less complex than ours, but it is also redemptive and forgiving, and there is little of his generosity in this novel. Adela, in fact, is one of only two main characters (George is the other) to possess humanly redeeming features. Bernard's determined jokey malevolence drives the novel and, in spectacular fashion, causes its conclusion. while his former army servant and former lover, Derrick Shortwell or Shorty (whose 'domestic status ... rather ruled out the use of his Christian name'),[176] is a squalidly meandering alcoholic. The fifth member of the quintet, Marigold Pyke, is a theatrical ex-childhood-friend of Adela's, now in her mid-seventies and given to expressions such as 'kiddle-widdles', 'thingle-pingles' and 'blackle-packles' (who she thinks might eat dog-food).

Jane, who remains a generous and perceptive reader of Kingsley's work, says that even though each of these characters is in some way intolerable, she nevertheless feels sympathy for all of them.[177] It's certainly possible to feel sympathy for Adela and something approaching affection for George. He is at first presented to us – together with his ludicrous dog, Mr Pastry – as essentially a nuisance, requiring dutiful attention; but this is the view of Bernard and Shorty, and so not to be trusted. He has had a stroke and now suffers from nominal aphasia, the inability to remember names for things, so his conversation is encumbered with long explanatory circumlocutions; formerly a scholar of some repute, he holds the title of Emeritus Professor of Central European History at the University of Northampton. In giving George Zeyer his name and academic status, and then punishing him with a failure of language, Kingsley creates a dark joke at the expense of his old Cambridge adversary George Steiner. Yet, towards the end of the book, George is cured to so alarming an extent that he can't stop using nouns: 'I was just saying to Bernard here that a sense of humour is more precious than pearls or rubies or any number of motor-cars or luxury yachts or private aeroplanes or castles . . .'[178]

Whether it's possible to feel any sympathy for Bernard is a trickier question. On the face of things, the answer is plainly no: he is the most distilled of all Kingsley's 'bastards', far nastier than, say, Roger Micheldene or Maurice Allington. But Bernard is dying from terminal cancer and has only months to live, and this prompts the novel's unsettling, unspoken question: how do we expect a dying man, who is also depressed and unfulfilled, to behave towards those around him? Bernard's reaction to despair is to plan a series of cruel and largely unsuccessful practical jokes – designed, for instance, to convince Marigold that her absent-mindedness is in fact senility – which inadvertently leads to his and everyone else's death. *Ending Up* challenges the reader to deny that in Bernard's position he mightn't do the same; it is this which turns a simple black comedy into something more disturbing. To provide an outside focus, Kingsley supplies a small number of younger visitors, connections of Marigold's, who turn up for a meal and later, heroically, for lunch on Christmas Day. They supply a chorus of mundane decency, but it is Keith, the young advertising executive, who embodies the authentic, Kingsleyesque reaction to the proceedings: 'Keith was seized by boredom – a poor word for the consuming, majestic sensation that engulfed him, comparable in intensity to a once-in-a-lifetime musical experience, or what would be felt by the average passenger in a car driven by a drunk man late for an appointment.'[179] Keith has the luxury of escaping from Tuppenny-hapenny Cottage in an hour or so; Bernard is stuck with it for the rest of his life. Like so many of Kingsley's anti-heroes, from Patrick Standish onwards, Bernard has to persuade us that in his circumstances we *might* behave almost as appallingly, and it is on this that the peculiar resonance of *Ending Up* largely depends.

There is, however, one other factor to be considered here, and that is the conclusion. The book's timescale runs appropriately from autumn into winter: the big climactic scene takes place on Christmas Day, while the main characters meet their accidental ends in the first week of the New Year. It thus belongs to a particular literary tradition concerning death and rebirth at the turn of the year, of which the most familiar example in English is perhaps *Sir Gawain and the Green Knight*. And rebirth there certainly is. Early in the novel, there lurks an insignificant-looking reference to the fact that Bernard's brief, unsatisfactory marriage to his Czech wife Vera had produced a son, Stanley, 'who had emigrated to Canada and never been heard of since'.[180] On the last page of the book, it is Stanley who arrives to discover the bodies: he is the inheritor, the survivor who begins a new civilisation after the demise of the old one, a familiar figure indeed in 'alternate world' science-fiction stories. Stanley's arrival adds an ambitiously symbolic dimension to *Ending Up* and gives this short novel an unexpected note of moral grandeur.

Perhaps because of its slightly eccentric publishing history, *The Crime of the Century* has been almost entirely ignored by commentators on Kingsley's work, but he viewed it explicitly as a companion piece to *The Riverside Villas Murder*:

I had recently (1973) published a detective novel, one of a particular type. It had a period, inter-war setting, a complicated method of murder, a great-detective figure with eccentricities, including an obsession with jazz, and plenty of clues and misdirections on the classic model. It was also appropriately domestic, small-scale, involving a limited local community. When the serial was suggested there seemed to be a perfect opportunity for me to have a go at the opposite type of detective story, the one with large thriller or action elements and large forces involved – half Scotland Yard, hundreds of coppers, top political and professional brass, the whole nation holding its breath and the whole of London scared stiff as a mass-murder prepares to strike again for some unknown but vast and terrible purpose – the crime of the century.[181]

This doesn't sound like a book to be completely disregarded. Admittedly, it has two major weaknesses: a cast-list so enormous that characterisation (and thus a clear sense of who's who) is skimped; and a denouement involving a deranged pop star and the blackmail of a secretly homosexual cabinet minister (topical in view of the Jeremy Thorpe affair, yet really belonging to the 1950s world of Dirk Bogarde in *Victim*). Against this, it is more successful and engrossing simply as a detective story than *The Riverside Villas Murder*, it contains ingredients which link interestingly with other novels and it embodies reflections on the very nature of fiction.

The book opens, cunningly, with an extract from a piece of detective fiction: a novel in progress, in fact, by Christopher Dane, featuring his regular sleuth James Fenton – a slightly unlikely transformation for the poet and *New Statesman* colleague of Kingsley's son Martin. But Dane is blocked, because the story he is writing so unnervingly resembles one 'actually' taking place and being reported daily in the newspapers. 'There's something horribly attractive about real crime which you just don't get in fictional crime,' he says. 'No way of doing it. A totally different kind of thrill.'[182] This pair of complicating ruses – the novel within the novel and the question of a 'reality' within the novel's world – seem to promise more literary reflexiveness than the book eventually delivers, although the solution to 'the crime of the century' is there (if only we could see it) in the opening extract from Dane's work. Dane himself is soon co-opted on to a grand committee whose members include the cabinet minister, a senior policeman, legal and medical experts, and the public-spirited pop singer Benedict Royal. Kingsley had evidently noticed that among the recent horrible noises to assault his ears was a group called Queen, whose song 'Killer Queen' was a hit while he was writing the novel. These committee members, in the traditional Agatha Christie manner, become the main suspects; there are also various other interested misfits, such as a fantasising loner and a fake Irish terrorist or two, to supply the equally traditional red herrings.

The neatness of the committee idea is that the probable criminal and the probable solver of the crimes – a continuing series of murders, accompanied by coded clues – become almost indistinguishable. As one of its members, Dr George Henderson, puts it: 'I took his point that Royal should be the guilty party, because of co-opting him; Dane, that is. It would be grander still if Dane set the whole thing up himself as a practical exercise in his art, with him playing both criminal and detective.'[183] There are plenty of entertaining diversions on the way to the solution, as well as motifs familiar from Kingsley's other books. One victim of a separate, imitative crime is given his 'fear of the Underground and of lifts and of heights';[184] one suspect committee member is made suspect in a different way by attempting a seduction to 'the strains of Mahler's First Symphony' on a 'black simulated-leather couch';[185] while the admirably commonsensical Dr Quintin Young briskly sorts out the fantasising loner: 'What you are is nothing much out of the way: a rather solitary man who's become fascinated with violent crime. No more abnormal, really, than the chap who likes reading about explorers or pirates. We all have our secret lives and fantasies, and you took yours a little further than most of us do. That's all.'[186]

9

The Amises left Lemmons in July 1976. Kingsley had never under-stood the place: he liked the idea of a grand house full of amusing people, but he had no aesthetic feeling for buildings – he once wrote, only half jokingly, that 'architecture ought to be comprehensively done away with'[187] – nor any grasp of the ways in which a house might embody spiritual values or even inspire love; the houses which

do this in English fiction – such as Mansfield Park or Howards End –
tend to occur in works by novelists he didn't much admire. Moreover,
he was completely indifferent to the finer details of his immediate
surroundings: the advertisement strapline 'Very Kingsley Amis, Very
Sanderson' had been a grotesque joke. In all these respects, Jane
was completely unlike him. Lemmons had been her project, and she
had over optimistically hoped that Kingsley would in time come to
see what it was about. He never did. One Sunday morning, he
announced: 'I don't want to live here any more. It's too bloody cut
off. I want to go back to London.'[188] And not just anywhere in
London: within walking distance of Hampstead Underground station
was his whimsical stipulation. Jane thought that 'it wasn't fair for
two people to live where one of them didn't want to' – generously
suppressing the corollary that it wasn't fair for two people to leave a
place where one of them wanted to stay – and that if Kingsley were
happier, so would she be: so would *they* be. Since he remained
constitutionally incapable of house-hunting, it was Jane and Colin
who discovered Gardnor House in Flask Walk, an elegant eighteenth-
century building with a walled (but shady) garden. Colin, Sargy and
various part-time members of the 'commune' – including Jane's
daughter Nicola, the painter Terry Raybould and his wife Jane, and
Daniel Day-Lewis – organised the clearing, packing and moving; Jane
herself was too upset to care. Kingsley, meanwhile, sat in his study
and wrote until his desk was taken away: his 'main job', he told Robert
Conquest on 5 July, had been 'drinking up all the nearly-empty bottles,
horrible stuff like cherry vodka, Mavrodaphne, raki etc.';[189] he had
also 'suffered a number of frightful ballockings from Jane for not
caring enough about her caring so much about leaving here'.[190] It is
at moments like this that he really does seem unforgivably obtuse.

Kingsley had a specific reason for wanting to live in London again:
he had become a great luncher-out. There were the Tuesday so-called
'fascist' lunches at Bertorelli's, where the regulars included Robert
Conquest (when in England), Anthony Powell, Bernard Levin and
John Braine, shortly to appear in a most unexpected fictional incar-
nation from Kingsley, as well as political journalists and occasional
Conservative MPs; the differently politically tinged Friday lunches,
these with an *Observer/New Statesman* air about them, at the Bursa
Kebab House, where Terence Kilmartin, Clive James, James Fenton,

Peter Porter and Martin Amis might be among those present; and any number of lunches at the Garrick Club. 'By the mid-1970s,' says Zachary Leader, 'he was making the hour-long commute into London at least three times a week after the morning's stint writing.'[191] To those of his own generation, or older, he was a dependably entertaining curmudgeon; to his juniors, an avuncular figure who could be relied upon to tease and, up to a point, be teased in return. Because the company was predominantly and often exclusively male, the conversation would have a certain broadness; a good deal of time was enjoyably spent deflating, or 'pissing on', figures and institutions of inflated reputation or excessive self-importance – George Steiner, say, or the Arts Council. This was the sort of stuff Kingsley had always enjoyed. The really striking thing is not that he was starting to turn into a grumpy old codger but that the social tone – scathingly disrespectful, yet with a ground bass of conservative values – so much resembled his undergraduate scurrilities with Larkin in Oxford and his pub talk with Jo Bartley and David Sims in Swansea. It was as if not only Cambridge (obviously) but the more gracious social aspects of his second marriage (still almost unthinkably) had been aberrations.

That this marriage was in dire trouble was widely known within Kingsley's circle: close friends such as Conquest, Larkin and Powell discuss it in their letters to each other though not to Kingsley himself. What was less known was that he had lost interest in sex altogether and had sought professional assistance. Initially, in the context of more general anxieties, he consulted his friend Dr Jim Durham and then, after suffering a panic attack in a tube train stuck outside Barnet station, one 'student of the mind' who practised in Windsor, 'a young and amiable South African called Hafner' and a 'Dr Wooster, so spelt in life' whose advice would find its way into *Jake's Thing*.[192] The *Memoirs*, though quite forthcoming about Kingsley's other phobias, are reticent about his sexual difficulties. Durham, however, suggested that he should see Dr Patricia Gillan, who practised in Harley Street and ran a sex-therapy clinic at the Maudsley Hospital. He and Jane also consulted Dr John Cobb, who 'called himself a psychologist, but what he really was, at least in his dealings with us, was a sort of highbrow marriage counsellor'. A novelist of Kingsley's satirical disposition, whose entire career had been kick-started by the intolerable preposterousness of Daddy B, could hardly fail to find such people ridiculous. So it proved: 'we were having trouble with our marriage, were we? Well, being nicer to each other would help, of course. Finding out what the other one liked to eat, where he or she liked going for the evening, etc., and acting on it could not fail to be useful. Specific tasks were set . . .'[193] This, too, was to appear in *Jake's Thing*. Meanwhile, the fact that Jane actually found some aspects of counselling useful didn't help Kingsley one bit. His 'growing boredom' was, he says, mistaken by Dr Cobb for 'surly defensiveness'; then he ruefully adds, 'perhaps it *was* surly defensiveness'. And if it was, who could blame him?

For writers, as Kingsley very well knew, don't take their neuroses to expensive quacks: they turn them into books. He had already touched on the idea of the sexless life in *Girl, 20*, where Douglas Yandell decides he'd rather be 'a monk in a world with music than a full-time stallion in a world without it'.[194] Now, in two novels which, like *The Riverside Villas Murder* and *The Crime of the Century*, approach a similar theme from two utterly different points of view, he asked: what happens to a man when sex is taken away from him? *The Alteration* (1976) began with a specific voice. Kingsley had been invited to review for *Records and Recording* two LP anthologies of singers from the EMI archives, among whom was Alessandro Moreschi, one of the last castrati, recorded at the age of forty-six in 1906. He found it musically very impressive.

> But the noise was indescribably depressing. You thought, this poor creature, singing away: big success, but no man at all. I was depressed for days . . . Then I thought, someone – he or his father – must have *consented* to this operation. And that decision brings out everything of importance in human life. Your arguments for and against your duty to God, to sing his music. Your duty to art. Sex. Love. Marriage. Children. Fame. Money. Security.[195]

He realised that something had to be done with this and at first couldn't decide what. A historical novel was one possibility, but its unsettling impact would have been blunted by chronological distance, while he rejected an eccentric-millionaire-on-Mediterranean-island scenario as a 'coward's way out' (too close to Bond territory as well, which would have created an unfortunate juxtaposition). His eventual solution was an 'alternate world' novel – he explicitly sanctions this Americanism in *The King's English* – set in a differently ordered present. The usual premise of 'alternate world' fiction is that some major event in the past has failed to occur: in this case, the Reformation. So England (like the rest of Europe) remains a Catholic country: its secular seat of government is London, but its ecclesiastical heart is the Cathedral of St George, which has 'the loftiest dome in the Old World' and 'the longest nave in Christendom', at Coverley (traditionally pronounced 'Cowley') near Oxford. The novel opens there, on the occasion of the funeral of King Stephen III; among those attending are 'the young King William V himself; the kings of Portugal, of Naples, of Sweden, of Lithuania and a dozen other realms; the Crown Prince of Muscovy and the Dauphin; the brother of the Emperor of Almaigne; the viceroys of India, New Spain and Brazil . . .' and so forth.[196] Outside, the processional route leads to nearby Headington Palace, which we are surely to imagine on the site of Headington Hall, where Kingsley (as we've seen) was briefly stationed in wartime and which was now the seat of Robert Maxwell.

The first few pages of *The Alteration* thus very clearly establish that this isn't quite the mid-1970s England that most of us remember. It is a world in which two 'aged representatives of the Holy Office', Monsignor Henricus and Monsignor Lavrentius, are 'known in their native Almaigne and Muscovy' by their familiar names, Himmler and Beria. Pope John XXIV, when we eventually meet him, turns out to be a Yorkshireman bearing a startling resemblance to John Braine (the Roman scenes make use of material from two trips to Rome Kingsley was persuaded to undertake in 1974 and 1975, accompanied not only by Jane but by Jim Durham and his wife Nita). There are inspired satirical transformations of other contemporary figures whom Kingsley didn't much admire: for instance, Monsignor Jean-Paul Sartre is the French Jesuit author of *Existentiae Natura*, while Lord Stansgate is put in charge of the London branch of the Holy Office at the Broad Arrow Tower (the reason why the real Lord Stansgate, who renounced his title to become Anthony Wedgwood Benn, was 'hated and feared', Kingsley told the *Daily Telegraph* in 1975, was 'that he looks and sounds as if he is off his head (which I, for one, am sure he is not), that he talks and acts as if he is intent on personal power (which I am sure he is), and that the combination appears dangerous').[197] Things worked out rather differently for earlier celebrated individuals too: Shakespeare was excommunicated and exiled to New England, but Mozart happily lived on to complete his Second Requiem, K. 878. Köchel seems to be among the relatively few people whose role was identical in the 'alternate world' and in the more familiar one. There's a great deal of this, and it is immensely entertaining despite the hazard of in-jokes becoming in-growing jokes, which sometimes they do.

The brilliant title of *The Alteration* has two meanings. One obviously refers to the 'alternate world' itself, in which almost everything is changed. The other more particularly is the name given to the operation which ten-year-old Hubert Anvil – whom we first encounter singing in that second Mozart Requiem – must undergo if his extraordinary voice, 'full-grown yet fresh, under total control yet spontaneous, sweet yet powerful',[198] is to be preserved. Kingsley's sly use of 'alteration' for 'castration' strikes precisely the right note of morally evasive nineteenth-century euphemism, like 'correction' for 'incarceration'. And it should alert us to the fact that this is a book about a moral dilemma; as with *Take a Girl like You* or *Ending Up*, the novel will be diminished if we close our minds to the apparently less sympathetic point of view. The central issues are those of choice and consent. How can Hubert and his worthy but conventional father Tobias Anvil voluntarily assent to something which will deprive him of an ordinarily fulfilled life? (It doesn't help that the Anvil household contains not only Hubert's standardly randy elder brother but a fornicating priest as well.) How can Hubert, despite seeking information from his brother, the fellow-choristers in his dormitory and a cheerfully explicit farm lad, know what it is he'll be missing? Yet all of us make choices every day which deprive us of unchosen and unknown things; and when we take into account the glory of God and the perfection of art – the two most potent factors imaginable in this Catholic world – we will see that the scales are more evenly balanced than the secular modern reader might at first assume. *The Alteration* is about a dilemma, not a foregone conclusion.

As it happens, the book's conclusion provides only a partial answer to its central question; what is expected to happen does happen, but not for the expected reason. Although God is glorified and art is served, the impossible choice has been replaced by a simple necessity, and this is less an evasion than an acknowledgement that life-shaping events are often rather like that (becoming a lecturer at Swansea, for example, may look like a choice while actually being a necessity). This is one of several ways in which *The Alteration* remains faithful to the world we actually inhabit. Another is the familiarity, rather than the expected strangeness, of minor details: when Hubert, like the other choristers, on his leisure day changes from 'chapel dress to the garb permitted for the leisure hours' – 'coloured cotton shirt, a furious indulgence for those limited on all occasions to white . . . loose trousers reaching to the ankle . . . and rubber-soled canvas shoes instead of the constant polished leather'[199] – we suddenly notice that he's wearing, without having quite the right words for them, the typical clothes of the 1970s teenager. When Protestant New England, to which Hubert hopes to escape, seems altogether too good to be true – informal, tolerant, even granting equal status to women, as he finds to his amazement when he meets the family of the New England ambassador, Cornelius van den Haag – we're sharply reminded that it also has apartheid (the ambassador's Dutch name is an early signal): 'You see, Hubert,' explains Pastor Williams, 'God created the Indians and ourselves for two different purposes and in two different ways, and he proclaimed this by making them a different colour from us.'[200] We are not to expect anything as simplistic, or as wildly unlikely, as a perfect world from Kingsley.

While a world out of time enables its author to produce unexpected insights into the here and now, it also grants him some linguistic and literary freedoms. *The Alteration* is written in a perfectly serviceable modern English yet spiked with unfamiliar idioms: 'Fuck a fox!' isn't an expression in common use, though one can see how it might be, nor are married women usually called 'Dame'. 'Where we are going to have some trouble is with the printer,' Kingsley wrote to his copy editor, 'to stop him normalising mustach to moustache, italian (windows) to Italian – and caffè to café, etc.'[201] Everyone's speech is appropriately tweaked (Latinate for the clerics, Pilgrim Fathers English for the New Englanders) with the exception of the tone-deaf Pope John Braine, who speaks in gloriously unreconstructed Yorkshire. Jacob, the Jew who kidnaps Hubert during his flight from Coverley, utters chunks of *The Merchant of Venice*. And the scene in which Hubert, aided by his canny chorister friend Decuman, makes his escape effortlessly shifts us into another fictional world: a young hero adventuring across England on horseback is, after all, a subject for Henry Fielding.

Kingsley was pleased with *The Alteration* and with its reception. 'Have had excellent reviews for my ballocks book,' he told Conquest,

'though they all get it wrong, can't read what's in front of them.'[202]
He also, more than once, expressed the hope that it might be filmed:
it could indeed make a stunning if fiendishly expensive film, but one
can't help feeling that he was mischievously intrigued to see how a
director might cope with the book in general and its final scene in
particular, surgical removal of 'ballocks' presumably not being an
option.

While Hubert is deprived of what he's never enjoyed, Jake Richardson in *Jake's Thing* (1978) no longer enjoys what he's accustomed
to have. Is that better or worse? Jake is Jaques (as in 'melancholy . . .'
with its lavatorial pun), which is not so distant from Jim, while
Richardson is Dick's son, which is Dixon; so this is what happens to
Jim when he gets unlucky and has trouble with his dick. As Kingsley
confirmed to John McDermott in 1985: ' "Jake Richardson" is a
deliberate reformulation of "Jim Dixon".'[203] He has a fat wife called
Brenda – as with Adela in *Ending Up*, Kingsley makes her physically
as unlike Jane as possible – of whom he is genuinely fond but in
whom he no longer has any sexual interest; nor, indeed, is he sexually
interested in anyone else. They live in a fairly recognisable bit of
North London, here called Orris Park, where theirs is the only
ungentrified house in Burgess Avenue. For as little of the week as he
can decently manage, Jake teaches at Oxford, where he holds the
unstrenuous post of Reader in Early Mediterranean History and is a
Fellow of Comyns College. We first meet him as he is consulting
his GP (who refers him to 'A very able man, Dr Rosenberg') before
going home to Brenda, buying a decent bottle of wine and a box
of chocolates for her on the way; there he finds her dreary friend
Alcestis, who is married to the even drearier Geoffrey and who is in
the middle of recounting a torpidly bathetic anecdote about a
plumber. This reminds Jake of Martial's epigram about the farting
ploughboy[204] and, as it dribbles to its conclusion, we learn (what
no one in the book seems quite able to fathom) the real cause of his
problem:

> Jake was close to tears. In that moment he saw the world in its
> true light, as a place where nothing had ever been any good and
> nothing of significance done: no art worth a second look, no
> philosophy of the slightest appositeness, no law but served the
> state, no history that gave an inkling of how it had been and

what had happened. And no love, only egotism, infatuation
and lust.[205]

He is suffering from depression. Life appears worthless and unendur-
able. This is exactly the note of James Churchill during his breakdown
towards the end of *The Anti-Death League* and, more recently, of
'Things tell less and less . . .'. It raises an important if ultimately
unanswerable question of cause and effect: whether Jake's loss of
libido is the consequence or the source of his depression. The point
matters because Jake, like Kingsley, seeks treatment specifically for
his sexual dysfunction. Kingsley also sought help in dealing with his
phobias; but neither actually gets to the heart of the matter, which is
clinical depression. Kingsley, like many creative people, must have
instinctively sensed that his creativity was inextricably bound up with
his depression, and he would have known that there were treatments
for depression, such as electro-convulsive therapy, to which a writer
couldn't willingly submit himself. So the question is evaded. Jake
joins a procession of Amis heroes, of whom Patrick Standish and
James Churchill are in this context the most notable, who display
depressive symptoms – which he, like his author, treats with understandable obtuseness. This was to have terrible consequences for both
their marriages.

Like *The Alteration, Jake's Thing* has a double-edged title:
although the 'thing' obviously refers to Jake's obstinately non-func-
tioning penis, it is also suggests his obsession, his 'thing' about everything going to pieces in late-1970s England. Moreover, the book –
which looks like a fairly straightforward linear narrative – really has
two strands. The predominant one concerns Jake's sceptical encounters with doctors, therapists and other charlatans, his angry rejection
of the whole business, and his eventual separation from his wife,
who is rather taken with 'GROUPS and WORKSHOPS and crappy
"new friends"' – but that phrase comes from a letter from Kingsley
to Larkin about Jane, which goes on to lament *his* 'total loss of
sex-drive'.[206] 'If there's one word', says Jake, 'that sums up everything that's gone wrong since the War, it's Workshop.'[207] The satire
is a bit too swashbuckling for its own good: Dr Rosenberg, whose
methods and opinions owe a good deal to Dr Patricia Gillan, turns
out to be a dwarfish Irishman, while the hectoring and humiliating
'workshops' conducted by an American called Ed take place at

premises owned by a Mr Shyster. There are other indulgences, such as a nostalgic trawl through shops off the Charing Cross Road and an informed analysis of the then-and-now state of soft-porn magazines (Patrick in *Difficulties with Girls* will do much the same), but the heart of this strand is Jake, his condition and what is to be done about it. 'Why did you come to me in the first place?' asks Dr Rosenberg, and Jake replies: 'I realized something that used to be a big part of my life wasn't there any more.' 'And you miss it,' Dr Rosenberg deduces without much trouble. But Jake, whose mind is a good deal more subtle than that of some other Amis heroes, instantly sees (though Rosenberg doesn't) the lurking paradox here: 'how he could be held to miss what he no longer wanted; you don't miss a friend you'd be slightly sorry to run into, do you?'[208] If 'desire' is what you've lost, how can you possibly desire its return? Kingsley's best shot at expressing rather than solving this conundrum comes not in the novel but in a Larkinesque short poem called 'Senex':

> To find his sexual drives had ceased
>   For Sophocles was no disaster;
> He said he felt like one released
>   From service with a cruel master.
>
> I envy him – I miss the lash
>   At which I used to snort and snivel;
> Oh that its unremitted slash
>   Were still what makes me drone and drivel![209]

We might call this grumbly acceptance the post-Jake position; or rather, it is the position Jake approaches towards the novel's end.

But before considering that conclusion we need to look at the secondary strand, which is so distinct in tone that it amounts almost to a book within a book. This is set in Oxford and, had it been developed, it could have represented Kingsley's one sustained attempt at an Oxbridge collegiate novel. It has some rather good characters of its own, starting with Ernie the porter, clearly a relative of the man who expressed astonishment when Kingsley asked for Lord David Cecil all those years ago, and including dons with names such as Damon Lancewood and Roger Dollymore. Its links with the London chapters are clear but arbitrary: Jake, concerned that his naked appearance before medical students will have become common knowledge, is met by protesters' shouts of 'Wanker Richardson' as he arrives at college; he is pursued to Oxford by a deranged and suicidal fellow patient called (though not named) Kelly; and the Master of Comyns, 'a distinguished crystallographer', wishing to discuss the proposal that their college should admit women, says, with unconscious and nicely placed irony: 'I must draw Jake aside briefly. I have to consult him about women.'[210] In fact, the scenes of university politics begin to move towards a different sort of book, one perhaps resembling J. I. M. Stewart's Oxford quintet, *A Staircase in Surrey*; and this is because they stem from a different impulse.

Martin was writing a piece for an anthology called *My Oxford*, edited by Ann Thwaite and published in 1977, and this prompted Kingsley to compare the place he had known as a student with the place it had by then become. In May 1976 he revisited Oxford to 'give a light-verse reading' – he was working on the *New Oxford Book of Light Verse* at the time – and stayed at the Randolph, 'which I used to like quite'. But, he told Conquest, just as he and Jane were getting to sleep at midnight, 'a sodding group sprang to life directly beneath'; next morning, having consequently overslept, they were late for and initially denied breakfast. As for the rest of the place: 'The town was horrible too: Rag week, boutiques, shopping precincts, pop music in every pub. I have a Betj-style poem on the way . . .'[211] The poem, 'Their Oxford', is more Larkin than Betj, resembling 'Here' in its method of sweeping in and then listing details:

> To reach the centre you turn left, not right,
> And drive halfway to Abingdon before
> You start to double back past building-site,
> Paella joint, hair-stylist, hi-fi store,
>
> By uncouth alleys to the old hotel,
> Now newly faced . . .

The hotel gets three stanzas contrasting the days when 'parents and fiancées drawled at ease' (his own included) with the diminished present, before he ventures out to the Cornmarket, which:

> Is now a precinct (not the sacred sort);
> Beyond We're Every-Wear there still exists

The Roebuck, once the unarranged resort
Of hearties, Bodley readers, botanists,

Where men in long top-coats would snort and scratch,
Meat-market porters gulp their morning break,
And stall-boys jostle: now, yards off, you catch
The surge and thunder of a discothèque.[212]

This is also Jake's Oxford, or at least the Oxford he has to put up with: 'Here, where you could have sworn there was nothing but a couple of colleges, some lodgings and an occasional newsagent or tobacconist, stood hairdressers' and clothiers' and trumpery-bazaars of a glossy meanness formerly confined to the outskirts of the large cities.'[213]

Jake is asked by the Master to present at a College Meeting the formal case for the admission of women, as a matter of academic advocacy rather than personal conviction. When the time comes, however, he is suffering from an excruciating hangover, the consequence of an evening of debauchery with an old and married friend, Eve Greenstreet: improbably successful sexually, it seems, though he was too drunk to be aware of it. Still, he manages to present his case, but he is then goaded – mostly by the dreadful 'writer in residence', a term not far behind 'workshop' in Kingsley's litany of shitty things – into revealing his true opinion. It's a set-piece: like Jim Dixon's drunk public lecture in *Lucky Jim* or Ronnie Appleyard's attack on Student Mansfield in *I Want It Now*, the kind of wish-fulfilling moment of self-revelation that too seldom happens in real life. 'I was asked to put a case, that's all,' Jake explains, before asserting, with authorial conviction, that 'it's the men who are going to be the losers':

When the first glow has faded and it's quite normal to have girls in the same building and on the same staircase and across the landing, they'll start realizing that that's exactly what they've got, girls everywhere and not a commonroom, not a club, not a pub where they can get away from them ... there will be women everywhere, chattering, gossiping, telling you what they did today and what their daughter did yesterday and what their friend did last week and what somebody they heard about did last month and horrified if a chap brings up a *topic* or an *argument*.[214]

It's a marvellous performance, ending with the suggestion that women should 'bugger off back to Somerville, LMH, St Hugh's and St Hilda's',[215] and only a careless reader of Kingsley – there have been plenty of these – would suppose that it represents anything as simple as misogyny.

This leads back to London and to Dr Rosenberg. Jake's considered opinion is that 'Rosenberg was a bit suspect' and 'Ed was a ravening charlatan.'[216] That, though, is before the disastrous 'weekend Workshop' from which Jake departs with another set-piece speech, this time addressed to Rosenberg himself. He scores some notable bulls-eyes, especially when he confronts Rosenberg's trendy drivel about 'repressive attitudes' – 'Repressive? In 1977? I was doing fine when things really were repressive, if they ever were, it's only since they've become, oh, permissive that I've had trouble' – and brilliantly shows how sexual permissiveness really means sexual competitiveness: 'No wonder you boys have got enough trade.'[217] When Brenda eventually leaves him for dull Geoffrey, it's because Geoffrey is actually interested in her, a piece of implied self-criticism which Kingsley must have fully intended. In the novel's final chapter, Jake is living, like Douglas Yandell at the end of *Girl, 20*, in tolerable solitude: 'in a perfectly bearable couple of rooms in Kentish Town'. It's a state Kingsley seems genuinely to envy and surely would have tried, if only he could have coped with being on his own. We leave Jake exactly where we found him, with his GP, who this time suggests they should 'run tests' to see if there's anything physically wrong with him, a proposal Jake has only to consider for a moment:

> Jake did a quick run-through of women in his mind, not of the ones he had known or dealt with in the past few months or years so much as all of them: their concern with the surface of things, with objects and appearances, with their surroundings and how they looked and sounded in them, with seeming to be better and to be right while getting everything wrong, their automatic assumption of the role of injured party in any clash of wills, their certainty that a view is the more credible and useful for the fact that they hold it, their use of misunderstanding and misrepresentation as weapons of debate, their selective sensitivity to tones of voice, their unawareness of the difference in themselves between sincerity and insincerity, their interest in importance (together with

noticeable inability to discriminate in that sphere), their fondness
for general conversation and directionless discussion, their pre-
emption of the major share of feeling, their exaggerated estimate
of their own plausibility, their never listening and lots of other
things like that, all according to him.

So it was quite easy. 'No thanks,' he said.[218]

Although there's a gesture towards distancing in 'all according
to him', this is very close to Kingsley's voice in his letters to Larkin
and Conquest. It's also the voice of someone who has loved and (in
the fullest, most straightforward sense) enjoyed women, and who is
devastated by the discovery that he no longer does so. Nevertheless,
after this there could be no going back.

10

Early one evening in 1979, John Baxter was sitting in the bar of the
Coach and Horses in Hampstead, waiting for Kingsley, who came
'shuffling in twenty minutes late':

> It was hard to reconcile this figure with the man I remembered. At
> fifty-seven, he appeared twenty years older. (In a letter to Philip
> Larkin later that year, he confessed the almost total loss of his
> once prodigious sex drive.) Stooped, almost shambling, he was
> myopic without his glasses, which he put on in the doorway before
> peering around uncertainly. Obviously, he was a regular. It wasn't
> only the suited business types who smiled and said hello but the
> men in grimy work jackets.[219]

The last detail is the most telling. Kingsley switched his allegiance to
the Coach and Horses when his former local, the Flask, was 'gentri-
fied': a phonier version of 'posh' and exactly what Jake Richardson's
house had so stubbornly resisted. It was as if he was trying to get
back to the Bryn-y-Mor in Swansea. Those had been the good times:
over the next few years, annual summer visits to stay with his old
friends Eve and Stuart Thomas in South Wales would constitute his
only regular absences from London and the Garrick, and the most
successful of his late novels would be set there. Soon, too, his
domestic arrangements were to alter so greatly that he would find

himself living for the most part in a bedsitting-room, gladly exchanging Jane's culinary excellence – all those dishes with mercilessly
parodiable names – for the simple, reassuring food of his youth. The
crucial point is that, although he and Jane were still together at
Gardnor House, this process had already begun.

When Alice, at the end of *Through the Looking-Glass*, shakes the
Red Queen, the irascible chess-piece turns into a kitten; and there are
times when one wouldn't mind trying to do much the same to an
actual person. But no amount of shaking could have transformed
Kingsley from what he was. Had he been differently made, he might
grudgingly have accepted that his loss of sex drive was the result
of advancing years and too much drink – and concluded that a life of
creative companionship in a handsome and comfortable home was
a pretty good deal in the circumstances. It didn't work like that: it
threw into relief everything about Jane that had once seemed so
entrancingly unlike himself and now only emphasised how incompatible her tastes and manners were with those of the boy from Norbury.
The reason why Jake Richardson's 'quick run-through of women in
his mind' is so devastating is that its detail doesn't, as he claims,
apply to 'all of them': point after point zeroes in on one kind of
woman in particular, an upper-middle-class Englishwoman. Curiously, Jake isn't married to one: Brenda is more down to earth than
that. But Kingsley was. Nevertheless – and here the temptation to
give Kingsley the Red Queen treatment returns – Jane is, as everyone
who has met her knows, thoroughly down to earth in her own way.
For instance, there's a blast of full-strength Amisian pungency when
she describes her feelings on leaving the garden she'd created at
Lemmons, dismissing the hope that the new owners would care for
it: 'The wife had twice come round the house, and while we were all
in cotton and sandals, she resolutely wore her mink coat and leather
boots that reached to her ritzy little knees.'[220] Her own hands-on
practicality was and remains as evident in the kitchen as in the
garden. She had seen tough times, especially in the years after the
break-up of her first marriage, and wasn't easily impressed by
unworked-for affluence. Though not a pubby person, she enjoyed a
drink and rolled her own cigarettes.

Such facets of her character, which had previously delighted
Kingsley, now merely fuelled his despair, for if Jane had obligingly
conformed to his stereotypical notion of 'posh', it would have been

so much easier to quarrel with her. But she didn't, and that is why
the ebb and flow of their relationship in the latter part of the 1970s
is so variously tinted with puzzlement and despair, anger and the
remains of love. Kingsley in his *Memoirs* says almost nothing about
this period, or indeed about Jane at all: she is airbrushed out, in a
way that at the time of the book's publication looked simply brutal
but which in retrospect seems desperately sad. Jane, in *Slipstream*,
catches the emotional complexity – and the hopelessness – of their
failing marriage perfectly in a few lines:

> I was standing by the window of our bedroom one morning,
> looking out of the window and feeling very sad. He came to me,
> put his arms round me and gave me a long, gentle kiss, and said,
> 'I used to be so much in love with you.' Before I could say
> anything, he turned and walked out of the room. It was like
> meeting a loving ghost suddenly, who vanished before I could
> respond. I stayed by the window until I stopped crying. But that
> evening, after work, when I tried to talk to him, he'd retreated.
> Insulated by whisky, he was withdrawn and dismissive. 'I don't
> think so, I don't want to do that.'[221]

He was terrified. To reach the place to which he'd retreated, Jane
would have had to get inside his fear; and that, perhaps, she never
quite did nor could she be expected to do so. He was to put a good
deal of this emotional helplessness and this habit of drink-fuelled
withdrawal, implicitly linking this with his South London background, into the central character of a novel; but not just yet.

Meanwhile, he was working with his usual astonishing self-
discipline. Quite apart from an output of novels which had achieved
almost Murdochian regularity, he had edited *The New Oxford Book
of Light Verse* and *The Faber Popular Reciter*, both published in
1978. The problem with such pleasurable-looking commissions is
that reviewers expect anthologists to have read every possibly eligible
poem in the entire history of literature and to have sound reasons
for each inclusion or exclusion. Larkin had discovered this, to his
cost, when he edited *The Oxford Book of Twentieth-Century Verse*
(1973), provoking among other responses a distressed, severely critical review by Donald Davie in the *Listener* (as well as a long and
impassioned subsequent correspondence in its pages). In March 1974,
Jon Stallworthy at OUP shrewdly suggested that Kingsley might like

to edit the companion light verse anthology: its title was an invitation
to include poems he actually *enjoyed* – the approach which had
landed Larkin in so much hot water – while the residual rivalry of
old friends made the proposal irresistible. 'Part of the pleasure', he
told Larkin in 1976, 'has of course been *keeping out* dull fuckers like
Dryden, Burns, Blake (A Petty Sneaking Knave I Knew: Why Don't
you stick your Prick up you?), *Don Marquis*, Ogden Nash (aaoh!
aoh! aaoh!), Harry Graham (especially HIM) and all the tribe from
Alan Brownj . . . [sketch of sign saying TOILETS] . . . varez . . .'[222]
Several friends suggested various candidates for the anthology, while
Larkin, anticipating the reviews, also supplied a little song, to the
tune of 'Daisy, Daisy':

> Davie, Davie,
> Give me a bad review;
> That's your gravy,
> Telling chaps what to do.
> Forget about style and passion,
> As long as it's in the fashion: –
> But let's be fair, it's got you a chair,
> Which was all it was meant to do.[223]

Kingsley replied that 'it would do for my LV anthol if it weren't for
the fact that in 20 years' time EVERYBODY WILL HAVE FORGOT-
TEN WHO DAVIE WAS'.[224] At that point, in December 1976, Davie
was nearing the end of his professorial term at Stanford, California.
With consummate irony, in 1978 he became Andrew W. Mellon
Professor of Humanities at Vanderbilt, and from there he wrote
'mad' letters to Kingsley – including one in which 'he says annoyingly
"You are remembered hereabouts" without saying in what spirit'.[225]
Whether mad or not, Davie was once again someone whom Kingsley
could have done with as a friend: he had, after all, devoted his life to
literary scholarship and was shortly to edit a rather different OUP
anthology, *The New Oxford Book of Christian Verse* (1981). He was
also a challenging, intellectually rigorous contemporary, a necessary
sort of companion supplied neither by Kingsley's clubbable cronies
nor by his younger admirers: had the two been on easier terms, their
nominations for each other's books might at the very least have
proved interesting and surprising, even if not actually useful. *The
New Oxford Book of Light Verse* proved an unexpectedly onerous

task, and Kingsley had to scramble to deliver it by the deadline of 31 August 1977; by comparison, he told Conquest, 'The Faber Book of Non-Trendy Verse has been easier and is going faster: a careful look through the Dict of Quots took me most of the way, then hymnals and old-fashioned anthologies.'[226]

A more ticklish matter was his own *Collected Poems*, which appeared in 1979. With *Jake's Thing*, he had left Cape for Hutchinson: this looked like (and was) a sound piece of advance-doubling negotiation by his agent, Jonathan Clowes, but it also had a symbolic significance. He had originally moved to Cape largely because of Jane's friend Tom Maschler; both he and Jane had remained there ever since, even though she too would move on (to Hamish Hamilton) for *Getting It Right* in 1982; since 1973, Martin too had been a Cape author. Going elsewhere at this point not only made financial sense, it gently insisted that he was his own man. Hutchinson, before its absorption into Random House, was a traditional general publisher, impossible to pigeonhole on the highbrow–lowbrow or literary–popular scale and hence very much to Kingsley's taste; its smallish poetry list was among the responsibilities of his first editor there, Anthony Whittome, who clearly felt that the success of *The New Oxford Book of Light Verse* had sufficiently reconnected Kingsley with poetry to justify a *Collected*.

When the novelist writes about himself, he continually qualifies this with properly fictional details, so that the reader won't know for certain which is which. The poet's self-revelations are harder to disguise, brief yet brightly lit, and a *Collected Poems* can't help seeming to present a sequence of significant moments from the author's life. Jane feels that Kingsley, while lacking the 'dedicated, chaste' commitment of Larkin, 'would have liked to write more poetry';[227] there was always a part of him which disdained the pubby, clubby outer man with his huge, dependent need for company. Kingsley deleted most of his first volume, *Bright November*, but he also had worries about some more recent pieces: 'There are five (no doubt there should be more) I feel dubious about: will they add to my reputation or tend to fuck it up?'[228] None of these five – 'Words', 'Progress', 'Kipling at Bateman's', 'Sonnet from Orpheus' and 'Hours of Waking' – survived into the published book, which is slimmer than it need have been and looks too blatantly like the work of a part-time poet; enormous early computer-set type adds to the sense of thin stuff padded out, whereas a complete poems 'in blunt ten-point' (or twelve) would have had more substance. At the same time, comparative sparseness clarifies the book's trajectory. Given the state of his marriage, Kingsley's decision to begin with 'Letter to Elisabeth', his heartfelt love poem to Elisabeth Simpson, becomes touching in a new way; the Movementish poems of the 1950s now clearly embody his most genuinely confident and witty voice; the Welsh retrospective sequence, 'The Evans Country', takes on an unexpectedly nostalgic sheen; while the last twenty poems, previously uncollected, sustain an almost unbroken note of valediction and regret.

This note springs from complex causes: recollection of childhood ('Bobby Bailey'), wartime ('A Reunion') or early married life ('Wasted'); dissatisfaction with the way things are now ('Shitty', 'Crisis Song', 'Their Oxford') or with the author's own ageing ('Ode to Me', 'Senex'). The penultimate poem, written in 1978, is 'Farewell Blues',[229] a parody of John Betjeman's 'Dorset' with its whimsical lists of those who 'lie in Mellstock Churchyard now': in three equivalent stanzas, it provides instances of the horrible new before lamenting the dead musicians who 'lie in Brunswick churchyard now' ('Brunswick' becomes 'Decca' in the second stanza and 'Okeh', where the stress falls wrongly, in the third). On 27 July he sent a draft version to Larkin, who wasn't impressed: in his reply, he tried to put Kingsley right, pointing out that some of his original nominees were still alive and that 'he should line up the chaps with the labels they chiefly recorded on'.[230] But Kingsley couldn't really get the hang of that, nor did he understand that, since for over thirty years American Decca records were released in England as Brunswick, the musicians in his first two stanzas were mostly interchangeable anyway. Larkin, for whom getting such things right was part of the pleasure of jazz, must have groaned when he read the published poem. Betjeman, however, was thrilled: 'I love your jazz poem. What a delightful surprise it was and how truly learned it is.'[231] Collected Poems was dedicated to him.

Appropriately enough, the novel on which Kingsley was working at this time, Russian Hide and Seek (1980), is simultaneously pessimistic and escapist. It is the last of his 'entertainments', or 'genre novels', and it would indeed be entertaining to any reader who came to it without prior knowledge of his other novels. In its untitled early stages, Kingsley gave it the code-name 'CHN III',[232] 'CHN' standing for 'country-house novel' and its two predecessors being *The Anti-Death League* and *Ending Up* (none of which is really a 'CHN' as a true practitioner of the genre – for instance, Elizabeth Jane Howard – might understand the term); but to those familiar with his work, it resembles a curious hybrid of *The Anti-Death League* and *The Alteration*. Like the former, it opens in some enigmatic rural place, whose details are described without providing any real hint of location (this version of up-a-bit-from-Hertfordshire turns out to be around Northampton); like the latter, it is set in an alternative England where characters speak a not-quite-right dialogue. The main dialogue is actually Russian – this is England in the far-off twenty-first century, some fifty years after its Soviet invasion – and when people lapse into what they comically imagine to be old-fashioned colloquial English they speak in italics, exchanging ludicrous pleasantries such as *'Fine to see you old customer'*,[233] politely exclaiming *'Fucking hell'*[234] and stumbling into misunderstandings such as this one, of a dog's tombstone: ' " *'To the memory of Pug,'* " he read out, " *'who departed this life June 24th 1754.'* Presumably a young child, though it seems odd to give just the nickname." '[235] English culture has, of course, disintegrated entirely, but the old policy of 'denationing' is being replaced by the NCPE, or 'New Cultural Policy for England'[236] – just the sort of phrase which might have been coined without irony by Tony Blair and an instance (there are several here) of Kingsley's satire rather unnervingly hitting the nail. This policy, as exemplified in the novel, has two main strands: one is artistic – including events such as a concert of 'works by Dowland, Purcell, Sullivan, Elgar, the composer of "Ta-ra-ra-doom-de-ay", Noel Coward, Duke Ellington (taken to have been an English nobleman of some sort), Britten and John Lennon'[237] and a disastrous performance of *Romeo and Juliet* which ends in a riot – while the other is religious, as an elderly, blind and deaf clergyman, the Reverend Simon Glover, leads a service in a rural church approximately restored for the occasion. Naturally, he chooses to use the Book of Common Prayer, a distinction to which the Russians are oblivious and another point well made: 'It was of course unknown to Commissioner Mets or to any of his advisers that about the middle of the previous century various amended forms of prayer, supposedly more accessible to the congregation of the day and certainly disencumbered by hard words like "*ye*" and "*unto*" and "*thee*", had begun to be used in English churches.'[238]

This is the level on which *Russian Hide and Seek* works splendidly: the satirical tweaking of those aspects of English life which were already starting to fall apart, given an extra nudge by invaders who are even more stupid and ridiculous than the natives. The actual plot, on the other hand, is a bit of a shambles. It concerns a young officer, Alexander Petrovsky, who with his friend Theodore Markov plots a ludicrously inept revolution which would give England back to the English. He seems at first to be a James Churchill figure – attractive, intelligent, yet something of an outsider – and there is indeed a military establishment at which the game of Russian hide and seek (it involves soldiers shooting at each other in the dark) takes place. There is also a grotesque equivalent of Lady Lucy Hazell in Mrs Korotchenko, who engages Alexander in some notably bizarre sexual games. The last of these, in which he has sex with her on a wheeled table attached to a rope manipulated by her naked twelve-year-old daughter – while being 'hurtled round the barn in a succession of vast unique elliptical orbits' before 'flying through the air with an altogether different motion, out into the sunlight and still locked with Mrs Korotchenko, now bawling her loudest near his ear, across the farmyard over the pigs and poultry and straight into the pile of cartons'[239] – has a fair claim to be the weirdest page in Kingsley's fiction, not least because the comic tone has come so strangely adrift. Kingsley, like Jake, was straightforward in his sexual tastes, and Mrs Korotchenko's peculiarities are meant to symbolise moral perversions, but any serious point is compromised by the sheer silliness of the scene.

Russian Hide and Seek suffers from a pervading air of creative weariness. There are too many peripheral characters including, as in *The Anti-Death League*, a surfeit of barely distinguishable army officers. Old motifs fleetingly appear for no particular reason: an echo of a scandalous Swansea evening – during which Kingsley disappeared into the garden with a succession of women – in Alexander's seduction by Mrs Korotchenko on the lawn of his father's house during a party; yet another nod towards Kingsley's parental short-comings when Alexander's mother reminds his father that 'being tolerant is so much less trouble'.[240] Above all, the journeyman prose, which neither falls below professionalism nor rises above it, seems temporarily to have lost its teeth. On publication day, Kingsley dined at 10 Downing Street and presented a signed copy to the Prime Minister; on being told it was about 'a future Russian takeover', Mrs Thatcher replied, 'Get another crystal ball.'[241] Nevertheless, he was rewarded with a CBE in the next New Year's Honours. The book, meanwhile, received 'some crappy reviews, but enough lengthy even if wrong-headed respect in some quarters to leave the ego only superficially damaged'.[242] By this time, the ego had other kinds of damage to contend with.

Jane says she decided to leave Kingsley during the fortnight they spent at that year's Edinburgh Festival. A confident Kingsley could have shone there, charming everyone with his intelligence and wit; on the other hand, Edinburgh was well stocked with ingredients – plays, concerts, dinners, 'posh' friends of Jane's and artists more distinguished than himself – likely to flip him into paranoia and fury. He flipped: after one disappointing night at the theatre, he refused to go to another play or allow Jane to do so; he wanted sandwiches in their room rather than dinner; and when at lunch he found himself discussing Mozart with Claudio Abbado, 'Kingsley told him, in so many words, that he didn't know what he was talking about.'[243] Later, when Jane suggested that it might have been possible to disagree more gracefully, he accused her of 'being upper class and suggesting people shouldn't say what they thought'. This was the division that was always going to come between them eventually.

She had booked a ten-day stay at Shrubland Hall, a health farm in Suffolk, for the end of October and the beginning of November: as with her previous absences, Kingsley would have Lily Uniacke – who had loyally moved with them from Lemmons to Gardnor House – to look after things, and a pre-planned succession of visitors to keep him company. In the weeks leading up to her Shrubland Hall visit, while he was enjoying his lengthy lunches at the Garrick, she packed suitcases of clothes and removed them to the house of her friend Ursula Vaughan Williams, where she would go after her stay in Suffolk. On the morning of her expected return to Gardnor House, Kingsley would receive a hand-delivered letter explaining her decision; that way, he'd at least have had some time to get used to being without her. She arranged for her part-time secretary to look after her dog Rosie – who had done service as the Furry Barrel in

Girl, 20 – so that she didn't become a hostage in any subsequent recriminations. On the morning of her departure, when she told Kingsley she was off, he didn't even look up from his paper. Had he been the Red Queen, or the kitten, he might have been shaken into noticing what was going on. But he wasn't, and he had no idea that she wasn't coming back.

5. FOLKS THAT LIVE
ON THE HILL

1

'But is there any comfort to be found?' asked Yeats, and for answer offered another question: 'Man is in love and loves what vanishes, / What more is there to say?'[1] Kingsley took some time to recognise the comfort and tried terribly hard to deny the love. Telling Larkin that Jane had 'just buggered off', he explained: 'She did it partly to punish me for stopping wanting to fuck her and partly because she realised I didn't like her much.' It took only a few lines for that mask to crack: 'Yeah, but not having her around and trying to take in the fact that she never will be around is immeasurably more crappy than having her around. I've had a wife for 32 years.'[2] He accurately foresaw that selling Gardnor House, dividing the proceeds and finding somewhere else to live was going to be an unpleasant and convoluted business. When he wrote to Conquest ten days later, his attempt at defiance – 'No word from the old bitch' – collapsed even more rapidly: 'By God she was hard to live with but living without her seems altogether pointless. I had no idea she meant so much to me.'[3] To Larkin, he added: 'Your godson' – his and Hilly's elder son Philip – 'is providentially around, having left his intolerable wife and been sacked from his job. I think he's the nicest fellow I've ever met.'[4]

Though not always quite the word for the tasks it's set, 'providentially' will do well here: Philip and Martin between them embarked on a programme of keeping their father company in the evenings and staying overnight, which they called 'Dadsitting', knowing that – while Mrs Uniacke, the Garrick and Kingsley's friends would between them look after his material needs – his fear of being alone simply couldn't be dealt with in any other way. Jane's first condition for returning to him was that he must give up drink completely, a suggestion which managed to be both sensible and impossible; her second condition, Kingsley speculated, might be 'that I saw off my head and serve it up to her with a little hollandaise sauce'.[5] During 1981, the selling of Gardnor House proved every bit as tiresome as anticipated, with the predictable squabbling about shares of the proceeds and the practical nuisance of 'People coming in droves to look over the house, at enormous length or for insultingly short periods, standing outside my study talking loudly in Arabic etc.'[6] But providence still had a smart trick up its sleeve. In August, with the house still unsold and surveyors making discouraging noises about it, Kingsley could tell Larkin that he'd 'found, and yesterday installed here, the couple who'll look after me. They are Hilly and her 3rd husband, Lord Kilmarnock. Nay, stare not so.' Apart from solving the problem of his loneliness and providing 'a bit of family', this astounding arrangement had a closely related and even more important consequence: 'the day this was decided on I started on a new novel, and the day they came, yesterday as I said, I got the plot of same sorted out. They have a little boy of 9. Yes, but he's very nice.'[7]

Kingsley hadn't thought the little boy – Jaime Boyd, born on 27 January 1972, before his parents' marriage and thus unable to succeed to his father's title – 'very nice' at the start. Kingsley, Philip and Martin, together with Hilly and Alastair Kilmarnock and Jaime, had gathered for an 'introductory dinner' at Gardnor House. All seemed to be going well until the dessert course, when an incident occurred which Martin describes as 'completely unbelievable'. At this point, Jaime reached towards the fruitbowl, which 'contained oranges, apples, grapes – and a single peach':

> As Jaime's fingers met its surface, Kingsley, like a man hailing a cab across the length of Oxford Circus during a downpour on Christmas Eve, shouted:
> – *HEY!!!*
> . . . It was an extraordinary manifestation, hideously harsh, hideously sudden. The sound Kingsley had uttered would have been just about appropriate if Jaime had reached, not for a peach, but for the pin of a hand grenade. There was no silence: everyone reeled back, groaning, swearing. Even Jaime whispered 'Jesus Christ' as he shrivelled up in his chair. I can't remember – I can't even imagine – how we survived the rest of the evening.[8]

It is, of course, very far from 'completely unbelievable' (and that isn't what Martin unironically means). On the contrary, Kingsley's outburst precisely encapsulates two interconnected aspects of his response to this strange occasion: one is the explosively released pent-up tension of a man who finds himself entertaining his happily married first ex-wife, shortly to be his housekeeper, in the house of his absent second wife; the other is the stark revelation of a self never far from his surface – the uncertain lower-middle-class boy with an instinctive greed for pleasure he might be denied. The deserted adult in him needed a companionable housekeeper; the insecure child needed a sympathetic mother. Hilly would have to be both.

Soon after he married Hilly, David Shackleton Bailey had been offered a chair at Michigan and in 1968 – the year Donald Davie left Essex for California – they moved to Ann Arbor; for a while Hilly and a friend, Connie Basil, ran an 'English' fish-and-chip shop there, stoically called Lucky Jim's. The marriage was rocky from the start. Two years later, after a summer holiday in Europe, she and Sally stayed on at Ronda in Andalusia instead of returning to America with Bailey; she worked for a year as a matron in the international school in Seville, where Sally became a pupil. Meanwhile at Ronda, they had met the proprietor of the nearby Casa de Mondragón language school, Alastair Boyd: this, like most of his ventures in the business world, wasn't a financial success, although the bar he and Hilly subsequently ran in Ronda was – so roaring a success, in fact, that it was closed down by the police. Alastair inherited his title, without money or property, in 1975; two years later, he and Hilly were at last able to marry. They returned to England, where Alastair took his seat in the Lords and inherited a cottage in Thornburgh, Buckinghamshire; there, to make ends meet, Hilly had yet another unconventional shot at catering, this time running a mobile hot-dog van with a friend from the village. But the Kilmarnocks felt isolated without a London base, and the only way they could afford this was for Hilly to take a job which included accommodation. She began to search for something suitable among the classified advertisements in the *Lady*. Then Philip rang, proposing almost exactly what she'd been looking for, with one unexpected twist.

The sale of Gardnor House dragged on until the end of the year, accompanied by escalating rancour. Although Jane had been the original property owner, Kingsley had contributed most to their joint bank account: much of what the house contained he had paid for, even if he hadn't seemed to notice it. Now he noticed with a vengeance: 'when she came to the house in my pre-arranged absence for her to collect her "share" of the contents she rifled the place, taking all the best crockery, glassware, etc., including the remains of a case of decent claret a club-mate had given me for doing him a favour'.[9] (Jane says, as seems more than likely, that the best crockery and glassware had actually been hers from the start.) Meanwhile, the conveyancing solicitor – Jane's solicitor, inevitably – wouldn't release Kingsley's contested share of the sale proceeds, which for a while seemed likely to scupper his chances of buying the house in Kentish Town which Alastair had found for them. In fact, at the start of 1982, after a few weeks in a rented flat, he and the Kilmarnocks moved to 186 Leighton Road, NW5: 'Not a bad area, no violent thick blacks to speak of, but all pubs full of pop. I can't bear the way there's a drum-beat on the third beat of EVERY SINGLE bar.'[10] (He adapted this for a grotesquely 'modernised' pub in *The Old Devils*, where 'a piece of rock music, with the compulsory slap on the third beat of every bar, started up all around them at enormous volume, giving the effect of an omission handsomely redressed'.)[11] To Conquest, he added that they were 'near a little down-market shopping centre where you can't get e.g. China tea or any malt whisky but Glenfiddich . . . The house itself is just right for the four of us, though not large.'[12] He had a small bedroom and a study on the top floor: Philip has perceptively remarked that it was like going back to Kingsley's parents' house in Berkhamsted.[13] It quite soon became clear that the place was too small – just wrong for the four of them, in fact – and three years later the ménage would move on, to a larger house in Primrose Hill.

In leaving Kingsley, Jane had freed both of them to live in the different styles which suited them best. But she had also freed them both as writers. Jane, after a long period of readjustment, would embark on the quartet of novels for which she is now best known: *The Light Years* (1990), *Marking Time* (1992), *Confusion* (1993) and *Casting Off* (1995), the books collectively known as *The Cazalet Chronicle*. These are in the grand English tradition of the country-house novel, and it seems highly unlikely that she would have been able to write them under the same roof as Kingsley. In the unhappy months after her departure, he worked fruitlessly on a book with a homosexual central character, which turned out to be beyond his range: he abandoned the novel, though not the title, *Difficulties with*

Girls. Then came Philip's providential intervention, the arrival of the Kilmarnocks, and the start of *Stanley and the Women*.

2

Stanley and the Women (1984) divides its readers more sharply than any other novel of Kingsley's. Many, including his son Martin, passionately dislike it; some rate it very highly, such as A. N. Wilson, who calls it 'the best of all Amis's novels, and that is saying something';[14] while a still smaller minority (this reader among them) have crossed the floor from the former position to the latter. To do this, of course, involves rereading the novel, something that most people who initially loathed it are unlikely to have done. It also involves acknowledging some colossal flaws, the most immediately striking one being the title, which is not only clumsy and unattractive but also plain wrong (Charlie Norris's helpful distinction between 'bullshit' and 'nonsense' in *The Old Devils* comes to mind). For the most crucial relationship in the novel is the one between Stanley and his mad son Steve, while beyond and underlying this is a series of deeply troubling questions. What happens if you share every aspect of Kingsley's background – Stanley Duke is at least as close to his author in this respect as Peter Furneaux or Robin Davies – but don't have the academic or literary talent? What happens if, in fact, you end up as the advertising manager of a newspaper, and owner of a flashy, ludicrously named car, who is eventually promoted (with a special irony for the non-driving Kingsley) to motoring correspondent? And what happens to this parallel-Kingsley when his son goes off the rails, as his unstable and alcoholic daughter Sally had, and his second wife leaves him, as Jane had? The book that starts from these questions deserves a less reductive title than *Stanley and the Women*.

The title announces, and most readers unthinkingly accept, that the novel's central, intemperate quarrel is between genders, whereas it is just as vitally between classes: specifically, between a rough-edged, hard-drinking man from SW16 and his bookish, privately educated wife from a few rungs further up the social ladder. Stanley Duke's background is of such importance because he feels it explains him. It's what has made him the sort of man he is; in this sense it becomes his apologia, and Kingsley's. Although Stanley tells us that

he 'left South London for good as soon as I had the chance', he hasn't
entirely escaped:

> what I saw from the Apfelsine was the same as ever, was cramped,
> thrown up on the cheap and never finished off, needing a lick of
> paint, half empty and everywhere soiled, in fact very like my old
> part as noticed when travelling to and from an uncle's funeral a
> few weeks back. Half the parts south of the river were never
> proper places at all, just collections of assorted buildings filling up
> gaps and named after railway stations and bus garages. Most
> people I knew seemed to come from a place – Cliff Wainwright
> and I got out of an area.[15]

Cliff Wainwright, Stanley's GP, 'came from one station up the
Clapham Junction line from me but had done a thorough job on his
accent, only letting out an unreconstructed SW16 vowel about every
other visit'.[16] The transformed accent resembles Kingsley's own,
sharply recalling his conversation on the subject (and brief reversion
to unreconstructed SW16) with Jane at Cheltenham; while the two
references to actual places explicitly identify Stanley's background as
Kingsley's, in marked contrast to the geographical sidestepping which
takes place in *The Riverside Villas Murder* and *You Can't Do Both*.
Explaining his fear of doctors, he urges his wife Susan to 'remember
I'm a boy from SW16 whose parents were so much in awe of the
doctor that they might have let him die of blood-poisoning rather
than do what the doctor didn't order'.[17] Towards the end of the
novel, when Susan has left him and he seeks temporary solace in the
arms of the Irish (and thus, to him, not class-badged) journalist
Lindsey Lucas, Stanley assumes not only his author's background but
his ancestry. Responding to Lindsey's assertion that he's 'not really
Jewish at all', he replies: 'No. My grandfather came from East
Anglia.' She then suggests that he's 'lower-class': 'I was before I came
up in the world, true, but lower-middle-class, not working-class. Very
important distinction. My old dad got really wild if you said he was
working-class. Worse than calling him a Jew.'[18] Kingsley's grandfather, as we've seen, came from East Anglia, and the distinction
between 'lower middle class' and 'working class' was a crucial one in
pre-war South London. As for the matter of Jewishness, Kingsley
elsewhere recalled that his father 'had a decent big nose that caused
him, so he said, to be occasionally mistaken for a Jew by Jews; our

name, with its closeness to Amos, may have contributed to this'.[19] Stanley's passing reference – in the face of his son's sudden and deranged anti-Semitism – to 'the kind of mildly anti-semitic remarks that came naturally to someone like me born where and when I was'[20] is also part of this context. To the unpoliticised lower middle class of pre-war Norbury, Jews were, like Welshmen or Irishmen or Indians, people with comical names and amusingly different customs, the stuff of knockabout humour. Kingsley never lost his innocent pleasure in such differences and sometimes caused unintended offence as a result – as when he adapted the name of his schoolfriend Richenberg for the party-giving Reichenbergers in *I Want It Now* – but he wasn't anti-Semitic. Nor is Stanley.

No, the defining baggage Stanley carries is that of class. It's the consequences of class, Lindsey Lucas suggests (and it's vitally important within the novel that this suggestion should come from a woman), that have made Susan 'mad. Off her educated head.'[21] Lindsey, who knew Susan before Stanley met her, explains that she was taken away from school and tutored at home: 'You think of what happens at school, at any school. There are two things everyone gets plenty of, enough and to spare, especially at first – opposition and competition. Susan hates those. She won't have them.'[22] At home, she was indulged, not least by her 'archetype of the ridiculously indulgent father who worships the ground his little gel walks on and, you know, fancies her quite a bit'.[23] At Oxford, she had a breakdown and didn't sit Finals. Much of this, apart from Oxford, which looks like an arbitrary stab at distancing, is cruelly close to Jane: she is the catalyst who supplies *Stanley and the Women* with its furious energy, just as Daddy B did for *Lucky Jim*. But to describe Kingsley's attitude towards her as one of 'hatred' or to call the novel 'misogynistic' is to miss the point: that facet of the book is a howl of disappointment and pain which, even more than *Jake's Thing*, could only have been written by a man who had invested everything in his love for the wrong woman. As Stanley says quite early in the novel, recalling the end of his first marriage and clearly voicing his author's feelings after the end of his second: 'Stopping being married to someone is an incredibly violent thing to happen to you, not easy to take in completely, ever.'[24] Here again, as in *Jake's Thing*, the tone of the last page is of huge importance. After Susan's presumed self-injury and departure, Stanley and his doctor friend Cliff get blokeishly drunk in a pub before returning to Cliff's home and wife Sandra, who embraces Stanley 'with all the warmth of a recent rape victim'. Then the phone rings.

> 'Oh Stanley, thank God you're there,' said Susan's voice. 'I was going to give up if you weren't. Can you ever forgive me?'
> 'What for?' I said.
> 'Well, for those terrible things I said to you.'
> 'Oh, those.'
> While she hurried on about having been so desperately frightened and upset and one thing and another I turned towards Cliff, who did the brief lift of the chin South London people use to mean Told you so or Here we go again or Wouldn't you bleeding know. People elsewhere too, I dare say. Perhaps all over the world.[25]

There isn't a finer conclusion in all Kingsley's fiction. On the one hand, that dumb-show of South London solidarity does much to justify Cliff's astringent presence in the novel, reaffirming and rounding off the class theme. On the other, the rueful note of resignation and acceptance that women are necessarily different from and mysterious to men – that this is a universal truth which we'll all have to live with – essentially qualifies the book's more excitable moments.

The intentionally shocking blasts of misogyny don't originate from Stanley. They are shrewdly placed. The ominously named Inspector Fairchild, who sorts out Steve's invasive attempt on an Arab embassy, dryly remarks of 'the Major Fuads of this world' that 'They do seem to have got the women problem sorted out nice and neat.'[26] (That grimly funny 'nice and neat' is characteristic of the novel's comic edge, as are the constantly swapping commercial attachés at the Penangan High Commission, who appear to Stanley to be called Mr One and Mr Two and who transform his own name, 'Mr Duke', into 'Mr Joke'.) Cliff Wainwright, whose origin 'one station up the Clapham Junction line' symbolically allows him views one notch more extreme than Stanley's, thinks that women are 'like Russians – if you did what they wanted all the time you were being realistic and constructive and promoting the cause of peace, and if you ever stood up to them you were resorting to cold-war tactics and pursuing imperialistic designs and interfering in their internal affairs';[27] this was certainly a view that Kingsley himself liked to put forward too, in his disconcerting, not-quite-joking mode of the time. That the villainous Dr Collings is a woman, though necessary to the book as titled, isn't initially the main point: at first, she is simply one more in Kingsley's procession of stupid, inhuman and destructive psychiatrists. It's the male (and plainly mad) Dr Nash who, having quite early on offered 'the proposition that all women are mad',[28] eventually completes Stanley's disbelieving formulation of what he's being told: ' "I thought you were saying . . . that Dr Collings was getting at me out of sheer malice, and I *thought* you meant that she was simply trying to . . ." "Fuck you up because you were a man," said Nash, disconcerting me to some extent.'[29] Beside Messrs Fairchild, Wainwright and Nash, Stanley himself appears hurt, vulnerable, impressionable and decent. 'You are a nice man, Stanley,' says his first wife, Nowell, and he later tells her: 'I miss you. Every day.'[30] Kingsley had said exactly the same of Hilly, not long after they parted in 1963; *Stanley and the Women* is dedicated to her.

Stanley's niceness renders him uncomprehendingly defenceless in the face of his son's schizophrenia. Because he doesn't understand what is happening to Steve, he is at the mercy of all those who think they do: his wife, his ex-wife, his GP, the doctors Nash and Collings (only Nowell, Steve's mother, seems actually to affect his behaviour positively, persuading him to go to hospital and to climb down out of a tree). At its most challenging level, the novel poses a series of questions about the nature of madness, of which Kingsley himself felt he'd had more than a glimpse at the time. Nash, whose own deranged state only becomes clear quite late in the book, gets most of the best lines, delivering a sound argument for Hamlet's madness being only a pretence as well as a robustly Kingsleyesque definition of sanity: 'The rewards for being sane may not be very many but knowing what's funny is one of them.'[31] But, as Polonius asks, 'What is't to be mad?' Everyone in the book seems to be, one way or another; even Stanley, for all his apparent straightforwardness, may be a far from reliable narrator. Appearances can, after all, be deceptive: thus, when Stanley encounters 'a tall thin woman with a froth of white hair, a tic, a frown and a mouth that moved vigorously' in the grounds of the mental hospital, St Kevin's, the only surprise is that she has 'a copy of the *Journal of Behavioural Psychology* under her arm, which I felt must have meant something'.[32] There are no simple answers, and it's a strength of the novel that none are cobbled together. In the end, Steve 'has a good chance', and there's a good chance too that Stanley and Susan will resume their marriage. It's the best they can hope for.

3

The furious energy that powers *Stanley and the Women* wasn't just the result of breaking up with Jane. It had other causes, both political and personal. When Margaret Thatcher became Prime Minister in May 1979, a disenchanted former lefty such as Kingsley couldn't fail to be delighted: 'Bloody good, eh?'[33] He had met her, through Conquest, in January that year and at the Conservative Party Conference in October delivered, at her invitation, a lecture called 'An Arts Policy': in it, he attacked the 'traditional Lefty view, the belief that anybody can enjoy art, real art, in the same way that everybody is creative' and the concept of 'community arts'[34] – the 'New Cultural Policy' of *Russian Hide and Seek*, in fact. He remained a staunch supporter of hers during and after the Falklands War; Larkin, on the other hand, had reservations which he intended to mention to her when they met in late 1982. Kingsley knew better: 'If you did tell her what you thought I'll warrant you got a flea in your ear. She doesn't like being disagreed with. FUCKING WOMAN SEE . . .'[35] By 1984, although he told Conquest 'I still bat for her,'[36] he acknowledged her waning popularity – and, beyond that, a sense that the shittiness of things in general hadn't notably decreased. The rudeness for which he was now famous grew more intense and more unpredictable, often directed at close friends. Zachary Leader cites the telling example of a dinner given by Donald Trelford, editor of the *Observer*, on 28 October 1982 at the Garrick, in delayed recognition of Kingsley's sixtieth birthday; the other guests were Martin, Anthony Howard, Terence Kilmartin, Blake Morrison, Clive James, Julian Barnes, Alan Watkins, Geoff Nicholson and Hugh McIlvanney – all friends with strong *Observer*ish connections. According to Watkins, Kingsley's reply to Trelford's toast began: 'I just want to make a few remarks. The first thing I've got to say to you is that the *Observer* is a bloody awful paper.'[37] The anger, like the rudeness, is rooted in internal conflict: the *Observer* might have been designed to set warring the lefty and Conservative factions within him. What does the instinctive, faltering liberal do when his world starts to fall apart? He rages against the dying of the light. Kingsley would also have relished his momentary transformation into Prince Philip, who once described the pugnaciously royalist *Daily Express* as 'a bloody awful paper'.

By some distance the shittiest thing to happen to him personally during the writing of *Stanley* was a nocturnal fall on 10 March 1982 which left him with a broken leg and six months' compulsory abstinence from alcohol. Earlier that day he'd attended the annual lunch of the Society of Snuff Grinders, Blenders and Purveyors, and found the Society 'as generous as ever with its hospitality'; on the way home he'd 'paused' at his club. Once home, he 'added a few lines to my current novel, drank some gin, ate supper, watched "Minder" on television, drank some whisky and, having taken a sleeping pill, one of the Mogadon group, eventually retired upstairs. Not an altogether exceptional day.'[38] He was keen, like most people who injure themselves while drunk, to play up the ludicrous and mitigating aspects of the accident itself, telling Larkin that 'I broke my right tibia standing up, trying to avoid an alcoholic fall'[39] and offering Conquest this piece of casuistry: 'A drunken fall? Well, yes, even if what I did was to break them [tibia and fibula] *standing up*, trying to avoid a fall which I would have done much better to give in to.'[40] During his three weeks' stay in the Royal Free Hospital, Hampstead, he experienced the 'peep round the twist' – 'nothing spectacular, just a few voices and non-existent cats' – described in *Memoirs*.[41] While he was there, Jane sent him a proof copy of her new and most Kingsleyesque novel, *Getting It Right*: 'I thought it was quite good, but at the same time not-much-good enough to encourage me a good deal to get on with mine.'[42]

He was delighted to discover that giving up booze was painless and free from side effects, but in gratefully noting that he had 'no chemical dependency' he was wise enough to realise that this didn't preclude a psychological one. Once home, he found the indignities of crutches and commode (which of course he called 'Kermode', after the distinguished critic Frank Kermode) only marginally offset by the pleasure of being a pampered invalid. What he most wanted to do was to get on with *Stanley*, but he ruefully realised that, being stuck in one room, 'you don't get much work done, words on paper that is, because you spend too much time at it. Essential to idle and get pissed half the time to accumulate energy etc. for when you do work.'[43] Although he couldn't drink, he could still eat: he began to take comfort in comfort food, including calory-intensive midnight raids on the kitchen. By November, he had become 'enormously fat, but feel slimmer as a result of buying trousers MEASURING FORTY TWO INCHES ROUND THE WAIST instead of wearing my old 38's I think about an inch and a half above my cock'. That same afternoon, he told Larkin (who would helpfully reply that he now wore trousers with a 46-inch waist), he was to 'go down to my dentist and he will put A METAL PLATE WITH FALSE TEETH ON IT into my mouth'.[44] He was still only sixty years old.

Despite all this, the early 1980s were in other respects a regenerative time for Kingsley. His new domestic arrangements suited him, and he had a brave stab at concealing any regrets at the passing of the old ones: spending Christmas 'getting drunk with old George Gale' seemed to him a better bet than traipsing round 'the effing Wess Tend' in search of expensive presents for Jane. His work on *Stanley* during 1983 went well, punctuated by enjoyable irritations such as Penguin's promotion of books 'by our leading young novelists' who were either 'no good in the sense you can't bear what they're doing' (Ian McEwan, Clive Sinclair, Graham Swift) or 'no good in the sense you can't see he's doing anything' (William Boyd). 'Don't know what to say about M**t** A***,' he added.[45] After delivering *Stanley* in February 1984, he took on the most improbable – and, he said, the most enjoyable – commission of his life: a year's stint as 'Poetry Editor' of the *Daily Mirror*, choosing a poem a day and adding a brief introductory note, until his contract was terminated by the paper's new proprietor, the 'mad Czech [Robert] Maxwell'.[46] But that year was marred by the death of his friend John Betjeman on 19 May, of whom he shrewdly remarked to Conquest: 'He'll go down to history as a genial teddy-bear figure beloved of all while a nice old softie like me will be taken as a curmudgeonly old shit.'[47] It troubled him that, among the drafts, manuscripts, typescripts and papers he was at that moment having to sell – to finance his purchase of 194 Regents Park Road – were eleven letters from Betjeman: 'No getting round that, I'm afraid.'[48]

Kingsley and the Kilmarnocks finally moved to their house in Primrose Hill on 17 July 1985. After some modest reorganisation, it was to become a place in which, as Eric Jacobs puts it, 'All parties could lead their own lives, interact with each other as necessary and

come together when they wanted.'[49] Writing to Conquest soon after
the move, Kingsley made his priorities clear: 'Here we are then, in
just a week ago, study, drinks cupboard and telly (one on every floor)
in operation, which is all that matters really.' So that was all right.
Meanwhile: 'My Welsh novel trudges on, coming up to 200 book-
pages.'[50]

4

That 'Welsh novel' was of course *The Old Devils* (1986). The idea
for it came to him during one of his regular summer visits to Swansea,
as he 'was putting his shoes on to go down to the Yacht Club' for a
lunchtime drinking session with his friends Eve and Stuart Thomas.[51]
It was an idea that had been waiting to occur since 1979, when he
judged the Arts Council's Fiction Prize and read Christopher Hood's
The Other Side of the Mountain. Noting among Hood's characters
'the television Welshman' and 'the perpetually over-reacting Englishman', Kingsley also observed: 'The South Welsh (never mind the
North) are hard to write about. Outsiders notice noticeable details
and produce a caricature; natives turn romantic (or Gothic) and
produce a fantasy.'[52] It sounds, even then, as if he were setting himself
a challenge; in other respects, too, the book assumes an inevitable-
looking place in the jigsaw of his fiction. It's an oblique sequel to
That Uncertain Feeling, a more sympathetic and inward portrait of
the Gruffyd-Williams set in later years; a partial revisitation of *Take
a Girl like You* in Rhiannon's Jenny Bunn-like episodes and memories; an airier, more expansive variation on the theme of *Ending Up*;
and a companion piece to its immediate predecessor – for, if *Stanley
and the Women* is partly about a lack of local identity (what happens
if you come from a place that isn't a place), *The Old Devils* has a
surfeit of the stuff. Ironically for someone who'd written three so-
called country-house novels without bothering much about the conventions of the genre, *The Old Devils* applies those principles – a
pack of eight or so main characters to be shuffled within a socially
insulated context – not to a country house but to a country.

The book is complicated by the ghostly presence of two poets.
One is Larkin, who was seriously ill while Kingsley was writing and
who died, on 2 December 1985, as the novel was nearing completion.

Its title points to Larkin's poem 'The Old Fools' and there are
numerous verbal echoes, such as Charlie Norris's quite contented
reflection that 'Life was first boredom, then more boredom'[53] (the
original, 'Life is first boredom, then fear', is in 'Dockery and Son').
Malcolm Cellan-Davies's jazz record collection, and his discographi-
cal expertise concerning it, is exactly in line with Larkin's tastes, as is
his gleeful response to the ghastly Percy Morgan's request for (late)
Basie or Ellington, Gil Evans, or 'Coltrane or Kirk or anybody like
that': '"Not a damn bit of use, boy," said Malcolm with hostile
relish. "And my Basies stop in 1939 and my Ellingtons about 1934.
And no, no Gil Evans – I seem to recall a baritone man of that or a
similar name playing with somebody like Don Redman, though you
obviously don't mean him."'[54] There's a good deal more of this:
Malcolm's views on jazz – soundly anti-modernist, like Larkin's
combative introduction to *All What Jazz* – are confirmation, in
Amis–Larkin code, of the admirable character beneath his social
awkwardness. As the book progressed and his friend's health deteriorated, Kingsley increasingly tried to involve Larkin in it: in his
penultimate letter, on 17 November, he mentioned that the novel
would include 'a Dylan-like character ... safely long dead' and
wondered whether Larkin might 'run me up half a dozen lines of sub-
Thomas to come swimming back into someone's head'.[55] He meant
to amuse the patient, but it was too late. The best Larkin could do
was to suggest recycling some of the earlier sub-Thomas from *That
Uncertain Feeling*.

For Thomas is, perhaps unexpectedly, the other poet who haunts
The Old Devils. At first glance, Kingsley's attitude towards him looks
unambiguous: Thomas's biographer George Tremlett asserted that he
had 'spent the past 30 years (ie 1958–88) abusing Dylan Thomas in
print',[56] and those dates exclude *Memoirs* (1991). In fact, he began
to abuse Thomas much earlier than that, while still at Oxford,
recognising him as a bad influence on his own (and on Larkin's)
work: 'I think I have traced the nastiness of my early words to the
influence of Mister Dylan Thos.' He found himself 'VIOLENTLY
WISHING that the man WERE IN FRONT OF ME, so that I could
be DEMONIACALLY RUDE to him about his GONORRHEIC
RUBBISH, and end up by WALKING ON HIS FACE and PUNCH-
ING HIS PRIVY PARTS.'[57] When the man *was* actually in front of
him, in Swansea four years later, he failed to carry out this plan but

remained unimpressed: 'that crazy Welch fellow came here to give a talk; I went to the pub and found him half-stewed before the meeting ... His conversation consisted of one or two written-out solos and a string of very dirty and very not funny limericks ... His talk was horrible: shagged epigrams topped up with some impressionistic stuff about America ... And the poems he spoke out with his mouth: ooh corks!!!'[58] *Memoirs* contains a detailed three-page account of this occasion, after which Kingsley adds: 'Thomas was an outstandingly unpleasant man, one who cheated and stole from his friends and peed on their carpets.'[59] In 1985, while at work on *The Old Devils*, he summed him up succinctly: 'Piss with froth on, you remember.'[60]

Yet when in 1986 Stuart Thomas invited him to become one of the Trustees of the Dylan Thomas Literary Estate, Kingsley not only accepted but conscientiously fulfilled his responsibilities. He still didn't care for the poems, despite managing on one occasion to assure Stuart Thomas somewhat disingenuously that Dylan Thomas's 'ear was always impeccable',[61] nor for the 'false, sentimentalising, melodramatising, sensationalising, ingratiating' portrait of Wales in *Under Milk Wood*;[62] but there were aspects of the prose – the young provincial in London of *Adventures in the Skin Trade* or the pub crawl to unreached Porthcawl in 'A Story' – that must have struck a more sympathetic note. Certainly, that pub crawl seems to lurk behind *The Old Devils*, as does the figure of Thomas himself, in the disguise of Brydan (1913–60), a poet whose work possesses all the characteristics Kingsley detested in *Under Milk Wood*, together with a popularity tinged with reverence to an extent which seems improbable even in Wales. The catalyst for the book's mostly low-key action is the return home, after years in London, of Alun Weaver and his wife Rhiannon. Alun is a poet and all-round hack, author and editor of books on Brydan and on Wales, as well as a television personality whose face is sufficiently well known to attract autograph-hunters (though not nearly as many as he would like). He is, in fact, a media-friendly Professional Welshman, rather in the way that Melvyn Bragg is a media-friendly Professional Cumbrian: it's probable that Kingsley had Bragg, whose *South Bank Show* he disliked and satirically disparaged in letters,[63] in mind as a model. But although he seems to belong in the line of irredeemable anti-heroes that began with Roger Micheldene, he is more complex and interesting than that.

To start with, he clearly has a good deal of his author about him:

Kingsley himself had, after all, come to regard Wales as a sort of
spiritual home and was a great returner to it; and the days had long
gone when he could poke fun at the studied rudeness and deluded
grandeur of a successful writer without the joke at least partly
rebounding on himself. From the moment we meet the Weavers in
the second chapter, travelling to Wales by train rather than by car
because having a fixed time and place of arrival is a better way to get
noticed, it's clear that Alun is to be treated with affectionate rather
than contemptuous wryness. He's an appalling sexual philanderer,
whose exploits in late middle age recall those of a much younger
Kingsley, somewhat mitigated by roguish charm. Although no one
who knows him well has an unequivocally good word to say for him,
they are actually glad to see him: he's at the centre of every scene in
which he appears. His set-piece rudenesses – for which, partly because
they look so orchestrated, so 'performed', he is applauded and
forgiven – have a pedigree stretching back through Ronnie Appleyard's attack on Student Mansfield all the way to Jim Dixon's lecture.
This, for instance, is what happens when the luckless Malcolm
demands an 'explanation' of the encounter which he (correctly)
suspects has taken place between his wife Gwen and Alun:

> 'You're the feeblest creature God ever put breath into,' said Alun.
> 'Why any woman should have spent thirty-three minutes married
> to you, let alone thirty-three years, defies comprehension. You've
> no idea in the world of what pleases a woman: in other words' –
> he seemed to be choosing these with care – 'you're not only
> hopeless as an organizer of life in general, you're a crashingly
> boring companion into the bargain and needless to say, er, peren-
> nially deficient in the bedroom. Correct?'[64]

Alun's startlingly sudden demise, also at the centre of a scene, is less
a moral judgement than a practical necessity: his disruptive energy
has to be extinguished before the book can reach its benign conclusion.

As with other novels centred on a group rather than on an
individual (*The Anti-Death League* is the best example), Kingsley
spreads himself between several characters. 'Keep the reader guessing
– wch the Amis char?' reads one of his notes for the novel in
progress.[65] One useful consequence of this is that it allows self-
contradictory bits of him to quarrel or to misunderstand each other,

as they did in reality. The two fat men, Charlie Norris and Peter Thomas, are cases in point. Charlie, who with his gay brother Victor owns a restaurant called the Glendower, shares with Alun, Peter and his creator a relish of (not necessarily deeply held) right-wing opinions, so together they have:

> a lovely time seeing who could say the most outrageous thing about the national Labour Party, the local Labour Party, the Labour-controlled county council, the trade unions, the education system, the penal system, the Health Service, the BBC, black people and youth. (Not homosexuals today.) They varied this with eulogies of President Reagan, Enoch Powell, the South African government, the Israeli hawks and whatever his name was who ran Singapore.[66]

Merely to create this list, in this mildly satirical tone, is to compromise it: 'seeing who could say the most outrageous thing' was precisely the game Kingsley himself so much enjoyed playing. But later in the novel Charlie has a much more serious and disturbing authorial experience. While visiting the coastal village of Birdarthur, famous as Brydan's retreat and as memorabilia-encrusted as Thomas's Laugharne, Alun unwisely shows Charlie the opening pages of a book he's writing about returning to Wales and is affronted by the bullshit-free response he receives. Partly in revenge, he allows Charlie – who, as he knows, shares Kingsley's phobias about darkness and being alone – to walk home from the pub to the cottage where they are staying, in the dark and on his own. Charlie's resulting panic attack, in which he turns 'a curious colour, that of a red-faced man gone very pale' and utters an unstoppable high-pitched wailing, is based on an attack experienced by Kingsley during a weekend party given by the philanthropist Drue Heinz and helplessly witnessed by Jane towards the end of their marriage. It is only terminated, and explained, by the arrival of Victor and a syringe of Largactil, a strong tranquilliser: 'He's not mad, if that's what you're wondering. An attack of depersonalization. Panic brought on by being cut off from the possibility of immediate help and then self-renewing. Very frightening, I imagine. Well, we haven't got to imagine, have we?'[67] In that carefully ambiguous sentence, Victor is saying not only that we don't need to imagine (because we've seen it) but also, and far more importantly, that we couldn't really imagine the experience even if we tried – any more than Jane was able to imagine what Kingsley was going through. And although Alun shortly afterwards admits to Rhiannon that 'It's the worst thing I've ever done,'[68] even this, given what we and she know of him, can't help seeming like damage-limitation. The complexity of the scene – one of the finest in all Kingsley's fiction – derives from the way in which Alun's prickliness about criticism and readiness to play a blokeish practical joke on a vulnerable friend are as much part of the author as the panic and depersonalisation. Kingsley knew not only that he was Alun as often as he was Charlie, but also that he was Alun *because* he was Charlie. Thus is the divided self transformed into fiction.

Peter, rather more straightforwardly, counters the boredom of a long and hopeless marriage (which will end when his wife Muriel quite amiably leaves him in the penultimate chapter) with nocturnal binge-eating which, like Kingsley, he blames partly on giving up smoking. His son William, as Peter squeezes with difficulty into his car, addresses him in the unmistakable voice of another son: 'You know you're enormously fat, do you? Fatter than ever? No-joke fat?' And Peter's reply is pure Kingsley:

> 'I'm very good during the day, marvellous during the day, a lettuce-leaf here and half a sardine there, and then I'm sitting on my arse with the telly finished and I start stuffing myself. Cakes mostly. Profiteroles. Brandy-snaps. Anything with cream or jam or chocolate. Also cake, Genoa cake, Dundee cake with almonds. Seed cake with a glass of Malmsey. Like some Victorian female only this is one o'clock in the morning.'[69]

In the comic symmetry of the novel's denouement, the deserted Peter's reward is a domestic ménage with the widowed Rhiannon, an event precipitated by the marriage of their respective children, William and Rosemary. Rhiannon is, indeed, an older and wiser Jenny Bunn: not only does her husband share several of Patrick Standish's least admirable qualities, her chaste excursion with poor Malcolm inevitably recalls Jenny's disastrous evening with Graham McLintock in *Take a Girl like You*. Her generosity – and indeed the very fact that Kingsley could again create a central female character for whom he felt such gratitude and affection – says much about Jenny's other older and wiser counterpart. Gratitude and affection are what Malcolm feels for her in the closing pages, as he tidies up his jazz records and resumes work on his translation, 'more of an adaptation, actually', of a medieval Welsh poem: 'If she had found love with Peter he was glad, because he had nothing to give her himself. But she had given him something. The poem, his poem, was going to be the best tribute he could pay to the only woman who had ever cried for him.'[70] If it's not precisely a happy ending, it's an accepting and consoling one – the kind of ending Larkin would have understood and endorsed. In his address at his friend's funeral on 9 December 1985, Kingsley identified these qualities in Larkin's poems: 'They are not dismal or pessimistic, but invigorating; they know that for all its shortcomings life must be got on with.'[71]

Yet *The Old Devils* isn't without its faults. One is the lack of focus which is the negative consequence of the 'group' arrangement; some readers find it difficult to engage with a bunch of rather similar characters whose main occupation is getting drunk in South Wales. Another is the unevenness of the writing, which includes passages of unusual carefulness (the subtly detailed pages on the Weavers' arrival at Swansea station, for instance) and alarming looseness (trailing sentences with their dependent clauses propped up by nothing more substantial than commas). *Stanley and the Women* is a technically sharper and better-organised novel, but it was *The Old Devils* which won the Booker Prize in 1986. The judges' decision wasn't by any means unanimous, despite the diplomatic efforts of the chairman, Anthony Thwaite, to make it appear so; and there was a suspicion, rebutted by Thwaite,[72] that the award was implicitly retrospective, taking in books such as *Jake* and *Stanley* which would have divided a judging panel even more deeply. Kingsley was thrilled, in his acceptance speech announcing his instant conversion from the view that literary prizes were trivial and worthless to a new-found respect for them. He was also encouraged to press ahead speedily with his next novel, *Difficulties with Girls* (1988).

The best and the worst one can say of this book is that Kingsley knew exactly what he was doing: 'when you're old enough you can get away with piss, cf G Greene', he told Conquest,[73] shortly before it was published. It's a fateful combination of two terrible ideas: an eight-years-after sequel to *Take a Girl like You* combined with some residual gay characters from the abandoned 'Difficulties with Girls'. Among the many pleasures of *Take a Girl like You* is the poised uncertainty of the ending, which doesn't actually state that Jenny and

Patrick will marry: a deliberate ambiguity which was sabotaged in
the Andrew Davies-scripted BBC television version by a clodhopping
epilogue in Patrick's voice, explaining not only that they did, which
is bad enough, but that the marriage turned out differently from that
portrayed in *Difficulties with Girls*, which is worse. *Difficulties with
Girls* finds Patrick, now a publisher, and Jenny, now a part-time
teacher of disturbed children in a local hospital, living just south of
the river in a flat whose address is 1B Lower Ground (close, we may
suppose, to Upper Ground and Lower Marsh). The story concerns
their relationships with their immediate neighbours – who include
Eric and Stevie, a gay couple, and Tim Valentine (*né* Vatcher), who
merely thinks he's gay – and with people in the world of publishing:
much the best of these is an elderly Irish novelist called Deirdre, 'not
merely an Irishwoman and an old Irishwoman but a bloody woman
as well',[74] whose beautifully manipulative lunch with Patrick brings
the book briefly to life.

Nothing else much does. The Tim–Eric–Stevie plot strand, which
comes pretty close to suggesting that cohabiting gay men spend their
lives quarrelling and ultimately stabbing each other, is too preposterous to bother with; so is Patrick's implausible North London
tryst with Wendy Porter-King (all that's missing is the tape-recorded
'Lucky sod' as he lets himself in with a latchkey); and so too is the
rather promising idea of a literary publishing house taken over and
sold down the river by its smarmy young managing director, which
needs but doesn't receive an Arnold Bennett-like attention to business
detail. Graham McLintock from *Take a Girl like You* puts in a cameo
appearance – he has been shortlisted for a teaching job in Surrey,
which he doesn't get – for no obvious reason except to show that he's
as obtuse as ever and Kingsley can still write his dialogue. Patrick
adds to the least admirable features of his younger self a smattering
of late-Amis exaggerated prejudices. Early on, he reflects that 'molest-
ing' his boss's wife in the office was 'no worse than the act of an
adolescent psychopath – round about par for him, in fact'.[75] Then, as
the novel progresses, there's a coded attack on Jane's fiction (books
about 'baa-lambs and kittens and babies and lovely gardens and
little old cottages');[76] an ambiguous response, anger masking guilt,
to Harold Porter-King's complaint about 'all these funny-looking
people coming over here from wherever they live and seeming to
think it's all right for them to settle down in any place of ours';[77] a

self-cancelling denial of anti-Semitism in 'He was so far from being anti-Semitic that a couple of his best friends really were Jews';[78] a milder version of Charlie's panic attack ('he felt as if his mind was not his any more, no longer his . . . he made a continuous babble on a low note with his lips and tongue').[79] With characteristic sidestepping, however, it's Eric who tells Patrick that women are like children: 'They're different from us. More like children. Crying when things go wrong. Making difficulties just so as to be a person.'[80] That sounds very like post-Jane Kingsley. In fact, it's an almost exact paraphrase – with one vital omission – of a draft poem Kingsley sent to Conquest on 23 April 1987, while writing *Difficulties with Girls*, which opens (and closes) with the couplet: 'Women and queers and children / Cry when things go wrong.'[81]

Jenny seems to have deteriorated since *Take a Girl like You*. She has learned to read Patrick shrewdly but very little else: she is staggeringly naive – especially about the gay neighbours[82] – and encumbered, in the sections seen from her point of view, with dreadful bits of cod-northern diction ('But it was right amazing . . .', 'an old man with something terrible wrong with one side of his face . . .').[83] Her soppiness over animals and plants is vaguely attributed to her childlessness – she has had a miscarriage some years earlier – and may or may not be cured by her announcement of pregnancy which ends the book. But it's as hard to believe that she's a woman in her late twenties, living in London in 1967, as it is to accept Patrick, with his dreadful old-buffer diction and his secret porno magazines, as a bright and attractive man of thirty-six. Kingsley evidently chose the year because it saw the legalisation of homosexual acts between men over twenty-one; one section is set on the day the bill was approved in Parliament. However, he seems to have forgotten everything else about it: a background which ought to be brilliantly coloured is drab and uncertain, while Jenny and Patrick would surely have noticed that this was the year of *Sergeant Pepper's Lonely Hearts Club Band* and the 'Summer of Love'. Someone should have reminded Kingsley that 'to be against the Beatles (late-middle period) is to be against life'.[84] Perhaps someone did, and he forgot.

5

The failure of *Difficulties with Girls* isn't simply a matter of a prize-winning author, in his mid-sixties but physically older than his years, complacently going through the motions and turning out a potboiler. Kingsley's most characteristic phases – the novels of the 1950s, the emotional modulation through *Jake* and *Stanley* to *The Old Devils* – are rooted in periods of anger and unrest. Once settled in Primrose Hill, he became settled in other ways: the force of habit which found him so reliably at his desk at set times each day had less desirable consequences. His life moved to a fixed schedule between fixed points: the Queen's, his local pub; the Garrick, where he could 'get pissed in jovial not very literary bright *all-male* company';[85] and, apart from the annual three-week outing to Wales, home. In September 1987, reeling under the strain of 'the raised alcohol level' and 'the eating of lethal food' during his Welsh sojourn, he told Conquest: 'My life is just work, family, club (plus Swansea) now and v nice too.'[86] His leisure reading had become confined to popular novels – detective stories, thrillers, science fiction – and in the evenings he watched *Coronation Street* and *The Bill* on television. He listened to music: jazz, which he found had lost some of its savour, on a cassette tape recorder; concerts, as long as they didn't include Mahler or anything much more recent, on Radio 3. But he seldom went out to a concert and never to the theatre, which he had always disliked; the visual arts meant nothing to him, of course. Most of us, as we grow older, become less receptive to the new, in accordance with Conquest's law that people are most conservative about what they know best; yet Kingsley had closed an awful lot of doors, shutting out not only the irritation and the pretension of high culture but also its possible stimulus. He had been working towards this all his life: the fault-line that runs through his career is the reluctance of the boy from SW16 to move in the highest intellectual, academic or artistic circles, preferring instead the safety of pub or club. This didn't matter while unexpected events were still hurling themselves at him, however inconveniently, and asking to be turned into fiction. Now, he found he had to recycle the past: each of his last four novels is essentially backward- or inward-looking.

He carried on writing because he had to. Larkin had been exactly wrong for once, when in the last year of his life he told Kingsley: 'My sodding job is the only thing that keeps me going, like the Garrick Club with you (yes, I know you didn't actually say that).'[87] Kingsley didn't say that, because for him it was the sodding job too: turning out a new novel was what kept *him* going. The novel he embarked on after *Difficulties with Girls* was *The Folks that Live on the Hill* (1988), which has a decent claim to be regarded as the most benign of all his books: almost everyone in it emerges in a better light than they deserve, while even those who don't – a hectoring wife named Desirée (like the potato, as someone points out), a poisonous lesbian .called Popsy, and Chris, the crooked manager of an off-licence – escape lightly by the standards of *Jake* or *Stanley*. The book shows the influence of Kingsley's evenings in front of the television: it's arranged precisely like a soap opera, with brief episodes involving minor characters interleaved between more substantial ones for the main players, and its climax (though not quite its final chapter) assembles the entire cast in a reconciliatory pub scene. It would work on television with very little adaptation, which is possibly why it hasn't been adapted.

As in *The Old Devils*, Kingsley divides recognisable aspects of himself between two characters: the brothers Harry and Freddie Caldecote. Harry, the book's engaging linchpin, is a twice-divorced, retired scholarly librarian who lives with his widowed sister Clare and her late husband's recalcitrant dog Towser. Their house is on Shepherd's Hill, and Harry spends much of his leisure time in his local, the King's, and his club, the Irving – so Primrose Hill, the Queen's and the Garrick aren't greatly disguised. Harry's relationship with Clare, like Kingsley's with Hilly, is one of non-sexual, mutually comprehending companionship; when Freddie's terrible wife Desirée makes impertinent suggestions about it, Harry wants 'to tell her that even in 1990 a man could love his sister as his sister and she him as her brother and nothing more', but he knows 'that would never do any good'.[88] Harry, however, has a degree of competence in managing his life which exceeds Kingsley's. It's the dreamy, stamp-collecting, poetry-writing Freddie (at work on a long poem which eventually makes him rich, so it must be worthless) who takes on his author's less practical characteristics, although he owes a good deal to Kingsley's Primrose Hill literary neighbour Peter Quennell, to whom the novel is dedicated. He also shares his author's relish for high-cholesterol vulgar foods, the less likely to be enjoyed by Jane (or Desirée) the better: having just tucked into a bacon butty in a café, he tells Harry that what he'd enjoyed most about it was 'The fact that it wasn't beef Stroganoff or sole bonne femme or steak en croûte or tripe à la mode de Caen.'[89] Several other characters in the book function as, or actually are, members of the Caldecotes' extended family: among them, Harry's charmingly feckless, money-scheming son Piers; his ex-stepdaughter Bunty, entangled with both her partner Popsy and her ex-husband Desmond; and alcoholic, disturbed Fiona, who is Harry's 'first ex-wife's sister's child', as Desirée helpfully explains, adding, 'It isn't as if she's your daughter.' 'Oh yes it is,' Harry replies. 'In every disagreeable and pestiferous way it's exactly as if she's my daughter.'[90]

This introduces in a delicate and good-humoured way the novel's other strand of autobiography, for Fiona is very clearly based on Sally Amis, even down to her trouble with an intermittent Irish boyfriend. Fiona is convinced that her drink problem is inherited from her great-aunt Annie, 'My mother's aunt who drank herself to death',[91] whom she thinks she resembles physically. Harry, when he discovers a photograph of this relative in his own mother's photo-graph album, rips out the page so that he can show it to Fiona and so demonstrate that there's no likeness: 'Not your lineage, not your branch of the family, not somebody who inherited something along with you, not your blood, not your stock. So you're not hemmed in by your ancestry.'[92] A good deal is encoded here; for, as Zachary Leader explains, it was strongly suspected by Kingsley and Hilly – and, from quite early on, by Philip and Martin, though not by Sally herself – that Kingsley was not Sally's father. Leader records Hilly's shock when Philip turned to her, after a male friend of hers had visited their house in Swansea, to say: 'What's Sal's Dad doing here?'[93] Kingsley, almost incredibly, seems never to have mentioned the question of Sally's parentage to anyone – not even in letters to Larkin or Conquest – until this slyly allusive point. Fiona is treated with great sympathy and by the end of the book may even be on the way to recovery, unlike Sally; yet her predicament exposes Kingsley to two charges. One is his recurrent self-rebuke that in being a permissive parent he had actually been a lazy and neglectful one: he ought to have done more to help Sally, just as Harry ought to have done more to help Fiona. The other is that in raising the doubtful question of inherited alcoholism he seems to disclaim responsibility for Sally's: just as Fiona's problems can't be traced to her great-aunt, after all, so Sally's are, genetically at least, nothing to do with him.

The Fiona/Sally subtext accounts for one's otherwise slightly puzzled sense that *The Folks that Live on the Hill* is a more serious book than it seems. Late-Amis preoccupations are batted past in a quite amiable way: we learn of Harry that 'Arms cuts, State education and the Arts Council were the sort of thing he thought he was equal to seeing off'[94] and of Freddie that 'he quite enjoyed novels, or those dating from before about 1950 when they stopped writing them'.[95] In other, less characteristic ways, *The Folks that Live on the Hill* often feels curiously like a travel book without the travelling: there's a spirit of innocent observation which values the entertaining above the strictly relevant – a succession of amusing minicab drivers, the Cypriot vodka fraudster at the off-licence, the comic double act of Asian brothers (they call themselves Charles and, yes, Howard) who run the local post office and convenience store. It's a book in which, rather as with life, important differences are made by things just turning up: that photograph, for instance, or the chalcedony ornament from Clare's late husband's baroque flute which, until the closing pages, we're led to believe might have been filched by Piers in his financially exiguous period. Lightness is all.

6

Kingsley was awarded a knighthood in the 1990 Queen's Birthday Honours List: on the day of his investiture, 25 July, his friends Geoff and Mavis Nicholson accompanied him to the Palace, which was just as well as he'd forgotten to bring his invitation and wouldn't have been admitted if a guard hadn't recognised Mavis from her television appearances. When Gavin Ewart congratulated him, he replied: 'Jolly kind of you to write. I was afraid Spike Milligan would score at the same time. Unworthy thought.'[96] Despite his often deliberately provocative Tory and monarchist views, he hadn't the temperament to become a 'pillar of the establishment'; apart from a few occasions when a pompously exhibitionist touch might lend weight to a good cause, such as the successful campaign to erect a Poets' Corner memorial to Housman in Westminster Abbey, he never mentioned his knighthood again.

Meanwhile, two large-scale non-fiction projects were encouraging him (as if he needed it) in his mood of introspection and retrospection. One was the collection of essays, articles and reviews published as *The Amis Collection* in 1990: the proposal for 'a sequel to *What Became of Jane Austen?*' had been suggested early in 1987 by John McDermott, who was then working on his study *Kingsley Amis: An English Moralist* (1989: its subject preferred the subtitle *An English Dancer on the Optics*).[97] Although the book is introduced by McDermott, it was compiled by a species of shuttle diplomacy – he sending bundles of photocopied uncollected pieces to Kingsley for his approval or disapproval. In the end, despite having expressed some pretty clear opinions, Kingsley found himself overcome by a 'sort of shyness': 'So I am leaving the whole thing to you, the publisher and Jonathan Clowes, though actually I will reserve the right of veto when the selection is made.'[98] This was quite a good way of retaining control without doing much actual work. The result is an extensive but unfocused collection of pieces, arranged in fairly arbitrary sections and not necessarily in chronological or other discernible order within them: a valuable resource which is somehow duller than it ought to have been. A freshly edited volume which combined the best of *What Became of Jane Austen?* and *The Amis Collection* would be a job worth doing well.

The other non-fiction book – one which many of his admirers wish had remained unpublished – was *Memoirs* (1991). The spirit in which he approached it is evident from a letter to Conquest in February 1990: 'Been v.g. fun doing autob., pissing on J Michie, Snowdon, D Cecil, Wain, Muggeridge . . . F Bacon, F Ayer, Wesker, Leo Rosten, Driberg and Roald Dahl, and cracking up Mrs T, Melford Stephenson, Eliz Taylor.'[99] Consequently, he can't, or shouldn't, have been entirely surprised by the 'great volumes of piss poured on me from most quarters' when the book appeared: 'What bad taste to show Muggeridge, Roald Dahl, F Bacon, T Driberg et al in a bad light!'[100] It's actually less the badness of taste, or of light, that does the damage than the boys-behind-the-bikeshed tone: an all-male muckiness, doubtless encouraged by (though surely not typical of) the company Kingsley kept at the Garrick, in which 'piss' figures all too prominently. For *Memoirs* contains not only the allegation concerning Dylan Thomas's treatment of carpets, already quoted, but also accounts of John Braine's drunken overnight stay in Swansea – he was discovered next morning 'with the electric fire full on and near enough to the bed to have caused it to burst into flames had he not rendered the sheets non-inflammable'[101] – and of Philip Larkin mistakenly trusting in the absorbent quality of his clothing after drinking too much beer before a meeting of the Literary Society at Shrewsbury School while Bruce Montgomery was teaching there, an incident recounted to Kingsley in the strictest and immediately regretted confidence. Many readers have thought this padding-out of his contribution to Anthony Thwaite's festschrift *Larkin at Sixty* with unflattering stories which he withheld during his friend's lifetime particularly ill judged.

But the real trouble with *Memoirs* – quite apart from its rancorous tone and surfeit of scurrilous anecdotes – is that it's a lazy and inaccurate book: the laziness is plain from the construction, a series of separate essays (including much recycled material) which don't combine into a coherent autobiography, and the inaccuracy from the disputed recollections of Walter Sullivan or from Kingsley's readiness to foist an anecdote denied by Conquest on to Philip Toynbee, 'whom it fits down to the ground, especially since he's dead'.[102] Even more hurtful than the corrosive portraits of former friends, who at least have the chance to come to a sort of life in them, is the way in which other individuals are airbrushed out completely: most notably Jane, who makes ghostly appearances as an unexplained first name or in unhappy phrases such as 'a then newish wife'.[103] As if to hammer this point home, the book is dedicated to 'Hilly, Philip, Martin, Sally, Jaime and Ali' and it concludes with 'Instead of an Epilogue', a poem in three loping, understated stanzas 'To H.'. The first stanza takes Kingsley back to 1932, when he found a Camberwell Beauty butterfly in his grandmother's Camberwell garden; the second, set in 1940, recreates that winter in Marlborough when 'every stalk and stem was covered in / A thin layer of ice as clear as glass'. This is the third:

> In '46 when I was twenty-four
> I met someone harmless, someone defenceless,
> But till then whole, unadapted within;
> Awkward, gentle, healthy, straight-backed,
> Who spoke to say something, laughed when amused;

> If things went wrong, feared she might be at fault,
> Whose eye I could have met for ever then,
> Oh yes, and who was also beautiful.
> Well, that was much as women were meant to be,
> I thought, and set about looking further.
> How can we tell, with nothing to compare.[104]

That generosity of spirit is exactly what the main body of *Memoirs* so often lacks.

Both *The Amis Collection* and *Memoirs* directly affected Kingsley's fiction. Among the most deeply felt of the essays – and the only one which is undated in *The Amis Collection* – is 'Sacred Cows', a brisk and surprisingly effective attack on the overinflated self-regard contemporary American literature accords itself. The piece works because it acknowledges the particular qualities of earlier American writing and sorrowfully records examples of more recent promise unfulfilled: for instance, Norman Mailer ('When *The Naked and the Dead* appeared, I thought someone the size of Dickens was among us') and J. D. Salinger, 'who did struggle on for one more decent effort after the marvellous *Catcher in the Rye*'.[105] Such praise lends authority to Kingsley's subsequent charge that 'America takes her writers too seriously,' regarding them 'as key operators in the national heritage business' and giving them 'too much too soon':

> The same desire to find and reward the 'great', and that character-istically innocent readiness to take the will for the deed if the will is signalled boldly enough, have elevated Nabokov and Bellow, neither of whom writes English. Nabokov, in a way peculiar to foreigners, never stops showing off his mastery of the language; his books are jewels a hundred thousand words long. Bellow is a Ukrainian-Canadian, I believe. It is painful to watch him trying to pick his way between the unidiomatic on the one hand and the affected on the other.[106]

There's mischief here: Nabokov and Bellow are among the novelists most admired by Kingsley's son Martin. But there's also something far more important than mischief: the assertion, which isn't to be lightly dismissed, that the writer's primary responsibility is to his language and the implication that literature – not only poetry, as Robert Frost famously remarked – is what gets lost in translation, even when the 'translation' is something which occurs in the author's mind before his words reach the page. These are among the issues at the heart of Kingsley's last major novel, *The Russian Girl* (1992).

One impulse behind this book can be traced all the way back to William Cooper's *Scenes from Provincial Life*, which raises the question of whether it's possible to love a writer without admiring the work: there, the manuscript of his unpublished novel which Joe gives to his girlfriend Myrtle remains unread. ' "How," I asked myself, "can Myrtle love me and not want to read my books?" '[107] Another went back to Kingsley's meeting in 1962 with the Russian poet Yevgeny Yevtushenko, of whom he had revised his good opinion when Yevtushenko's name was put forward for the post of Professor of Poetry at Oxford in 1968. His election 'would have installed a trusted ally, if not a total minion, of the Soviet régime in a highly sensitive and influential spot';[108] in the event, the successful candidate was Roy Fuller. And a third impulse was the collapse of the Soviet Union, which occurred during 1991. Kingsley suspected, like the minor character Julius Hoffman who is introduced specifically to voice this opinion, that 'what is replacing it is no better, no less violent, no less tyrannical, no less ugly, dirty, barbaric, illiterate, boorish, no less complete and irrremediable a cultural desert'.[109] This context is essential in underpinning our sympathy for the Russian girl of the title, the beautiful but talentless poet Anna Danilova, who is in London to organise a petition for the release of her brother Sergei (languishing – justly, as far as we can gather – in a Russian gaol) and who settles on Dr Richard Vaisey of the London Institute of Slavonic Studies as the instrument to bring this about. Richard is an academic Stanley: he too comes from an inauspicious background (in his case somewhere up on the left-hand side of England), drives an absurdly flashy car (this one is called a Viotti TBD) and is naturally encumbered by an impossible wife, Cordelia. She is Kingsley's most outrageous elaboration of the Jane theme: her condition is one of elegant stasis – in her drawing room a chess game and a *Times* crossword rest perpetually in a state of suggestive incompleteness – complimented by her monstrously affected diction and her strange capacity to have gullible friends attend to her every need. Towards the end of the novel, having discovered Richard's relationship with Anna and locked him out of the house (it's her house, her money), she suddenly acquires astonishing vindictive ingenuity, hiring actors to impersonate policemen and security guards, causing books and possessions to vanish from both his home and his office, and the wheels to fall off his Viotti TBD. Somewhere in this progress, the novel – which began by looking quite like a book by Kingsley Amis – has been transformed into something rather unexpected.

The heart of this transformation is in the twelfth and thirteenth chapters, which include Richard and Anna's country visit to the exiled Russian author Anton Kotolynov, who has metamorphosed himself into an American thriller-writer called Andrew Cottle, their lunch at the wittily named Cor Anglais, and their return to London; Richard's doorstep ambush by Arkady Ippolitov, of the 'Ad Hoc Committee for Cultural Relations' and the revelations which follow over several Scotches in a surreally dreadful bar; his subsequent nightmare progress to Angelus Crescent in search of his ex-brother-in-law and confidant Crispin Radetsky; and his further confused journey home to find that his wife has vanished. This sequence of events is curiously reminiscent of Iris Murdoch's aptly titled *The Flight from the Enchanter*, a book of which Kingsley once complained that it seemed 'very *unreal*' and full of 'abnormal' characters. One wouldn't be at all surprised to bump into a Murdochian character such as Mischa Fox in *The Russian Girl*, which has a good deal of unreality and abnormality about it (its title may incidentally remind us that Murdoch wrote a novel called *The Italian Girl*). This suggests something paradoxical about the development of Kingsley's fiction: although he had come a long way from the straightforward social comedy of his early novels, he had arrived in 1992 at a place very close to where Iris Murdoch had been in 1955. Yet that clearly isn't the whole story; and there was, in any case, a good reason for it.

Just as the well-disposed reader of Murdoch's fiction accepts odd characters and implausible plots as a modest price to pay for novels of ideas, so in *The Russian Girl* everything becomes subservient to the book's intellectual propositions: Kingsley's views on literature and culture are here articulated more clearly, and more persuasively, than anywhere else in his work. This seriousness of intent is announced in the opening pages, where a faculty meeting (boycotted by a bunch of trendy women, naturally) is debating the question of literature in translation. Richard believes that literature needs to be read in its original language; he sees the opposing view, that reading in translation is better than nothing, as a capitulation to the 'more

will mean worse' drift in higher education. Meanwhile, the honourable but temporising head of department, Tristram Hallett, attempts
to mediate, agreeing that the best candidates must read Russian
literature in Russian while arguing that 'it is a great deal better that
some young people should read *Crime and Punishment* in English
than not read it at all'. Is it, though? 'The knowledge they'll have
will be of information only,' says Richard. 'You know as well as I do
that every word Dostoevsky writes is written in a way only he can
write it.'[110] This distinction between literature and 'information' is
crucial, since only by reading the words the author actually wrote
can we establish whether a work has any *merit*. Richard, of course, is
bilingual in English and Russian, which gives him an advantage over
most of the other characters in the book and enables him to conduct
some crucial conversations in whichever language an unwanted eaves-
dropper won't understand; but it also presents him with his central
moral dilemma, when he falls in love with Anna. For not only is
Anna's poetry entirely without merit, as even we may guess from a
wickedly brilliant translation, complete with illiterate misprints, by
a 'sympathetic' American called McKinnon;[111] she herself is indifferent to the idea. She can't see that the fact that Richard dislikes her
poetry 'makes a very great deal of difference' both to his ability to
support her petition and indeed to their (at this point undeclared)
emotional relationship; and when he suggests to her that it's essential
at least that 'you believe in your poetry . . . that you think it's good,
it has *merit*', she merely replies, 'It pleases me, it amuses me.'[112] When
she reads her work, in Russian, before an enraptured audience at
the Institute, Richard can't help knowing that this is 'a victory for
something hostile to what he thought valuable'.[113] Before the reading
is over, he is in tears, 'but not the sort of tears that might have been
intended or allowed for. He wept that all that honesty of feeling, all
that seriousness of purpose, all that sincerity that had found
expression through such outstanding dramatic gifts, as again they
undoubtedly were, should have come to nothing.'[114]

Anna is indisputably a genuine Russian, and a highly attractive
one, but as an artist she is a complete phoney (her name, and
something in her manner, recalls that other seductive phoney, Anna
Le Page in *Take a Girl like You*). Her bogus creativity symbolises
nothing less than the twentieth century's capitulation to the glitzy
charms of novelty over coherent cultural values, as we discover

towards the end of the book. By this time, Hallett, unwell and
unbearded, has taken early retirement. When Richard visits him,
he produces a draft paper on which he's been working and reads
from it:

> 'The eclipse of merit. Beginnings. The role of modernism in the
> rendering irrelevant and passé of artistic merit and questions of
> merit. As soon as originality became important, the days of artistic
> merit or excellence were numbered. The question *Is it any good?*
> had always been hard to discuss, and only to be settled after a
> lapse of time and by the judgement of the wider public. This
> irritated intellectuals, who found it easier and more agreeable to
> ask *Is it new?*, together with *What does it mean?* and *Is it art?*,
> questions easy to discuss and never to be settled. Examples from:
> music, visual arts, verse, minority performing arts, minority prose
> writing such as to exclude the wider public. There have been more
> recent encroachments from political or quasi-political art, such
> that it is agreed to be irrelevant or unseemly or even actually
> dangerous to ask *Is it any good?* Example,' and at this point
> Hallett refrained fom doing what he might well have done and
> change his style of delivery, however briefly, 'the poems of Anna
> Danilova, which although not or not systematically political in
> themselves are used for a political purpose, and the question of
> their merit is irrelevant and to raise that question unseemly among
> other things. To further their use for this purpose is to participate
> in, and to spread further, the attack on artistic merit.'[115]

This splendid passage summarises the Amis–Larkin aesthetic position
in a manner which, unusually, is neither reductive nor intemperate.
It is, of course, a position in danger of imminent extinction. When
Richard rather complacently remarks, 'Artistic merit's safe enough as
long as there are people like you and me around,' Hallett has to
remind him: 'I've retired and you've capitulated.' He does capitulate.
He becomes, with well-judged irony, a simultaneous translator in
Brussels. The petition turns out to be irrelevant, since Anna's brother
conveniently dies in prison. Richard, as Hallett observes, has 'signed
away what he must have seen as his good name for nothing'.[116]
Whether or not this is too high a price to pay for 'the divine Danilova'
(and, it must be said, for getting shot of Cordelia) is left unstated.

7

The folks that lived on the hill must have seemed, to the casual observer, to be getting on fine; but this was because their familial existence was so ordered that they seldom came together. Ali spoke for the SDP on health and social services in the House of Lords, a political allegiance and a brief that Kingsley found too lefty by half: it didn't help that he read the *Guardian*, or 'the traitors' gazette'. Kingsley's daily routine consisted of a morning's work; lunchtime drinks at the pub followed by Hilly's cheese-and-pickle sandwiches or lunch at the Garrick; a bit more work in the late afternoon; supper on a tray; telly, Scotch and bed. Their worlds tended not to intersect and when they did – if all three found themselves dining or entertaining together, for instance – the atmosphere wasn't easy. Julian Barnes acutely suggests that 'Ally filled a vaguely similar role to Colin [Howard],'[117] with whom, despite his companionable usefulness, Kingsley had some spectacular disagreements. Hilly's devoted shuttling between the two men in her household was nothing short of heroic, for they were 'completely different animals'. 'Separating Kingsley and Ali used to give me the jumps,' she says.[118]

That Kingsley in his later years quite often behaved appallingly, in the style of his rudest and most bigoted invented characters, is well known and plentifully documented. What is a little more surprising is a lack of understanding, even among people who knew him well, of *why* he did it. Two slightly earlier incidents involving Julian Barnes are worth considering here. The first took place a little before the Amis–Kilmarnock household moved to Primrose Hill; Kingsley had invited Barnes round for 'a bite of supper' in his sitting room, and the tray containing their food was duly delivered by Ali, deputising for his wife as he sometimes did. 'Ali was barely out of the room,' Barnes remembers, 'when Kingsley said: "Not bad for a boy from Norbury, eh? Get your dinner from a peer of the realm." '[119] On another occasion, in 1986 – after the successful publication of Barnes's *Flaubert's Parrot*, which wasn't at all Kingsley's sort of book and can't have helped matters – Kingsley invited Barnes and his wife Pat Kavanagh to dinner at the Garrick. Additionally needled by the fact that Barnes had visited South Africa and his wife had grown up there, Kingsley snapped into racist mode, offering opinions such as 'You should shoot as many blacks as possible' (at which point Pat Kavanagh left in distress).[120] He also complained afterwards to Martin that Barnes hadn't treated him with the deference due to 'a senior writer'; Barnes's reaction when told of this was that 'the senior writers he respected "didn't refer to themselves as senior writers" '.[121] Perhaps surprisingly, the racism, in being merely ridiculous, is less significant than the remark about a boy from Norbury being waited on by a peer of the realm and the insistence on being treated as a 'senior writer'. For these betray Kingsley's chronic insecurity: they are the utterances of someone who'd always felt precarious in his grasp on the ladder of upward mobility and who now feared he might be losing it.

Friends and commentators have variously seen arrogance, contempt, grandeur and self-parody in Kingsley's late rages and ravings; but I see panic, despair and that childish urge to shock and offend which panic and despair can produce. These outbursts are the equivalent of the abusive upper case in his early letters to Larkin: they are what happens when the civilised lower-case courtesies of ordinary prose fail. And it's absolutely no coincidence that some of his most volcanic eruptions should have been directed at post-*Flaubert* Julian Barnes. When, in 1983, Barnes had 'made the mistake' of telling Kingsley what he was working on, he was greeted by 'an expression poised between belligerent outrage and apoplectic boredom'; and when sent a copy of *Flaubert's Parrot*, Kingsley 'let it be known that he had never got beyond the third chapter'.[122] There was, says Ian McEwan, 'a serious aesthetic rift between the generations'.[123] For Kingsley, Barnes and his sort of unfinishable fiction were the threatening future: the 'senior writer' was under siege. Barnes himself modestly disagrees with this diagnosis. He doesn't think that Kingsley was 'insecure about clever young novelists: he just genuinely thought they were no bloody good – me, Ian [McEwan], Martin . . . with Ian McE: "You can tell he's no bloody good because he wears those little round gold glasses . . ." '[124] Either way, as wily Enobarbus remarks in *Antony and Cleopatra*: ' 'Tis better playing with a lion's whelp, / Than with an old one dying.'

Kingsley's gathering sense that his creative powers were diminishing and time was running out partly explains one of his most extraordinary changes of mind. In July 1992, Eric Jacobs, a Garrick

Club member and freelance journalist who had previously worked for the short-lived newspaper *Today*, asked Kingsley's permission to write an authorised biography. Kingsley's response was a firm but courteous rejection: 'If the answer must be No, please rest assured that, far from thinking your suggestion in any way appropriate, I take it as a great compliment.'[125] Yet, little more than a fortnight later, he wrote again to Jacobs: 'I am very glad that you propose to write my biography. Yours will be the authorised biography, and I undertake not to give any other biographer any co-operation for three years.'[126] What had intervened in a mind-changing way was lunch. When Jacobs asked what might persuade him to agree to the project, Kingsley specified not only the meal but the location, Simpson's-in-the-Strand, a refinement which Jimmie Fane in *The Biographer's Moustache* fails to inflict on *his* biographer Gordon Scott-Thompson, although the result in each case was similar: 'So we had lunch there, about which I can remember only that we drank a lot, it cost a lot and we were somehow in business at the end of it.'[127] Unlike the justly neglected Fane, however, Kingsley remained in the public eye, for the time being at least, and wanted to make sure he remained there. He must also have sensed that an authorised biography by an amiable if somewhat pedestrian journalist – one, moreover, who vowed to avoid the kind of critical appraisal over which he had fallen out with the American academic Dale Salwak and his *Kingsley Amis: Modern Novelist* – would go some way towards redressing the omissions and distortions of his own *Memoirs*. What Jacobs can't have anticipated was that his book would, by the time it appeared, be buttressed by two related novels: Kingsley's reconfiguration of his early life in *You Can't Do Both* (1994) and his mischievous examination of the subject–biographer relationship in *The Biographer's Moustache* (1995).

You Can't Do Both is a fascinating and enjoyable book but an unsatisfactory novel. The problem is partly that the background and daily life of fifteen-year-old Robin Davies in the first of its three episodes bears too close and cannibalistic a resemblance to that of fourteen-year-old Peter Furneaux in *The Riverside Villas Murder*, and partly that the book as whole goes against the principles Kingsley himself sets out in 'Real and Made-up People', where he argues that all was well with fiction until 'D. H. Lawrence started writing about himself, people he knew and what there was of what had actually happened to him, and his knowing or unknowing heirs are all around us today.'[128] Kingsley joins them, knowingly, in *You Can't Do Both* – which might, had the title been available, very plausibly have been called *Sons and Lovers*. Although he had scarcely a good word to say for Lawrence throughout his literary career, and indeed subjected him to some of that enthusiastic upper-case abuse ('a GRINDING SHIT' who was 'INSULTINGLY BAD IN E X A C T L Y THE KIND OF WAY YOU'D EXPECT FROM THE WAY HE BEHAVED'),[129] that is the novel for which he once made a grudging exception: in 1948, he told Larkin that he'd 'begun *Sons Lovers*, by that touched Mexico-loving type, which seems rather good to me'.[130]

Coincidentally or not, Lawrence haunts *You Can't Do Both* almost as disconcertingly as Dylan Thomas haunts *The Old Devils*. He makes his appearance as part of Jeremy Carpenter's early attempt to educate, and if at all possible seduce, young Robin: 'Take old Lawrence. He's the only writer I know who writes about it [sex] in a completely honest and straightforward way and keeps just the right balance between, well, what you think and what you feel.'[131] But when they meet again later on – Robin is by this time in the army, on leave, having interrupted his Oxford degree, while Jeremy is a conscientious objector who's spent time in prison – Jeremy's view of Lawrence is much modified: 'Lawrence had a great appeal for the sick and infirm. It's a funny thing, I've never come across any kind of Lawrence-disciple, queer or not, who wasn't in a proper pickle about sex.'[132] That Jeremy is a 'made-up' character – who successfully goes against late-Amis stereotyping by being sensitive and intelligent as well as pacifist and homosexual – shouldn't obscure the fact that his literary tastes, his fondness for jazz and even his sexuality owe a lot to the young Larkin. Nor does the Lawrence (and Larkin) subtext end there. At first glance, Robin's agricultural Welsh relatives – God-fearing Cousin Emrys and his mildly deranged family – seem chiefly indebted to *Cold Comfort Farm*; but Kingsley certainly intends a Lawrentian echo, a farcical version of the Brangwens perhaps, as well as an artfully concealed reference to his old friend Philip. The key is Larkin's poem, 'I Remember, I Remember', in which a fleeting visit to his birthplace, Coventry, reminds him of how his 'childhood was unspent' and of all the magical things that didn't happen to him, including 'that splendid family':

> I never ran to when I got depressed,
> The boys all biceps and the girls all chest,
> Their comic Ford, their farm where I could be
> 'Really myself'. I'll show you, come to that,
> The bracket where I never trembling sat,
>
> Determined to go through with it; where she
> Lay back, and 'all became a burning mist' . . .[133]

Larkin said of 'I Remember, I Remember': 'Really that poem started off as a satire on novels like *Sons and Lovers* – the kind of wonderful childhoods that people do seem to have . . . It wasn't denying that other people did have these experiences, though they did tend to sound rather clichés: the first fuck, the first poem, the first this that and the other that turn up with such wearisome regularity.'[134] *You Can't Do Both* takes those apparently irreconcilable opposites and shows that in this case you can, indeed must, do both: Robin's growing up, despite its exemplary drabness, does contain 'the first fuck, the first poem, the first this that and the other' which drive the novel's progress.

This progress, as we've already seen, is essentially its young author's through school and university, love and marriage. But the book suffers from an uncertainty of tone and intention: some scenes – for example, those involving Robin and his parents or Robin with his girlfriend Nancy Bennett in Oxford – are taken directly from autobiography; others are given thin and arbitrary disguises, as when Nancy's proposed but abandoned abortion is shifted inexplicably from London to Cardiff; still other scenes (the Welsh farm) and characters (Robin's somewhat Larkinesque friends Jeremy Carpenter and Embleton who, like Inspector Morse, is known by no other name) are invented. The seams show: a certain skittishness lightens the true fiction, not always to its advantage, while some of the passages concerning Robin's mother drift towards uncharacteristic sentimentality. And the episodic structure is out of character, too: the book feels like several bits of something much vaster, a Proustian autobiographical epic, and it ends on a tentative, downbeat note, as if half expecting an impossible sequel. Its most memorable and touching feature is the fictionalised portrait it provides of Kingsley's parents, especially his father.

Although we've already had one version of the earlier part of this, in *The Riverside Villas Murder*, Robin's father Tom Davies is a fuller and a chronologically more extended portrait. In one crucial respect, he is unlike William Amis. He is Welsh, 'the remnants of his Cardigan accent showing' when he tells his son he can't possibly visit a schoolfriend at teatime and fulfil a family obligation in the evening: 'I'm sorry, old boy. You can't do both. I'm sorry.'[135] The mournful relish he takes in prohibition (for it genuinely brings him no pleasure) is true to the spirit of William Amis, and the Welshness is an inspired addition: it supplies not only a fig leaf of fictional distance but, once we've met the farming relatives, a convincing explanation; by now, of course, Kingsley felt he'd earned the right to make mild fun of the Welsh. Even in the book's first section, Robin regards Tom and his home-life in general with an amused tolerance which disappoints Jeremy, who'd hoped to hear something more transgressive than this: 'At the moment I quite like home, I like being there. Oh, my father and I rub each other up the wrong way some of the time, but that's only to be expected, isn't it . . .'[136] This tolerant affection is beautifully caught when Robin, returning from his holiday in Wales, is met at the station by his father: 'As always on the rare occasions when they had been parted for some time, Robin was impressed by the extravagant normality of his appearance: appropriate office get-up, folded newspaper under arm, bowler hat on head, no Red Indian's eagle feathers or pirate's cutlass and eyepatch.' His father's expression, he notices, 'told only of simple pleasure'.[137]

We need this adolescent–father relationship to be clearly established, because without it Tom Davies would be completely unbearable when we next meet him. The occasion is the deeply ill-advised weekend visit of Robin, now an Oxford undergraduate, and his younger girlfriend Nancy to the Davies's South London home. It begins worryingly, when Mr Davies's 'tremendous show of cordiality' merges into 'one of the sustained bouts of clowning he went in for a couple of times a year',[138] and is clearly destined for a disastrous end when the Davies parents are called away by a family emergency, leaving the young couple alone on the Sunday. It doesn't take Mr Davies long to deduce on his return that what he calls 'something improper' has taken place during his absence. 'For the first time in your life, old boy,' he tells his son, 'I wish you'd told me a lie'; but he speaks 'without rancour'.[139] His practical reaction – to send the girl packing – seems extreme and his emotional reaction absurd, although ludicrously endearing: 'I've had a nasty shock, in fact I can't remember when I had a nastier, and I'm not firing properly on all cylinders yet.'[140] Kingsley's ear for dialogue was seldom sharper than in his rendering of pre-war South London, with its strategies of embedded irony and consolatory cliché. It's a register which is capable of articulating distress combined with surprising dignity; for it's Mr Davies, not his son (who is too busy preventing himself from fulfilling a long-held ambition to swear vividly at his father), who wonders, 'Why has there got to be this terrible conflict between the generations?'[141] The lovers depart, though not without some surreptitious financial help from Robin's mother, and spend the night with his useful elder brother George.

If the emotional note of that scene owes a good deal to the occasion on which William Amis discovered condoms in his son's pocket, the scenes describing Tom Davies's final illness, death and funeral – which take place twenty years before William's – are more properly fictional. Robin's final visit to his father in hospital catches precisely the right note of understated reconciliation: 'We've both of us respected the other chap's point of view,'[142] says Robin, which wasn't quite how he once felt; and when his father asks his forgiveness for (of all things) not sending him to Sunday school, he replies, 'Dad, there's nothing to forgive.'[143] Before the cremation, George has to read out a brief oration written by his father asserting his atheism, to the puzzled consternation of Cousin Emrys: it's a neat and conclusive demonstration that Tom was, in his quiet way, at least as bold an iconoclast as either of his sons. He is not long survived by his wife, who does however approve of Robin and Nancy's marriage, tactfully acknowledging its necessity: 'Well, for what it's worth I give the two of you my blessing. The three of you. I can't help feeling pleased about that.'[144] She also persuades Nancy's parents to attend the ceremony, just as Kingsley's mother did with the Bardwells.

The Robin Davies of whom we take our leave in the book's short fourth section is a mixture of young Kingsley and Jim Dixon. A cackhanded adulterer (with Welsh Dilys), he is easily discovered and apprehended, at least partly to his relief, by Nancy: their life will resume, as Kingsley's and Hilly's did. But the more subtle hint that things will work out for him comes at the start of the section, where we learn not only that his office door is labelled 'DR ROBIN R.

DAVIES READER CLASSICS DEPT' but also that, on closing it behind him, 'he went into a vigorous silent routine of obscene gestures involving most of the top half of his body and accompanied by the pulling of hideous faces. This sequence he performed every morning in term-time or nearly.'[145] We know whom he most resembles. He will be lucky.

8

Since 1978, and *Jake's Thing*, all Kingsley's full-length books had been published by Hutchinson; but his relationship with his editors there, in particular Richard Cohen, hadn't been an easy one, as his letters make clear. 'Have had difficulty with R COHEN at Hutch,' he grumbled to Conquest on 18 July 1986. 'He *changes* things.'[146] By that December, Jonathan Clowes was 'auctioning me round the publishers so I may be able to quit Cohen on grounds of greed'.[147] Nothing came of this; but when in 1994 Hutchinson offered £40,000 for the successor to *You Can't Do Both*, Clowes did find a substantially better bid, £135,000 for *The Biographer's Moustache*, as part of a two-book deal with HarperCollins. Although that house would also publish *The King's English* posthumously, *The Biographer's Moustache* was the only novel he wrote for it and the last he was to complete.

The book is a dampish squib: a little cluster of quite entertaining ideas that, even at just under 300 pages, seems monstrously over-extended. Its starting point is clearly Jacobs and his biography: Jimmie Fane is an elderly writer, his biographer Gordon Scott-Thompson is a younger freelance journalist, and several of their meetings take place at Fane's London club, Gray's. But there – despite some wry and perceptive observations on the problematic nature of critical biography – the resemblance ends, for the novel is really grounded in three of Kingsley's abiding preoccupations: class, sex and drink. Jimmie is something of a toff (though not half as toffish as Willie, Duke of Dunwich), whereas Gordon shares, and is acutely conscious of, Kingsley's lower-middle-class origins: one of the novel's recurrent motifs concerns the pronunciation of class-defining words. It opens with Jimmie obstinately defending his use of 'luncheon' for 'lunch'; at their first meeting, much is made of Gordon's reference to his 'c.v.', which is unimproved by his pronunciation of 'curriculum vitae'; only near the end of the book does Gordon's patience finally run out, in a way which doesn't disconcert Jimmie in the slightest, when he's asked to repeat the sentence 'I've no complaints, none at all':

> Gordon started to do as he was asked, then stopped and stared. 'You old bugger,' he said without either hostility or affection. 'You wanted to be sure about whether I say *c'mplaints* or *kommplaints* and whether I say *none* or *nonn*. I suppose if I got them wrong you'd have to decide between me being culpably Yorkshire–Lancashire or criminally tainted with spelling-pronunciation. You old *bugger*.'[148]

To which Jimmie can only 'confess I am a little bit naughty like that once in a way, but we all have things like that about us, don't we? Childish things?' It's a sly attempt at excuse and apology for Kingsley's own, often pedantic, contentiousness, as is Jimmie's equally unfussed reaction to Gordon's description of him as 'not a reluctant shit and certainly not an unconscious shit' but 'a self-congratulatory shit'.[149] He is, in fact, merely refining something that Willie Dunwich has already said to him: 'But he's not a *bounder* exactly, m'm? More of a shit.'[150]

We've met plenty of these in Kingsley's fiction. Often, their shittiness is combined with some recognisably authorial characteristics, and Jimmie is no exception: he's an ageing novelist with a lecherous past and a present fondness for drink and linguistic pedantry, his club and his cronies. He is, however, not much good and neither, we may suppose, is his biographer (it's odd, incidentally, that this book about the relationship between two indifferent writers should have appeared at the same time as Martin's on a similar theme, *The Information*). Neither is sufficiently interesting to carry the book's weight, while the musical-chairs sub-plot – Gordon's affair with Jimmie's much younger wife Joanna, Jimmie's proposed return to his second wife (of four) Rowena, Gordon's girlfriend Louise's eventual marriage to the preposterous Willie Dunwich – seems cobbled together in an entirely arbitrary way. The class theme is developed in ways which suggest a degree of thwarted Dickensian ambition: on the one hand, there's a very impoverished old flame of Jimmie's, Madge Walker, and her disabled deaf husband Alec, 'The

Captain', who is treated in exactly the same way as Wemmick's Aged Parent in *Great Expectations*; on the other, there's the world of eating, drinking and falling off horses at Hungerstream, seat of the Dukes of Dunwich. Willie Dunwich is funny enough as a slapstick aristocrat – 'By some prodigy of phonic aptitude he had managed to get his message across without apparently bringing his jaws together at any point. Seen at closer quarters, his possibly psychopathic look came down largely to his not having much in the way of eyebrows or eyelashes and a kind of blistering effect over the cheekbones'[151] – but this is a type which, ever since Lord Edgerstoune in *Take a Girl like You*, had obstinately remained no more than a type. Dickens, in *Bleak House*, first parodies but then humanises Lord Dedlock, while Chesney Wold comes alive through its peculiarities; by contrast, the description of Hungerstream remains obstinately formulaic.

The writing seems tired, too: those interminably trailing late-Amis sentences in *The Old Devils* have given way to a style which is syntactically sparser yet drawn to ornate, almost solicitorial effects (the later prose of both Anthony Powell and Roy Fuller comes to mind). Sometimes, the result is at once jaded and childish: 'It was an Italian restaurant that was unusual in having Brian Harris in it.'[152] And where Kingsley's prose at its best fizzes gently, here the sparky moments stand out too clearly: 'A girl of about thirty answered his ring apparently clad in an excerpt from the Bayeux Tapestry.'[153] This, we discover, is Fane's ghastly daughter Periwinkle, who briefly seems as if she may join the company of Kingsley's demented young things (Simon in *I Want It Now*, Sylvia in *Girl, 20*), but of whom we don't see nearly enough.

The consolatory pleasures of *The Biographer's Moustache* mainly arise from Kingsley being naughty: the book is generously stuffed with in-jokes. When Jimmie, at the very start, describes himself to his wife as 'a very impressive man whose impressiveness has not been diminished by the passage of time',[154] he parodies Kingsley's description of himself to Julian Barnes as a 'senior writer'. When Gordon successfully talks his publisher into giving him 'an advance on that advance',[155] he recalls a much younger Kingsley's almost equally improbable success in doing the same with Victor Gollancz. Jimmie's *Who's Who* entry lists his recreations as 'visiting churches in Tuscany and Umbria, good food, conversation', but Joanna's gloss on this turns him emphatically into a version of Kingsley: 'I've never known him go near a church anywhere, though he might venture near an Italian one if it was next door to a kosher palazzo that had a proper duchessa in it he could chat up ... Yes – good food; he likes expensive food, as you well know, but that's about as far as it goes. I don't think he's much of a taste-buds man, do you?'[156] Lunching at Gray's, Jimmie remarks that 'I'd have suggested to you that we should go straight in to where one eats if that didn't sound such a dismal notion':[157] Kingsley's sentiments exactly. But the running joke of course concerns the fraught relationship between novelist and biographer (although *The Biographer's Moustache* appeared too late for Jacobs to be warned or instructed; the novel doesn't even feature in his bibliography).

Fane is sufficiently vain – an echo already used for Sir Roy Vandervane, in *Girl, 20* – to feel that any book about him will do his reputation good, which is one way of saying that his reputation has sunk pretty low. He allows himself to be persuaded, although he can't quite countenance the expression, that Gordon's book 'will *trigger off* a large revival of interest in what I've written'.[158] Gordon's publisher, on the other hand, is acutely aware of the book's problematical nature, combining the 'critical' and the 'personal': 'I'm sorry to say ... more people are going to be interested in the second than the first. From what I know of you, my old Gordon, you're likely to be more interested in the first than the second.'[159] This sound but uncommercial instinct of Gordon's seems to have been inherited from his father, a retired schoolteacher: the quiet chapter dealing with his evening visit to his parents is one of the best things in the novel, recalling that feeling for domestic warmth which makes *The Folks that Live on the Hill* so enjoyable. But Gordon's biography will never be written: partly because Jimmie is 'such a ... massive and multifarious shit that I disdain to be associated with you in such ways as having my name with yours on a title-page,'[160] but more pressingly, as his editor Brian Harris tells him, because his contract has been cancelled. This (and it's the most audacious in-joke in the book) is all to do with what's happening in publishing:

'All these financial deals going on, who cares a toss who owns this or who's paid a hundred million quid for that, I agree. The trouble comes when one of the bloody philistines who've bought you up

start looking at the books, and I don't mean the books of exciting new poetry or the books of vibrant innovative prose, I mean
the *books*, the sodding account-books. One fine day one of the
bastards happens to glance at the page that shows the annual
profits on turnover of the various enterprises the company owns,
and the fellow starts making a few comparisons. He's one of the
smart ones who can count on his toes as well as his fingers . . .'[161]

Sneaking this into a book published by HarperCollins, a firm owned
by Rupert Murdoch's News International, must have been almost as
much fun as putting Roger Micheldene's thoughts on the stinginess
of small publishers into *One Fat Englishman*.

As for that wretched moustache: Kingsley himself had grown one
in 1982 – he resembled a character who ought to have been played
by Peter Sellers – and he soon got rid of it. Gordon's begins with his
'dissatisfaction or boredom with his own unadorned looks' and a
memory of his grandfather, 'a striking-looking man';[162] it is ceremo-
nially demolished in furtherance of his affair with Joanna, despite
her recollection of someone having once 'said that being kissed by
a man without a moustache was like having to eat a boiled egg without salt'.[163] Jimmie also approves, finding the naked-faced Gordon
'younger, more optimistic, altogether less . . . what shall I say, less
gangling, more sophisticated' (he means 'less *common*');[164] at the end
of the book, however, its regrowth has begun, which Louise interprets
as a signal 'to show the world you're back in your old life', although
Gordon insists that 'it's more like a reminder to me, if it's anything
more than just a moustache'.[165] This seems a disappointingly modest
significance for the symbol which gives the novel its title.

It was clear to everyone, when *The Biographer's Moustache*
appeared in the late summer of 1995, that it belonged among the
minor Amis novels; but these had been scattered throughout his
career and there was no reason to suppose that he wouldn't return to
form. In early August he set off as usual for his extended stay in
South Wales, a habit whose unwisdom had been increasingly clear,
even to him, for some time. 'You probably wondered if I was dead,'
he told Conquest in 1987; 'well, I nearly bloody am, or at least my
demise has been brought appreciably closer by a couple of weeks in
Wales (with another to come)'.[166] In 1989, he added that 'the . . .
drinking that goes on there makes the Old Devils look like – well not

a vicarage teaparty because in Swansea I bet they get arsehole[d] there too';[167] and in 1989 his doctor fixed him up with 'a clinical psychologist with an interest in alcohol-related problems. Amis saw him twice.'[168] He would have known, and quite possibly told, the story of the theatre critic Robert Benchley who, when warned that excessive drinking meant a slow death, replied 'So, who's in a hurry?' and took another sip; while his son Martin, in *Night Train*, describes alcoholism as 'suicide on the instalment plan'.[169] For many years, Kingsley stayed with the prodigiously drink-consuming Stuart and Eve Thomas, but after Stuart became seriously ill in the early 1990s Michael and Virginia Rush succeeded them as his hosts at Mumbles. In some ways, though not in others, he travelled light: Swansea-based Jack Prince, who undertook the heroic task of driving him there and back, remembered that he was always ready and waiting at 194 Regents Park Road, with 'his raincoat, his typewriter, a sheaf of paper, a case of Macallan ten-year-old Scotch and a plastic bag'.[170] The bag contained his clothes – these were no more important to him now than they'd been when Hilly first caught sight of him in 1946 – and also, if he was bothering to take them, an increasingly complex menu of drugs.

He knew that Stuart Thomas was dying. The previous year, in his thank-you letter to Virginia Rush, he'd written: 'It was odd saying goodbye to Stuart this time; I wanted to give him a hug or the equivalent but it doesn't do to let people see you're not all that sure you'll see them again.'[171] In fact, he *had* seen him again, when he and Hilly paid a brief visit to the Thomases in December 1994, curtailed when Stuart was taken to hospital on Christmas Eve. When Kingsley arrived in Wales on 13 August 1995, he immediately wanted to see Stuart, but was distressed to be told by Eve that this wasn't convenient; Stuart died the following day, and three days after that Kingsley delivered a eulogy at his funeral. In a trite and obvious sense, it wasn't the best start to his holiday, yet, despite Michael Rush's sense that Stuart's death 'triggered something in Kingsley's own condition',[172] the closure it represented may actually have been less depressing than a hopelessly drawn-out continuation of his friend's terminal illness. He was, in truth, very far from well himself. On 20 August, after lunching with friends at their cottage in Laugharne – where he had once stayed, using it as the basis for that memorable Birdarthur scene in *The Old Devils* – he walked

unsteadily down the steps to the garden gate, staggered, fell, and hit
his head. He seemed not too badly hurt and he was, in any case,
always falling over; that he was foul-tempered and complained of
back pains scarcely counted as a novelty. But it soon became obvious
that something was seriously wrong: his friend, doctor and fellow
Garrick Club member Ronald Zeegan was eventually contacted and
arranged his admission to the Chelsea and Westminster Hospital. He
left Wales on 31 August, accompanied by his authorised biographer
Eric Jacobs (whom he had summoned, possibly to record some
memorable last words, and who was faultlessly attentive), after
signing the Rushes' visitors' book 'Kingsley Amiss'.

Kingsley discharged himself, against his doctor's advice, after less
than a week. Back at Primrose Hill, he was more impossibly demanding than ever, before becoming seriously deranged: his random
self-dosage of the pills he kept rattling about in a shoe-box, washed
down with Scotch, seemed at least partly to blame for this. He was
readmitted first to University College Hospital and subsequently, after
apparently suffering a stroke, to the Phoenix Ward at St Pancras
Hospital. Just after eleven on the morning of Sunday 22 October,
with his daughter Sally at his bedside, he died in his sleep. It was
almost time to put the clocks back.

6. MARTIN AND THE MODS

1

According to his mother, Martin Amis 'looked like Orson Welles in a black rage' on the day of his birth, 25 August 1949.[1] The earliest published photograph shows him and his elder brother Philip, aged one and two respectively, sharing a bath in a butler sink beneath the outside taps in the yard of their home in Mumbles Road, Swansea. It's easy to misread this as evidence of quaintly dated deprivation – 'I was very short of money when I was a baby,' says Martin, with a wretched attempt at winsomeness. 'I slept in a drawer and had my baths in an outdoor sink'[2] – or of Bohemian eccentricity, but it isn't really either of these. For this was provincial Britain in 1950. I was born the year before Martin and cheerfully spent my own early childhood in a house without either mains electricity or drainage in rural Surrey, a mere twenty-five miles or so from London: we are both children of rationing, which didn't completely end until 1954. Most young families in the post-war years had to make do in numerous and inventive ways: in this respect, as in his early schooling, Martin's childhood was absolutely ordinary.

In other respects, it wasn't. Writing is a contrarian's trade, and most writers begin by seeking to irritate, affront or simply assert their difference from their parents: Kingsley, reacting against his own father's timid and conventional mediocrity, is a perfect example. Composers and painters, where one generation hands on specialised skills to the next, are quite likely to appear in family clusters, but words are our common property. So father-and-son literary firms are extremely rare: Martin mentions Dumas *père et fils*,[3] and the most notable modern English example, apart from Kingsley and himself, is that of Roy and John Fuller – an interestingly rule-proving exception, since Roy Fuller combined his literary career with that of a building society solicitor, thus simultaneously providing the requisite conventional self for his son to react against. When a hapless reader in a newspaper question-and-answer feature asked Martin, 'How do think you might have ended up spending your working life if your father hadn't been a famous writer?', he received a scathing reply: 'Well, John, that would depend on what my father had chosen to do instead. If he had been a postman, then I would have been a postman. If he had been a travel agent, then I would have been a travel agent. Do you get the idea?'[4] But what (I suspect) the questioner meant to imply was something more subtle: how did having a famous writer for a father affect him and his own literary development? For affect him it did, and from an early age.

Kingsley's parents knew exactly where they belonged – not working class, not middle class, but lower middle class – and had a clear sense of how they and their son ought to conduct themselves as a result. Martin's childhood lacked both the constraint and the safety net that came from such certainties. For one thing, his father's occupation as a university lecturer was in itself a badge of class exemption: when other middle-class people spoke of the '*professional* middle-class', they implied among other things a degree of naivety or even frivolity, as if 'professional' people weren't to be taken as seriously, and certainly didn't work as hard, as businessmen who actually knew where the money came from. For another, there was an element of domestic anarchy which, when they glimpsed it, puzzled and offended both sets of grandparents, 'Daddy B' and 'Mummy B' (the Bardwells) only slightly less than 'Daddy A' and 'Mummy A' (the Amises): it was 'definitely bohemian by lower-middle-class standards', says Martin. 'I'd find my mother with her feet on the table smoking cigarettes and playing jazz, and that shocked even me'[5] (despite, one might add, his middle-name kinship with the greatest of jazz trumpeters). The literary world was never far away and it was usually drunk. Writers came to stay and sometimes, as in the cases of Johns Braine and Wain, behaved badly; the boys' respective godfathers, Philip Larkin and Bruce Montgomery, would appear too – the one twinkly but parsimonious, the other recklessly generous and once, 'on the afternoon of an unforgettable Guy Fawkes' Night', giving them '*ten bob* for fireworks'.[6] There were numerous parties which, as Philip told Zachary Leader, were 'big, jazzy, with lots of people getting very drunk, shouting, dancing'; meanwhile, the two brothers would eavesdrop from the stairs, 'hoping that someone would come up and give us 2/6 or something'.[7] But Martin also remembers an evening when he sat on the stairs, overhearing 'a terrific row' between his parents and 'next morning, father coming up with a breakfast tray, dodging the missiles being thrown at him'.[8] For Kingsley to have achieved so domestic a feat, the situation must have been serious indeed.

The post-party wreckage at 24 The Grove would have been uncomplainingly dealt with by Eva Garcia, who began working for the Amises in 1951 and who, according to Martin, was 'terrible and great . . . one of the divinities of my childhood'. She was also 'Welsh, classic Celt-Iberian, as was her husband Joe, a kind, cubiform, semiliterate, longsuffering grafter who was actually *taller* sitting down than standing up'.[9] Her tasks were more numerous than one might expect of a part-time help at this point: the Amises were doing all right by the mid-1950s, but the extent of Eva's employment nevertheless suggests extravagance or carelessness on their part. Martin recalls coming home from school to find her making his tea, either singing raucously (her 'great' mode) or pallidly suffering from a migraine (then she was 'terrible'). While the Amises enjoyed a degree of social ambiguity and, in Swansea terms at least, upward mobility, there was nothing at all ambiguous about the Garcias' social status: they lived in Maryhill, an impoverished area of the city where cars were rarely seen, and Hilly would drive Eva home at the end of the day, her Morris Minor exciting comment not least because she drove straight across the roundabouts. It was in this car that the family were travelling, with Eva, one day in about 1956, when they were held up by a serious accident on the Mumbles Road. There was a general concern for Sally, two or three years old, who might see something upsetting; Martin, at any rate, observed and cheerfully filed away the memory of 'a twitching blood-bespattered figure half covered by an old overcoat'. They were apparently 'safely past when Eva propped Sally up on the back seat and said, "Look at him, Sall. *Writhing in agony* he is."'[10] Eva was an enthusiastic connoisseur of others' misfortunes and disasters, which greatly cheered her up: an aspect of her character which she would later deploy with devastating effect on Martin. Some parents wouldn't have stood for it.

Both Hilly and Kingsley were negligent parents – the point is inescapable, and it will recur – although their negligence was of two quite distinct varieties. Creative eccentricity was part of Hilly's upbringing: her folk-dancing, funny-language-learning father and her education at progressive Bedales had seen to that. For her, permissiveness was a matter of principle: 'I let him do *everything*. I let *you* do everything,' she told Martin in 1977, as he anxiously tried to prevent his five-year-old stepbrother Jaime from falling out of a tree. 'She did. She let us do everything. We spent all-day and all-night car journeys on the roof rack of the Morris 1000, the three of us, in all weathers, slithering in and out while my mother frowned into the windscreen . . .'[11] That sort of carelessness or carefreeness, depending on one's point of view, would have been prohibited only by Kingsley's anxiety, not by his sense of propriety, had he been present. *His* negligence was mostly characterised by absence – 'He was in his study. He was always in his study' – and by indolence. He was at once wary of being an effective parent, with the discouraging example of his own father before him, and quite certain of his inability to be any such thing; as with financial arrangements and other domestic responsibilities, his sense of his own incompetence elided neatly with his laziness. Anything to do with the great outdoors was naturally beyond him, so it was Hilly who approved her young sons' plan to canoe along the Welsh coast from Swansea Bay to Pembroke Bay: a misadventure grandly headlined 'THE SAGA OF THE AMIS BOYS' by the *South Wales Echo*, although only one Amis boy, the other one, carried on with the attempt after Martin 'asked to be dropped off' and 'called home from the snackbar at Caswell Bay'. By the time the coastguards had been alerted, Philip too, acknowledging defeat, was 'drinking Tizer and trying the phone in the snackbar on Caswell Bay'.[12]

When, rarely, Kingsley was called upon to fulfil a disciplinary role, the results were tragi-comic. Martin recalls the occasion at 24 The Grove, which makes him less than seven years old, on which he was finally apprehended for stealing money and cigarettes from his mother's handbag and coat pockets: he was 'sent upstairs to be beaten, or at any rate hit, by my father in his tiny study at the end of the long corridor'. He has no memory of the beating, if indeed it took place, but does recall his father's face 'in quarter-profile (and shouldn't this have been *my* face?): childish, softly frowning, entering a plea for mitigation, for leniency, asking for things to be seen in a kinder light'. Afterwards, Martin learned from Hilly that Kingsley had 'wept that night, as he always did when he hit us'.[13] On another evening at about the same time, when the boys took to sneaking downstairs repeatedly and hiding behind the furniture during a party,

'Kingsley eventually took a hairbrush to us, but so limply that we giggled about it for an hour after he had gone downstairs'; they turned the giggles into apparent and audible 'wails of anguish', and once again it was Kingsley's tears that were 'unfeigned'.[14]

It was after the family moved to 53 Glanmor Road in April 1956 that Hilly's and Kingsley's different forms of negligence began to fuse into something altogether more worrying. Instead of selling their previous house, they let it at a peppercorn rent to Eva and Joe Garcia: this enabled them to go away whenever they liked, meanwhile parking their children with the Garcias in what was, after all, the home in which they'd grown up. For Martin, who was 'an equable little boy, easily the "easiest" of the younger Amises',[15] this wasn't too upsetting: the truism remains true that, for the future writer, everything that happens during growing up is material – and for most writers this is something we seem intuitively to register at a very early age. The rather less equable Philip found it 'bloody awful': 'I hated it. But we were forced to do it because Hilly and Kingsley were having such a wild time.' Eva 'had a temper on her'; Joe would arrive home 'filthy' and sometimes drunk; and they had 'grim-looking' friends from Maryhill with 'horrible' children.[16] There was drunkenness and swearing in the Amis household, but it was offset by intelligence, wit and a residual awareness of the good manners that were being affronted: all this was lacking at the Garcias', and both Philip and Sally were terribly unhappy there. Martin was made of sterner stuff: at least he liked to think so.

2

Yet the swagger of Martin the child, as of Martin the writer, is a far wobblier affair than it first appears. One of the many thankless paradoxes about growing up is that a permissive, unprotected childhood may turn out to be more sheltered than one which is structured and disciplined. Put crudely: the boy of Martin's generation who went through the traditional rigours of prep and public school (as many an academic's son would have done) experienced a sequence of emotional and intellectual shocks and dislocations which the free-ranging young Amises were largely spared. According to one sort of orthodoxy, they ought to have been happier as a result; but two of them were often very unhappy indeed. The third learned to swagger: it proved an effective stance, except on a few occasions when Martin, confronted with events which his prep–public school alter ego might have found unremarkable, crumpled into a distressed heap. There's little point in taking sides over this: either kind of upbringing, while equipping children to take some things in their stride, is likely to fail monstrously in other ways; and each is a mirror image of the other. Or as Kingsley put it: you can't do both.

'Hold on to your hat – he's going to tell us the big one,' the ever-so-knowledgeable seven-year-old Philip muttered to his younger brother when they found themselves summoned to their father's study one day in 1955. Kingsley recalled the occasion in *Memoirs*: 'The short monologue I gave them slipped out of my head afterwards at the first opportunity, though I know I did conscientiously get in a certain amount of what might be called hard anatomy and concrete nouns, although again I must have used the word "thing" a good deal and talked about Dad planting a seed.'[17] He added: 'I have never loved and admired them more than for the unruffled calm and seriousness with which they heard me out.' Closely separated brothers – so close that Martin would irritate his father by demanding to know if he and Philip were really twins – become much more fully, if not necessarily reliably, informed in such matters than only sons, simply through their competitive need to acquire forbidden information. A couple of years later, upstairs in the house in Glanmore Road, Martin and his cousin Marian Partington took off their pyjamas and climbed into bed together, then 'lay in the dark for a long time and busily whispered'. Martin asked, 'Will you marry me?'; Marian replied, 'Yes'; and he, aged eight, 'thought something like, well, it's a bit early – but it's sometimes good to get these things out of the way'.[18] He didn't know everything yet.

Martin found the times he spent with the Partingtons 'arcadian'. Roger Partington – the 'Old Rodge' satirised in Kingsley's letters to Philip – had married Hilly's sister Margaret in 1947: they had two daughters, Marian and Lucy, and two sons, David and Mark. Whereas Kingsley had been infuriated (though also entertained) by their bucolic eccentricities, Martin discovered the refreshing innocence of the village as opposed to the grubbiness of the city. The symbolic embodiment of this was a camping holiday at St David's with his aunt 'Miggy' and her four children: 'When we got ready for bed in the great tepee I felt I was shedding my towny complexity and mire, and that I was entering a calmer universe than the one I would (eventually) return to.'[19] He thought of the Partingtons as a parallel family, Miggy 'my mother and yet not my mother', David 'my brother and yet not my brother': 'for much of my childhood I earnestly wanted David to be my brother, and he wanted it too'.[20] Although one shouldn't read too much into this, there's a clear sense of his real family not coming up to scratch, especially in the department of shared outdoor activity. In the low late-afternoon sun, thanks to some freakish syzygy, a 'tennis ball would cast a shadow two yards long', while Martin's and David's approach was signalled by their shadows when they were still forty feet away: 'We were growing boys. We were immensely proud of our long shadows.'[21] In all Martin's childhood, it's the moment when he seems most like a child of the conventional *Swallows and Amazons* kind.

This wasn't to last: Martin's formative landscape, like his father's, was that of a city's residential suburbs, and neither of them would ever possess a deeply rooted relationship with the natural world or a place called home. It's notoriously easy to become isolated in suburbia, lacking the village's supportive kinship or the city's crowded energy, and Martin evidently felt himself to be something of an outsider. In *Experience* he provides a sharply etched memory of this which is both archetypal and painfully specific. It begins with him, aged eight, trying to push a 'plump pebble' through the bars of a drain, 'to hear that satisfying plop as it joined the waterways of the city's innards'; the time, as so often with such memories, is a dark, wet winter afternoon. He's interrupted in this typical lonely-boyish occupation by a swarthy, curly-haired fifteen-year-old, 'his good looks undermined by his fraudulently bright green eyes', who demands to know what he thinks he's doing and then makes a proposition: a Rollo, 'or possibly two', if Martin will 'Just show me . . . ewe willie'. Martin doesn't: he walks away and then finds himself crying, not from fear but from something 'more like *grief*' (and perhaps pity, too). With the unshakeable instinct of small boys on such occasions, he says nothing to his mother. But a few weeks later he's again confronted by the green-eyed boy, this time accompanied by a stocky little henchman, a 'terrible toddler' called David. 'What ewe doing here on my road?' and 'Who said ewe could walk past my house?' demands the green-eyed boy and, after each of Martin's unsatisfactory replies, instructs his companion, who must have 'enjoyed Rollos by the tubeful': 'It him, Dai.' Dai does as he's told; when Martin returns home with a bruised face, Hilly sets off in pursuit with her three dogs, returning – of course – 'still furious and unavenged'.[22] (Had she been successful, things wouldn't have been any better: just wrong in a different way.) Every boy who's ever walked home from school has this story, or one very like it, and knows how it redefines and complicates every relationship it touches: to the green-eyed boy, who for a moment looks like a hero-worshipable friend; to Dai, a potential ally corrupted beyond rescue or redemption; to Hilly, whose intervention is as just as it's fruitless. It's one of those moments in childhood when, as Graham Greene says, a door opens and lets the future in.

But a year or so later, a door opened in a more literal and troubling way. In the early summer of 1959, as Kingsley's academic year at Princeton was drawing to a close, Martin had gone unsleepily to bed while his parents gave one of their parties, 'like a baritone schoolyard, several walls away'. The bedroom door opened and a 'dapper middle-aged man' came in, 'followed by a woman in a grey silk blouse beneath a black jacket, dark-haired, handsome, even distinguished'. She remained at the door, while the man 'introduced the notion that he was a doctor and that it would be a good thing if he examined me': this, says Martin, 'went as far as what is usually called "fondling"'. Subsequently, although he had no recollection of the man, he vividly remembered how the woman 'leant against the open door, maintaining her tall-eyed, all's-well smile as she turned, every few seconds, to glance down the corridor'.[23] The memory is significant, for what makes this disquieting little incident truly odd is the presence not just of a third person but of a third perspective. That sense of an additional semi-detached gaze reminds me, in a fittingly oblique way, of Thom Gunn's haunting poem 'The Corridor'.[24] There, a voyeur at a hotel bedroom keyhole glimpses *another* pair of eyes, watching him, in a pier glass at the end of the passage. And in each case the image owes part of its power to our recognition that this is what the writer does, standing slightly aside from the action, with one eye on the subject and the other on the reader.

For Martin, there wasn't a better place to be than America in 1958–9 (not, as he misremembers it in *The Moronic Inferno*, 1959–60), for this was a time when, in the eyes of a nine- or ten-

year-old, everything American was cool in the way that, unthinkably, everything English was to be half a decade later. America
had invented and continued to dominate popular culture, above all
in the iconic form of pop music; of the fourteen hits to reach No. 1 in
the *New Musical Express* charts while the Amises were away in
Princeton, all but four were American. Unsurprisingly, therefore, the
boys lost no time in transforming themselves, even inventing rock-
star versions of their own names, so that Philip became Nicky (from
Nicol, his middle name) and Martin Marty. He'd arrived short-
trousered, like any little boy from Wales. 'Soon I had long trousers, a
crew cut, and a bike with fat whitewalls and an electric horn. I ate
Thanksgiving turkey. I wore a horrible mask on Hallowe'en.'[25] Being
culturally stateless – brought up in Swansea but emphatically not
Welsh – made assimilation that much easier: Martin quickly picked
up elements of an American accent and diction which he has never
lost in his own speech and which pepper his prose with blistering non-
English anachronisms (and not just in his Atlantic-hopping fiction,
either: for example, when he's writing about London in *Experience*,
distances are measured in 'blocks', rather than streets, and buildings
are ascended not by lift but by 'elevator'). 'I feel fractionally American
myself,' he says, and the strange thing is that these fragments still so
often have the air of those phrases we'd try out in the playground, at
nine or ten, to persuade disbelieving friends that our non-existent
American aunts and uncles were on friendly terms with Marilyn
Monroe and Elvis Presley. Though tangibly and sometimes horribly
real, Martin's view of America has retained the shadings of childhood
fantasy.

3

When he was eleven, Martin became a pupil at Bishopgore Grammar
School in Swansea, but he had barely settled in there when Kingsley's ill-considered move to Peterhouse whisked him, and the rest of
the family, off to Cambridge in 1961. What happened next is, alas,
another instance of negligent parenting on his father's part. It needs
to be remembered, on the one hand, that Kingsley now held a senior
academic position at a Cambridge college and, on the other, that
the town possessed two distinguished boys' schools, the Perse and the

Leys: why then, while Philip was sent to board at the Friends' School, Saffron Walden, did Martin end up in the anonymous mediocrity of the Cambridgeshire High School for Boys? Money shouldn't have been a problem, if only the Amises had made an effort to manage it more sensibly; Kingsley's political allegiances were already moving well away from the doctrinaire left; and his association, not much later, with the Black Papers on Education makes his indifference to Martin's schooling look hypocritical as well as culpably careless.

The following summer, the family travelled to Majorca so that Kingsley could write his profile of Robert Graves; everyone has a last summer of childhood, and this was Martin's. He remembers an evening in Spain, on the journey home, his engrossed attention to a pinball machine interrupted by Philip again saying: 'Quick, Mart. Dad's telling us the lot.' The 'lot' was a 'less anatomical induction' to sex than the one previously attempted in his Swansea study, and Martin 'came away with all the very best thoughts and feelings: my father and my mother loved each other, and I and my brother and my sister were somehow the creation of that . . .'. North of Barcelona, something began to go wrong with the car – an event which would be replicated five years later in much the same place though in altered circumstances – and Martin 'spent my thirteenth birthday helping, quite happily, to push it up the Pyrenees'. His family life had never seemed better, but: 'Six weeks later, Kingsley met Elizabeth Jane Howard.'[26]

It was the autumn of the Cuba Crisis, and at the Cambridgeshire High School for Boys the imminent danger to the future of the human race prompted an eccentric response. Martin's form-master 'regularly told me to get down on the floor and hope that my desk lid would protect me from the end of the world',[27] a strategy of limited usefulness, he thought; but he wondered whether another incident which took place that last week of October 1962 might also have been 'crisis-borne'. This is the third of the childhood 'violations' he describes in *Experience*:

> I was returning from the playing-field when I was jumped on by a group of older boys and dragged into a classroom. Some major inadvertency (perhaps this was connected to the crisis, too) had brought it about that an entire school outbuilding was left uninvigilated all afternoon – long enough, at any rate, for eighteen or

twenty of the younger children to get the treatment that was
waiting for me. The maximal resistance I gave was the result of
primitive panic and remained unsubdued by blows and threats as
I was spread out on the absent master's desk and roughly stripped.
On the blackboard someone had chalked up a kind of manifest; I
thought for a moment that it was a school timetable, but in fact it
was just a scorecard, giving each victim's name, his age, his form,
and the state of his sexual development, if any. For the record, my
entry concluded: TINY. NO HAIRS AT ALL . . . Well, I could
live with that. *That* wasn't the end of the world, I thought, as I
ran away clutching my belt in one hand and a shoe in the other. If
fear is simply the intense desire for something to be over, then I
had indeed been horribly frightened, that day. Frightened by their
hysteria, their self-goading mob energy, all splutter and grinning
spittle. Was there nihilism in it? Who cared? We were all dead
anyway. But the essence, the gravamen, was the forcible restraint
and what that does to the spirit.[28]

The event belongs with the green-eyed boy rather than with the
Princeton couple, in the sense that it's the kind of thing that schoolboys do, a commonplace sort of experience, though none the less
frightening for that. But Martin makes two interesting assumptions.
The first is a connection with Cuba, both in the doubtful matter of
the empty classroom (school classrooms are often empty on games
afternoons) and in the throwaway 'Who cared? We were all dead
anyway.' The second is the moral weighting of the last sentence: 'the
forcible restraint and what that does to the spirit'. Both assumptions
seem highly questionable: adolescent rituals are very unlikely to be
directly influenced by global events and such rites of passage may
actually be part of the spirit's necessary education. To believe otherwise is to elevate niceness into an ideal rather than to attempt an
understanding of good and evil: it is the self-deluding error of the soft
left, whose glum legacy is 'political correctness' and among whose
most frightening aspects is the righteous fascination with which it
regards human violence, as something externalised and cartoon-like.
The question which *Experience* doesn't pose, and to which Martin's
nomadic teenage years were to provide no certain answer, is this: if
he had stayed on at the school, would he in two or three years' time
have been among the 'older boys' perpetrating some such 'violation'
and thus perhaps in some sense completing a process? Or would he

have dissociated himself with a virtuous 'Not me'? Actually, schools were changing so rapidly during the 1960s that the circumstance probably wouldn't have arisen, yet the notional answer to the question has at least some bearing on the kind of writer he became.[29]

So, more immediately, has his home life during the eventful year and a half the Amises spent at Madingley Road: the house 'differed from every other don's house in the city' – the most sympathetic side of Kingsley's quarrel with Cambridge – as it was so often full of students who stayed the night, drove the car, cooked the meals or simply 'read or dozed in the garden'. According to Bill Rukeyser, it was 'the locus of considerable sexual activity', but of this Martin was (but only just) still largely unaware. At Madingley Road, 'the atmosphere was lawlessly, and in some way innocently, convivial' and it wasn't unusual to find 'my mother and our family friend Theo Richmond, both of them exhausted by laughter, riding through one of the sitting-rooms on Debbie, our pet donkey, who, every morning, would stick her head through the kitchen window and neigh along with Radio Caroline'.[30] (Debbie was evidently a clairvoyant donkey, since the Amises left Cambridge in 1963 and Radio Caroline didn't start broadcasting until Easter 1964.) It was here, too, that Martin began his tentative metamorphosis into a Mod, appearing one day in his self-designed made-to-measure suit from Montagu Burton, 'the tailor of taste': it was 'a genuine dog's dinner, the trousers as tight as tights, the jacket a blunt denial of the human shape, with two gold buttons, no lapels, and no collar either except for a hank of black velvet at the back of the neck'. The shortness of the jacket posed its own problem for, as Philip noted in his diary, Hilly had 'found Mart crying in the night about the size of his bum. I do feel sorry for him, but a) it *is* enormous, and b) it's not going to go away.'[31] To Martin's bum, at his own insistence, we shall return in due course.

While the Amis household at Madingley Road attempted to recreate the carefree enjoyment of earlier days in Swansea, it also had an anachronistic hint of the dawning hippie era. This couldn't last, and it only needed a suitably grand prophetess of doom to announce its end: fate supplied a perfect one in Eva Garcia, up from Swansea for a visit, unaccompanied by cubiform Joe, in the spring of 1963. With perfect timing, she launched her missile across the kitchen table at Martin: 'You know your father's got this fancy woman up in London, don't you?' 'Has he really?' Experience had long ago taught him that Eva regarded 'the dissemination of bad news' as 'a privilege to be vied for', and this was clearly to be one of her big moments: 'She addressed me with the narrowed stare and flat smile of reckoning I remembered from my childhood in the valleys. She said gauntly, – Ooh aye.'[32] Kingsley had had plenty of affairs, but 'fancy woman' and 'London' made this different – even though part of that difference lay in an abrupt shift to Eva's Welsh working-class perspective. A couple of days later, while driving Martin to school, Hilly told him that she and Kingsley were going to separate; she chose the moment, Martin remembers, so that he wouldn't have time to brood on the news. This seems to conflict with the unpremeditated manner of the Amises' separation later that summer, yet it's likely that Hilly's decision hadn't hardened into planning practical arrangements and that, even if it had, Kingsley wouldn't have taken these in. When he set off on 21 July, en route to his Spanish holiday with Jane, he persuaded himself that his family would still be there when he got back. There was something furtive about his departure, all the same. 'I know a scuttle when I see one,' says Martin, 'and my father definitely scuttled down that gravel drive on the day he left the house in Madingley Road, Cambridge, in the summer of 1963. He was carrying a suitcase. A taxi waited . . .'[33]

The following month, Hilly and the children 'absconded' to Soller, Majorca. The term is Martin's and not entirely fair. They had rented the villa and now they intended to live in it, so they were merely carrying out an agreed plan; yet the notion that Kingsley would somehow manage to join them there was self-evidently absurd. Once he and Jane had returned to England and it was abundantly clear that he intended to stay there, Philip and Martin established a 'silent routine' of sitting on the wall, waiting for the postman, in the hope that he'd bring something more substantial from their father than his 'occasional notes and postcards'. The house was intended to be a holiday villa and had no proper heating for the colder months: by late autumn, Hilly was becoming seriously depressed and the boys were 'almost comatose', so she packed them off on a plane to London. She sent a telegram to announce their visit.

But the plane was late landing at Heathrow, the explanatory telegram hadn't arrived (was it ever sent or, if so, correctly addressed?), and it was midnight when the two tired boys turned up on the doorstep at Basil Mansions. Martin – adding to the stock of self-delusion that both his parents had been accumulating during the year – had contrived to imagine Kingsley, possibly the least domesticated father anyone had ever known, 'in the unlikely role of a functioning, indeed rather houseproud single man'. What now confronted him was Kingsley in his striped pyjamas and, beyond him in the corridor, the 'fancy woman' whose existence Eva had so delightedly revealed: 'It wasn't just that he was surprised to see us. He was horrified to see us. We had busted him *in flagrante delicto*: in blazing crime . . .' Except that Jane wasn't the 'fancy woman' who, in Martin's imagination, would have been 'all bangles, cleavage, and electric red hair'. What he now saw was someone altogether different: 'In her white towel bathrobe, with her waist-long fair hair, tall, serious, worldly . . . already busying herself, cooking eggs and bacon, finding sheets, blankets, for the beds in the spare room.'[34] He at once recognised in Jane 'the glamour and mystery of life lived' and, crucially, understood that it was possible to respond to this without being disloyal to Hilly; he was fourteen but, in this one respect, more mature than his fifteen-year-old brother, who immediately decided that Jane was 'obviously someone who didn't like children'.[35] Their stay in London turned out to be an alternating sequence of tearful and angry discussions with their patient father – Martin remembers that Philip called Kingsley a 'cunt' and got away with it – and 'expert treats': 'gimmicky restaurants, the just-released *55 Days at Peking* in Leicester Square, a new LP each . . .'[36] It was the third week in November 1963: George Gale came to the dinner he didn't stay to eat on the day John F. Kennedy was murdered in Dallas, Texas. The times they were a-changing.

As soon as they'd flown back to Soller, the boys found themselves enrolled in the 'casual and cosmopolitan and above all coeducational' International School at Palma. They quickly learned to appreciate the unEnglish freedoms of their new life: they rode (and crashed) the dirt-track motorbikes that Hilly, not to be outdone in the expert-treat department, bought for them; they drank beer in cafés after school and, on one momentous occasion, cognac before it; they watched films the English censor would have denied them on the grounds of their age, such as Hitchcock's *Psycho*; and they advanced their sex education in, among other places, the Soller–Palma train. They were both happier, now that they'd in some sense reclaimed their father; they had also inadvertently acquired positions of near-adult privilege

and enhanced negotiating rights with their parents. When their
Mediterranean stay came to its end and they returned permanently to
London, in the late spring of 1964, they had established that in either
place they could do more or less as they pleased.

4

We know what Kingsley was like at this age: he resembled Peter
Furneaux in *The Riverside Villas Murder* and, even more closely,
Robin Davies in the first section of *You Can't Do Both*. He had spent
his fifteen years in the same South London suburb and the last four
of them as a diligent pupil at the City of London School; his parents
treated him like a child and in many ways he still behaved like one;
adult freedoms in general, and sexual experience in particular, were
the stuff of fantasy. Martin at fifteen had no settled parental home
and had attended four schools in as many years; he had the freedom
of the streets of London and any moment now he would lose his
virginity with a girl he'd met that same day in a Wimpy Bar. It's
tempting to conclude that teenage life had altered out of all recognition and in one easily recognisable direction, yet here the paradox
of permissiveness recurs: in crucial respects – specifically, the way in
which he related to the established adult world – Martin was actually
less confident and secure than his father had been at the same age.
He also lacked the powerful stimulus of parental opposition which
had spurred on Kingsley's interest in jazz and forbidden books.

The flat in Ovington Gardens, Knightsbridge, to which Hilly and
the children temporarily moved in May 1964 was impossibly small,
with only two bedrooms for the four of them; they stayed there only
a few weeks before taking on a dilapidated house in the Fulham
Road. Kingsley paid the rent in each case – Robert Conquest found
himself having to provide 'a reference for Mr. W. Kingsley Amis to
pay for a flat for Hilly'[37] – but the arrangements were handled by
their solicitor friend in Swansea, Stuart Thomas. Philip returned to
the Friends' School, Saffron Walden; Sally went to a private school
locally; once again, it was Martin who drew the short straw, which
in this case was called Sir Walter St John's School, Battersea. Martin
remembers it as 'a violent school with violent pupils and violent staff.
It seemed to me that you could do *anything* there and expect just an

hour's detention.'[38] 'I was beaten up on a pretty regular basis,' he says. 'My only two defences against the playground bruisers were the many stolen cigarettes I dispensed and my growing reputation as a palmist.'[39] With his children's education, as with their home, Kingsley didn't want to know. He'd pay the bills; the rest was up to Hilly. But Hilly was in no state to cope: one night, after dinner with Sybil Burton, at which they drank too much and talked in a maudlin way about being the ex-wives of famous men, she took an overdose of sleeping-pills at the Fulham Road house. Sally, unable to wake her mother and remembering that terrible day when her grandmother too had been beyond waking, was hysterical when Mavis Nicholson, worried by an earlier phone conversation, rang to enquire after Hilly. It was a drunk and reluctant Kingsley whom Mavis eventually persuaded to go, with Colin, to Fulham Road; he called an ambulance and accompanied Hilly to hospital where, when she recovered consciousness, he berated her (Sally, meanwhile, had been taken to stay with the Nicholsons). Hilly's recovery was 'swift and total. When she talked about it afterwards,' Martin writes, 'she said she had been depressed because she was still in love with my father.'[40] Their states of denial made both Kingsley and Hilly unyielding towards each other and irresponsible towards their children. As soon as Hilly had recovered, she took Sally off to stay with the Gales at Wivenhoe, leaving Martin to fend for himself. Just before leaving, she rang Jane: 'Well I'm off now, it's all up to you.'

When George Gale arrived at Fulham Road one afternoon, he 'went from room to room in solemn consternation. Every cupboard he opened had a fourteen-year-old girl in it.'[41] He alerted Kingsley; but of course it was Jane who actually went round to see what was going on, discovering 'Martin alone in the house in bed, fully dressed, with a high fever'. He was, Jane remembers, frightened as well as hostile. 'I said, "You don't look very well, would like some tea or an egg? And while you have them I'll make your bed." Well, of course, there wasn't any tea in the house, there wasn't an egg and there wasn't a single piece of clean linen.'[42] Martin passes over this episode in *Experience*, but it stayed with him. The memory informs the feelings he gives to nine-year-old Terence Service in *Success*, who is accidentally abandoned in his parents' house after his murderous father's arrest: 'And for a week I picked my terrified way through the dead rooms, through the rank scullery-world of thickened milk and glaring butter, through the nights on that nail-bed of nerves, and through the slow time of the pendulous afternoons. Can you imagine?'[43] Jane, says Zachary Leader, 'found the confusion and dirt of the house nauseating' and she remains disinclined to condone Hilly's behaviour. She decided that she and Kingsley must move in at once and sort things out, which in practice meant that while Kingsley spent the days writing at Blomfield Road, she and Colin cleaned and decorated the house from top to bottom. It took them a fortnight.

During this time, Jane bumped into an old friend, the film director Alexander Mackendrick and he – as Martin puts it – 'stopped by for a drink', something that an adult mightn't willingly have done at 128 Fulham Road a couple of weeks earlier. Mackendrick was about to leave for the Caribbean to film *A High Wind in Jamaica* but lacked one juvenile lead: a fourteen-year-old boy. Jane thought Martin might be ideal for the part, Mackendrick agreed, and Hilly had no sooner returned from Wivenhoe than she was off to the West Indies with Martin and Sally (a 'busy extra'). This expedition took place in the second half of the summer term: it's ironic that Jane, who would shortly become the only person to take some trouble over Martin's education, should have been responsible for this latest disruption of his schooling. In an ordinary pupil's life, it would have been the summer before O Levels: a time when grammar schools, reasonably enough, expected their pupils to sit end-of-year exams which would determine their academic sets and likely candidacies for the vital following year. Moreover, 'There was some kind of semi-illegality involved in taking children abroad for work, and 20th Century Fox thought it prudent to wait until we were out of the country before notifying the school.'[44] Neither Hilly nor Jane had received an orthodox school education but Kingsley, not for the first time or the last, ought to have known better and at least have tried to present the case against.

Even so, it would have been a hard opportunity to pass up. Apart from acting with a group of frighteningly precocious children, Martin 'played chess with my co-star, the consistently avuncular Anthony Quinn, and the divinely pretty daughter – Lisa Coburn – of my other co-star, genial James, fell in love with me and followed me everywhere'. He was paid £50 a week, a colossal amount of money, despite the fact that during the filming his voice broke and had to be dubbed; when they all returned to London, the rest of the summer was spent finishing the film at Pinewood. Martin didn't summon the courage to watch *A High Wind in Jamaica* until years later, partly because of the dubbed voice and partly because he worried that his bum would look big in it (it does, he says). In September, on the first day of the new academic year, he presented himself at Sir Walter St John's, in a brand-new blazer, only to learn that he'd been expelled for chronic truancy: the headmaster had written formally to Hilly in Jamaica but the letter, naturally, hadn't reached them there. The expulsion seemed terrible and humiliating, made all the worse by the new blazer; then, crossing Chelsea Bridge, Martin flung his school cap into the river and felt much better, 'comforting myself with the obvious thought that I had far less to fear than those who remained'.[45]

Philip had left the Friends' School, Saffron Walden, and enrolled at Davies, Laing and Dick, a well-established 'tutorial college' or crammer, in Holland Park; there the expelled Martin joined him. The crammer, largely staffed by retired or unsuccessful teachers, was 'chaotic': one of them, an elderly mathematician whom the boys called 'Flash Crunch', becomes Mr Greenchurch in *The Rachel Papers*, where crammers in general get a pretty rough ride. Not that the Amis boys spent much time at Davies, Laing and Dick: Martin soon returned to his holiday routine of 'cruising all day and playing Scrabble all night'. Kingsley and Jane were far away – using up the unexpired lease on the villa in Majorca while Colin oversaw the renovation of their new home in Maida Vale – so the one pair of potentially watchful eyes was averted while Martin played truant and life at Fulham Road relapsed into a Bohemian mix of 'Tellies and trannies, cats and lodgers, fires and floods – and dope, and speed'.[46] All this was too time-consuming to allow much time for reading ('when I did read I read comics, and after I'd done that, I reread them': this at the age of fifteen or so) but, feeling vaguely that he wanted to be a writer and that he was good at English, he precociously attempted an A Level in the subject. He was 'reeking in bed one morning' when Hilly shouted up the stairs: 'Martin!' 'My mother usually called me Mart. The full Martin was always a . . . "You *failed*." Not even an E. An *F*.'[47]

By this time, he and Philip were spending the weekdays at Maida Vale and returning to Fulham Road at weekends: the arrangement had been bravely suggested by Jane when she and Kingsley returned from Spain in November 1964. Thus, early in 1965, she 'embarked upon the extraordinarily difficult business of being a stepmother',[48] a role which in this case carried particular burdens: not only did the boys blame her for the break-up of their parents' marriage, they also deeply resented the elements of order which she was determined to bring into their lives. Martin remembers this as a kind of social culture shock: 'The kitchen was a prosperous one, good looking but also potently stocked, it seemed to me, and continually replenished by men in white topcoats. *Jane* was quite posh, after all, and I felt I had gone up in the world.'[49] But Kingsley was no help at all. Jane cites the telling example of a second-hand pub bar-billiards table they bought for the conservatory: it had a shilling-in-the-slot mechanism, and everyone agreed that the money collected should go to charity; except that there was never any money, because the boys had found a way of emptying it. Kingsley simply replied, 'Well, it isn't very much money,' when Jane raised the matter. 'This was in front of the boys, so they *knew* I was a prig, and their father was a good sort.'[50] They were unused to parental discipline: in their home lives, at least, they had until now been curiously immune to the 'generation gap' about which so many of their contemporaries were noisily protesting. Hilly's Bohemianism and Kingsley's indifference had effectively defused generational opposition; but here it was, personified in the shape of a 'wicked stepmother'. In such circumstances, even the best-meant gestures are sure to misfire. Jane remembers making 'a sitting room for them with their hi-fi' and adds: 'There was a lot of pop music and it smelt of hot socks.'[51] You can hear the generation gap – the uncomprehending distance, the mild distaste – even now; so there was absolutely no chance of Philip and Martin missing it at the time.

This is the moment at which Martin becomes decisively unlike his father, and also the moment when the 1960s really do begin to seem utterly different from the 1930s. There is almost always a fault-line in popular culture which divides the hot from the cool: these are, of course, predominantly jazz terms, and the young Kingsley had pre-ferred the 'hot' New Orleans tradition to the 'cool' modernists of his own generation; it was a temperamental choice, of a piece with his liking for pubs and his unconcern about the clothes he wore. By the 1960s, the terms of pop culture had spread out to embrace most aspects of an adolescent's life, but the fault-line was still there: Rockers were the inheritors of the hot, Mods of the cool. In the spring of 1964, a period straddling the Whitsun rioting of Mods and

Rockers at Clacton, Charles Hamblett and Jane Deverson carried out
a Mass Observation-type survey, assembling the written and recorded
views of British teenagers into a mosaic which they called *Generation
X*. One (unnamed) respondent described the Mod boy of June 1964
in precise detail:

> At the moment they're wearing ... Ivy League-style suits with
> three buttons on the jacket and narrow lapels and two vents at the
> back. Trousers have seventeen inch bottoms, boots have round
> toes and are in imitation crocodile or python. Blue suits and blue
> shirts with peg collar – giraffe collar three inches high – they very
> uncomfortable and crease up.
>
> The shirts are about 39s 6d and a mod will pay thirty guineas
> for a suit and up to £5 for a shirt. Most popular is John Michael,
> the Mod Shop in Carnaby Street, Soho. The Dunn's shops are fab
> for hats. We pay up to £5 for shoes and £2 10s for a hat ...
>
> Mods go to dance halls, Hammersmith Palais, the Marquee,
> and the various 'discotheques' – clubs where they play gramo-
> phone records; there's a very popular one in Wardour Street ...
>
> The Mod boys are the smartest dressed every time, they might
> look a bit effeminate but they're not really. People talk about them
> taking Purple Hearts, but not many of them do ... The Mods
> don't watch TV programmes except teenage programmes – *Ready
> Steady Go* and *Thank Your Lucky Stars*. They read James Bond
> because they fancy themselves with women like the ones he has.
> Oh, and Micky Spillane.[52]

Another contributor, David Holbourne, said: 'If you're a Mod, you're
a Mod twenty-four hours a day; even when working with other
people, you're still a Mod ... But I'm past it now, I'm too old, 19.
You've got to be sixteen to be a Mod, to be able to wear high heeled
boots and long hair and not care what anyone thinks.'[53] When Martin
returned from Jamaica that summer, he made his sixteen-year-old
brother a generous present of £50: 'He told me what he was going
to do with it. He was going to hail a taxi (we only used taxis in
emergencies) and say, "*Carnaby* Street." '[54]

It's a world away from Kingsley's youth, not just in its conventions
and fashions but in kind: this obsessive attention to detail simply
wouldn't have ocurred to previous generations of teenage boys. While
the young had quite often irritated their parents by being disorganised

and dirty, Mods terrified their elders by being simultaneously fastidious and subversive (at my school, where a regulative loophole allowed black ties as an acceptable alternative to striped ones, we tormented the staff with our ingenious variants: knitted ties, string ties, leather ties; button-down collars, tab collars, stand-up collars . . .). Carnaby Street, Philip's unhesitating destination, was the Mods' sartorial mecca, while the offshore stations Radio Caroline and Radio London supplied the soundtrack: for *Generation X* contributors, this was predominantly blue beat, a predecessor of reggae, but during the next couple of years the pirate radio stations promoted an avalanche of new Mod bands, including Georgie Fame and the Blue Flames, the Kinks, Moody Blues, Small Faces, the Who. The use of dope and amphetamines (first 'purple hearts', then 'speed') became commonplace in the city life of Mods, who rode scooters – Philip acquired his Vespa in 1965 – when sufficiently unstoned to drive or, sometimes, when stoned enough to fall off. It was a fantastic time to be young, if you didn't have to worry about exams: there was a perfectly unshakeable sense that no one in the history of humanity had known how to have fun until now.

Sex was a central part of this fun. Here, Kingsley did have a view on his sons' conduct: his guiding principle was that it should be diametrically opposite to his own father's. So, having 'cheerfully and encouragingly and almost gloatingly' established over dinner at Biagi's, an Italian restaurant near Marble Arch, that 'both his sons were sexually launched', he took them out to lunch in Soho a few days later in the summer of 1965: 'After lunch he led us to an ambiguous little outlet in a side street north of Piccadilly. Some will consider it appropriate that he bought for us there, among the Brylcreem jars and the jockstraps and the hernia supports, a *gross* of condoms.'[55] No doubt he remembered his own nervousness in the same quest, his need for moral support from his friend George Blunden when shopping for condoms in wartime Oxford; no doubt, too, his action was of an admirably neurosis-dispelling sort which is all too rare among fathers of teenage sons. Yet one doesn't have to be a prude to see the problematical side of it, tactfully acknowledged by Martin in 'almost gloatingly'; Kingsley ought by now to have recognised that there was more to life than a good fuck and that his chummy encouragement of his sons in this respect was no compensation for his negligence elsewhere.

Two other subjects which he might most usefully have broached over one of those meals were drugs and truancy. A year later, after a typically exhausting truant's day of gambling, girls and dope, Martin returned home to find himself summoned to the sitting-room by Kingsley, Jane and Colin: 'I sensed Howard knowhow in this triumvirate of adult unanimity.'[56] They knew he was using drugs, they said; Philip had already admitted as much, during an interrogation prompted by Jane's discovery of 'a box with PHIL'S DRUGS written on it in eyecatching multicoloured capitals' among his clothes, a neat symbol of the way in which behaviour acceptable in Hilly's world didn't always transplant well into hers. Philip, in fact, had already left home and taken refuge with his girlfriend; he would never return, nor would he ever forgive Jane. Martin, full of apparent remorse and assurances of future good behaviour, was taken out to dinner at Biagi's, 'awed, and sumptuously relieved, to find myself in a restaurant rather than in a jailhouse' (or indeed, since this was London, a prison);[57] but when he went to bed that night he discovered a note from Philip, telling him that he hadn't given Martin away. There'd been no need.

But the truancy went on: 'What I liked was bunking off school and hanging out with my friend Rob and betting in betting shops (not the horses: the dogs) and mincing up and down the King's Road in skintight velves and grimy silk scarves and haunting a coffee bar called the Picasso, and smoking hash (then £8 an ounce) and trying to pick up girls.'[58] Rob was Rob Henderson, an amiable and companionable Westminster School dropout, a perfect friend and a reliably bad influence; the crammers really didn't stand a chance, given the competition. Weeks and months passed in a haze of narcissistic indecision, while Martin and Rob wondered whether or not they'd go to the Picasso. Kingsley, who had made an art out of not noticing, continued not to notice; Jane, particularly after Philip's departure, knew she had to tread carefully. And Martin, though he jealously guarded what he supposed was his freedom, was steadily sinking into what he'd later call 'a bottomless adolescent *cafard*' in which 'it could take you an entire day to transport a single sock from one end of your bedroom to the other'.[59]

In allowing this to happen, or at least so completely to take over his life, his parents and stepmother were once again to blame. They seem not to have bothered to encourage him to do anything else.

Other boys of his age with literary ambitions were reading widely and avidly in contemporary fiction and poetry; were picking up the *TLS* and the *Spectator*, *Encounter* and the *London Magazine*; were acting and learning musical instruments; were going to concerts and opera and the outstanding productions of Laurence Olivier's recently formed National Theatre Company at the Old Vic. And other parents, with far less in the way of literary and cultural expertise than Kingsley and Jane, were encouraging their children to do these things. The point matters because, in the space where some sense of high cultural values might have been planted in Martin as a necessary counterbalance to the vernacular world of the streets, there was a vacuum: this was to have lasting consequences, for the architecture of good prose, its tone and cadence, is something best learned through imitation, early on. Kingsley's boyhood reading shaped his adult work in ways that proved indelible.

Jane's grasp of chronology – like Martin's, though for different reasons – is shaky here. She can't put a date to the moment when she asked him what he wanted to do and he replied: 'Be a writer.' 'But you never read anything,' she told him. 'If you're so interested in writing, why don't you read?' She gave him *Pride and Prejudice*: a slightly improbable choice, but – after being rebuffed when he asked Jane to tell him how it ended – he enjoyed and finished it. 'That was when he started to read properly,' she says, with justifiable pride.[60] It was also the moment when, despite having failed to establish any rapport with his brother, she realised that she might be able to do something with Martin. This clearly involved getting him out of London, away from Rob and the King's Road and the Picasso.

5

'Sussex Tutors was the end of the road: my last-gasp saloon.'[61] It was a boarding crammer in Marine Parade, Brighton, situated in a rambling building high above the beach and surrounded by similar houses which had been turned into nursing homes. Sussex Tutors was owned and run by a Mr Ardagh and his mother Mrs Gibbs; and they were evidently no fools. Jane remembers telling Ardagh: 'This boy is virtually illiterate. He's been very badly taught, but I think he's scholarship material. I can say this because I'm not his mother.'[62] By the summer of 1966 Martin, at seventeen, had managed to pick up a mere three O Levels; during the academic year 1966-7 he would squeeze in four more *and* three A Levels with good enough grades for him to sit Oxford Entrance the following November. The fact that he was so studiously settled in Brighton was one reason why Kingsley and Jane felt able to go to Nashville in the autumn of 1967. Philip, too, was by this time settled in a place of his own and as a student at Camberwell School of Art, at the instigation of Colin Howard's friend Sargy Mann, who taught painting there. Not only were both boys at last following the paths which would determine their future professional lives, as writer and painter; they both owed this new sense of direction to the Howard side rather than the Amis side of the Maida Vale ménage. At about this time ('late teens' says Martin), Kingsley asked his two sons what they proposed to do with their lives. Philip said he wanted to be a painter, Martin a novelist. ' "Good," said Kingsley, rubbing his hands together rapidly, even noisily in that way he had. "That means the Amises are branching out into the other arts while keeping their stranglehold on fiction." ' [63] This remark, delighted and amused as it is, exactly catches the tone and the extent of his involvement.

Unlike his father, Martin isn't much of a letter-writer; nor is he much of an archivist, so letters *to* him (including Kingsley's and Jane's) are as scarce those *from* him. Nevertheless, he scatters through *Experience* a sequence of his letters to his father and stepmother, several of which date from his final year in Brighton: they are fascinating documents, often as interesting for their style as for their content. The first one in the book (dated 23 October 1967) opens in a manner which few eighteen-year-olds would have adopted towards their elders – 'Thanks awfully for your letter. So we all appear to be working like fucking fools' – before switching instantly to describe a state characteristic of Charles Highway in *The Rachel Papers* or the see-sawing foster-brothers of *Success*: 'I seem to be flitting manically from brash self-confidence to whimpering depression . . .' (The state may be common enough, but the adjective 'whimpering' stamps it as 'early Martin Amis'.) He's enjoying the English, having chosen, on Mr Ardagh's advice, 'about 6 chaps' to know 'pretty thoroughly' – cautious choices, leaning a good deal on the preceding A Level syllabus: 'Shakespeare; Donne and Marvell; Coleridge and Keats; Jane Austen; Owen; Greene; and possibly old Yeats as well' – but, like many another Oxbridge candidate, worried about being jinxed by a failure in minimum-entrance-requirement O Level Latin. The former non-reader has caught the adolescent reading bug a few years later than most, and is perhaps all the better for that: in London, he'd read *Middlemarch* in three days, *The Trial* ('Kafka is a fucking fool') and *The Heart of the Matter* in a day each, and even back in Brighton he's knocking back 'a couple of novels a week (plus lots of poetry)'. His considered opinion of *Middlemarch* is that it's 'FUCKING good – Jane Austen + passion + dimension', which isn't a bad formula. And he slyly turns down an invitation to spend Christmas in Nashville, of which he's heard quite enough, partly because Oxford interviews could take place well into December and offers through UCCA might arrive as early as 1 January, and partly because American television is so 'lousy'.[64]

At Brighton, he says, he was 'in love with literature – particularly with poetry'.[65] This first proper engagement with books is invariably fresher and less compromised than what succeeds it, and Martin was still an absolute beginner: in his next letter (4 November 1967), he reports that he now has 'a hallowed library of about 25 books', a startlingly meagre collection for an Oxbridge candidate. But his reading is steadily branching out from its old A Level base, which included the book he calls Lawrence's *The Rainbore* ('so I feel qualified to say why he's no good'), and his literary opinions are often pungently similar to young Kingsley's: Pound is a 'Trendy little ponce', Auden 'Good, but I feel he *must* be an awful old crap'.[66] Meanwhile, however, 'that veritable little hobgoblin Mr Ardagh' has 'put a burning queer in the room next to mine', who 'rushes in without knocking every night between 12 and 1, with eyes aflame, hoping to catch me at some stage of undress'.[67] Here Martin sounds surprisingly and rather disagreeably young – inexperienced, in fact – though in other respects the style anticipates his future work: Mr Ardagh will henceforth always be a goblin or hobgoblin, and such cartoonish or (at best) Dickensian stock epithets are characteristic of Martin's fiction; as are the caricature of the 'burning queer' and the list of possible retaliations – 'putting bogies in his coffee, spitting on his toothbrush, stealing his shampoo, soiling his pyjamas, etc.' – which will grow into the grotesque practical jokes of 'Johnny' in *Dead Babies*.

If it seems unfair to subject an eighteen-year-old's letters home (or,

in this case, abroad) to effortful scrutiny, we need to bear in mind
not only the prominence Martin gives them in *Experience* but also
his own clear sense at the time that he was joining the family firm
and becoming a writer: these are letters intent on trying out literary
gestures in front of their expert recipients. The next one was written
only three days later, and the shape of its opening is pure Kingsley –
'Another letter so soon, you see, because I want to ask some rather
delicate questions . . .'[68] – except that Kingsley might have reached
for the mock-posh 'you sam' of Bertrand in *Lucky Jim*. On the
assumption that he'd still have an exam or two to mop up the
following summer, Mr Ardagh had proposed that he should get a
part-time job teaching in a prep school at Rottingdean; it had now
dawned on Martin that he might make a plausible case for having a
flat of his own during this period, to enjoy some independence which
naturally wouldn't 'entail riot, insurrection, disregard of personal
health, and general wanton behaviour'. (In the event, things were to
work out differently and involve a good deal of commuting from
London on the Brighton Belle.) When he wrote again, on the last day
of November, he was in a doubly gloomy state: his Oxford papers
had gone badly, he thought, since he'd sat them in the aftermath of
'a complete break-down . . . a mild glandular fever: head-ache, fiendish sore throat, sweating, temperature 104!';[69] and an interview at
Rottingdean had revealed that he'd be expected to teach Maths and
Games rather than English and History. The goblin agreed that his
papers weren't up to his best standard and the goblin's mother
arranged for a medical certificate to be sent off with them, but it was
the surname on the scripts which ensured that Martin would at least
get interviewed.

   He describes himself at this stage as Osric, the fawning courtier
in Act V of *Hamlet* whom Kingsley had coincidentally played in a
university production at Swansea: 'Thus has he – and many more of
the same bevy that I know the drossy age dotes on – only got the
tune of the time and, out of an habit of encounter, a kind of yeasty
collection, which carries them through and through the most fanned
and winnowed opinions,' says Hamlet. Osric is Shakespeare's Mod.
He's fashionable, narcissistic and empty-headed, in touch with 'the
tune of the time' and wholly subservient to it. Martin wasn't quite
like that: he was more independent than Osric, though not much

more substantial. As 1967 turned to 1968, he found himself caught up in the same game of chance as every other university applicant. When he was interviewed at one of his standby choices, Durham (only just: Colin's erratic mail-forwarding from Maida Vale almost jinxed it), he sensibly talked himself into almost believing it might do: 'I thought Durham a beautiful town I must say, and the college looked very comfortable from all points of view.' There was an interview at Exeter University in the pipeline too, but the back-up he really wanted was Bristol. Then came the summons from Oxford. He had an unusually short haircut for the occasion: 'I think I look like a particularly nasty and petulant Baboon.'[70]

At his father's old college, St John's, he was interviewed by John Carey, who ought to have enjoyed his enthusiasm for Donne but was 'embarrassed' by the state of his languages; while at Exeter College, Jonathan Wordsworth, who wasn't bothered about the languages, 'and, I suspect, is rather proud of the fact that he doesn't care about that', offered him an open exhibition.[71] Another younger don at Exeter gamely remarked, 'You certainly know all the clichés, don't you?' to which Martin replied: 'Well, you can't be too careful.' Osric would have been very proud of that remark, not least because it would have been beyond him, and so was the petulant baboon. Nevertheless, since nothing more surely tickles an admission tutor's fancy than a bright candidate with a truly catastrophic school record, Martin was always going to get a place; the exhibition – Kingsley described his own as 'a kind of cut-price scholarship' – provided a modest financial bonus of £40 per year. When Martin rang his father in Nashville with the news, it had to be explained to Kingsley that, no, he wasn't talking about the West Country university but the Oxford college; and the confusion, although understandable given that his son had applied to both places, was also typical of Kingsley's lack of interest and attention. 'I said hesitantly, "Exeter? You do mean Exeter, Oxford?" to which he replied, "I don't mean the University Fucking College of the South West of England. I mean EXETER COLLEGE OXFORD." I told him that answered my question.'[72] Martin certainly knew who to thank: 'VERY *seriously* though, thank you, O Jane, for quite literally getting me into Oxford. Had you not favoured my education with your interest and sagacity, I would now be a 3-O-levelled wretch with little to commend me,' he wrote on 9 January 1968. 'I have a huge debt to you which I shall work off by being an ever-dutiful step-son.'[73] True enough, even if the tone is a strange brew of Osric plus irony.

Although he had rather surprisingly scraped a pass in O Level Latin, he'd need something more solid than that to cope with Oxford Prelims, 'unpleasant and meaningless exams which befall the student at the end of his or her second term'; he claims that in his entrance papers his 'attempt at the Latin unseen had consisted of a single word, mistranslated: I had rendered *igitur* as "the general", whereas I gather it in fact means "therefore" '.[74] So, once a week during the spring of 1968, he travelled back to Brighton for Latin coaching with a tutor who – as described by him on 12 February 1968 – resembles a character who might have appeared in a novel by *either* of the Amises:

> I go to an old shag called Mr Bethell who, I should say, is experiencing puberty for the second, or possibly the third time. This old dullard can speak seventeen languages fluently, including Latin, Ancient Greek, Welsh, Anglo-Saxon, Romney [*sic*], and the language of the tinkers. He says things like: 'There are 140 first conjugation deponent verbs': I say 'Well I never' and he says 'They are Venor, Conor' and so on and on and on. He is also a high-priest of B.O. well versed in its most secret arts, and master of the most esoteric precepts of his craft. He still enjoys frequent use of his limbs, although they taper off, after the second joint, to gangrenous supporating [*sic*] threads.[75]

There are two voices here: the first, which uses phrases such as 'old shag' and 'old dullard' and turns Mr Bethell into a variant of Daddy B, is Kingsley's; the second, in which the tutor's physical character-istics are exaggerated in the manner of a grotesque cartoon, is Martin's. Though they run together plausibly enough in the informal context of a letter, they are completely different: at length, the author of the first would find the author of the second impossible to read.

When he wasn't being entranced by Latin deponent verbs, Martin was now working for Colin, who ran a hi-fi business based in Rickmansworth; later, during the summer, the pair would also take on the rewiring of Lemmons, which the Amises bought in July and to which they would eventually move in November. Martin's own recollections of this period are, as usual, a bit fuzzy in matters of chronological detail: in *My Oxford*, he says that he can 'account for only *five days* of the traditional mind-expanding months between school and university, in which I had worked in my step-uncle's record shop in Rickmansworth';[76] in *Experience*, he spent 'three weeks' there, 'sitting behind the till'.[77] His point in *My Oxford* is that he'd neither been working in a factory nor had he 'walked from Oslo to Peking and back'. But he had been travelling, all the same. In fact, he'd been about as stereotypically pre-studentish as you could possibly get in 1968. He and Rob Henderson – and a couple of friends, who *were* a couple, called Si and Fran – had all driven off to Majorca in a Mini-Moke, wearing 'the usual chaos of flowered scarves and crushed velvet'. While they were there, they decided to go and visit Robert Graves.

When Rob asked him how they should behave with Graves, Martin (who should have known better) replied: 'Just go on as if he's a god.' The resulting dialogue between the two Roberts is transcribed in *Experience* thus:

– Make that mountain open up.
– What?
– Turn it into a volcano.
– What?
– Go on. You can do it. Make that cloud go away.
– Oh, you're –
– Summon a tidal wave.
– You little –
– Make the moon come out.
– Ooh, you –
– Make the –
And Robert got hold of Rob and roughly tickled him.[78]

They parted on the friendliest terms: causing Graves to be effectively teased was one of the generational continuities between the Amises. But on the way back, having left Si and Fran in Majorca, things went seriously wrong. For the second time in his life, Martin found himself pushing a broken-down car up the Pyrenees; the difference was this one, broken even beyond coasting, had to be pushed down as well. They had no money: currency restrictions meant you could take only £50 out of the country and Rob, after an unsuccessful visit to the bookmakers', hadn't been able to raise even that: they were stuck,

hungry and homeless. They'd bought Spanish cigarettes in bulk and
they shared these with more seasoned hikers, who bewilderingly
asked them whether it was possible to get work in the docks at
Barcelona. As if they'd know: 'Rob and I looked at each other: our
pallor, our want of inches, our soiled flower shirts.' Kingsley and
Jane were themselves away in Greece and couldn't be contacted;
Rob's mother, when phoned, said, 'Get a job'; but eventually Colin
managed to arrange for some money to be sent through to them. By
the time the car had been repaired, they had fifteen francs left, and
with this Rob contrived to buy an unsustaining and indeed nauseous
combination of glacier mints, coffee-cream biscuits and orangeade.
Martin gashed his hand on the orangeade bottle which broke as he
opened it, was violently sick, and ended his one stint as driver when
a flicked cigarette-end went down the back of his jeans. 'That week
in Perpignan was my only experience of privation, of hunger,' he
writes.[79] Imaginatively, he was going to make the most of it.

After they'd got back to England in August, Martin went off to
work with Colin and Sargy on the rewiring of Lemmons. Meanwhile,
the Russian army was gathering on the border of Czechoslovakia
and the Beatles' seemingly endless 'Hey, Jude' was playing, seemingly
endlessly, on the radio. On the morning of 21 August, Martin
remembers, Kingsley appeared in the courtyard at Lemmons, where
the electricians were taking a break, and called 'in a defeated and
wretched voice: "Russian tanks in Prague." ' In time this might seem
to be, as indeed the Beatles put it elsewhere, the end of the beginning,
rather than the beginning of the end, but it didn't look that way yet.
As for Martin: 'I turned nineteen four days later. In September I went
up to Oxford.'[80]

6

'No,' says Osric, 'I was a Londoner, thanks, far too flash and worldly
to countenance the pompous hicks and dumb Henries I expected to
find in boring old Oxford.'[81] His assumption on going up was that
'only two types of people ever went to Oxford, and I knew, for a
start, that I belonged to neither'. These two types were the 'craven
swot from somewhere called Heaptown' and the 'haughty cretin from
one of our public schools'; and they can indeed be found, sharing

rooms, in Philip Larkin's *Jill*, where they are called John Kemp, from Huddlesford (which is close to Heaptown), and Christopher Warner, late of a public school called Lamprey College. Martin, of course, intends this contrast in a spirit of self-deprecation: experience, he implies, would prove the inadequacy of such stereotypes. Except that for him it wouldn't, quite: caricatures including the pair he half mocks here recur as a problematical feature of his work.

Oxford supplied 'more fragmented and less corny' types than he'd anticipated – those two among them – and they included political people, God people and sport people. There were also 'gnome' people, 'humble clerks of the new literacy', and 'cool' people, who 'had among their number all the cockiest and best-looking youths in Oxford; they drank alcohol and took drugs, and they were as promiscuous as anyone well could be there',[82] Martin reckoned himself to have been an incongruous mixture of the gnomic and the cool – a combination less unlikely but more troublesome than he recognised. For the two groups had much in common: they were classless and they were uncommitted to the external ideals of the political, God and sport people. The trouble was that at a more local level, including the most local of all levels inside one's own head, they tended to pull in opposite directions. On the one hand, he had to develop the habit of gnome-like dedication, the solitary study which is also very like the writer's life, partly to repair the deficiencies of a scattered education and partly to meet the unignorable challenge of his father's First from Oxford. Kingsley, as Jane recalls, gave him an open account at Blackwell's, and he made good use of it.[83] On the other, he couldn't shake off the legacy of Osric the Mod: 'there I was, in my black velvet suit, my snakeskin boots and eagerly patterned shirt, a relative tike by Oxford standards, with quite a few metropolitan girlfriends and one metropolitan love-affair under my belt, a famous Oxonian father, hardly a perfect stranger to human contact, not unpleasing (though small) to look at, a £9-a-week allowance – and nothing to do'.[84] That vein of narcissism, though clearly characteristic of our generation, is exceptionally strong and apparently inextinguishable in Martin, and it's worth re-emphasising how very different this makes him from his father in his student days: what Hilly noticed about Kingsley were his awful clothes; what Martin notices about himself are his splendid ones. And it's a characteristic hardly tempered by the passage of time, for as recently as 2000 he could say of the 1970s: 'It amazes me, now, that any of us managed to write a word of sense during the whole decade, considering that we were all evidently stupid enough to wear flares.'[85] It's an effortful joke, of course, but only an author who retained a chunk of unreconstructed Mod within him would think that writing has much to do with the cut of one's trousers.

When he was recalling his student days for *My Oxford* in 1977, he was still young enough to want to demystify, for instance by asserting that 'There will, for example, be no more Oxford "generations"'[86] – which, quite apart from being demonstrably untrue, isn't something a man still in his twenties could possibly have known. At the same time, he was constructing his own anti-mythological myth. Explaining the 'element of candid terror' in his first reaction to the place, he describes himself as 'Originally a child of the lower middle classes', a claim Kingsley in his day could make with perfect justice but not one to be accurately applied to the son of a novelist and university lecturer. His sense of insecurity intensified when at first he found himself sharing rooms with an Old Harrovian – his reaction wasn't so far from John Kemp's on encountering Christopher Warner, after all – although in this he was loading all his anxieties on to the convenient scapegoat of class. In an early letter home from Oxford, he describes his room-mate's allergies (chocolate, spices, alcohol) after he's suffered 'some sort of attack' and speculates on ways of inducing another one: 'Take the silly grin off his face.'[87] Halfway through the term, he managed to negotiate an exchange with 'a credulous Classicist' which gave him a room of his own, only to find that he and the now ex-room-mate, Marzys or 'Marzipan', subsequently became the best of friends.

Anyway, there were bigger worries than that about being an exhibitioner at Oxford. What, like many of his generation, he really suffered from was cultural deprivation: pop culture had proved so intoxicating during the 1960s that the intellectual infrastructure of taste and reference simply hadn't developed. For instance, he still knew far more about the Beatles than about Bach, a deficiency others would have sought to remedy, though he apparently didn't: for there's a truly shocking moment in *Experience*, where he refers to 'Bach's "Concerto for Cello"',[88] in four words conveying ignorance of musical history, the composer's oeuvre and the difference between a concerto and a sonata (of which there are in any case six by J. S. Bach). His father had been able to take a scurrilously disrespectful view of received culture precisely because he knew a good deal about it from quite early on. Martin didn't have that luxury; hence, despite his plumage, he had to become a successfully diligent gnome.

His tutor was 'urbane, pooh-poohing Jonathan Wordsworth, the distinguished nepotic scholar',[89] although pooh-poohing perhaps wasn't a habit in which Martin needed to be encouraged. Wordsworth had taken a chance on him and he treated his protégé with a touch of interested favouritism, privileging him over his tutorial partner, whom Martin liked no better than his room-mate: 'a coy little turd . . . who, after 40 minutes of bulging his eyes and pouting his lips, tried things like curling up in a little ball, humming nursery rhymes, and gasping at the sunset over the chapel'.[90] This, had he known it, was his first encounter with a literary 'Martian', for his tutorial partner was the poet Christopher Reid; they too subsequently became good friends. Towards the end of this first term, in November, a keenly contested election took place for the vacant Professorship of Poetry, which had become vacant on the resignation of Edmund Blunden. Kingsley, who was among the sponsors of the successful candidate, Roy Fuller, was invited to a lunch party at the campaign headquarters – the home of Roy's son, the poet and Magdalen don John Fuller – to which he asked if he might 'bring my son along, now in his first year at Exeter, and a tractable lad'.[91] Martin glumly remembers the occasion as one to which he invited his girlfriend, Rosalind Hewer, seeking and failing to impress; there is a photograph, taken in the back garden, of the worthies impressively assembled, Kingsley among them but Martin conspicuously absent. John Fuller recalls that Martin 'spent much of the time sitting on the sofa telephoning his girl-friend',[92] although Anthony Thwaite's recollection is that Rosalind *was* there, sharing the sofa: either way, Martin's priorities were clearly and unsurprisingly those of a moony nineteen-year-old rather than an aspiring novelist anxious to get himself snapped standing next to Anthony Powell. Thwaite, corroborating Kingsley's unlikely sounding description of his son as 'tractable', remembers Martin as 'shy' and also that father and grown-up son embraced and kissed when they met, an unusual gesture of affection which was to remain habitual with them.[93] After the party, the Thwaites drove Kingsley back to London while Martin returned, alone, to his room, filled with the ridiculous and unconquerable despair so characteristic of his age and situation:

> The famous skylines I could see from my window, the stained-glass hagiographies of the chapel opposite, the Songs and Sonnets of John Donne laid out tenderly on my desk – suddenly all this was second-hand, mere leftovers, junk. I sat there for several hours, and when I couldn't bear sitting down I stood up, and when I couldn't bear standing up I sat down. About 9 o'clock there was a tap on the door. It was she, bearing apologies and a persuasively worded invitation to return with her to her flat. Intimacy (with the author in rather less than colossal form) took place, and a happy few months began.[94]

He had met Ros through one of his few friends in his first term at Oxford, Tim Healey (son of the then Defence Secretary, Denis Healey), who was at Balliol; she gets a slightly rough though anonymous ride in *My Oxford*, but she appeared in Martin's life at a vital moment and rescued him from a period of painfully self-reinforcing undergraduate loneliness. For what seemed to him an eternity – but can't in fact have been more than a few weeks – their friendship was irreproachably chaste, despite a moment which would have struck an ironic chord with his father: one evening, searching his jacket pocket for matches (something Amises seem very ready to let other people do), 'she accidentally produced a wallet of contraceptives instead. "Well, you never know your luck," I said.'[95] In *Experience*, she appears only parenthetically in one of the Osric letters, misdated naturally: 'Fucking thanks for the lunch Dad (and from Ros too).'[96]

This elegant acknowledgement properly belongs to the spring of 1969, for Martin was 'getting quite delirious' about Prelims, to be taken at the end of that term. Among the five papers were 'one on Old English grammar, all indecipherable inflection changes and vile vowel movements, and a Latin paper, requiring from the candidate two translations from Books IV and VI of the *Aeneid*'.[97] He was desperately unconfident in academic matters, and overworked – often setting his alarm clock for 4 or 5 in the morning – to make sure he passed. The result, apart from the fact that he did pass with ease, was an almost exact replica of the state he'd got himself into over Oxford Entrance: 'I've never felt so ill in all my life . . . Wednesday featured a feverish chill; Friday – a bulging headache, and on Saturday I had what felt like a coronary. Yawn, but I always have this before exams.'[98] With the passing of Prelims, his relationship with Ros passed too.

His second-year (and more permanent) girlfriend was Alexandra Wells, or 'Gully', a first-year historian at St Hilda's whom he'd met much earlier in London: she was to be the dedicatee of *The Rachel Papers* and their relationship would last 'in its intermittent way about as long as the average marriage. Ten years?'[99] With Gully, he says, he 'tasted some of the conventional sweets of Oxonian life',[100] and it's certainly true that his Oxford had more in common with *Brideshead Revisited* than his father's. This generation, like Waugh's, was one given to flamboyant showing off and simply having a good time: 'it's so nice here in the summer', he writes languidly, 'that it's difficult not to spend the whole time lying drunkenly in punts or in the Fellows' garden pretending to read'.[101] It's the voice of Charles Ryder, whose ambiguous social status, like Martin's, made the observation worth recording (Sebastian Flyte would have taken it for granted). He was happier and more confident, partly because he'd discovered – as intelligent second-year undergraduates usually do – that he could get away with it: quite apart from having a more relaxed and successful social life, he'd found that he could 'rather shine' with 'derivative and journalistic essays'. At the same time – and perhaps the dissonant yet unmissable chiming of 'Gully' with 'Hilly' was a subconscious factor here – he was wary of becoming too committed while still a student. In that revealing letter from the summer of 1969, he writes: 'Things are more or less O.K. with Gully but I keep on wishing I weren't tied down and that I'm wasting the best years of my life etc., since, as far as I'm concerned, the relationship isn't getting any better: it just seems to consist of me trying to maintain the illusion that I'm as keen on her as ever (which I'm not).'[102] But he's 'at that awful stage where I think I'd be equally pissed off without her'. At least, unlike Kingsley, he was granted the uncomfortable luxury of having to make up his own mind, rather than having his hand forced by inadequate contraception. His plan was that they and some other friends should share a house in the country during his final year, 'somewhere quite far out' from Oxford. What they ended up with was certainly 'far out'.

Living at the Old Forge at Shilton, near Burford, entailed a fifteen-mile commute into Oxford in Martin's Mini. One letter – as usual undated but clearly belonging to the autumn of 1970 – describes the events of a weekend there: the dramatis personae were X and Y, the husband and wife who rented the cottage; another house-sharer, Z; Martin and Gully; and two guests – a supposed girlfriend of Z's and Rob Henderson. By the time Martin sent his account of the weekend off to Jane, Z was in 'the local looney bin'. On Friday, he had beaten up the girl 'whom he'd asked for the w.end & found in bed with another guest' (Martin's friend Rob); next day, this was followed by 'a suicide bid (some sleeping pills)' and 'an 80 m.p.h. mercy dash to the Radcliffe'. By Sunday Z was back to scuffle with Y, who called the police: 'He went to the bin (where he's since had a *fit*) and Y has gone to the London Clinic . . .'[103] It wasn't an altogether helpful atmosphere in which to prepare for Finals although it was, Martin presciently noted, 'novel-fodder': the novel it would feed was *Dead Babies*. Eventually, Martin and Gully made their escape in the traditional moonlight flit, loading up the Mini and driving off in the early hours. For Martin, it was back to gnomedom and Exeter House, the college's annexe on the Iffley Road, where for two terms he worked with the obsessive discipline and concentration needed to match his father's First – which he did, coming third in his year. In a way that hardly anyone ever admits, this was a good deal more enjoyable than sharing 'a house in the country with unstable and profligate friends' where 'work was fatally eased out by pleasure, most of it pleasureless'.[104]

And indeed, the really curious thing about having been a student in the late 1960s is this: in the end, I don't think our generation – Martin's and mine – had nearly as much fun at university as Kingsley's. Pleasure-seeking and comfortably off, with our permissive preconceptions about sex and our easy access to cars and booze and drugs, we'd never quite match the warmth and the camaraderie of a smoky pub, a crowded tea-room or even a jazz-record shop in wartime Oxford; meanwhile, that potent mixture of awed deference and subversive ridicule with which previous generations of students had regarded their teachers – 'Men big enough to be worth laughing at', as Kingsley put it[105] – was slipping away too. Something subtle and nuanced about the human atmosphere had already been lost for ever, and it's a loss that translates straight into the impoverished fabric of fiction.

7. RACHEL AND THE 1970s

1

'Any London house would have published my first novel out of vulgar curiosity,' says Martin in *Experience*.[1] Read, but not necessarily published; and less out of vulgar curiosity than out of commercial expediency. He was a hot property before *The Rachel Papers* appeared in 1973: young, good-looking, bright, with a First from Oxford and a job at the *TLS*, famously parented and step-parented. To borrow the terms of John Wain's infamous remark to his father, Martin certainly wasn't Joe Soap. But rather than troubling any other London houses with the task of reading and just conceivably rejecting it, Pat Kavanagh, a family friend, quietly placed the book with Kingsley's publisher, Tom Maschler at Jonathan Cape. This made perfect sense and had every advantage but one: *The Rachel Papers* was never submitted to the chastening attention of an editor who knew nothing about it, apart from being quite sure he wasn't going to like it. Nor did it ever go through the process of critical negotiation and thorough revision that honed 'Dixon and Christine' into *Lucky Jim*. Its one substantial dose of pre-submission reworking stemmed from the morning, late in 1972, when Kingsley enumerated the failings of his own early story, 'The Sacred Rhino of Uganda': the careless multiplicity of *-ings*, *-ics*, *-ives*, *-lys*, *-tions* and prefixes. After lunch, Martin spent the afternoon with *The Rachel Papers*, deciding it was 'doggerel . . . all "the cook took a look at the book" . . . like a nursery rhyme' before getting down to work on those intrusively chiming prefixes and suffixes, as Kingsley had implied he should. 'It was the only piece of literary counsel he ever gave me.'[2]

Although it is in most important ways a quite different sort of novel, *The Rachel Papers* possesses the same curious relationship with its decade as *Lucky Jim*: that is, we think of it (correctly) as a book which is characteristic of the 1970s in spite of the fact that its social mores and points of cultural reference are those of the late 1960s, just as the quintessentially 1950s *Jim* is grounded in the immediately post-war years of the late 1940s. It has another striking affinity with Kingsley's first novel: its hero, Charles Highway, is as ambiguously placed in relation to his author as Jim Dixon. Both of them are at once teasingly autobiographical and resolutely made up; the difference is that Charles is very much easier to dislike. This is only partly because he, like his author, is younger than Jim: the book's frame is an hour-by-hour countdown to the midnight of his twentieth birthday – a curious chronological landmark, given that the really significant birthday was always one's twenty-first. However, according to Charles, 'Twenty may not be the start of maturity but, in all conscience, it's the end of youth.'[3] He was described by a reviewer as 'both a gilded and a repulsive creature', and Martin not only agrees with this judgement but, as we have seen, extends it to include his own younger self: 'I accept this description, for my hero and for myself. I was an Osric.'[4]

The short life on which Charles looks back is populated partly by caricatures and partly by characters adapted from actual people, a common and often unavoidable strategy in first novels by young writers. Among the caricatures are his immediate family: a wealthy, successful father, indolent, disorganised mother, and five siblings, who include an older married sister, Jenny, and a predictably noxious nine-year-old brother called Valentine. Norman Entwistle, Jenny's oafish husband, is a caricature too, and supplies the template for a sequence of working-class Londoners culminating in Mal from 'State of England' (1996). The Highways live in the country near Oxford, the Entwistles in Campden Hill Square (a place much favoured by fictional creations of the Amis family), but neither location is very convincingly imagined, with the exception of the narrator's bed-rooms, whose contents are itemised with adolescent obsessiveness. Kingsley had stayed much closer to experience for the domestic settings of his early novels, adapting his first Swansea digs for Jim Dixon, his and Hilly's first Swansea flat for the Lewises, and so forth. The crammer where Charles picks up the missing bits of his education required for Oxford entrance has a terrible cheating principal and a battily camp off-campus English teacher, but the mathematician Mr Greenchurch is based on 'Flash Crunch' from Davies, Laing and Dick. Although Charles Knowd at Oxford has rather different literary interests from Martin's tutor Jonathan Wordsworth, he takes the same line on admitting Charles, while Charles's friend Geoffrey is

affectionately and extravagantly modelled on Rob Henderson. Rachel
was a Sephardic Jewess from Golders Green, of whom Rob 'resignedly said that she was the most beautiful girl he'd ever seen' and
whom Martin 'de-exoticised' in the novel, somewhat to his own later
puzzlement.[5] She is pursued by Charles's arch-rival, a parodic American called DeForest Hoeniger (the name 'DeForest' perhaps comes
from a songwriter's credit), who is all too clearly a spiritual cousin of
Student Mansfield and Tupper Saucy. As for Charles, despite his
superficial disguises – the spectacles, the reedy voice and the extra
couple of inches in height – it's clear that his interior self has much in
common with his author's.

But *The Rachel Papers* is a mass of self-contradictions. Not only
is Charles Highway younger than Jim Dixon; whereas Jim is a grown-
up graduate with a job, Charles is an adolescent who hasn't even got
to university yet. Unlike Jim, he's too immature to have acquired a
convincing style of his own: the novel he narrates is all over the place,
as in a sense it has to be, but its very success in replicating the comic-
grotesque ramblings of the late teenage psyche both makes it a lesser
sort of book than *Lucky Jim* and supplies a practically unassailable
excuse for its inconsistencies. Take the narrative voice, for instance.
Charles is supposed to be the child of well-off middle-class parents
(though the language of his exchanges with his father makes him
sound more like the child of Kingsley Amis) and he detests, partly
because he envies, Americans: his memorable attack on them, which
reads like a concise version of one of his father's set pieces, begins by
citing their violence and racism ('go out blowing niggers' heads off,
roast a Jew or two, disembowel a Puerto Rican') but ends with him
much more vulnerably hating 'their biceps and their tans and their
perfect teeth and their clear eyes'.[6] Yet, from the start of the novel,
his diction and syntax keep lapsing oddly into American: he says that
his mother 'came on all vague and spiritual' when he means 'came
over';[7] or 'I told her to be sure and have a good time', rather than 'to
be sure to'.[8] It's impossible not to see these false notes of Charles's as
false notes of Martin's, legacies of that year in Princeton when he so
wanted to be American. Moreover, the book is full of things that
don't seem quite right syntactically, and these range from straightforward imprecisions such as 'At the age of ten I must have had
more teeth in my head than the average dentist's waiting-room,'[9]
which overlooks the fact that waiting rooms don't have teeth, to self-

collapsing striving after effect: 'Then I wrote to Pepita. Did I write to Pepita. I still have the reply somewhere.'[10] The second sentence, an early example of the variant-repetition tic which often threatens to wreck his prose, only has its intended effect if spoken in a kind of camp stage-American; on an English page, it simply looks wrong, while the missing question-mark would merely serve to emphasise its redundancy (if she replied, he must have written). We need to be more thoroughly convinced that this is the narrator's gangling awk-wardness of utterance – as, on the same page, 'Erections, as we all know, come to the teenager on a plate,' where the clunkingly apposite verb is almost as excruciating as the Salome-esque visual image, surely is – and not a longer-term problem of his author's.

Another way of addressing this question would be to ask: where does the narrative voice of *The Rachel Papers* come from? With *Lucky Jim*, the answer could be found in coherent if not altogether expected places: early Evelyn Waugh; William Cooper's *Scenes from Provincial Life*; Christopher Isherwood's Berlin books. With *The Rachel Papers*, Martin's childhood infatuation with America signposts one literary source: Holden Caulfield in *The Catcher in the Rye*. He supplies the adolescent perspective and the demotic slanginess – a style that David Lodge, in *The Art of Fiction*, calls 'Teenage *Skaz*', identifying charac-teristics such as repetition, hyperbole and compacted syntax which are as evident here as they are in J. D. Salinger[11] – and it is this that makes Charles appear to be younger than he actually is. Take, for instance, his compilation of an 'Anxiety Top Ten' (with 'Last week's positions in brackets'): it's brilliantly done and it's exactly the kind of thing that a lonely and uncertain teenager would do – Martin makes good use of his surprising experience of loneliness in his first year at Oxford – but it's mainly composed of mid-teen anxieties. The jokey list is an Amis family tradition; yet young Kingsley's versions of it, in his spoof jazz personnels and cricket teams, seem mature and sophisticated by comparison with this:

(–)	1	Clap
(1)	2	Rachel
(2)	3	Big Boy
(7)	4	Loose Molar
(10)	5	Owing Norm Money
(3)	6	Bronco

(6)   7   Being Friendless
(9)   8   Insanity
(–)   9   Rotting Feet
(4)   10   Pimple in Left Nostril

Ones to watch: Having a smaller cock than DeForest; incipient boil on shoulder-blade.

Clap has taken the charts by storm, ousting Rachel after her confident two-week run. Spot in Nose is definitely following Disintegrating Toenails on its way out of the Ten – but watch for Boil on Back![12]

The difference between father and son here, though partly explained by the latter's extreme youth at the time of writing, is both qualitative and, above all, generational. For it isn't entirely Martin's, or Charles Highway's, fault that the major formative influence in his narrative voice comes less from literature than from pop music and its attendant patter; this invasive presence of popular culture in the development of a literary style represents a kind of pressure which Kingsley didn't have to endure. We haven't yet done with Martin the Mod.

The central scene in *The Rachel Papers*, the one in which Charles momentously induces Rachel into his bedroom, takes place to a specific soundtrack: the second side of the Beatles' *Sergeant Pepper's Lonely Hearts Club Band*. Charles reckons this is 'a safe choice, since to be against the Beatles (late-middle period) is to be against life',[13] a judgement which is more fraught with ironic qualification than at first appears. He describes his carefully planned though incomplete seduction – the scene is interrupted both by the repeating groove of gobbledegook with which the 'cheeky Beatles' have ended their LP and by the arrival of Charles's father and his mistress elsewhere in the house – with the chilly forensic detail of his own *Conquests and Techniques: A Synthesis*: his sex manual is precociously home-made, unlike that of Robin Davies in *You Can't Do Both*. He is more cynical, more experienced and more competent than Robin, though far less sympathetic, and his concentration on sexual strategy to the exclusion of human feeling resembles that of a quite different Kingsley anti-hero, Patrick Standish in *Take a Girl like You*, planning his thwarted Saturday afternoon assault on Jenny. Patrick, of course, would have settled for jazz, but Charles's choice of background music is wryly appropriate: before the couple become so engrossed with each other that even the tumultuous 'A Day in the Life' escapes their notice, Rachel actually manages to sing along with 'When I'm Sixty-Four' and 'Lovely Rita', the two songs which despite their jaunty surfaces most clearly reveal the Beatles' underlying callousness and contempt for other people. They are the perfect theme music for *The Rachel Papers* as a valediction to the decade in which 'All you need is love' became a mantra of indulgent self-regard.

Charles's self-absorbed perspective is chronically adolescent and incurably Mod, and this applies not only to people but also to his sense of place. Other people are of interest to him for one of two reasons: if they are young, they are potential sources of gratification, either sexual (Rachel, girls generally) or druggy-social (Geoffrey); if they are old, they are objects of satirical contempt; and if they fit neither of these models, they're simply to be ignored. Similarly, his perception of places is restricted to interior detail, the surfaces from which to construct a semblance of self: he can see rooms, but not buildings or landscapes. When he first arranges his own room at Campden Hill Square in anticipation of Rachel's arrival, he does so in order to polish up a personality he doesn't quite own:

> Not knowing her views on music I decided to play it safe; I stacked the records upright in two parallel rows; at the head of the first I put *2001: A Space Odyssey* (can't be wrong); at the head of the second I put, after some thought, a selection of Dylan Thomas's verse, read by the poet. Kleenex well away from the bed: having them actually on the bedside chair was tantamount to a poster reading 'The big thing about me is that I wank a devil of a lot.' The coffee-table featured a couple of Shakespeare texts and a copy of *Time Out* – an intriguing dichotomy, perhaps, but I was afraid that, no, it wouldn't quite do. The texts were grimy and twisted after a year of A-Level doodling. I replaced them with the Thames and Hudson *Blake* (again, can't be wrong) and *The Poetry of Meditation*, in fact a scholarly American work on the Metaphysicals, although from the cover it could have been a collection of beatnik verse: Rachel could interpret it as she wished. Unfortunately, the *Time Out* had a rangy, black-nippled girl on the cover. What instead? Had I got time to run off and get a *New Statesman*? Not really. I looked round the room. Something incongruous, arresting. After a quarter of an hour, I decided on a Jane Austen, the mellow *Persuasion*, face down, open towards the end, by my pillow.[14]

This is a meticulous re-creation of a typically late-adolescent process: one that recurs in other contexts, such as the selective self-presentation of a university interview, which is Charles's other major preoccupation. But as the constituent material of a narrative persona, it can't help becoming wearisome. Moreover, it grows into a repetitive tic: when Rachel visits the Highways' home in the country, we get a parallel inventory for Charles's room there, its 'posters of Jimi Hendrix, Auden and Isherwood, Rasputin, reproductions of works by Lautrec and Cézanne', the chess set and the postcards and the bookcase which 'retold my adolescence', as indeed does the whole book.[15] And when we eventually reach Rachel's own bedroom, there's a girlified version of the same thing, a bed covered with 'crappy gonks and teddy-bears and dolls' to whom, in their owner's absence, Charles addresses a few words: ' "How's Wollidog den?" I said. "Where's your mummy, Winstonchester? How would your fwend Munchy like his fucking face—?" '[16] It's very funny and effective, yet terribly constricting as a narrative viewpoint; Jim Dixon is so much more liberated in his anarchic adulthood than Charles in his obsessive adolescence.

Naturally, Charles knows what's wrong: 'cosmic angst, metaphysical fear, a feeling both claustrophobic and agoraphobic, the teenager's religion . . . An Angus Wilson character terms it "adolescent egotism", thereby almost driving me to suicide last Christmas.'[17] Later in the book, his self-analysis becomes at once more critical and more flattering: 'Me? Me, I'm devious, calculating, self-obsessed – very nearly mad, in fact . . .'[18] Because he's quite a bookish chap, even when he pretends this is a pretence, the literary resonances must be intended. The nearer and stronger echo is of Prufrock's 'No! I am not Prince Hamlet . . .' stanza with its similarly ambiguous catalogue of *his* qualities:

> Deferential, glad to be of use,
> Politic, cautious, and meticulous;
> Full of high sentence, but a bit obtuse;
> At times, indeed, almost ridiculous –
> Almost, at times, the Fool.[19]

While Prufrock sees himself as Polonius, the best Charles can manage is Osric. But Osric in his ridiculous way aspires to be Hamlet (the more distant and fainter echo) who, having 'lost all my mirth, foregone all custom of exercise', is 'but mad north-north-west'. Hamlet's condition, though its causes are more substantial, looks very like teenage angst to a teenager.

Several echoes and pre-echoes remain in *The Rachel Papers*. There's a strange double echo of *Brideshead Revisited*, a book not much regarded by either Amis yet nevertheless inescapable in each's imaginative development: Martin thinks it an example of 'Lasting schlock, the really good bad book.'[20] The scene in which Charles and Rachel visit her elderly nanny in her little room gently parodies Waugh's scene in which a similar visit is paid by the other Charles and Cordelia to *her* nanny. Later, after Charles's Oxford interview and despite his lame attempt at denial – 'Oxford skylines offered spurious serenity in the form of gold and stone against sharp blue, which I of course refused'[21] – there's a hint of the sentimental undercurrent which makes this, in spite of itself, the most Oxonian-aspirational novel since *Brideshead*: a point his uncoincidental namesake Charles Ryder would have perfectly understood. There are also striking reminders that young Martin is his father's son. One concerns Kingsley's 'mild anti-Semitism' (a point elaborated in *Experience*),[22] which is shared by Charles's father, Gordon Highway who, on learning that his son-in-law Norman's mother's maiden name was Levi, 'said to my brother as they walked away, "Looks like I owe you a fiver" '.[23] Kingsley would later allude back to this by making 'Levi' and its anagrammatic possibilities an obsession of the deranged anti-Semitic Steve in *Stanley and the Women*. Another is the prejudice against public schoolboys, unhappily bundled up with homophobia, already glimpsed in *My Oxford*: here it appears in his description of the likely clientele at Rachel's crammer (which is posher than his) as 'Cuntish public-school drop-outs, dropped out for being too thick, having long hair or dirty boaters, unseaming new boys in multiple buggery, getting caught too many times with an impermissible number of hockey sticks up their bums';[24] the portrait of the doting English tutor Mr Bellamy, and Charles's unforgivable treatment of his gift (an early edition of *Paradise Lost*), is clearly part of the same hostile animus. And a third reminder is presciently voiced by an elderly Oxford friend of Gordon Highway's: 'The so-called new philosophy, "permissiveness" if you like, seen from the right perspective, is only a new puritanism, whereby you're accused of being repressed or unenlightened if you happen to object to infidelity, promiscuity, and so on.'[25] This is almost exactly what Jake tells the dreadful Dr Rosenberg in *Jake's Thing*. At moments such as this, it's clear that Martin had already become a fully contributing member of the family firm.

2

When *The Rachel Papers* was published in November 1973, Martin was sharing a 'small but fancy' (and, of course, unaffordable) maisonette in Knightsbridge with Rob Henderson and his girlfriend Olivia. They held a celebratory party: Kingsley was there, and Robert Conquest; Philip – who contributed, Martin recalls wonderingly, 'a *magnum* of whisky' – and Sally; Christopher Hitchens and Clive James. Two literary generations were thus represented, although there was no question of a baton being passed, and by the time the 'shocking rout' ended at four or five in the morning, Hitchens had taken Sally off to the Cadogan Hotel. When Rob and Olivia went to bed together upstairs at dawn, Martin was left alone downstairs wearing their present to him, a blue T-shirt with *The Rachel Papers* 'embossed on it in purple capitals'. Within a few weeks, the unaffordability of the place became apparent, and he decamped to a bedsit in Earls Court.

'I still felt like a student,' he says in *Experience*, a point amply corroborated by his novels of the 1970s. The post-university pressures on Kingsley, who because of military service and postgraduate research was slightly older, had been those imposed by marriage, a young family and a teaching job; a direct literary consequence of this is the early appearance of married central characters and family lives in *That Uncertain Feeling* and *I Like It Here*. Martin's post-university pressures were completely different. He was single and, at this point, without a fully committed girlfriend; his financial lurches were all his own, uncomplicated by other mouths to feed or mortgage payments to find; and his approach to the matter of earning a living was casual to an extent which, a generation earlier, would have been the prerogative of the immensely privileged or the dottily Bohemian. (There was one overwhelming pressure, though, bottled up in the jar marked *success*.) Before joining the *Times Literary Supplement* as an editorial assistant, he had worked for four months at a small Mayfair art gallery, 'showing the punters around the place, dusting frames in the basement, making the tea and coffee, hand-addressing the invitations to the private views, and reading about a book a day'[26] – the origin of Gregory Riding's job in *Success* – and then for three weeks as a trainee copywriter at J. Walter Thompson: excluding editorial stints on periodicals and the more bookish bits of newspapers, these, along with the brief spell at Colin Howard's hi-fi shop, are the only 'proper' jobs on Martin's CV. Moreover, going to work at the *TLS*, in its pre-Wapping days in an annexe off New Printing House Square, was like going back to university: 'The *TLS* felt like a library, the sessions with the literary editors felt like tutorials, and my articles felt like weekly essays.'[27] This feeling was compounded by Martin's student-like clothes, his Earls Court bedsit, his solitary meals and instant coffees. By contrast, Lemmons, 'a citadel of riotous solvency' with its 'in-depth back-up, a cellar, a barrel of malt whisky, a walk-in larder', fulfilled the role of the solid parental home, where he was 'so secure': 'and, clearly, so insecure elsewhere'.[28] In the early 1970s, it had quite suddenly become possible for many graduates to behave like students for half their adult lives; the surprise was that this seemingly indulgent state of affairs didn't feel at all comfortable.

For, although we were in superficial ways more sophisticated and more experienced than our parents had been at the same age, graduates of Martin's generation were often at a deeper level far less mature: prosperity, permissiveness and pop (an alliterative trinity that forms itself as inescapably as Pound, Picasso and Parker, Larkin's modernist villains) invited us to remain childlike or even childish. Most of Martin's novels are centred on men who haven't grown up: their games and their fantasies, their toys and their cars, their sexual and scatological maunderings: all these are signals of retarded adolescence. They have no settled values and no cultural resources; they abuse what vestiges of literacy they possess. They are addicted to drink or gambling or pornography or all of these. And when in due course we meet the character who most exactly embodies this catalogue of terrible vacuities, he will be called John Self.

Like *Lucky Jim* two decades earlier, *The Rachel Papers* won its year's Somerset Maugham Award. Its author, a less reluctant traveller than his father, headed to Spain, where his mother was in her bar-running phase at Ronda, in the summer of 1974; Jaime, his half-brother, was then two years old, although it would be another three years before Hilly and Ali were able to marry. Hemingway once recommended Ronda as the ideal place for an elopement, an accolade made all the more ambiguous by its bestower, but Martin found it a congenial place to write: there, in a room of the Palacio de Mondragón, he worked on his second novel, *Dead Babies*, including the short retrospective episode where Andy and Diana meet (even if they don't quite elope) in Ronda. Maugham had died almost a decade earlier and was thus unable to observe that, while Amis *père* had spent his money writing a book about someone who hated 'abroad', Amis *fils* produced a novel set almost entirely in a demented version of the English home counties.

There was another visitor at Casa de Mondragón that summer: Hilly's emotionally exhausted sister Miggy. The arcadian Partingtons had supplied Martin with the rustic innocence his Swansea childhood so conspicuously lacked: he once told his cousin David, 'You're a country bumpkin and I'm a city slicker,' to which David ingeniously replied, 'No, you're a city bumpkin and I'm a country slicker'[29] (an exchange appropriated by Charles and Geoffrey in *The Rachel Papers*). But now, something had happened to destroy the Partingtons' treasurable innocence for ever: on the evening of 27 December 1973, David drove his sister Lucy into Cheltenham to visit her friend Helen Render. Lucy hoped to study medieval art at the Courtauld Institute, and the two friends were polishing up her letter of application; that task completed, at 10.15, Lucy left Helen and set off on the three-minute walk to the bus stop. She was never seen again.

3

The world hadn't yet heard of Fred West: it would do so over twenty years later and then it would once more hear of Lucy Partington. Yet Fred West was there all along, in his unquenchably violent perversity a figure precisely of the 1970s: he appears in several of Martin's novels, wearing different names, long before his real name was revealed. This, for instance, is Philboyd B. Marshall, Jr, of Tara, Tennessee, the father of Skip Marshall in *Dead Babies* (1975), the book Martin completed in Spain in the summer of 1974: 'Philboyd had once *raped* him . . . because he had caught Skip emptying the latrine with a shovel, rather than with his bare hands . . .'; 'Philboyd bought from the knackers a three-legged mule, which he installed in an enclosure and went out to visit torments on twice-daily with kitchen knives, meathooks, branding-irons'; 'on Skip's return that night Philboyd clubbed his son round the kitchen with a frypan for three-quarters of an hour'; 'Philboyd stumbled home . . . and dejectedly hosepiped his wife to death.'[30] The boomeranging irony of all this is that it's intended as a satire on the specifically American violence detested by Charles in *The Rachel Papers*, reaching back to Kingsley's grim impressions of the South while he was at Vanderbilt: Tara, Tennessee, is meant to be so unlike own our dear Cheltenham. On the other hand, a pornographic video described towards the end of the book is unmitigated by any such geographical distancing:

> A porker had indeed made a young lady his, and there had been an additional coupling between a twelve-year-old boy and a representative of the monkey tribe. Large helpings of excrement had been consumed ('oh, wretched evacuees!' Quentin cried), people had showered in urine, and they were shown a genuine sex-death, in which an elderly actress was asphyxiated on a brace of craning phalloi. The remainder was a jangling bestiary, in whopping close-up, of gaping vaginas, rhubarb penises and gouged behinds.[31]

The viewers are marginally redeemed by finding this unstimulating – the decorous period scene which they watch next proves, puzzlingly, to be far more erotic – but it would, one imagines, have been entirely to the taste of Fred West.

Dead Babies is US military slang from the Vietnam War for civilian casualties which generate maximum negative publicity: those, that is, involving dead babies. The very title was so offensive to its first paperback publisher that for a while it became *Dark Secrets*, which sounds more like a box of chocolates. The book is an eager attempt to escape the curse of the second novel: Martin's chosen escape route is the hybrid genre subsequently employed by Kingsley in *Russian Hide and Seek*, a subversive combination of the country house and the futuristic. This country house is ominously called Appleseed Rectory – Apple was the Beatles' record company, so this is what happens when the 1960s and 1970s go to seed – and is a much expanded version of the Old Forge at Shilton. The future date, though established by details of transport and topography as well as new drugs and drinks (some of them comically Kingsley-baiting, such as an *Irish* version of Glenfiddich), is uncertain and inconsistent; at least the British motor industry has unexpectedly prospered, for there's a Jaguar I-type as well as an MGE. *Yes*, the very 1970s-sounding student magazine edited by Quentin Villiers, has 'won outspoken praise from William Burroughs, Gore Vidal, Angus Wilson',[32] all of whom were far from young in 1975 and would have been improbably old by the time the book's contextualising changes had taken place. Moreover, the characters, while their excesses may belong to the dystopic future, are unmistakably our contemporaries in ways beyond those implied by the epigraph from Menippus: '. . . and so even when [the satirist] presents a vision of the future, his business is not prophecy, just as his subject is not tomorrow . . . it is today'.

Some of them, indeed, are not merely our contemporaries but our elders. Among the post-hippy freaks who are paraded at the start of the book in an Angus Wilson-style 'Dramatis Personae', a gesture whose marginal out-of-dateness further skews the chronological angle, are some notably backward-looking stereotypes. Of the Appleseeders, as opposed to the catalytic weekend visitors, Quentin Villiers is a malevolent version of the old-fashioned public-school toff whom Martin so often dismisses with contempt; Keith Whitehead is an extreme form of the grotesque comic dwarf typified by the 1950s comedian Charlie Drake; and, perhaps most intriguingly and anachronistically, Andy Adorno, although a child born into a 1960s hippy commune, is in his Harley-Davidson-riding physicality the natural object of Martin the Mod's awe – a Rocker. There are also Giles Coldstream, the first of Martin's creations to experience – indeed, to be wholly defined by – dental problems, and two women: Celia Villiers, married to Quentin (although marriage in this milieu bears little resemblance to marriage outside it), and Andy's girlfriend Diana Parry. The visitors are a trinity, or a 'troy', of Americans – Marvell Buzhardt, Skip Marshall and Roxeanne Smith – and Lucy Littlejohn, 'silverhaired, jovial, a golden-hearted whore'. There is hardly anyone here whom the reader is likely to find sympathetic or even interesting.

So what happens? Everything and nothing. The chemistry of the weekend – which in its literal and extreme sense is the province of the metaphysically forenamed Buzhardt – is in every respect catastrophic. The only escape from the claustrophobic environment of Appleseed and its wrecked pastoral surroundings occurs on the Friday evening, when the participants visit the even more terrifying future London: they go to the Psychologic Revue, held at 'a semi-derelict 1920s cinema

in what used to be Kilburn High Road', for a performance by the
Conceptualists, whom Marvell says are 'Something between old-style
Hell's Angels and Chuck Manson'[33] – a description rejected by Andy
with snarling disgust, partly because he has been close to the Con-
ceptualist movement himself and but also, surely, with a glimpse of
self-recognition. This fractured urban landscape, with its jangling
catchphrases of 'street sadness' and 'cancelled sex', is one we shall re-
encounter in Martin's novels. Here, the diminished world of which it
forms part is the explicit legacy of the 1970s, the book's authorial
present: 'That's what they did. In the 'seventies. That's what they
achieved. They separated emotion and sex.'[34] The phrase 'dead babies',
having started off in the novel as a random expletive, modulates by
the middle of the book into something altogether more desolate:
'Marvell hung his head again. "Babies," he muttered. "Dead, dead
babies." '[35] Then, just before the final catastrophe starts to unfold,
there's a further modulation into elegiac wistfulness:

> Yes, it was seven o'clock and a pall of thunder hung over the
> Rectory rose-gardens. The formerly active air was now so weighed
> down that it seeped like heavy water over the roof. Darkness flowed
> in the distance, and the dusk raked like a black searchlight across
> the hills towards them.
>
>   But pity the dead babies. Now, before it starts. They couldn't
> know what was behind them, nor what was to come. The past?
> They had none. Like children after a long day's journey, their lives
> arranged themselves in a patchwork of vanished mornings, lost
> afternoons and probable yesterdays.[36]

This isn't quite what it seems. The elegiac tone is compromised both
by that cumbersome 'formerly' in the second sentence and by a sense
of ventriloquism – of tone and imagery at odds with the prevailing
narrative voice – in the third. And then there's the injunction to
'pity the dead babies': the word 'pity' itself is troublesome, with its
inevitable echo of Wilfred Owen and its puny failure to attain
the 'woe or wonder' of tragedy. Anyway, why should we pity them?
Their fate has been to an unusual extent in their own hands; the
'past' which they so conspicuously lack is something they could have
acquired quite easily by reading and thinking; and their resemblance
to tired children is entirely wilful. No, they don't deserve our pity, they

deserve our contempt; and that is a peculiar state for the entire cast of a novel to be in as it nears its conclusion.

While *Dead Babies* is a satirical reinterpretation of the country-house novel as a genre – with darkly ironic glances in the directions of Iris Murdoch and Elizabeth Jane Howard – it also has a more specific source: *Mansfield Park*. There, too, the unattended pleasure-seeking young cause mayhem, egged on by amoral and catalytic outsiders, the Crawfords: in Jane Austen, the damage is naturally less extreme, though more affecting, and the action is underpinned by moral rules (which nevertheless sanction Sir Thomas Bertram's involvement in the slave trade), yet the parallel is inescapable. *Mansfield Park* may also remind us of the awkward truth that all fictional creations are products of their author's imagination: when Mary Crawford makes her outrageous joke about rears and vices (she is purportedly talking about admirals), there's no escaping the fact that her pun comes from inside Jane Austen's head, just as the almost intolerable obscenity of *Dead Babies* comes from inside Martin Amis's. However, the sexual excess, the drug-taking, the violence and the whole vision of a dystopic future also owe much to a very different influence, William Burroughs, and once again to a specific book: *The Wild Boys*, published in 1972 at exactly the time Martin would have been thinking about his second novel. Like *Dead Babies*, *The Wild Boys* is set in the 'future' of the late 1980s; its fictional world is similarly manipulated by a 'joker'; its 'Penny Arcade Peep Show' prefigures the 'Conceptualists'; and we know that Martin read it carefully, because he reviewed it for the *Observer* in June 1972. In his review, he scolds the blurb-writer for describing *The Wild Boys* as 'science fiction' and 'prophetic':

> But this is precisely how not to read him. SF always tries to be realistic. Burroughs never does. Some critics are confused by his lack of realism and get depressed because they feel that the world is a rather more decent and wholesome place than he would have us believe. But the only time an educated and well-balanced person has any business being depressed by a book is when its author is simply a bore.[37]

As a young literary critic's swashbuckling polemic, this is fair enough; as self-exculpation for the novel he was beginning to write, it takes on a rather different complexion. Martin's future-world does aim for the 'realism' absent in Burroughs, even if it entails implausible feats of endurance (the improbability, for instance, of Little Keith actually remaining alive by the novel's closing pages), and it does contain elements of prophecy. Readers will, however, probably decide that the world has remained a bit more 'decent and wholesome' than *Dead Babies* anticipates, at least in terms of the English social life described in the book. But 'an educated and well-balanced person' – or simply an intelligent reader who wouldn't necessarily claim either of those qualifications – ought to protest at the assertion that he only 'has any business being depressed by a book . . . when its author is simply a bore', because here Martin is writing himself a blank cheque. That reader might very well feel that a capably written piece of poisonous rubbish (and some have thought *Dead Babies* to be just that) is far more depressing than an illiterate one, not least because it's such a conspicuous waste of talent.

'I felt the squeeze of immediate hurt,' says Martin, 'when Kingsley, who claimed to have liked my first novel, said he "couldn't get on" with my second.'[38] There's no reason to doubt that – one is *always* hurt when family or close friends don't enjoy one's work – but he must by then have possessed a fund of self-criticism sufficient to mitigate his surprise. The love-child of Jane Austen and William Burroughs was always going to turn out to be an awkward bastard.

4

In retrospect, there are perfectly good reasons for regarding the English literary landscape of the mid-1970s as an amenable place. There were generous and informed books pages in the serious weeklies – the *Listener*, *New Statesman* and *Spectator* – and in the quality Sunday papers; *Encounter* and *London Magazine* were flourishing; the range of established literary periodicals was boosted by three ambitious reincarnations of existing magazines, *Granta*, the *New Review* and *PN Review*; publishing houses, not yet visibly bunched into conglomerates, seemed to be falling over each other to discover promising new authors, who were generally less susceptible to group identity than their counterparts of two decades earlier. The 1960s had seen clusters of poets with shared geographical origins – Ulster, Liverpool – and the latter part of the 1970s would see the arrival of the 'Martians' (Craig Raine in *The Onion, Memory* (1978) and Christopher Reid in *Arcadia* (1979), both incidentally published by Oxford University Press), but among the less easily classifiable debuts were those of James Fenton (*Terminal Moraine*, 1972) and Andrew Motion (*The Pleasure Steamers*, 1978). Among novelists, the publication of Ian McEwan's collection of short stories, *First Love, Last Rites*, in 1975 and of Julian Barnes's first novel *Metroland* in 1980 marked the arrival of writers who had a good deal in common with (and in Barnes's case had been perceptibly influenced by) Martin. Of these writers, all except the Sussex-educated McEwan had been at Oxford where, with the exception of the slightly younger Motion, they had overlapped with Martin. So much for his contention that 'Oxford generations' were a thing of the past.

Yet the young English novelist of the 1970s had a far less settled idea than his 1950s counterpart of what a novel was and what it was *for*. The common ground shared by many of the Movement generation – that modernism had resulted in one lot of pretentious tosh, the 'apocalyptic' excesses of the 1940s in another, and it was time to get back to intelligent common sense and honest craftsmanship – had the advantage of clearing a space in which the writer could get on with his job. Twenty years later, the taste for straightforward English social comedy had become less dominant: young readers in particular were turning to Latin American authors such as Gabriel García Márquez and Jorge Luis Borges or rediscovering the differently labyrinthine Hermann Hesse; if they looked back to the 1950s, they looked towards America, to Jack Kerouac or William Burroughs. A lot of this was to do with the dying days of hippiedom, an aspect of the 1970s viewed scathingly from the future perspective of *Dead Babies*, and it owed more to drugs and cloudy thinking than to considered literary taste. At the same time, the main English novelists associated with the 1950s, most of them as yet no more than middle-aged, were still publishing: William Golding (after a fallow period), Iris Murdoch and Angus Wilson added major works to their oeuvres during the 1970s. So, of course, did Kingsley Amis.

Martin reviewed books by two of these now senior novelists – Murdoch and Wilson – just as his father had done twenty years earlier; and his pieces disclose, often simultaneously, both the prickly relationship between generations and the younger writer's readiness to learn or to borrow. Writing on Murdoch's *The Black Prince* in February 1973, his indignation is roused by its trickery: 'The book, which is offered by its narrator as both a "true story" and a "work of art", is itself presented by an "Editor" who in turn supplies "Postscripts" from the other characters, all of whom distort the story and accuse the story of distortion.' The reader, 'desperate to know *what happened (was it art or life?)*', is rewarded with 'the "Editor's" final scotching of the rumour that he and Bradley are "the invention of a minor novelist". Now you see her, now you don't.'[39] This is precisely the sort of trick which was to be played on the reader in Martin's two substantial novels of the following decade, *Money* and *London Fields*. Of *The Sacred and Profane Love Machine* – a title whose juxtaposition of the pretentious and the pornographic suggests the recipe for another aspect of his own fiction – he decides that 'it is bloated and it sags' and ascribes to Murdoch working methods which are notably like his father's: 'She can't, in the nature of things, revise much and probably she never re-reads; she just "gets on with the next one".'[40] In fact, Martin's admiration for Murdoch was much warmer and less qualified than Kingsley's: in *Experience* he brackets her and Elizabeth Jane Howard as the two most interesting women novelists of their generation.

He wasn't so kindly disposed towards Angus Wilson. Reviewing *As If by Magic* in June 1973, he took some unwise pot-shots at jokey names – Alexandra Grant is a student (the student Grant),[41] ' "Hamo" is (small wonder) the homo' – of just the sort which populate his own later novels and at 'Americans saying "Noo York" and "anyways", hippies using "like" as if they were rustics, the word "delicious" appearing seven times in as many pages, the whole book riddled with repetitions, unintentional rhymes, jangles, even solecisms',[42] a catalogue of effects which he would in due course gleefully replicate. More substantially, he found that when Wilson describes the young, 'the hilarious inaccuracy of his observations renders this half of the book a more or less total write-off':[43] this indeed seemed undeniable at the time, and any young reader of *As If by Magic* would have cringed – just as we cringed at comparable inaccuracies in Anthony Powell's *Hearing Secret Harmonies* (1975) or, to an admittedly lesser extent, in Kingsley's *Girl, 20* (1972). Yet perhaps the way in which an older novelist *hears* the young is not so much wrong as different: the result of a steady retuning in the process of selection and emphasis, which comes to focus mercilessly on their silliest verbal habits. There's nothing disgraceful in Martin's indignant twenty-something reaction to *As If by Magic*, though that can't quite be said about his haughty piece on the 'amateurism' and 'hobbyist brio' of Angus Wilson's critical writings: those terms seem merely impertinent when applied by a relative beginner to someone who'd been a professional author for over thirty years and a Professor of Creative Writing too.

People used to say, when vexed by our generation, that a couple of years in the army would have done us the world of good. They had a point. Intelligence and experience are as out of balance in Martin's early reviews as in his fiction: the broader sympathies of young Kingsley's writing, grounded in his understanding of ordinary people, are missing. Living in London, working in literary journalism, didn't help – it encouraged him to create a brittle, sometimes abrasive mask of confidence to cover an inner self which was 'tractable' (Kingsley's word) and 'shy' (Anthony Thwaite's). He knew this, obviously: the conflict between brash exterior and inner hollow man becomes almost a definition of a Martin Amis central character. And others noticed it too. Frederic Raphael remembers a chance encounter with Claire Tomalin, then literary editor at the *New Statesman*, in a wine bar in Lamb's Conduit Street: she was meeting 'someone from the office', who turned out to be her deputy, 'Martin Amis, a short, pleasant-looking boy of twenty-seven, with innocent gigolo eyes and an air of candid *arrivisme*'. Raphael at first told Martin that he'd been reading 'bits' of one of his two novels, then modified this to professed enjoyment of *The Rachel Papers*: ' "I only said I'd read bits because I didn't want to spoil you." He seemed placated, the modest glow-worm, Gary Glitter in mufti.'[44] It's almost too good – almost, indeed, the sort of lethally effective formulation (though not quite the style) that Martin himself might have employed. Precisely this matter of deceptively layered appearances – apparent success as a mask for underlying emptiness, and the intimately related obverse of this illusion – was to be the theme of his next novel.

One of the riddling paradoxes of fiction is that an unambitious form is in one crucial respect more ambitious than an ambitious one: it is, in this sense, easier to write *Ulysses* than a novel by, say, Barbara Pym or C. P. Snow. *Ulysses* competes only with itself, with its own ambition; a novel by Pym or Snow competes with a thousand others about middle-class women, strange clergymen and mendacious academics. *Success* (1978) looks like Martin's simplest novel and is, for that reason, hugely ambitious. The most restrained of all his books, it is also the most exposed, with a sparseness which leaves both characters and author vulnerable, like chamber musicians denied the shelter of a symphony orchestra. But none of Martin's novels is structurally quite straightforward – even *The Rachel Papers* is punctuated by the clock ticking towards Charles's birthday midnight and *Dead Babies* by roman-numeralled character biographies at every tenth short chapter – and *Success* plays a narrative trick of the kind which was to become much more complicated in his later books. It's divided into twelve chapters, for twelve months, a template as simple and arbitrary as those of its two predecessors; but one half of each chapter is narrated by Gregory Riding and the other by his flat-sharing foster-brother Terence Service. The joke is that neither narrator is remotely trustworthy.

Terry tells us this: 'Gregory is a liar. Don't believe a word he says. He is the author of lies.'[45] And eventually Gregory admits as much: 'I tell lies. I'm a liar. I always have been.'[46] Is there any reason to suppose that Terry is likelier to tell the truth? Initially, yes: his world is more impoverished, and therefore less fantastic. But the sceptical reader will become increasingly suspicious of him as the foster-brothers' apparent fortunes see-saw. One possible interpretation of the book is that *all* success is illusory, founded on self-deception and on deceiving others. Even what we learn about Gregory's and Terry's apparently verifiable existences – their backgrounds, their jobs, their friends – is compromised in the telling. Gregory, according to Gregory, is the only son of prosperous parents, who live with his sister Ursula in landed luxury near Cambridge, tended by servants; he was educated at archly named prep and public schools, Repworth and Peerforth; he saw himself as 'the village princeling and household cosset, the toast of the family, the *mignon* of the minions, the darling of the staff'.[47] Now he lives in an inherited West London penthouse and idly passes his days employed at an art gallery whose doting owners, Odette and Jason Styles, fawn over him and continually solicit his sexual favours; his evenings, meanwhile, are spent in bisexual debauchery, often at the salon of his friend Torka, where he seems to prefer boys, although he only ever brings girls home – unless, that is, he's off on 'an expensive romp' with his 'two chums' Kane and Skimmer, visiting cocktail bars and 'the grandest restaurants', for all the world like Simon Smith and his

Amazing Dancing Bear.[48] Much of this is nonsense, of course. Crucially (since everything else follows from it), the family estate, which will be derelict and dismantled by the end of the novel, is no more than a modest country house whose 'staff' consists of a single housekeeper: something rather less grand than Kingsley's and Jane's establishment at Lemmons. This matters, because social class, grudgingly misinterpreted in the usual Amis manner, is a major theme to which I'll shortly return.

But what, first, of Terry? We might expect him to be the more sympathetic of the pair, given the implied social viewpoint; given, too, that he is the first and mildest member of that procession of anti-heroic yobs whose later representatives include John Self in *Money*, Keith Talent in *London Fields*, Steve Cousins in *The Information* and Mal in 'State of England'. We learn that he spent his early childhood in Cambridge but was adopted by the Ridings at the age of nine, soon after his father had murdered his seven-year-old sister Rosie; his mother had died, also at his father's hands, three years earlier. It's a heavy burden for a character to bear – the terrible father is part of another fictional procession, the apprentice Fred Wests – but one of the book's subtler implications is that it may nevertheless be lighter (because, cruelly, more useful as preparation for the real world) than Gregory's inheritance of self-deception and insanity: Terry suspects that 'Gregory finds madness posh, like gout or incest'.[49] He is more troubled by the colour of his hair, which is ginger, and by the humiliation of being called 'Ginger', which is what his foster-sister Ursula does. He has a job which appears to involve teleselling – 'What *do* I sell? Whatever it is, they pay me £50 a week for it'[50] – but about which he remains extraordinarily vague, possibly a consequence of the Amis family ignorance about what workplaces are really like. He is serially unsuccessful with women: at the start of the book, he dolefully notes that his most recent sexual encounter was on the previous 23 July, while during the novel's twelve-month span his conquest of the office temp Jan is interrupted by Ursula's attempted suicide and his conquest of Ursula swiftly followed by her actual suicide. But even this bothers him less than his ginger hair, and even his ginger hair ceases to bother him as he becomes a success.

'Don't tell me he's becoming a success,'[51] wails Gregory, before arriving at the perception that Terry 'does, in some important sense in which I do not, look like a *person*, one put together with this life in view'.[52] Terry, indeed, has become serviceable: a joke all the more effective for being implicit, unlike the tiresome banter of his workmates ('Here's old tea service again'[53] and so forth). In fact, a large measure of his success is crudely redistributive: it proceeds from his discovery that Gregory is in every respect a failure. When he re-encounters Jan, assumed to have spent a wild night with Gregory after Terry's dash to Ursula in hospital, he learns of his foster-brother's impotence; when Gregory 'resigns' from his art-gallery job, Terry pseudonymously applies for it, thereby discovering not only that it is menial and ill paid but also that Gregory had been *sacked* from it. Gregory's veneer of self-confidence has by this time entirely disintegrated: he suffers, like Kingsley, from panic attacks on the tube and recognises that a 'whole layer of protective casing has been ripped off my life';[54] moreover, his own decline coincides with the end of the family fortune and his father's death. Terry, of course, has become much the higher earner of the two. This he owes to a dubious union official called Stanley Veale, whose most memorable attributes are his reckless consumption of spirits bought cheap, by the case, and his 'posh emphasis on the terminal *t*' which confusingly turns 'carport' and 'runabout' into 'carports' and 'runabouts'[55] – a habit first identified by Kingsley in a 1970s television commercial and memorably exemplified in a cab-driver who remonstrated with him, saying, 'Why d'you want to go and get yourself into *this* states.'[56] This is how Dickens treats his minor characters, picking up and playing with a verbal quirk, and it goes some way towards disguising the fact that the Stanley Veale business really doesn't work, for it isn't at all clear why Terry is singled out for such preferential treatment nor when and how he attends the four-nights-a-week course at the City College prescribed by Veale. It's a matter which cries out for some accurate knowledge of how such things work; and it also, since there are so many other working-class crooks or *cheats* in Martin's fiction, brings us back to the author's highly ambiguous treatment of social class.

Some personal background is relevant here. Martin's girlfriend while he was working on *Success* was Emma Soames, the granddaughter of Sir Winston Churchill. She was much admired by Kingsley, both personally and for ancestral reasons, and in *Experience* Martin mentions the one visit Jane and Kingsley paid to the Soameses' country home while Martin was staying there. Emma's father, Sir Christopher, asked Kingsley: 'Would you like to wash your hands before we go in?'

To which Kingsley replied: 'No thanks, I washed them behind a bush on the way down.'[57] This is clearly quite funny and it seems not to have caused offence, but Terry would have had a word for it, and the word is 'chippy'. According to him (fairly near the start of the book, remember), 'chippy' means 'minding being poor, ugly and common'.[58] Kingsley wasn't these things, though he'd been close enough to the first and last of them in his time; nevertheless, his reply was unmistakably 'chippy' in its implicit resentment of a 'posh' civility, since chippiness doesn't evaporate entirely with changed circumstances. Recalling this little incident, Martin adds: 'But, lor, how much stuff there was about class in those days. Whatever else she did, Margaret Thatcher [who became Prime Minister the year after *Success* was published] helped weaken all that. Mrs Thatcher, with her Cecils, with her Normans, with her Keiths.'[59] It's only a matter of chance, then, that her cabinets didn't include a Terry or a Stanley. But this is carefully disingenuous because, while Martin seems to take the approved line that class is a Bad Thing, he also, from the sanctuary of his own classless forename, repeatedly stigmatises lower-class characters with ridiculous speech mannerisms and self-mocking names – the drubbings meted out to *his* Keiths are especially merciless. Terry knows 'everything there is to know about class': he remembers a magazine quiz – 'anyone who completed this quiz, the idea was, would know at once how posh they were' – in which the last question asked what the participant's children would be called: would his son be '(a) Sebastian, Clarence, Montague, or (b) Michael, James, Robert, or . . . (c) Norman, Keith, Terry'.[60] And despite Terry's insistence that none of this matters, that it's 'crap', it continues to underpin the novel. Indeed, two related points seem worth making in unfashionable defence of class: one is that, at least since the mid-eighteenth century, class in England has been extraordinarily fluid, enabling immense social leaps to be made within individual lifetimes (think of Fanny Burney or George Crabbe); the other is that this fluidity coincides with the rise of the English novel, which has made class – in its nuances, misunderstandings and unexpected transitions – one of its major themes. For the novelist it remains an indispensable resource and Martin, for all that weird 'But, lor . . .' business, isn't one to do without it. Behind *Success* stands, once again, *Mansfield Park*, and behind Terence Service stands Fanny Price.

Personal background is also relevant in a more retrospective way,

for *Success* takes full advantage of seeming to be not at all autobiographical by being very autobiographical indeed. Terry's abandonment
in his squalid parental home after his father's arrest owes something
to Martin's experience of being left alone at Fulham Road, as we have
seen; his recollection of 'scrawling cloacal obscenities in the Fat Boy's
Letts Pupils' Diary'[61] is the schoolboy Martin's of stealing 'the diary
of a fat, speechless classmate' and filling it 'with a year's worth of
bestial, obscene and quite imaginary antics';[62] the notes he sticks on
his alarm clock, 'saying things like FUCKING GET UP'[63] are the
undergraduate Martin's, 'saying things like *Oh Really Get Up* and
BLOODY GET UP!';[64] while Gregory's art-gallery job is Martin's on
coming down from Oxford. There are private borrowings from Kingsley – the panic attacks, the joke about inadvertent plurals – and literary
ones too: the catalogue of fifty-eight composite words containing 'fuck'
which opens Terry's March chapter[65] directly echoes Garnet Bowen's
list of composites ending in 'bum',[66] themselves an echo of the 'usual
valediction' in the Amis–Larkin letters; and when Terry accepts 'the
largest whisky I had ever seen, heard or read about'[67] from Stanley
Veale, this sharply contrasts with the hospitality of Professor Welch
when he pours Jim Dixon 'the smallest drink he'd ever been seriously
offered'.[68]

Yet the most powerful and disquieting way in which Martin's own
past informs *Success* concerns Gregory's childhood relationship (and
to a lesser extent Terry's adult relationship) with Ursula. Gregory
fantasises this into something rather more sexual than Terry and we
eventually understand to have been the case, but its importance
remains considerable: it seems to blight Ursula's subsequent feelings
about sexuality and contribute to her general instability; but at the
same time Gregory's account of their adventure on an island in a small
lake – it begins with them 'playing with our raft, an uneven and
treacherous affair roped together out of logs, cracked doors, spare
timber and fat petrol tubs'[69] – most vividly recalls the *Swallows and
Amazons* idyll of Martin's childhood relationship, also mildly sexual,
with his cousin Marian Partington. Further ambiguities crowd in when
Terry begins his disastrous affair with his foster-sister; for the sister
who isn't quite a sister, who is unstable and ultimately suicidal, is also
Sally Amis. The shadowy but pervasive Ursula is a fusion of Marian
and Sally, the two most influential girls in Martin's childhood.

The sparse construction of *Success* throws into relief Martin's emerging thematic and stylistic tics. The reader of his two previous novels meets again the Swiftian astonishment that 'girls now go to the lavatory'[70] from *The Rachel Papers* and the idea that 'the past has gone, and from now on it is all future tense'[71] from *Dead Babies*. The lethal beer called Particular Brew, which Terry unwisely consumes in the Intrepid Fox, and which metamorphoses into Peculiar Brew, will figure in Martin's subsequent London novels, as will his glumly obsessive interest in pornography. Recurrent quirks of style include the use of private slang (here, 'tonto' for 'mad') as if it's universal, a semi-ironic application of the adjective 'powerful' ('my powerful green car', 'my powerful Grundig'), and an inability to resist empty riddling: 'the surest guarantee of sexual success is sexual success (you can't have one without the other and you can't have the other without the one)'.[72] Most worrying, because it becomes so pervasive in his later work, is that habit of fruitlessly emphatic repetition, which in its simplest form produces a chapter opening such as this: 'Gregory Riding is my foster-brother. He is.'[73]

My final point about this short but fascinating novel concerns its last page or so. This, the shortest of all the twenty-four half-chapters, finds the ruined and desolate Gregory wandering in the bleak winter landscape which was once his childhood home. Terry has returned confidently to London – 'I sip my drink. I'm going to be all right' – and Gregory recognises that 'This was the part he was meant for.' Dusk is falling:

> It really is dark. I pause again. Can I get there and back before nightfall? The woods are drenched, dripping with dreams and death. A wind blows. The trees attempt to shake their shoulders dry. Why won't the wind let the leaves alone? The lake is trying to warn me – danger in the streets of the trees. The wood is fizzing. A long rolls over on its back. One bird sings.[74]

This is clearly meant as a scene of failure and despair. Yet (and here I suspect myself of wilful misreading) it seems to me infinitely both more reassuring and more real than the numbingly amoral, intolerably vacuous urban world in which Terry has sought and found success. But Martin's fiction would from now on inhabit Terry's world, not Gregory's.

5

Success is the key to success. As with his father's third novel, *I Like It Here*, there's a temptation to regard the book as slighter and lighter than it actually is; but the mannerisms and the quirks, the obsessions and the limitations, of what we must begin to call middle-period Martin Amis are all there. By comparison, *The Rachel Papers* and *Dead Babies* are in one important sense much more conventional novels, for in *Success* every aspect of the narrative is rigorously honed to fit the demands of a fictional conceit – the balanced characters switching places in balanced chapters over the span of exactly a year – in the way which was to characterise Martin's subsequent novels, not always to their advantage.

And Martin was a success. James Fenton remembers him at this time as the pivotal figure in the Friday lunches, at the Bursa Kebab House and then at Bertorelli's, where 'people wanted to talk like him, pick up his language, his verbal mannerisms, his attitudes and so on. All the people who came to the lunches were best described in some kind of relation to Martin.'[75] This was rather different from the ironic awe with which his father was regarded on these occasions, as a smouldering repository of outrageous wisdom, and it was arguably less healthy. Many who attended these lunches recall an air of camaraderie laced with competitive edginess which could turn cynical and brutal, a carelessness with manners and feelings, doubtless encouraged by the predominantly male company. This tone feeds into Martin's fiction, as does the appropriation of Amis–Hitchens private slang from 'street sadness' and 'tonto' in the early novels through to John Self's references to his 'sock' (flat) and 'rug' (hair), which when cut undergoes a 'rug rethink'. The Martin-generation lunchers at the Bursa – including Julian Barnes, James Fenton, Christopher Hitchens, Clive James, Ian McEwan, Craig Raine and Christopher Reid – paradoxically formed a group which was far more intimate personally yet far less coherent in literary terms than the Movement in the 1950s. McEwan remembers the political diversity, the way in which the *New Statesman* contingent (Fenton, Hitchens) would be offset by the right-of-centre Piers Paul Read and Clive James; he points out too that Martin was 'brilliantly detached from politics', scathing about discussions about 'ball-bearings' or 're-tooling British industry'. There was also, McEwan adds, an overlapping group with another axis at the *New Review*, where 'every day was a Friday lunch'.[76] One can't help noticing that where the Movement writer's other self was usually a university lecturer, members of this group were likelier to earn their non-literary livings as journalists. Otherwise, it's difficult to decide what they stood for: indeed, 'standing for' was in some cases less to their taste than 'standing back from'.

That was the position of 'Martian' poets such as Craig Raine and Christopher Reid: to view earthly reality with the puzzled curiosity – the apparent incomprehension which may actually be a different comprehension – of someone from another planet. In truth, this notion was most vividly embodied in a television advertisement for dehydrated potato, which showed aliens chortling helplessly over the spectacle of earthlings peeling, cutting, cooking and mashing the things. But as a tool to enable the writer to see familiar things afresh, it had something to be said for it. Familiar people, too: coincidentally, both Raine's and Reid's first books included poems about butchers. In Raine's, the butcher is found 'smoking a pencil like Isambard Kingdom Brunel' and his shop contains 'coral necklaces of mince' and 'chickens stripped to their aertex vests';[77] in Reid's, a quintet of pigs' heads 'relax on parsley and smirk about / their newly disembodied state'.[78] In each case, the combination of a skewed perspective and a commonplace yet mildly grotesque subject is typically Martian. Nevertheless, the style has two inherent drawbacks which can cause problems: one is that the necessity of seeing differently inhibits the author from using what he and we already know about a subject; the other is that the innocent alien's eye must be scrupulously exact in perceiving things as they seem to be. A brilliant image can be derailed by one simple inaccuracy – a mistake the putative Martian would spot at once – as in these lines from Raine's 'Return Ticket':

> Left behind, the traffic lights
> exchange three words across the street,
> blinkered in Jane Austen bonnets,
> like the three sisters longing for Moscow.[79]

It's an arresting and original way of looking at traffic lights, despite the awkward lurch in chronology between Jane Austen and Chekhov, until we realise that the lights exchanging words must, alas, be facing in different directions, pointing down different streets, with their backs or sides to each other; they have no eye contact, so they can't be exchanging anything. If the Martian view could prove tricky to handle within the limits of the lyric poem, it was even more fraught with difficulty when stretched to novel length. But this is what Martin attempts in his fourth book, *Other People: A Mystery Story* (1981), which he wrote in Paris, 'during the fiscal year 1979–80, when I was abroad', as he carefully puts it in *Experience*.[80] His father put the point rather more robustly to Philip Larkin: 'Did I tell you Martin is spending a year abroad as a TAX EXILE? Last year he earned £38,000. Little shit. 29, he is. Little shit.'[81]

That perhaps didn't help Kingsley to warm to the novel when it appeared. 'Young Martin's new novel is out,' he told Robert Conquest on 9 March 1981, before going on to identify the book's central problem in two merciless sentences: 'Tough going I find. You see there's this girl with amneisa shit you know what I mean, so she's forgotten what a lavatory is and thinks the cisterns and pipes are statuary, but then how does she know what statuary is?'[82] Like Raine's conversing traffic lights, it's a conceit which doesn't work. The girl who calls herself Mary Lamb after an overheard nursery rhyme (an astute move for someone who barely understands what a name is, let alone how to choose an allusive pseudonym) is, for all but the novel's brief Part Three, a maddening mixture of literal-minded naivety and inappropriately sophisticated knowledge. At the outset, she appears to be released from the care of the 'white-clad keepers'[83] in a hospital, although the damaged state of those she encounters outside, and whom she immediately classifies into six types, immediately suggests that this isn't the normal world. There's also a warning shot of the false pastoral, which, here as elsewhere in Martin's work (the elegiac dusks in *Dead Babies* and *Success*), means something other or less than it seems: Mary discovers 'a good place to hide' – a concealed pun, as we later discover – in the 'moist hollow at the foot of a leaning tree'.[84] Thereafter, she is improbably adopted by a socially ascending sequence of people, all of whose lives she innocently wrecks. First, there's alcoholic Sharon, her gay brother Gavin, and her parents, the Bothams; then, after a hostel interlude, a squat-inhabiting bunch of misfits she encounters through working in a café; and thirdly, via a strange meeting at a television company, a wealthy loser called Jamie (like Gregory in *Success* he has learned that

'The rich have special terrors . . .')[85] and his dissolute entourage. Mr Botham is crippled for life; Alan, of café and squat, commits suicide; Jamie ends up in rehab: it's all, or so she thinks, her fault.

But is it? Because of her condition, Mary Lamb is, most unusually, a central character as free of responsibility as she is devoid of personality. Like the Dead Babies, she has no past; moreover, she has no clear understanding of time, which she realises is closely connected with something equally mysterious called money and whose passing she observes in a spirit of dispassionate curiosity. What she does and doesn't understand is continually problematic. An inability to cope with idioms and metaphors is one early symptom of her condition, so that when Sharon says, 'It's lucky the weather's turned,' she reflects: 'The weather had turned. It was lucky. Everything was coming right.'[86] Yet when, only a little later, she wonders why in the pub 'people kept using that word *fuck* and its cognates so often', this is a linguistically subtle thought to which she adds the striking codicil that 'they used it so often that the air seemed to quack'.[87] On page 54, she is still discovering how her own body works, even down to such rudimentary details as learning to blow her nose 'by watching Mr Botham, who did it often and expressively';[88] a page later, she's reading Shakespeare, Jane Austen and Dickens. Although her comprehension of what she reads is deeply eccentric, the fact that she can get anywhere at all with these books presupposes an extensive working vocabulary. Seventy pages later, when poor bald Alan says, 'I really love you, you know, Mary,' she replies: 'What does that mean, exactly?'[89] Could she have read Jane Austen *at all* without forming at least some idea? Her emotional blankness is essential to the narrative but impossible to square with the quite complex information she seems capable of handling; and her relationships with the external world are similarly inconsistent. Halfway through the book, she doesn't know how to climb into a car, nor does she appreciate how a car relates to a road and to other traffic,[90] although by this time she's working as a café waitress, dealing easily with a range of chores as well as with customers. She has a sure grasp of London geography – the television company, for instance, is just across the river from where the Bothams lived – yet she has to navigate her way by memorising a 'graph' (she doesn't know what a map is) and is subsequently surprised to find that the Circle Line doesn't go anywhere.

However, *Other People* isn't 'her' book: its puppeteer is, or seems to be, a policeman called John Prince, with whom she will eventually end up, or seem to end up (some day my Prince will come?). His name may also suggest Lucifer, Prince of Darkness, and he has the green eyes of the Devil and of the boy who threatened Martin as a child. He is the narrator who periodically appears to express his concerns about Mary and to offer his advice and opinions to the reader: the trouble with him is his narrative voice, one we hear a good deal in Martin's work, which is far less policeman-like than Amis-like. Prince functions within the main body of the novel in two main ways. Firstly, he conducts a dialogue of comic misunderstandings with the hopelessly literal Mary:

> 'I, I want forgiveness.'
> 'I beg your pardon?'
> 'That's right.'
> 'Sorry?'
> '*Yes*.'
> He laughed again. 'I can't get enough of this,' he said. 'But let's be serious for a while . . .'[91]

> Mary said, 'What do you get if you break the law?'
> 'Time.'
> 'What do you get if you murder someone?'
> 'Life.'
> 'What's life like?'
> 'Murder.'
> 'Is it?'
> 'Hell,' he said and laughed. 'Don't ever try it.'[92]

This sort of joke soon becomes wearisome (a subsequent variant has Mary trying to explain about her literal loss of memory, to which dead-babyish Jamie can only keep saying that it happens to him all the time). Secondly, however, Prince presents a point of view which is both quasi-authorial and offensive. His sections strike a note of complacent cynicism – 'Trev and Jock are criminals, I'm afraid'[93] – laced with cranky homophobia: 'Queers, they just want shelter from the lunar tempest. But *you* know what queers are like.'[94] Later, his generalised untruths become more sententious: for instance, 'Life is made of fear.'[95] At least Larkin allowed life the doubtful privilege of having some boredom to start with, and he wrote with the redemptive irony of his generation (Kingsley's poetry, too, receives its allusive nod: 'She read somewhere else: "A woman's solitary thoughts are almost exclusively romantic" ... but men weren't like that').[96] Prince's dislikeability is made all the more disturbing by his complete lack of background and by our intuitive sense that his apparent protectiveness towards Mary can only do her harm in the end.

As, in a sense, he does. On the way there, however, *Other People* has qualities which seem to belong to a less fussy and finicky novel, one less wrapped up in its own conceit. Many of the low-life characters – the Bothams, Alan and Russ and their circle – are treated with at least fleeting touches of warmth. The episode involving the television presenter Michael Shane is preposterous, but Mary's shacking up with the wealthily dissolute Jamie has its moments too, including some drinking wisdom borrowed from Kingsley: 'The trick is to drink very heavily every lunchtime. It saves a lot of effort in the early evening.'[97] But it's there that Mary rediscovers her earlier identity, as Amy Hide – an identity already discovered by John Prince but not, oddly, by her former lover Michael Shane. Amy Hide is, to use a term we shall meet again, a murderee; and the fate Prince leads her towards is her re-murder. So this life of re-learning and re-enacting is an afterlife and the air Mary/Amy breathes with such gratitude in the book's opening sentence belongs to the world hereafter. That is one way of looking at it. Another is to focus on the brief penultimate section, in which the adolescent Amy wakes from a terrible dream, which begins with precisely the same sentence: 'Her first feeling, as she smelled the air, was one of intense and helpless gratitude.'[98] In that case, the whole novel might become, eerily rather than reassuringly, an extended dream world: a variation on Lewis Carroll's two *Alice* books. Yet, even at that very moment, the policeman, the murderer, waits in the wings with his compromising Epilogue.

6

Martin's first four novels, like Kingsley's, belong unmistakably to the decade they just overrun and represent the clear first stage of a writing career. They are in obvious respects a much more disparate group. Each of Kingsley's is centred on a recognisably author-like figure who is either married (John Lewis, Garnet Bowen) or moving towards an apparently stable relationship (Jim Dixon, Patrick Standish); and each belongs, in formal and structural terms, to the mainstream of English social comedy. Of Martin's, only *The Rachel Papers* fits into this general pattern, and that in a youthfully subversive way: the other three are, depending on one's point of view, either strikingly eclectic or flailingly uncertain in direction. Nevertheless, there's a notable respect in which Martin's are more unified than his father's: three of them are set in London, while the Hertfordshire of *Dead Babies* is close enough for the entire cast to spend an evening in the wrecked capital, which is where most of them also spend their weekdays. His imaginative world is metropolitan where Kingsley's, even when reluctantly dragged abroad to Portugal, is provincial. One possibly unexpected consequence is that it's Martin's fiction which lacks contextual depth. In the city, and especially in the urban dystopia which with *Other People* becomes his special territory, it's easy for the streets to produce not much more than 'street sadness' and for other people to become other types of people. Kingsley's local habitations – those small towns in England, Wales, Portugal – have far greater social coherence: people have pasts, and families, and futures; they know who lives next door, across the street, who's to be found in the pub and the corner shop. It's a very British scale of things, one which Kingsley would cherish and admire all his life (one of the subtler achievements of *The Folks that Live on the Hill* lies in his reclamation of his part of London as a village). But Martin wanted none of it.

This is how Charles Olson begins *Call Me Ishmael*, his magnificently eccentric monograph on Melville's *Moby-Dick*: 'I take SPACE to be the central fact to man born in America, from Folsom cave to now. I spell it large because it comes large here. Large, and without mercy.'[99] In his 1982 essay on Saul Bellow, which opens *The Moronic Inferno* (1986), Martin recasts the idea: 'American novels are big all right, but partly because America is big too.'[100] In a later essay, also on Bellow, he claims that by 1970, the year E. M. Forster died, 'English fiction (which still awaited the crucial infusion from the "colonials") felt, well, hopelessly English – hopelessly inert and inbred. Meanwhile, and as if in obedience to the political reality, American fiction was assuming its manifest destiny.'[101] And at a conference in California, in 2000, he told his audience: 'The project is to become an American novelist.'[102] In fact, what Martin wanted to do after *Other People* was to write the equivalent of a big American novel. He would make no fewer than four attempts at this, and they were to define the middle period of his literary career.

8. THE STATE OF ENGLAND

1

When Margaret Thatcher became Prime Minister on 4 May 1979, Martin was in his Parisian exile: from there, he viewed her achievement both more distantly and less affectionately than his father. It's already becoming hard to reimagine the fanatical detestation that literary intellectuals of our generation felt for her,[1] though it's high time to acknowledge that this wasn't altogether a matter of politics. For Thatcher wasn't one of us: she was a chilly, philistine meritocrat who had married a successful businessman and climbed the ladder of power with a determination we might grudgingly have admired, were it not for our intuitive certainty that she had little time for books or culture or artistic fripperies. She wasn't funny, and she wasn't particularly bright, but she was terrifyingly effective; there was about her a quality we'd glimpsed, to a lesser degree, in Mary Whitehouse – that scornful, commonsensical repudiation of the permissive arty world which went down so reliably in parts of Middle England. Kingsley, as we've seen, was on the whole delighted by Margaret Thatcher; yet a major component of his delight was her apparently effortless ability to infuriate the silly little lefties of the next generation. What the next generation might usefully have done, however, was to make more effort to understand her appeal.

As it happens, Martin was to write directly about Margaret Thatcher at the end of the 1980s, in a review of Hugo Young's *The Iron Lady* (originally published in the UK as *One of Us*). His piece is a farrago of incomprehension. 'Mrs Thatcher is the only interesting thing about British power politics; and the only interesting thing about Mrs Thatcher is that she isn't a man,' he says.[2] But it's clear, even from his own review, that this is untrue. He is interested, first of all, in whether or not she is 'sexy' (Kingsley and Philip Larkin both thought so, and to the latter I shall have to return) and, more curiously, on the sexiness or otherwise of British politics in general: 'Describing a gradient of sullen and insular decline, British politics has long ceased to be sexy,' he writes, finding himself yearning 'for the banjos, the majorettes, the misappropriated campaign donations, the sweating vaudevillians of the American scene'.[3] This is as much as to say that he regards grown-up political debate as rather dull, even though 'the balloons and spangled confetti' of the previous year's Republican Convention in New Orleans were a 'childish spectacle'.[4] Thatcher's 'early years form a tale of almost macabre banality', he grumbles, before outlining a provincial progress which might well have appealed as fictional material to Arnold Bennett or perhaps even to the young Kingsley Amis (there's something of it, indeed, in the upwardly mobile Gruffyd-Williams set in *That Uncertain Feeling*). This is certainly interesting, as is the well-made point that 'Mrs Thatcher broke the unions by dividing the class they represented';[5] but much of the latter part of the review concerns her vocal, cosmetic and sartorial makeovers, a topic which a writer as vain as Martin Amis might have approached with more caution (he also, in this section, criticises her use of the royal 'we', which is of course quite unlike his own in such phrases as 'The holy book we mentioned . . .' a dozen pages later in *The War Against Cliché*).[6] However, the most revealing moment in his article comes when he discusses her response to the urban riots of 1981. 'When she saw the first footage of the riots and looting, the urban Morlocks in their ecstasy of hatred and despair, Mrs Thatcher responded as follows: "Oh those poor shopkeepers!"' On which Martin comments: 'Women! But *is* she one? Well, yes and no.'[7]

This is an ambitious claim, and possibly a reckless one, but Martin's failure to understand Margaret Thatcher's remark about shopkeepers supplies one key to his failure as a novelist. Arnold Bennett, again, and Kingsley, again, would have known exactly what she meant and sympathised with the plight of the hard-pressed, hard-working individual pitted against the mindlessly undiscriminating violence of the mob; for although England may not be precisely a nation of shopkeepers, it is a nation whose culture – and, therefore, whose fiction – honours and values the local and the individual. Martin's contemptuous dismissal, in which the contempt is as alarmingly characteristic as the dismissiveness, is a rejection not only of the perspective which English novelists had hitherto found invaluable but of England itself. Yet the alternative project was perilous: during the twentieth century, an Irishman had matched and a Frenchman had surpassed the scale of the big American novel, but hardly anyone in England had got close. Perhaps success had gone to Martin's head.

Bill Buford, then editor of the recently reborn *Granta*, would later recall Ian McEwan's observation that it was easy 'to be a young celebrity writer at the end of the seventies, because there was no one else [apart from Martin Amis and himself] around'.[8] McEwan now rightly points out that the very sense of a 'celebrity writer' was less familiar then, before the arrival of Waterstone's bookshops and the media circus surrounding the Booker Prize;[9] before, too, the replacement of the lead book review by the author profile. It was Buford himself who set out to remedy this state of affairs in 1983 with *Granta 7: Best of Young British Novelists*. Although self-evidently comprising prose rather than poetry, his anthology retains the same power to impress as Conquest's *New Lines* from 1956: it too contains an astonishingly high proportion of winners. Thanks to the luck of the alphabet, it kicks off with 'Money', 'the first chapter of the new novel that Martin Amis is currently completing':[10] in fact, *Money* (1984). John Fowles, in his diary entry for 24 March 1983, noted that the magazine was 'headed by the vogueishly bitter (if not actually sick) Martin Amis, who makes his father seem like a warm-hearted humanist by comparison'. He regretted 'A literary century gone very sour', inevitably sounding pretty sour himself, but more usefully discerned 'a marked shift away from common reader–writer assumptions into a generally waspish personal hatred'.[11] Other contributors to *Granta 7* included Pat Barker, Julian Barnes, William Boyd, Kazuo Ishiguro, Adam Mars-Jones, Ian McEwan, Salman Rushdie, Graham Swift, Rose Tremain and A. N. Wilson. It's worth dwelling for a moment on Swift, whose brief contribution, 'About the Eel', was from a 'longer work in progress'. This work, *Waterland* (1983), is by any reckoning among the most considerable English novels of its time. In its steady accretion of chronologically disparate fragments, it doesn't lack structural ambition, yet its movement – historical, geographical, genealogical, social – through generations of Atkinsons and Cricks roots it deeply in England. It demonstrates, just at the moment when Martin was setting out to prove otherwise, that the big novel needn't be remotely American.

2

Money is Martin's flawed masterpiece, and the cliché for once means exactly what it says. Writers are usually well advised to put everything they've got into a book (they may not live to write another), but *Money* both redeploys motifs from *Success* and pre-empts too much in *London Fields* and *The Information*. Philip Larkin is never far from either of the Amises, and the book's central character, John Self, seems to owe at least his name to Larkin's poem 'Self's the Man' in which the exemplary, married, unselfish Arnold (but, after all, his chosen life was just what he wanted, and therefore selfish) is played off against the solitary who's better 'At knowing what I can stand ... Or I suppose I can'.[12] John Self, too, is going to find selfishness harder to define, and to achieve, than he thinks. In fact, he acquired his name quite late in the novel's evolution, for in the *Granta* version of the opening chapter he's called John Sleep, presumably because he's sleepwalking into financial ruin. This is by no means the only difference between the two versions, between 'Money' and *Money*, and comparing them clearly reveals how thoroughly Martin crafted and polished the book. One example, from very near the beginning, must suffice. This is the second paragraph of the second short subsection in *Granta*:

> I looked for cabs, and none came. I was on First, not Second, and First is uptown. All the cabs would be heading the other way, getting the hell out on Second and Lex. So now I get to take a stroll down Ninety-ninth Street.[13]

Not much wrong with that; but here's the corresponding paragraph from *Money*:

> I looked for cabs, and no cabs came. I was on First, not Second, and First is uptown. All the cabs would be turned the other way, getting the hell out on Second and Lex. In New York for half a minute and already I pace the line, the long walk down Ninety-Ninth Street.[14]

The revisions are meticulous, but they point in contrary directions, towards the literary and the colloquial. The first sentence has now picked up a famous echo – 'And could not hope for help and no help came' from Auden's 'The Shield of Achilles'[15] – and this isn't quite an unmixed blessing: it adds resonance, certainly, yet it also exemplifies Martin's susceptibility to literary reference, even when not obviously relevant. (An absurd instance comes later in the same chapter, where a single sentence – 'So now I must go uptown to meet with Fielding Goodney at the Carraway Hotel – Fielding, my money-man, my contact and my pal'[16] – manages to allude to three separate authors, Henry Fielding, F. Scott Fitzgerald and, again, Philip Larkin; Self stays allusively at the Ashbery, which perhaps explains why he understands so little of what's happening around him.) On the other hand, 'turned' for 'heading', in the third sentence, seems neatly to substitute local New York demotic for conventional English, while the recasting of the final sentence turns an entirely neutral statement into one fraught with menacing deracination.

A young English writer who so confidently sets his novel's long first chapter (it's the best part of fifty pages) in New York is, of course, telling the reader something about himself and his ambition. This chapter had been some time in the making: it has its roots in 'Problem City', an uncollected piece which Martin wrote for the *New Statesman* in 1976. 'Problem City' supplies the New York background for *Money* in two and a half columns. The cabby who has unceremoniously dumped John Self in the wrong part of town, after an experimental exchange involving the word 'scumbag', would recognise these city streets – 'the roads are everywhere so lumpy that it is impossible to avoid hourly ablutions of slush' – for in the very opening lines of 'Money' John Self's cab hits 'a deep crater in the road' (or, in *Money*, 'a deep welt or grapple-ridge in the road'). 'Problem City' describes a cinema audience's mob reaction while watching *One Flew Over the Cuckoo's Nest* and the extension of filmed pornography into 'snuff movies'; it's witheringly sceptical about the solemn 'installations' of a 'Constructivist' sculptor called Mark di Suvero. And it picks up the tics of spoken language – there's so much talk of problems that Martin 'soon developed a problem problem' – and of signage:

On the buses you are usefully reminded NOT TO CREATE AN UNSANITARY CONDITION. In the passage of my hotel I received the twice-daily caution, NO SMOKING – *This Means*

You; 'Who, *me*?' I used to think, megging my giant Pall Mall
(of which I smoked about a carton a day, such was my nicotine
problem out there). LITTERING IS FILTHY AND SELFISH SO
DON'T DO IT say signs on midtown lamp-posts, debriefing any
would-be litterer who might have thought the habit was a fastidious and altruistic one.[17]

This is exactly the tone of voice and the accumulation of verbal
detail, laced with highly personalised slang ('to meg', according to
Jonathon Green, is 'to direct a film', which doesn't help), that so
often typifies the narrative style of Martin the novelist.

Except that, in *Money*, the matter of narrative voice is even more
problematical than it was in *Other People*. Just as Mary Lamb seems
to possess a vocabulary which is altogether too expansive for her
condition, so John Self – a semi-literate maker of ludicrous commercials who finds even *Animal Farm* heavy going – is blessed with an
expansive fluency very like that of Martin Amis: 'it is the novel that
John Self, the narrator, has in him but would never write'.[18] For
seventy pages or so, the reader might reasonably suppose that among
the resonances of 'Self' is the obvious one of an authorial disguise.
But then John Self, back in London, casually informs us that 'a *writer*
lives round my way too . . . He gives me the creeps . . . The writer's
name, they tell me, is *Martin Amis*. Never heard of him. Do *you*
know his stuff at all?'[19] It's perhaps not such a daft question at this
point, since the appearance of 'Martin Amis' in his own novel might
well prompt the reader to wonder just how much he knows about
'his stuff'. Or, in a way which yet again recalls Lewis Carroll (as both
Amises so unnervingly do), we may be unsure of who's dreaming
who: we had this sense of narratives enfolded within each other in
Other People and we shall meet it again in *London Fields*. Next time
the 'Martin Amis' character turns up, it's clear that various sorts of
fun are being had. For a start, there's John Self's (quite common)
misapprehension about the size of the literary audience: 'Sold a
million yet?' he asks Martin, drunkenly but not unseriously; this is an
idea later to be refined into an effective short story, 'Career Move'
(1992), which imagines that the relative incomes of film-makers and
poets are reversed. Then there's John's surprisingly knowledgeable
remark: 'Your dad, he's a writer too, isn't he? Bet that made it easier.'
To which Martin replies: 'Oh, sure. It's just like taking over the

family pub.'[20] Of course, this is funny in itself, since (as we've already seen) it's exactly how writers don't ordinarily operate; but it's even funnier in retrospect, when we discover that John Self, who does indeed think he's heir to the family pub, is no such thing. If it begins to look as if this 'Martin Amis' has been put here to subvert the expectations of his own novel, that's not so far from the truth. He is also there to redefine these expectations: 'The distance between author and narrator', he tells an uncomprehending John Self, 'corresponds to the degree to which the author finds the narrator wicked, deluded, pitiful or ridiculous. I'm sorry, am I boring you?'[21]

Certainly, 'Martin Amis' supplies two of the best jokes in . . . well, in Martin Amis. One occurs when he asks John Self whether he's 'the guy who made those commercials, the ones they took off the air' and, on discovering this to be the case, adds: 'I thought those commercials were bloody funny. We all did.'[22] John, unlike the sceptical reader, takes this as an unambiguous compliment. The other, completely outrageous, is when John phones Martin in an attempt to persuade him to revise his disastrous film script. Eventually Martin asks, 'What exactly are we looking at here?', a question John worryingly fails to understand until it's been reformulated: '*Money*. I'm in the book. Call me when you know.'[23] But Martin comes close to destroying the book which (in the other sense) he's in, the one called *Money*, by almost turning John's disastrous film project – 'Good Money' or 'Bad Money': the latter is naturally the British title – into a success. This unmade film might almost have been an ironic *homage* to the work of Brian De Palma, of whom Martin wrote in a *Vanity Fair* profile, 'There is no conventional sex whatever in De Palma's movies: it is always a function of money, violence or defilement, glimpsed at a voyeuristic remove or through a pornographic sheen'.[24] However, the whole point of it, since John is to be the victim of an elaborate confidence trick, is that it should turn out to be a fiasco. (The purple car he drives – 'a beautiful machine, a vintage-style coupé with oodles of dash and twang . . . my pride and joy'[25] – is aptly named a Fiasco, and by the time we reach the book's italic postscript it's deteriorated into one that '*doesn't like it when it's cold . . . doesn't like it when it's hot either, or when it's rainy. To tell you the truth, the Fiasco nearly always screws things up when it comes to getting you anywhere.*'[26] By then, it's become '*my grand folly*' though it's also still, with touching absurdity, '*my pride and joy*'.[27] The car's downhill progress mirrors its owner's, in precisely the same way as Gregory's allegedly sporty green machine does in *Success*. The idea loses just a little force through repetition, like the convoy of pastiche car names: Autocrat, Culprit, 666, Torpedo, Boomerang . . . Kingsley's more recherché versions of this joke are Stanley Duke's Apfelsine FK3 in *Stanley and the Women* and Richard Vaisey's Viotti TBD in *The Russian Girl*.)

Fielding Goodney's confidence trick is the novel's clockwork motor, and it raises interlinked questions about motivation and plot. Why does he do it? How effectively does it drive the plot? Martin is briskly dismissive of the first consideration – 'motivation has become a depleted, a shagged-out force in modern life' – and ambivalent about the second: 'It has been said that the plot is almost a distraction in this book, but I think it's important that Fielding Goodney is an artist. I don't understand it fully yet, but I'm sure it all has to do with that idea.'[28] The first point is certainly worth making: it may well be the case that the novel tends to exaggerate motivation, whereas people in their daily lives do all sorts of things for no very clear reason. Yet this really only applies to certain types of novels – those with at least a hint of genre about them – and to specific actions rather than to larger moral considerations: the reader never quite knows *why* Mr Knightley became an admirable man and Mr Tulkinghorn a villainous one. Plot is harder to dismiss. Even if we accept that it doesn't matter why Fielding Goodney devises the manipulative scheme which turns him into the book's third shaping spirit, alongside John Self and Martin Amis, it's important that the plot should at least tick over, especially in a book so heavily indebted to popular cultural forms. And it doesn't: *Money* is about a man whose life is so culturally impoverished that he can only think about making money; he thinks, too, that he is rather good at this, whereas in fact he's hopelessly inept. The plot by which he's manipulated and ruined, on the other hand, needs to be financially much smarter. But its cogs just won't turn: crucially, although having John Self double-sign financial documents not only as a counter-signatory but also as 'Self' is an amusing idea, those documents would be unbankably worthless and the sums floating around would prompt some close scrutiny of specimen signatures. Moreover, even a man who drives a purple Fiasco couldn't be quite as naive in his business affairs as this.

That may seem a laborious point, and perhaps also a trifling one. Nevertheless, it signposts one of the major fault-lines in Martin's mid-period fiction: the unresolved tension between his accumulation of realistic detail and his disdain for realism itself. 'Realism is a footling consideration,' he says,[29] and 'Martin Amis', cunningly quoting his alter ego's 1982 essay on Saul Bellow,[30] agrees with him: 'Even realism, rockbottom realism, is considered a bit grand for the twentieth century.'[31] In practice, the attention he gives to some aspects of realism in *Money* – the carefully researched authenticity of his New York, the scrupulous way in which the action is synchronised with the Charles and Diana wedding of 1981 – is very far from footling; a sceptical reader might feel that it's the necessary and pedestrian aspects of realism, such as making sure that the plot adds up or having a rough idea why people do what they do, which get neglected. The book suffers from this neglect, though not fatally, for it has an untrumpable card of a character in John Self.

John Self is the twentieth century in its terminal decline. He represents, in a crude sense, the state of Thatcher's England; as Martin wrote in a 1981 *Observer* review, 'even the most well-adjusted vandal – the most helpless product of junk food, adult videos and mangled cityscapes – must find plenty that is cheerless in his new surroundings'.[32] This is John Self's world (as it will be Keith Talent's and Steve Cousins's). He scans the news in the *Morning Line*: noting there's 'a major rumble brewing in Poland', he reckons Moscow should beat them up; an item about Lady Diana's trousseau reminds him of a 'famous snap' in which 'you can see right through her dress'; there are stories about a barmaid cudgelling 'her landlord boyfriend to death' and a grandmother 'mob-raped in her sock by black boys and skinheads'. But he saves his most passionate response for the piece about a teenaged girl apparently dying from her allergy to the twentieth century. His problem differs from hers: 'I'm not allergic to the twentieth century. I am addicted to the twentieth century.'[33] He recognises that this is a problem, because the twentieth century has turned terribly sour since his youth: 'I came of age in the Sixties, when there were chances, when it was all there waiting.' Like much of his interior narrative, this analysis of the contrasting present possesses a degree of articulate perception which is totally at odds with his oafish exterior:

Now they seep out of school – to what? To nothing, to fuck-all.
The young (you can see it in their faces), the stegosaurus-rugged
no-hopers, the parrot-crested blankies – they've come up with an
appropriate response to this, which is: nothing. Which is nothing,
which is fuck-all. The dole-queue starts at the exit to the playground. Riots are their rumpus-room, sombre London their jungle-
gym. Life is hoarded elsewhere by others. Money is so near you
can almost touch it, but it is all on the other side – you can only
press your face up against the glass.[34]

His mistake is to assume that he's on the other side of the glass, with
the money, instead of being on his way downhill to join the under-
class. His journey there, like Gregory Riding's, has surprisingly elegiac
notes, as when he reflects on the condition of urban wildlife – 'a
pigeon clockworked past on the pavement, eating a chip. A *chip* . . .
The stooped flowers in their sodden beds endure back-pinch and rug-
loss, what with all the stress about'[35] – as well as some wry inward
humour. In that same finely poised long paragraph, he treats himself
to 'a burn-up in the Fiasco' which ends in 'a jam on the Bayswater
Road', and there 'a frazzled wasp' flies in through the open window,
gets trapped in his trousers and stings him. It's a neat reworking of
the incident with the flicked cigarette-end when nineteen-year-old
Mart was driving in France. But gradually, even John realises that
he's a helpless puppet: 'I sometimes think I am controlled by someone.
Some space invader is invading my inner space, some fucking joker.'[36]
    A whole pack of jokers, in fact. Not counting such relatively
minor ones as his former business partners Terry Linex and Keith
Carburton, and his criminal friend Alec Llewellyn, there's Martin
Amis and 'Martin Amis', Fielding Goodney and his anonymous-
calling alter ego, and the sexually and financially voracious Selina
Street. Beyond all this, even, there's the further complication of his
parentage. He thinks he's the son of Barry Self, landlord of the
Shakespeare, where the employees include 'Fat Vince and Fat Paul,
two generations of handyman-and-bouncer talent';[37] but readers alert
to the influence on Amis *père et fils* of Henry Fielding, whose plots
usually turn on displaced parenthood, are given several clues that
this may not be the case: 'Me and Fat Paul – we're like brothers,'[38]
John guilelessly observes. 'You are your dad and your dad is you,'
he tells the ridiculous American actor Spunk Davis, adding: 'It's the

twentieth-century feeling. We're the jokes. You just got to live it, Spunk. You just got to live the joke.'[39] The joke that John unwittingly lives is that Barry Self isn't his father: Fat Vince is (just as in *Yellow Dog* Mick Meo isn't Xan Meo's father: Joseph Andrews – of course – is). And from his point of view, the joke isn't at all improved by his discovering it immediately after a sexual encounter with Vron, John Self's gruesomely pornographic new wife, which in turn leads to him being expertly beaten up by Fat Paul and disinherited by the man he'd previously assumed to be his father. By this time, he's very close to his destitute (and infinitely more likeable) end.

There's another and quite different side to *Money*, as Martin recognises in *Experience*: 'But I see now that the story turned on my own preoccupations: it is about tiring of being single; it is about the fear that childlessness will condemn you to childishness.'[40] John is offered a glimmer of redemption in New York by Martina Twain, the first and pretty much the last properly civilised woman character in Martin's fiction. She makes him read George Orwell and takes him to the theatre (*Othello*), though he misunderstands the significance of both; she eats well, drinks moderately and lives in an apartment with a plant-decked balcony and acrobatic bees; she also, a little ominously, adopts a stray dog called Shadow, whom she loses. She loses John, too, because he doesn't understand civilisation: after spending an evening with her, he nips off to 'a gogo bar on Broadway', feeling that it's 'a big relief – to be back in civilization again'.[41] Towards the end of the novel, they visit a Manet exhibition together. 'Women are more civilized,' John thinks, recalling and refining Kingsley's 'Women are much nicer than men': 'Maybe that is what's happening to me – I'm getting chicked.' He 'looked at Martina as she looked at Manet: the civilized pleasures and sacraments duly celebrated, with nothing pinched or over-correct',[42] yet he remains outside, excluded, like Philip Larkin at the dance in 'Reasons for Attendance'. Martina's 'shine' transforms the scenes in which she appears – partly, no doubt, because many readers will feel that this at last is the world and the set of cultural values with which we're at home and which Martin so very seldom gives us. Partly, though, it's the same shine that Catharine Casement brings to *The Anti-Death League*: that of an author 'getting chicked'. 'Martina' is both the feminisation of 'Martin' and an anagram of 'Martian'; for John Self, at least, her world will remain alien.

'Don't know whether you saw,' Kingsley wrote to Larkin on 18 June 1984, 'but young Martin has rung the bell. Put his girl in pod. Wedding bells to come but no hurry it seems, so it may be in every sense a little bastard that appears around Yuletide. Girl nice but we are not quite grand enough for her.'[43] In fact, Martin married his American girlfriend Antonia Phillips, a lecturer in philosophy, on the day that *Money* appeared; the book is dedicated to her. 'My first son, Louis,' he adds, 'was published four months later,'[44] on 15 November 1984. Kingsley, naturally, didn't think much of *Money*, which contained exactly the sort of post-modern trickery he liked least: 'I hated its way of constantly remind[ing] me of Nabokov. But of course I'm very old-fashioned.'[45] His own *Stanley and the Women* had just appeared too, and he very much enjoyed hearing that Louis's godfather, Hylan Booker, had told Martin: 'I bought your book today; I bought your daddy's book too.' 'That sentence', Kingsley remarked happily, 'will only get said once in the history of the world.'[46]

3

Martin had always held opinions; now he began to acquire convictions. From his father's point of view, they were mistaken ones: 'Talking of Martin, he has as I said gone all lefty and of the crappiest neutralist kind, challenging me to guess how many times over the world can destroy itself, writing two bits of ban-it bullshit in the Obs (of course) . . . He's bright, you see, but a fucking fool, and the worse, far worse, for having come to it late in life, aetat. nearly 37, not 17,' he told Conquest in June 1986.[47] The 'Obs' was of course the *Observer*, with whose editor, Donald Trelford, Kingsley had quarrelled in 1982 and where Martin (in an instance of that affectionate goading which typified the father–son relationship) was now 'Special Writer', taking on a variety of literary and cultural assignments. Kingsley hoped Conquest might come up with 'some book' to sort out Martin's ideological muddle, and in the same paragraph he optimistically adds that 'having now a 2nd baby has given him (M) other things to think about'. But in this assumption Kingsley was wrong, for it was fatherhood which had focused Martin's attention on humanity's possible self-extermination. He was of the generation whose teenage years had been haunted by songs such as Bob Dylan's

'Masters of War', in spite of which he had now dared to bring children into the world. *That* had given him something to think about.

'I first became interested in nuclear weapons during the summer of 1984,' he says in the 'Introduction: Thinkability' to *Einstein's Monsters* (1987), citing a 'coincidence' in which the 'two elements were impending fatherhood and a tardy reading of Jonathan Schell's classic, awakening study, *The Fate of the Earth'*.[48] When he wrote for *Esquire* on the 1988 Republican Convention – 'history now, and history didn't look too good down in New Orleans' – he felt he had to preface his report with 'a few words about my family':

> I have a wife and two little boys. Over here to cover the Convention, I happened to miss them very much. Why, just before I left, my three-year-old gazed up at me with those big blue eyes of his and said I was the best daddy in the world. My wife and I love our boys. And they love us. Okay?[49]

Okay, certainly, but we don't have to look far to discover why Kingsley found his son's passionately anti-nuclear stance infuriating. It was partly, perhaps even mostly, a matter of tone – that heavy-handed, ingratiating irony in the passage just quoted is a symptom – and here 'Introduction: Thinkability' is the key document. It too opens with misfiring irony, as Martin reminds us that the date of his birth, 25 August 1949, was four days before Russia's first successful atom bomb test: 'So I had those four carefree days, which is more than my juniors ever had. I didn't really make the most of them. I spent half the time under a bubble . . . To tell you the truth, I didn't feel very well at all. I was terribly sleepy and feverish. I kept throwing up. I was given to fits of uncontrollable weeping . . .'[50] All this reaches towards an inadvisable cuteness; it also, as with the Republican Convention piece, places the argument to come within an emotively personal context, as if to immunise it from attack. 'I am sick of them – I am sick of nuclear weapons,' he writes, making a metaphor of the infant's throwing up. 'And so is everybody else.'[51] But that isn't quite true, even at the closest personal level: 'My father regards nuclear weapons as an unbudgeable given.'[52] Father and son would argue furiously and end amicably – affectionate goading again – with Kingsley 'saying something like, "Think of it. Just by closing down the Arts Council we could significantly augment our arsenal. The

grants to poets could service a nuclear submarine for a year . . ." [53]
At some filial, familial level they were of course in agreement,
knowing there is no answer. Neither of them wanted to destroy the
world of Louis and Jacob Amis, to whom the book is dedicated;
what has gone so badly adrift in 'Introduction: Thinkability' is more to
do with method, tone, style. There are moments of terrible bathos:
'We have only one planet, and it is *round*.'[54] Worse still, and exempli-
fying a habit which wouldn't go away in his writing, is his way of
dealing with those who take a different view from his own, such as
Robert Jastrow: 'He is wrong, and in this respect he is also, I contend,
subhuman, like all the nuclear-war fighters, like all the "prevailers".'[55]
Describing one's opponents as 'subhuman' (and where does this place
his father?) is no way to conduct an argument. Throughout the piece,
in a manner which the world would later come to associate with
Tony Blair, he uses his emotional instincts to justify his intellectual
position, instead of using his intellectual position to test and verify
his emotional instincts.

   This kind of writing, when it's as strategically placed as 'Introduction: Thinkability', is intended to reduce the reader to a state of
critical helplessness: if he wants to suggest that the stories in the book
are strident and heavy-handed, then the 'Introduction' will seem to
scream, '*Of course* they are: that's the modern condition, the world
we live in, the nuclear nightmare for you.' And screaming – in the
sense of shouting very loudly – is what *Einstein's Monsters* mostly
does. Precisely because it's so slender a book, it demonstrates all the
more clearly that although Martin possesses an on/off switch, he has
very little in the way of a volume control and nothing at all for tone.
That the problem of tone won't be confined to the 'Introduction' is
evident from the first words of the first story, 'Bujak and the Strong
Force': 'Bujak? Yeah, I knew him.'[56] The force of that gratuitous
'Yeah' is to shift the focus immediately from the central character
back to the narrator. Who is this speaker? He is, we learn, a man
in his early thirties (so younger than his author) whose physical
feebleness is hilariously offset by his name, Samson, a joke Martin
likes so much that he'll reprise it for the narrator of *London
Fields*; Bujak's first name, as we discover quite late in the piece, is
Adam. Bujak's 'life went deep into the century' – which is perhaps
the kind of thing we should be shown rather than told – and, as a
member of the Polish resistance, 'he visited (and this is a story of

violence, of visitation) many neat tortures on Nazi collaborators'.[57] This is to become a predictable mid-Martin formula: the quasi-erotic juxtaposition of a bookish non-physical type with a violent strong-man. These two originally met in 'the late spring of 1980 – or of PN 35, if you use the post-nuclear calendar he sometimes favoured'[58] (a Kingsleyesque voice is needed to deal with that, the one which says things like 'Well, you *could* call it that, but it would be *very silly*'). Here we encounter them as Sam struggles to change a wheel and Bujak simply picks the car up with his hands.

But it is Bujak who loses his strength when the urban violence which so frequently afflicts Martin's characters strikes his family. At least, he loses physical strength but gains redemptive generosity, turning from an Old into a New Testament figure. Observing this, Sam suddenly sounds like a narrator not in Martin Amis but in Somerset Maugham: 'Incredibly, his happiness was intact – unimpaired, entire. How come? Because, I think, his generosity extended not just to the earth but to the universe . . .'[59] In the meantime, however, 'The world looks worse every day. Is it worse, or does it just look it?' As for the world's inhabitants: 'We live in a shameful shadowland. Quietly, our idea of human life has changed, thinned out. We can't help but think less of it now. The human race has declassed itself.'[60] As in 'Introduction: Thinkability', the style attempts to hector us into acquiescence. Do we 'live in a shameful shadowland'? Do *we*? And if, just possibly, we want to insist that we don't, then the writing excludes us in an aggressive manner which seems hostile to literature itself.

If the present is in a bad state, two other stories in *Einstein's Monsters* provide glimpses of imagined post-nuclear futures. 'The Time Disease', set in 2020, opens with the skewed technologies traditional to science fiction: there are 'zip trains', things to eat called 'a *hero*, and a *ham salad*' (the latter evidently not a ham salad), while on the television the 'Therapy Channel' provides programmes of stupefying boredom – until, that is, the 'outercom' sounds and Lou, the narrator, switches 'from Therapy to Intake'. We've been here before: in E. M. Forster's 'The Machine Stops' (1908), even though this isn't acknowledged among the sources. The additional conceit here is that healthiness has become unhealthy and that the only way to survive *time* is to lead a life not that dissimilar from that of Forster's Vashti. Happy Faraday – 'the TV star. *The* Happy Faraday'

– who plays 'the stock part of a glamorous forty-year-old with a bad case of *time*-anxiety'[61] – is terminally ill because she's actually turning into a glamorous forty-year-old. Reality and television are not simply confused (Keith Talent will have this trouble too) but inverted, despite Lou's assurance to Roy, his amanuensis: 'It's just TV, Roy. She writes that stuff herself. It isn't real.'[62] Although apparently inspired by Martin's dislike of Los Angeles, the story reads almost like a forty-years-later sequel to *Dead Babies*, as a passing mention of 'Greg Buzhardt' perhaps signals. This, too, is about the consequences of the twentieth century ('The twentieth century was all it took') and it finally strikes the same note of elegiac wreckage: 'The sky hangs above me in shredded webs, in bloody tatters. It's a big relief, and I'm grateful. I'm okay, I'm good, good. For the time being, at any rate, I show no signs of coming down with *time*.'[63]

'The Little Puppy That Could' is far more problematic. Here, the post-nuclear future is anti-technological (the distant literary ancestor, as of Kingsley's *The Alteration*, is Richard Jefferies's *After London: Wild England*). A village settlement is terrorised by an enormous dog, the 'Natural Selector', 'eight feet long and four feet high': he has become 'exclusively, even religiously homovorous', even though he looks 'bad on this diet', a clear 'demonstration of the fact that you shouldn't eat human beings'.[64] Andromeda, who has changed her name from Briana and is possibly the daughter of Tom (or Tim or Tam) and certainly of, alas, Keithette, discovers a puppy which she names Jackajack and which will quite accidentally confound and destroy the marauding dog before turning itself into a boy called John. 'Well, you *could* call them that, but . . .' says the Kingsleyesque voice again; and that's without the other village women (Clivonne, Royenne, Kevinia), without Keithette's division of the week (Shunday, Moanday, Tearsday, Woundsday, Thirstday, Fireday, Shatterday), without 'Blametakes' and 'Faultfinds'. This village society is pugnaciously matriarchal: Keithette is 'a rosy, broadfaced woman, stocky and flat-chested (the standard female form these days)',[65] her husband a helplessly put-upon slave. There are compounds for children – Andromeda is threatened with being sent there – and for Queers: the dog is munching his way through the latter, although some are too repulsive even for his taste. Kingsley, we will remember, wrote a scurrilous unpublished little poem about 'Women and queers and children' which was both vulnerable and unfunny. In this story, the casual demonisation of all three is merely poisonous.[66]

4

'Every morning, six days a week, I leave the house and drive a mile to the flat where I work. For seven or eight hours I am alone,'[67] Martin tells us in 'Introduction: Thinkability'. It was in this 'working pad' at Leamington Road Villas that John Haffenden interviewed him in 1985. Haffenden describes it as 'a flat in a solid and gabled Victorian edifice' located in 'Westbourne Park, that outland of North Kensington, a crow's mid-course between Wormwood Scrubs and Paddington'.[68] Haffenden's brief but evocative account also notes the fig tree outside, with its 'Martian-green tongues'; a pinball machine in the kitchen; curtainless windows in the sitting-room; 'a wall of hardback novels, TV set, video'; and 'a tide of working books' in the study. There are screaming children in an adjacent playground: 'Riot lessons',[69] Martin calls this, and it isn't entirely a joke. For we're very close here to the cityscape of his big London novels, *Money*, *London Fields* and *The Information*; and even though he insists to Haffenden that he's 'completely distinct as a writer and as a person', and that 'writing takes place in this odd capsule where I work',[70] it's surely interesting that he should choose so harshly twentieth century a capsule for himself. He isn't a writer whom one can readily imagine writing at a desk with a view of sea, or mountains, or even trees: the urban hardness of his chosen environment permeates, and arguably limits, his imaginative world.

One other aspect of Haffenden's scene-setting is especially notable. Martin, he says, 'is kitted out for tennis, and in due course rushes out to his car ... to meet the match suggested by his gear'.[71] There's tennis in the opening chapter of *Money* – where John Self is predictably humiliated by Fielding Goodney – and again, in what is surely too close a rematch, between Richard Tull and Gwyn Barry in *The Information*. Indeed Martin, in direct contrast to his father (who may have surprised himself by briefly enjoying rugby in his Marlborough exile, but thereafter would have none of it), has a startling range of sporting enthusiasms: startling, because most writers of his generation, finding themselves as teenagers in schools where arties couldn't be hearties, acquired a practised contempt for all games – except, perhaps, cricket with its subtle writerly narratives and its five-act dramas called Test matches. Martin, however, didn't really go to school in that sense and became instead a compulsive player of games across the whole physical to intellectual spectrum. Sargy Mann remembers how, at Maida Vale, Mart and Phil were constantly playing games such as poker, badminton and bar billiards.[72] In 1982, Martin actually devoted an entire book, *Invasion of the Space Invaders*, to an electronic video game. The author photograph on the dust jacket of *Money* has him glowering across a chessboard, although in his *Observer* piece on the 1986 Kasparov versus Karpov World Chess Championship he modestly claims that his 'chances of chess brilliancy are the "chances" of a lab chimp and a typewriter producing *King Lear*'. Nevertheless: 'Oh, I have thrown 180 at darts – twice in a lifetime. On the snooker table I have brought off violent pots that would have jerked them to their feet at the Sheffield Crucible. As for tennis, I need hardly hype my crosscourt backhand "dink", which is so widely feared in the parks of North Kensington.'[73] In what must strike the games-immune reader as an odd pair of commissions, *GQ* invited Martin and four other writers 'to spend an evening playing poker and then report on the experience for its pages'[74] in 1990, while *Esquire* asked him and Julian Barnes 'to dispute the best of five frames of snooker and then write about it'[75] in 1991. He was by now clearly spending a good deal of time on such pursuits, because in the same year he casually refers to 'my local sports club in Paddington, where I do most of my male bonding'.[76] That, possibly, is the key to a good deal, for reviewing Bill Buford's *Among the Thugs* (also 1991), he writes: 'Every British male, at some time or another, goes to his last football match. It may very well be his first football match. You stay home, thereafter, and watch it on TV.'[77] I can readily imagine the scorn with which he would greet my admission that I've never been to a football match and seldom watched one all the way through on television. (There are weary questions lurking here: Don't women watch football? Don't men go to the opera?) Of cricket, apart from a passing reference or two, Martin says nothing at all.

Nevertheless, it's evident that these other assorted games and sports are highly significant both for the author and for several of his male characters; most of them, too, involve questions of skill and strategy. But *darts*? 'Hand, projectile, target, through a medium of thin air – and that's that. Remove one umpire, both batsmen and all the fielders from a cricket pitch, and you get some idea of the dourness of darts.'[78] This comes from a rather strange piece which Martin wrote for the *Observer* in 1988 profiling the then World Darts Champion, Keith Deller: strange, partly because of its undisguised disappointment that Deller doesn't turn out to be 'half-drunk in some roadhouse, smothered in tattoos and darts magazines' but, on the contrary, 'genial, straightforward, considerate, clear-eyed' and devoted to his 'pretty wife, Kim';[79] and partly because Martin's fictional darts-player, who embodies all those grotesque preconceptions and more, is called Keith Talent, with a wife Kath and a daughter Kim, all of which seem hugely unfair to Keith and Kim Deller.

Keith Talent is, of course, the central character in *London Fields* (1989). Or is he? For, in what by this point is beginning to seem a predictable manner, the narrative voice is so multilayered that it's hard to tell quite where the book's centre of gravity lies. The apparent narrator and would-be manipulator is Samson Young, an American novelist of no great ability, author of *Memoirs of a Listener* and *On the Grapevine*, who has house-swapped his way to London. The house he's swapped himself into belongs to Mark Asprey, an even more worthless though far more successful writer who has a greater presence in the novel than his transatlantic absence implies: it's he, surely, who's the author of the notably ill-written prefatory note, which is signed with the initials 'M.A.' Yet these initials also belong, rather obviously, to Martin Amis. And they belong to Mark Asprey's alter ego within the book, Marius Appleby, author of *Crossbone Waters* – 'Now *that's* non-fiction.'[80] So we have at least three layers of authorship: who are we to trust?

Who, indeed, is Keith Talent to trust, as his familiar world of the Black Cross pub – with its regulars (among them Curtly, Dean, Fucker, Zbigs One and Two, Bogdan, Piotr, Norvis, Shakespeare and Thelonius [*sic*]), its barmen God and Pongo, its sign 'TV AND DARTS AND PIMBALL' which sounds like an utterance of Sir Roy Vandervane's – is turned upside down by these oddly demanding interlopers, Nicola Six, Guy Clinch and Samson Young? We know, at least, what Sam thinks of Keith: 'The moment I set eyes on him

I thought Keith Talent was an anachronistic kind of character. I thought that time and inflation and the new demographics would have mopped him up by now or sent him somewhere else: to the North, or at least to the suburbs.'[81] Keith, however, is in his own terms a success: he has 'the Cavalier [a real car, for once], the printed brochure, the dreams of darts'. He is, moreover, also 'anachronistic' to Sam – though not, surely, to Martin, whose fiction is stuffed with such people – 'in this matter of his libido', for he's 'an obsessional tailchaser':

> He drools and slurps at everything remotely bim-like on the street; he regales the entire pub with the things he does to Analiese Furnish and Trish Shirt; he'll even give you fifteen minutes (no berk protocols here) on how it went with Kath the other night. On top of all this he makes no secret of his heroics in the handjob realm. And on his diet I'm amazed he even gets around.[82]

When it comes to food, sex and pornography, in fact, he has a good deal in common with John Self.

'Man, am I a reliable narrator,' says Sam.[83] 'Boy, am I a reliable narrator,'[84] he insists later on – in case we've forgotten, or even started to believe him. For he is anything but. It suits his purposes for us to understand, at the outset, that Keith, who is 'a bad guy . . . a very bad guy. You might even say that he was the worst guy,'[85] is to be the murderer; while Nicola Six, who is 'tall, dark, and thirty-four',[86] will be the murderee: only one-half of this is true. This terminology, incidentally, comes from Rupert Birkin in *Women in Love* (Martin, like his father, is happy to borrow from authors he doesn't much like): 'It takes two people to make a murder: a murderer and a murderee. And a murderee is a man who is murderable. And a man who is murderable is a man who in a profound if hidden lust desires to be murdered.'[87] That it is self-evidently nonsense is, in the context of *London Fields*, part of its charm: what happens if you create a character, in this case a woman, who in an articulate and literate way profoundly desires to be murdered? You get Nicola Six: 'She welcomed and applauded the death of just about anything. It was company.'[88] The greater of the two main problems she poses lies in deciding – and Martin's scornful dismissal of motivation makes this tricky – why on earth she should feel like this; she seems, after all, to have better reasons than anyone else in the book, apart perhaps from the mysteriously prosperous Mark Asprey, for finding life enjoyable. But she is haunted – in a way which can't help seeming external to the novel, since it so clearly belongs to its author's own preoccupations – by Hiroshima and its aftermath. She has invented a parallel self, which will remind us of Amy Hide and Mary Lamb except that hers is called Enola Gay: 'Enola wasn't real. Enola came from inside the head of Nicola Six.'[89] But this subtext is diminished by becoming part of her ludic manipulation of other characters: Guy doesn't get her references to 'Enola Gay' and 'Little Boy' – 'And a little knowledge might have helped him here. A little knowledge might have saved him'[90] – even though it seems strange that he hasn't read, say, John Hersey; while Keith, predictably enough, associates only one thing with the name 'Bikini'.

Moreover, her death, which she preposterously treats as a kind of artistic endeavour, is to be synchronised with an event of cosmic symbolism: the eclipse on 5 November 1999, at the very end of the millennium, in anticipation of which the sun has already become lower in the sky, casting the long shadows which Martin remembered from his childhood holiday with the Partingtons in Wales. Everything about this is troublesome. Nicola's 'artistic' status, from which the author (whoever he may be) doesn't appear to dissent, for we're told that she emerges from 'the kind of mid-project doldrums that all artists experience, the windless solitude halfway between outset and completion',[91] is entirely in line with Martin's slack use of the word 'artist' elsewhere: for instance, in his lazy-ironic assertion that everyone in *Money* is 'a kind of artist – sack-artists, piss-artists, con-artists, bullshit-artists'.[92] On the other hand, the cosmic portentousness, unassisted by having a sell-by date which has now quietly passed, sits oddly in a novel whose main register is bludgeoningly yet narrowly comic. If the book's humour were more inclusive, Nicola would be presented as no more than loopily deluded and would probably carry a placard saying 'The end of the world is nigh.'

The lesser of the two Nicola problems, though the one which caused the greater fuss when *London Fields* was published, is conveniently stated by Sam, when he tells her: 'I'm worried they're going to say you're a male fantasy figure.'[93] They did; and it was the objections of two women judges, Maggie Gee and Helen McNeil, which led to the novel's exclusion from the shortlist for the 1989 Booker Prize.[94] Family history seemed to be repeating itself: after all, it had been rumoured that the alleged misogyny of *Jake's Thing* and *Stanley and the Women* scuppered Kingsley's chances of winning the Booker with them. But that, as I've already suggested, seems to me to have been a misreading, and so too were the feminist objections to *London Fields*: partly because Nicola really only exists in her own self-defined symbolic terms – she rejects all Sam's possible categorisations of her with the simple if unhelpful statement 'I'm a Murderee' – and partly because the pornographic elements within the book are so relentlessly anti-pornographic, rather in the nature of aversion therapy. It's a curious defence of the novel to say that Nicola is so sketchily and implausibly alive that it's very difficult to care much about what happens to her.

Guy Clinch, the foil, is 'a good guy – or a nice one, anyway . . . But when he woke in the morning there was – there was no life. There was only lifelessness.'[95] Must goodness or niceness (and the distinction is in Murdochian terms a vital one) be so ineffectually lifeless? He has a wife, Hope, who is 'intelligent, efficient . . . brightly American (and rich)' and a monstrous infant son named Marmaduke. As is often the way with mid-period Martin, the set pieces involving Marmaduke's increasingly grotesque escapades threaten to run away with the book; he is eventually subdued by Nicola in her role as one of the book's two unlikely childminders (the other, Keith, teaches him to smoke and swear). Guy's only purpose is to fall for Nicola in both senses, but his gullibility in the face of her increasingly convoluted deceptions – which are made all the more transparent to the reader by the book's restlessly unstable point of view – would be hard to put up with in a novel which aspired to realism. If we couldn't care less about Nicola, we care less still about Guy.

So what is driving *London Fields*? Sam warns us not expect 'Not a whodunit' but 'More a whydoit',[96] yet that's among the central questions the book fails to answer. It remains polarised between two extremes of humour – the conceit and the joke – and both of them are too effortful for their own good. The wonderfully evocative title reminds us that although there is indeed a locality called London Fields it's very far from being an agricultural one: it seems, however, to promise a work of Dickensian scope. According to David Lodge, 'Martin Amis is a late exponent of the Dickensian tradition of urban Gothic';[97] the crucial difference is that urban Gothic isn't *all* Dickens does. In fact, the novel specifically invokes Dickens to reaffirm the notion that money is filthy: 'Look at Dickens . . . the old man up to his arms in Thames sewage, searching for treasure; the symbolic names of Murdstone and of Merdle, the financier.'[98] There's even a brief appearance by a Mr Tulkinghorn (a name which evidently tickles Martin, for it crops up elsewhere in his work), but expectations of Dickensian depth and range are disappointed. No one seems to earn a living in any recognisable way; the only members of the professional class are people such as Sam and Guy, slumming it in a world not their own; and as for the aristocracy, we have a potentially touching cameo in Lady Barnaby, who is there to be cheated and ruined by Keith, although the book has no sympathy to spare for her. The fields of the title, then, are magnetic fields, 'force fields' which push and pull this small group of oddly assorted characters together and apart: it's a promising conceit but a half-empty one.

As for the jokes . . . It would be reasonable to assume that a comic novelist must have a sense of humour, and Martin is certainly unsparing of those who seem to him deficient in this respect. Robert Bly, for example, 'is one of those writers, like F. R. Leavis and Hermann Hesse, whose impregnable humourlessness will always prompt a (humorous) counter-commentary in the reader's mind'.[99] Yet a sense of humour, which Kingsley so evidently possessed, is perhaps a more generous and inclusive quality than the ability to know when something is funny. *London Fields* is well supplied with funny things, and some of them are very good indeed: Nicola invents a couple of academics called Professor Barnes and Professor Noble; the editorial assistant at Sam's American publisher, seemingly called Janit Slotnick and whose actual name we must assume to be Janet Slotneck, continually uses words such as 'treatmint', 'disappointmint', 'achievemint'; the books Nicola presses on Keith (as with Martina Twain and John Self) have jokily allusive subtexts, leading via Keats to the reflection that 'a book called *Keith and Embarrassment* would be a short book, trailing off after two or three pages . . .'.[100] On the other hand, a sense of humour might have led an author to ration the quantity of ridiculous names: we have not only Keith's women (Trish Shirt, Analiese Furnish, Debbee Kensit) and the Black Cross crowd, but also Ella from LA, Rheo from Rio, Merouka from Morocco; blonde girls called Juniper and Pepsi; thugs called Ashley Royle, Lee Crook, Kirk Stockist; and – in the great Marquis of Edenderry darts match – a bunch of 'darters' called Duane Kensal, Alex O'Boye, Paul

Go and Teddy Zipper. (Terry Linex and Keith Carburton from
Money turn up here too.) Though he sticks to lager with his darts
and buys six-packs of the ubiquitous Peculiar Brews, Keith also drinks
something called *Porno* (though this sounds innocent compared to
the *Blowjob* cocktail offered to Xan Meo in *Yellow Dog*). After all
this, do we need a pub called the Foaming Quart, or shops such as
BestSave, CostCheck and GoodFicks (where they don't ficks anything
properly), or Guy contemplating his breakfast cereal and wondering
'whether MegaBran shouldn't rename itself HumanShit'?[101] Isn't
there just possibly a limit to the quantity of this sort of joke that
English prose (or the reader) can stand?

And the prose itself is hugely problematical: despite its astonishing
energy and its nervously patchy eloquence, *London Fields* is in places
a hideously ill-written book. For this, of course, we may be intended
to blame Samson Young, or perhaps even Mark Asprey, although
the stylistic tics are often worryingly close to those of Martin Amis.
Sometimes, it's a register so overloaded with demotic clashes and
mixed metaphors that it becomes almost incomprehensible: 'additional blondes were pure gravy for the brothers because they kept the
black bird-pool high';[102] or 'His head, no larger than an avocado,
blazed out above an inverted pyramid of organ meat.'[103] Elsewhere,
and often, there's Martin's established trait of maddening repetition:
'The kiss was called the Jewish Princess – unforgivably. But then the
kiss itself was unforgivable. The Jewish Princess was unforgivable.'[104]
There's the woozy strain of cosmic tosh which is going to reappear in
The Information: 'The love force that swathes the planet, like
weather, found a messenger or an agent that night, in Guy, who had
never felt so so fully elemental.'[105] And there's the catalogue of
identically prefixed or suffixed neologisms, which was funny when
Kingsley did it with 'bum', because it made respectable words ridiculous, but which is merely tiresome when it occurs as 'horrorday',
'horrorclock', 'horrordust', 'horrortoe', 'horrornail', 'horrorman',
'horrorzip', and so on for three pages.[106]

Keith and darts; Nicola and death; Guy and love: E. M. Forster
would have called them, and the interminable cast of minor villains
and idiotic women, 'flat' characters rather than 'round' ones because
they do what's expected of them, reliably fulfilling the expectations
of their names and their verbal tags like minor comic characters in
Dickens. Except Keith: Keith surprises us, as John Self does in *Money*,

by turning out to be mysteriously more likeable and even a little more decent than we could have at first guessed. He seems to belong in a novel which could have supplied him with a roomier context of more varied places and more believable people than this one. 'And meanwhile time goes about its immemorial work of making everyone look and feel like shit,'[107] as Sam says, early in the book; to make sure that we've got the point, he immediately repeats it, adding a couple of commas. But this isn't an opinion universally held nor is it necessarily a productive one with which to underpin a novel. Although *London Fields* is dedicated to Kingsley, he seems not to have finished reading it.

5

Set entirely in England – and, with the exception of Keith's interestingly routed excursions to Heathrow, in London itself – *London Fields* ought to seem more like a state-of-England novel than the Atlantic-hopping *Money*. If it doesn't, this is largely to do with its symbolic ambitions, its parodic locations and its deracinated main characters, Keith once again excepted; but it's also a consequence of the literary life Martin was leading, as he suggests in his introduction to *Visiting Mrs Nabokov* (1993). There, he makes a distinction between, on the one hand, book-reviewing, 'the lowest and noblest literary form', and novel-writing, both of which are 'about not getting out of the house', and, on the other, the kind of roving journalistic assignment which 'might mean a fifteen-hour flight or a ten-minute drive to the other side of Regents Park'.[108] The interesting point about this distinction is its elimination of an intermediate state, the one which might contain the ordinary transactions of daily life: the world of Mrs Thatcher's shopkeepers. He's either indoors at his desk at Leamington Road Villas or out on a specific assignment. And this, of course, is all of a piece with the nomadic childhood and the discontinuous education; the early wish to be an American, the later wish to write like one, the recent consequences of a transatlantic marriage (which turned, in 1993, into a transatlantic separation, with trips between London and Cape Cod to visit, collect or return his sons Louis and Jacob). He isn't a writer who's ever wanted to allow himself roots.

The result is that his fictional worlds, even at their most ambitious, seem insubstantial: typically, they rely on ingenious conceits to disguise their lack of solid foundations and, like conjuring tricks, they work wonderfully until quite suddenly they don't. This is especially true of the short novel *Time's Arrow* (1991), which tells the story, backwards, of Odilo Unverdorben, a doctor at Auschwitz, who successively becomes Hamilton de Souza, John Young and Tod T. Friendly – which is his name when we first encounter him, an old and dying man who has suffered a stroke 'in washing-line and mailbox America, innocuous America, in affable, melting-pot, primary-colour, You're-okay-I'm-okay *America*'.[109] There is a huge and serious theme here, and the novel – particularly in its grim later, chronologically earlier, stages – is clearly the product of careful research. But the backwards-told story leads to excruciating anomalies. A novel actually written backwards, with every letter of every word of every sentence in reverse order, would be not only unintelligible but pointless, since the reader's only recourse would be to start on the last page. Fortunately, the initial back-spelling of dialogue, in which 'Oo y'irrah?' is 'How are you?' and 'Dug' is 'Good', only occurs briefly, to startle the reader into an apprehension of what's going on. Thereafter, conversations run backwards, speech by speech, whereas narrative merely records the reversed time-scheme. We soon get the hang of, for instance, people knocking on doors after they've backed out of rooms; yet the conceit takes on the familiar appearance of an overextended running joke:

> Around midnight, sometimes, Tod Friendly will create things. Wildly he will mend and heal. Taking hold of the woodwork and the webbing, with a single blow to the floor, he will create a kitchen chair. With one fierce and skilful kick of his aching foot he will mend a deep concavity in the refrigerator's flank. With a butt of his head he will heal the fissured bathroom mirror, heal also the worsening welt in his own tarnished brow, and then stand there staring at himself with his eyes flickering.[110]

The question *Time's Arrow* seems to prompt is this: is it possible or proper to write a novel grounded in the events of the Holocaust in so playfully absurd a mode? And the answer, surely, is yes: the book ends up far less compromised by its methodology than anyone could conceivably have expected. Yet this question disguises what I suspect is an even more difficult one: to what extent is the daring, even outrageous technique of *Time's Arrow* actually an evasion? For the comic quirkiness of its opening – so markedly different in tone from the pages describing the time when, as Odilo Unverdorben confesses to Father Duryea, 'We lost our feeling about the human body'[111] – effectively closes down the possibility of anything approaching tragic redemption for Odilo/Tod. Tragic redemption, indeed, would have been a still more audacious task: one perhaps not within the author's gift, demanding the incomparable genius of Shakespeare. Macbeth, we may remember, commits the most appalling crimes imaginable within the world of the play – his murderous career embraces both infanticide and regicide – and yet he engages our unqualified sympathy in his great Act V speeches. *Time's Arrow* necessarily falls short of that. It is, nevertheless, the most powerfully moving and in some ways the most self-disciplined of all Martin's novels.

6

Although this represents nothing more than a chronological coincidence, Martin's life in the early 1990s contained a series of shocks and changes which might almost have been designed to rival and surpass Kingsley's in the early 1960s ('mid-life crisis' is, I think, a phrase to be regarded with suspicion, for crisis is no respecter of such footling qualifications as the midness of life). His first marriage, about which his father had so wryly expressed his doubts at the start, ended with painful gradualness: in *Experience* he records a visit to Cape Cod, in 1993, 'to see my children, and their mother – to whom I had become a stranger, from whom I was *estranged*'.[112] He and Antonia were divorced in 1996. But by that point in the decade he had already experienced five other, highly distinct interventions by chance, fate or the simple cussedness of things.

The first was Fred West. After West – the nature of whose crimes had been uncannily suggested in *Dead Babies*, as he was committing them – was arrested in 1993 and the grisly secrets of 25 Cromwell Street, Cheltenham, became public knowledge, it was discovered that his victims had included Martin's cousin Lucy Partington. She had last been seen at a Cheltenham bus-stop on 27 December 1973; a memorial gathering for her was held on Sunday, 10 July 1994, at the

Society of Friends Meeting House in the town. 'Very soon it was clear to me that something extraordinary was happening,' says Martin. 'As I wept I glanced at my weeping brother and thought: how badly we need this. How very badly my body needs this, as it needs food and sleep and air. Thoughts and feelings that had been trapped for twenty years were now being released.'[113] Lucy Partington's is one of two photographs he keeps on his desk.

The other photograph is of Delilah Seale, his eldest daughter. Martin had a brief affair with her mother, Lamorna Seale, in 1973; three years later, he had lunch with her and she gave him a photograph of a two-year-old girl. Shortly afterwards, he showed this to his mother, then recently returned from Spain with Ali, in the impoverished interregnum before they took on the challenge of Kingsley: 'Lamorna says I'm her father. What do you think, Mum?' Hilly considered it from various distances. 'Without looking up she said, "*Definitely.*"'[114] Lamorna Seale committed suicide in 1978 and Delilah remained an absence in Martin's life until, early in 1995, she wrote to introduce herself to him. They arranged to meet in the bar of a Knightsbridge hotel and, when Delilah entered the room, Isabel Fonseca (who would become Martin's second wife in 1998) said: 'It's *you*.' 'Then hugs and kisses for the girl with my face':[115] sometimes, after all, happy endings are allowed.

The third crisis concerned his parting from his agent, Pat Kavanagh, and his resulting quarrel with one of his oldest literary friends, her husband Julian Barnes. Martin, who once claimed not to have opened his bank statements for fifteen years, shares with Kingsley an approach to money curiously compounded of naivety and greed. It's a troublesome mixture which led Kingsley to fall out with Victor Gollancz and Tom Maschler; in 1994, as he finished writing *The Information*, it persuaded Martin to go 'all in with my American agent, [Andrew] Wylie', which 'meant breaking with my English agent of twenty-three years, Pat Kavanagh'.[116] By this time, he was operating in a financial league not often familiar to literary writers and in which, arguably, they have no proper place; but it's perhaps natural for a novelist so conditioned by pop culture to expect pop cultural rewards. However that may be, he was surely naive in his expectation that Julian Barnes would, as he puts it, recognise the difference between 'church and state' and continue the friendship without noticing that one of his wife's most celebrated clients had just ditched her. Barnes, understandably and rather nobly, refuses to say a word about the incident, so we only have Martin's account. From this it's clear that Barnes did indeed write an intemperate letter in January 1995, ending with the words 'Fuck off'; and it's equally clear that Martin's undated reply, which he reproduces in *Experience*,[117] though carefully crafted and more temperate, is designed to be offensively sententious. It's rather as if Kingsley had quarrelled with Larkin or Conquest, and meant it, and stuck to it. Meanwhile, Wylie sold *The Information* to HarperCollins, ending (though only temporarily) the Amis family connection with Cape.

Fourthly, and not unconnected with the advance Andrew Wylie obtained for *The Information*, there were Martin's expensively mended teeth: about these, more than enough has been written already.

Finally, there was Kingsley's illness and death in October 1995; and to the death of fathers we shall return.

7

Money is subtitled 'A Suicide Note', but it's *The Information* (1995) which truly deserves this description. For thirty pages, it looks as if this might be the book in which Martin emerges as a steadier sort of novelist, with a more subtle touch and greater self-control. It's true that the characters we meet – literary rivals, slightly out-of-focus wives, mismatched twin children, pastiche yobbos in an orange van – are familiar citizens of Amisland, yet the pace is well judged and the prose keeps its feet on the ground. Until the last short section of the first, unnumbered chapter: 'Outside there hung the crescent moon. It looked like Punch. But where was Judy?' That's merely silly, a rhetorical question not worth its rhetoric, and so is the next paragraph, which begins: 'Fly a mile east in our weep ship to the spires of Holland Park . . .' Our 'weep ship'? What sort of language is this? It gets worse, rapidly. 'Why do men cry?' asks the mostly invisible narrator, who has just popped in with his first person: 'Because of fights and feats and marathon preferment, because they want their mothers, because they are blind in time, because of all the hard-ons they have to whistle up out of the thin blue yonder, because of all that men have done.' Quite apart from wanting to shout 'No,

they don't!' (and what about bereavement, loss of love, illness, age?),
one can't help recoiling from the dreadful prose, which stumbles
wearily from alliteration to incomprehensibility to bathos. Even the
final one-line paragraph, placed to create page-turning expectancy, is
actually meaningless: 'And then there is the information, which comes
at night.'[118]

We know that Martin isn't a hopeless writer; so why does he do
it? If there isn't necessarily any such thing as a mid-life crisis, there
might more plausibly be a mid-career crisis: the point at which an
author powerlessly realises that he's writing the same book all over
again. *The Information* is full of the most painful striving after effect,
because effects are all it has to strive after. It is a novel almost wholly
devoid of novelty. At its heart is the unfriendly rivalry between two
talentless authors, Richard Tull and Gwyn Barry. They belong to the
types identified by Anthony Burgess as the 'A' novelist and the 'B'
novelist, thus summarised by Martin: 'The A novelist, apparently,
writes in what we commonly regard as the mainstream: he is interested in character, motive and moral argument, and in how these
reveal themselves through action (yes, oh dear me yes, the A novel
tells a story).' The misquotation from Forster is presumably deliberate. On the other hand: 'The spunkier and more subversive B novelist
. . . is at least as interested in other things too: namely the autono-
mous play of wit, ideas and language (no, the B novel doesn't
necessarily tell a story at all).'[119] Martin adds, incidentally, that
'ambitious novelists', himself no doubt included, 'tend to get more B
and less A', without noticing that his father remained very satisfactorily loyal to 'A'. Successful, readable Gwyn, therefore, is an 'A'
novelist; whereas Richard, whose book entitled *Untitled* is so impen-
etrable that every editor who tries to read it becomes ill within a few
pages, is plainly a 'B' novelist with knobs on: 'Essentially Richard
was a marooned modernist. If prompted, Gwyn Barry would probe-
ably [have] agree[d] with Herman Melville: that the art lay in pleasing
the readers.'[120] Gwyn lives with his titled wife Demeter in affluent
luxury, while Richard (who has a wife, Gina, and twin sons) scrapes
by with a couple of unconvincing part-time literary jobs: he edits for
a vanity publisher, Tantalus Press, and is also literary editor at the
Little Magazine which, although it indeed has the modest staff of a
little magazine, seems to have the deadlines and frequency of a weekly
such as the *New Statesman* or *Spectator* (which it is perhaps meant

to resemble). It wasn't ever thus: 'In the old days Gwyn was just a failed book reviewer (Richard's designation) and publisher's skivvy.'[121] So their roles have reversed – even to the extent of Gwyn having come from the poorer background – in exactly the same way as Gregory's and Terry's in *Success*. And there's an earlier literary parallel: 'Whatever happens, we balance each other out,' says Richard. 'We're like Henchard and Farfrae. You're part of me and I'm part of you.'[122]

Whether this rivalry – expressed through games from tennis to chess and through a seemingly interminable American tour during which everything goes right for Gwyn and wrong for Richard – is enough to sustain a rather long novel is one question; whether the 'B' novelist would ever go to such elaborate lengths as Richard does to harm his 'A' novelist rival is more debatable still. (Perhaps, since *The Information* is a pretty 'B'-ish book, this sort of plausibility doesn't matter.) Anyway, Richard enlists the services of a thug called Steve Cousins or Scozzy, although he might equally have been called Keith Talent or, for that matter, Mal from the short story 'State of England'. Like Martin's other full-time yobs, Steve actually becomes almost engaging by comparison with the vacuous idiots he is there to cheat; he also, amazingly, 'had what it took to get through *Untitled* without his head falling off, but that was the extent of his merits'.[123] Steve has a seventeen-year-old black sidekick called 13, whose real name is Bently; and these two are also conveniently connected to Lizette, who babysits for Richard and Gina, and to Demeter's surreally misinformation-dispensing driving instructor Crash, who happens to be 13's elder brother. The main purpose of this group is to provide episodes in the criminal–sexual London underworld already familiar from *London Fields*. Also familiar from *London Fields* is the idea of ironically twinned infants: there, Kim Talent and Marmaduke Clinch; here, the actual but utterly contrasting twins, Marius and Marco, of Richard and Gina Tull. The business with Samson Young's ludicrously named American editors is only slightly tweaked into business with a ludicrously named agent, Gal Alpanalp.

It would be perfectly possible to put up with all these revisitations of an established fictional world, if only the book were better written (one doesn't, after all, tire of Jane Austen). But this is the novel in which the earlier amber lights concerning Martin's style finally turn red. There's slang so arcane as to be incomprehensible: 'Gwyn's trex was loved by the world; his trex was universal . . . The world loved trex; the world was trex.'[124] This modulates into whole passages which will mean nothing at all to anyone who wasn't within a mile's radius of Westway in 1995. Half a page on 'street names', for instance, along these lines: '13 had a little cousin whose street name was Emu . . . E stood for Ian; and Ian liked music: hence Emu. Brill.'[125] Or this, towards the end of an excitable section, apparently about Crash: 'It was called Thresher's, but Crash called it Pressures. On the way up Keith Grove he realized what it was: him, in the fruit juice bar, saying to Scozzy, and *laughing*: "*Oh* yeah. She's definitely Experienced." 13: that *bad* kid.'[126] Or, finally and entirely bafflingly: 'No one had as yet written a novel called *Quacko*. And for good reason. This novel would have no beginning, no middle and no end – and no punctuation. This novel would be all over the fucking gaff.'[127]

Sometimes, idioms stumble and collide, as when 13 drives 'down the wrong way of the M20 in a stolen GTi with five blue-and-whites up his pipe'.[128] This seems doubly unEnglish, making the motorway sound like a single-track road as well as using a colloquialism for police cars imported from New York. Sometimes, important-looking statements turn out to mean nothing: 'They all suffered from pains. These pains were informers sent by death.'[129] Or: 'But we see accidents, everywhere, on the information highway. We see hazard-lights and freezing fog. We see jackknife and whiplash.'[130] And, scattered throughout the book, there are those dreary adolescent vulgarities which seemed just about excusable in *The Rachel Papers* or *Dead Babies* but which are unseemly in the work of a middle-aged author. One will be enough: 'he sat down in the kitchen and ate a fruit yoghurt so rubbery with additives that it reminded him in texture of one of his so-called hard-ons'.[131]

There is one more puzzle about *The Information*, which may not seem vastly important within the context of the book but which spreads out beyond it; and that is a subtext, apparently voiced by Richard, which is hostile to literature itself. It comes out in his philistine materialism: 'He liked poets because they had no power and no money';[132] 'poets . . . were the only living writers who were lowlier than he was'.[133] It comes out, too, in the books he has to review which – with titles charting an upward gradient of obscurity, from *Robert Southey: Gentleman Poet*[134] to *Time's Song: Winthrop Praed 1802–1839* or *AntiLatitudinarian: The Heretical Career of*

Francis Atterbury[135] – are meant to sound impossibly dull but often look rather interesting to the literary reader (just as Jim Dixon's proposed learned article on 'The Economic Influence of the Developments in Shipbuilding Techniques, 1450 to 1485', one of the few missed targets in *Lucky Jim*, would actually appear fascinating to a specialist in the period). And it comes out, above all, in a curiously digressive passage which begins with Richard thinking ('if thinking is quite the word we want') that 'you cannot demonstrate, prove, establish – you cannot know if a book is good'. This is nonsense, of course, as Martin, who elsewhere rightly insists that 'all criticism of living authors should be evaluative',[136] obviously understands. Yet the passage then veers into an argument with the 'literary philosophers of Cambridge' and a startling misreading of the line 'Thoughts that do often lie too deep for tears' which, says Richard, contains an 'identifiable flaw: that *do*, brought in to make up the numbers'.[137] But it doesn't: that 'do' is not merely essential for the scansion but deliberately emphatic, and anyway permissible given the diction of the period. Richard (or is it Martin?) is merely betraying ignorance and a faulty ear. A few lines later – 'But life and literature were not the same. Ask Richard' – we've slipped away from Richard's point of view towards that of the shadowy omniscient, ambiguously authorial narrator; and where *he* stands on this or any other matter is anyone's guess.

9. FATHERS AND SONS

1

Martin's father died on 22 October 1995. My father died the previous year, on 28 June 1994. Nature's 'common theme', so Claudius assures Hamlet, is 'death of fathers', but he has a particular reason to play down the subject. For the rest of us, the surprise comes from the recognition that one's father's death is a beginning as much as a conclusion: he is the one person a man has no hope of seeing clearly in his lifetime. We rebel against our fathers, we argue with them, we deliberately misunderstand them; we proceed from the firm assumption that their opinions must be wrong and their advice bad; we do everything in our power to assert our generational difference and our personal distinctness. Then, when our fathers die, we begin to see not only how alike we were but how well we understood each other all along. For a writer, this realisation will sooner or later form itself into what Wordsworth called a 'timely utterance'. Kingsley seemed barely to register his father's death in 1963, yet four years later he memorialised William Amis both in verse ('In Memoriam W.R.A.')[1] and in prose ('A Memoir of my Father');[2] while in 1973 he used him as the basis for Captain Furneaux in *The Riverside Villas Murder* and in 1994 he affectionately returned to him for Tom Davies in *You Can't Do Both*. Martin's response to Kingsley's death was *Experience* (2000).

He also alludes to Claudius: 'But I know it is common; all that lives must die, passing through nature to eternity. My father lost his father, and my children will lose theirs, and their children (this is immensely onerous to contemplate) will lose theirs.' He realises – though it hasn't saved him from that overburdened parenthesis – that the book he's writing presents special problems of tone and organisation: he resolves 'to speak, for once, without artifice', but the habit proves an impossible one for him to break. His 'organisational principles', he says,

> derive from an inner urgency, and from the novelist's addiction to seeing parallels and making connections. The method, plus the use

of footnotes (to preserve the collateral thought), should give a clear view of the geography of a writer's mind. If the effect sometimes seems staccato, tangential, stop-go, etc, then I can only say that that's what it's like, on my side of the desk.[3]

It's an audacious conjuring trick: for, the footnotes apart, the episodic approach is familiar enough from his fiction. And 'the geography of a writer's mind' surely glances at 'the growth of a poet's mind', Wordsworth's programme for *The Prelude*: 'geography', though, implies a spacial scattering in contrast to the ordered chronology of 'growth'. Curiously, of these two memoirs, it's the blank-verse *Prelude* which seems more honestly 'without artifice' than *Experience*.

As is repeatedly the case with Martin's later work, an appearance of formal daring masks a kind of evasion: because his patchwork of non-chronological fragments is, by definition, full of endings, the business of remembering what happened next, or what ought to follow here, is continually avoided. This is especially frustrating in the passages about Martin's childhood. The reader who wants to make orderly sense of it will find himself going back and forth, as if trying to reconstruct the original state of a cut-up text by William Burroughs, and will still be defeated by mysterious lacunae and inconsistent dates. The succession of juxtaposed brief episodes, which is also very much the method of *Yellow Dog*, has clear affinities with journalism and pop song, but it's also something of a family trait. Kingsley in *Memoirs* also eschewed calm chronological narrative in favour of short and sometimes tenuously related essays. Yet where *Memoirs* gives the impression of being a lazy book, *Experience* is a busy one; and a consequence of this busyness is that the father–son portrait at its heart is compromised and modulated – even in the one long section about Kingsley's final illness and death, 'One More Little Hug' – by other memories and by those famously lengthy footnotes. (The phrase 'father–son portrait', incidentally, will recall one of the most mystifying moments in Kingsley's *Letters*: his furious rejection, in 1987, of a proposal by John Hayes, Director of the National Portrait Gallery, that he and Martin should sit for a joint portrait, as 'one of the most amazingly inept and tactless suggestions that has ever been made to me'.[4] It sounds, on the contrary, rather a good idea and it is just what *Experience* attempts in words.)

The unusual quality of Kingsley's and Martin's father–son

relationship, which Anthony Thwaite noticed in Oxford as long ago
as 1968, has been reaffirmed by Martin in a recent interview. 'Christopher Hitchens says he's never seen a father and son get on as well
as we did,' he told Mariella Frostrup; 'there was almost always
enmity between father and son, but there was never any of that generational stuff between him and me.'[5] This is the other side – the
good side – of Kingsley's neglectful permissiveness as a parent:
because he never ceased to empathise with the irresponsibility of the
child or adolescent, he never created the tensions with his children
that a more responsible father could scarcely have avoided. Moreover, while most of our fathers went off to work in the morning and
didn't return until after teatime, Kingsley's daily routine was nothing
like this during Martin's formative teenage years. The fact that size-
able chunks of these years were spent with Hilly in various sorts of
limbo, while Kingsley's relationship with Jane progressed from affair
to marriage, actually served to strengthen the exceptionally close
bond of male complicity between father and son. From the Soho
condom-buying expedition in 1965 until his death thirty years later,
Kingsley's attitude towards his second son – despite their furious literary and ideological disagreements – was one of chummy, bloke-to-
bloke equality. 'Say as little as you want or as much as you want,'[6]
he told him over dinner in 1993, when Martin went to talk to him
about the break-up of his marriage to Antonia. Such unembarrassed
openness is rare in father–son conversations between these two, or
perhaps any two, generations.

At best, this enables Martin to view his father with unusual
steadiness: 'Kingsley was never much of a tolerance-cultivator; and
his failures were big failures.'[7] The failures he has in mind here are
those of Kingsley's later life, and they range from his fatness – 'With
him, getting fat was . . . like a project, grimly inaugurated on the day
Jane left him in the winter of 1980'[8] – to the strands of misogyny and
anti-Semitism which Martin detects in *Jake's Thing* and *Stanley and
the Women*. 'What's it like, being mildly anti-Semitic?' he asked; to
which his father replied, 'It's all right.'[9] It wasn't all right, of course,
but in Kingsley's case it wasn't so terribly wrong either: as he skilfully
demonstrated in *Stanley*, it came with the psychological furniture of
growing up in pre-war Norbury and it meant no harm. We know this
because when Martin, stung into irritation, told him about a passage
from Primo Levi's *If This Is a Man*, Kingsley broke down in tears

and said: 'That's one thing I feel more and more as I get older. Let's *not* round up the women and children. Let's *not* go over the hill and fuck up the people in the next town along. Let's not do any of that ever again.'[10] For Kingsley, his apparent anti-Semitism – like so many of his racist and sexist outbursts – was a way of masking despair, panic, anxiety, chronic depression.

I'm not sure that Martin, understandably beguiled by the matily engaging father he wants to remember, ever quite gets the hang of this. When he writes of Kingsley's 'lavish array of phobias', he does so with uncomfortably forced lightness and gets a crucial detail wrong: the 'five-bob flip' at Croydon Aerodrome, after which Kingsley never flew again, is magically transported to the seaside and thus quite literally distanced. Martin says that in his late twenties he too began to experience panic attacks, but that they were cured by one sentence spoken to him by his father's friend and psychiatrist Jim Durham: 'Just remember that the worst thing that can happen to you is that you might make a fool of yourself.'[11] Although this may be good advice, and it may have worked for Martin, it's no cure for the kind of panic which prevented his father from using planes or tube trains, going out in the dark or being left alone in a house at night. Martin sees a world around him increasingly defined by terror; Kingsley had terror bottled up inside him.

There's a moment quite early in *Koba the Dread* (2002), in one of the passages which awkwardly juxtapose historical and personal memory, where Martin recalls another of his father's friends, 'the defector historian Tibor Szamuely'. Kingsley, he says, once complained to Tibor's wife Nina that her husband was an unusually late riser; whereupon she explained that he sometimes needed to glimpse the dawn before he could sleep, 'to be absolutely certain that they won't be coming for him that night'. And Martin comments: 'We cannot understand it, and there is no reason why we should.'[12] Kingsley, I suspect, would have understood perfectly. So (for the personal note prompts a more personal response, both here and below, than might have been appropriate earlier on) do I: for reasons which are less tangible though no less terrifying, I have nights when I'm awake until the sky begins to brighten, needing the dawn chorus to assure me that all's well and it's safe to sleep. My guess is that this isn't startlingly unusual; why then does Martin find it so? Does it perhaps go back, as I've already tentatively suggested, to a childhood which, however unsettled it may have been, somehow failed to acquaint him fully with the dark night of the soul? He is continually fascinated by terror, yet he remains at an intuitive level innocently detached from it; and this gives books such as *Time's Arrow*, *Night Train*, *Koba the Dread* and *House of Meetings* their peculiar flavour of unintended prurience.

It also perhaps explains those intrusive notes of artifice, of writerly rhetoric, in 'One Last Little Hug', which otherwise stands unquestionably among the great accounts of a father–son relationship's closing stages. The period of tragi-comic delirium at Primrose Hill between Kingsley's self-discharge from hospital and his final readmittance provides a notable example. Martin describes how his father 'got up in the middle of the night and showered and dressed – and packed'. Even though he'd happily cram his clothes for his Welsh holidays into a plastic bag, this time he packed a suitcase:

> On that night he told Hilly that he had to take a train – Kingsley, alone, in the middle of the night, taking a train? He was expected at a very important meeting. Advised against it by my mother at the doorstep, he went out into the street and approached a driverless parked car and demanded to be taken to the Garrick. He called to my mother,
> – Why won't he take me to the Garrick?[13]

Martin leaves implicit the important point that in his dementia Kingsley at last challenges his principle phobias: darkness, being alone, travelling by train. Instead, he turns the incident into an anecdote by shifting the focus to the 'driverless parked car' and leaving it hanging on Kingsley's pathetic, unanswerable question. He follows it immediately with another equally crafted snapshot, of a brief afternoon visit in which he discovers his father 'comatose in his chair' and is 'surprised when he speaks':

> – What time is it?
> – Two.
> – Two in the afternoon? What day are we?
> On my way out I look at the sheet of paper recurled into Kingsley's typewriter. I see no *seagulls*. He is still on page 106 of his new novel. It has been page 106 ever since the fall. Something seems to have been added. The page ends with the words: ' "On the contrary," countered Holmes.'[14]

The just-wrongness of 'What day are we?' crackles with authenticity; *seagulls* was a word he'd been obsessively typing, presumably trying to hang on to it, urged by herring gulls attracted to the nearby canals; while the novel was the unfinished *Black and White*, about the relationship between a heterosexual black woman and a gay white man which, like the suitcase-packing, sounds as if it might have been a late challenge to ingrained habits and perceived prejudices. The 'fall' refers obviously to the accident in Wales, yet Martin's mid-Atlantic diction admits the suggestion of a pun, 'the start of autumn': again, there's just a hint of self-conscious artifice.

Thus, almost inadvertently, Kingsley becomes mythologised. He is Lear; he is Prospero. He's also someone nearer than that: for ages I couldn't think who, until I realised that he has a bucolic cousin in H. E. Bates's Uncle Silas. Lecher, raconteur, incorrigible drinker, Silas at the end begins to 'turn day into night': 'he would doze all day and then, in the dead of night . . . he would wake and ferret in the cellar or mow his wheat and dig his potatoes and gather his elderberries for wine'. So, surely, would Kingsley have done, had he been a countryman. Even Silas's conversation with the authorial narrator has the same tone as Kingsley's with Martin: ' "What's the weather?' he said. "It rains," I said. "Let it," he whispered.'[15] And that's the most unsettling thing about *Experience*. Kingsley, when he isn't being viewed specifically as a writer, starts to sound like a character in his own or in someone else's fiction. He rather less often sounds like a *father*. But then, what are fathers like?

2

Ian Otho James Powell, 'Jim', my father, was a decade or so older than Kingsley and died on the eve of his eighty-third birthday. He was born and grew up in Ponders End, an unglamorously named and indeed an unglamorous bit of North London. His father, my invisible grandfather Otho, died when he was twelve; two years later, to help support his mother Agnes – they had moved to Fulham Road, where she ran first a shop selling baby clothes and then a teashop – he left school and got a job, thanks to his decent French, at Lepersonne's, a firm of glass importers (the identical trade to that of J. J. Amis). Eventually, he became Managing Director of a differently named but essentially similar company, Chairman of the Glass and Allied Trades Association and among the most respected authorities in England on anything to do with glassware. Much of this expertise was unceremoniously shared during lunchtimes, just round the corner from his offices in Charterhouse Street, at the Old Mitre in Ely Place; it was there that he once drew on the back of a peeled-off beer-mat the original design of the classic Guinness mug, for which his reward was a pint of best bitter. He was continually tickled by the oddities of his trade: when, during the early 1960s (and therefore pre-VAT), the little indented cigarette-rests vanished from pub glass ashtrays, it was because he'd discovered that those with them were classed as 'smokers' requisites', attracting the highest rate of purchase tax, whereas those without were 'nut dishes', attracting the lowest. A few years later, in my student local, there were brilliantly coloured rectangular ashtrays advertising the products of a big drinks combine: blue for beers, green for spirits, purple for wines. The only trouble was that they were exactly the size of jacket pockets, into which they constantly vanished. When I told him this, he was delighted: it was just what he'd intended. You couldn't, he explained, *buy* advertising space in people's living rooms, but you could induce them to provide it for nothing.

During the Munich crisis of 1938, he joined the Fire Service, rapidly becoming so indispensable that they prevented him from going off to serve (as he'd have wished) in the army when war broke out. It was in the Fire Service that he met my mother, Dulcie Delia Lloyd. Both of them were already married and, because of the delays in obtaining immediately post-war divorces, my mother changed her surname to his by deed poll before I was born in 1948: I've always thought that quietly heroic, characteristic of the pragmatic ways they found of getting on with things. Later that year, they were at last able to marry, and in 1950 the three of us moved from a flat in East Sheen to a small cottage – they called it their 'shoebox' – in rural Surrey. There, at Leigh, Jim became in some mysteriously unobtrusive and inevitable way involved in everything that went on in the village: the cricket club, the football club, the Cottage Garden Society, and if he wasn't Chairman he was Secretary. Was he also a Parish Councillor? Almost certainly. When we moved, later on, to Kent, he was definitely a District Councillor (Conservative, of course) at Sevenoaks; and in his fifties, he'd be found on a Saturday cafternoon running along the football pitch at Ide Hill as a linesman. I've never met anyone who devoted so much unpaid time to serving his community with so little pomposity or fuss.

But almost no one knew that he suffered from something worse than Kingsley's phobias: from clinical depression. I certainly didn't. While we were still living in Surrey – by this time, in a house tucked into the North Downs outside Reigate – I was sent off as a boarder to Sevenoaks School: partly, I now see, so that I'd be unaware of my father's illness and treatment, including ECT and at one point hospitalisation. I thought that his silences with me, the distance that had crept into our relationship since the easy sweetshop-indulging and model-railway-building days of my early childhood, were symptoms merely of what can go wrong between fathers and their difficult adolescent sons. I felt frozen out, and I froze him out, for years. My own attempt at a 'timely utterance' emerged seven years after his death, in the form of a three-page poem; I hope one day I'll be able to write about him at greater length.

In Baldock, Hertfordshire, a quarter of a century or so ago, I used to drink in a pub where an old man called George had his stool in the corner by the bar. George was both cantankerous and extremely deaf; he would become offended very gradually, responding to something he'd partially heard and misapprehended some time earlier by eventually raising his walking-stick with the words, 'I think I might have to take exception to that.' One evening, some of us were talking about the tricky relationships between parents and children, fathers and sons, and I remember someone saying that the word 'love' didn't always quite cover what you felt across the generation gap. No, I said, which is why the Biblical formula, 'Honour thy father and thy mother', is so subtle and so telling. We'd gone on to talk about something quite else by the time George raised his stick and said to me: 'I think I might have to take exception to that. I can't put up with a man who says he doesn't love his father.' I tried to explain, without much success, what I meant: that 'honour' in this context embraces both love and respect, bestowing dignity as well as affection. And that is the sense in which I honour my father.

Jim Powell wasn't a writer: it was my mother's letters, easier and chattier, to which I looked forward at school. He'd spent too much of his life in the business world to sound relaxed on paper, but his jokes were good and intelligent. Once, I found to my surprise that he'd stuck two stamps alongside each other on a page of his letter, one simply glued there and the other with neat diagonal cuts to its middle. 'This is a wasted stamp,' he'd written beneath the first and, beneath the second: 'This is a waisted stamp.' He was, of course, correcting a misspelling in my last letter home, and it seems (as it were) to have stuck; but that was really about the extent of his literary enterprise. Nevertheless, he was as complex and interesting a father as Kingsley Amis, and I can't help regarding his unliterariness as something of a blessing. For the artificial tone that mars *Experience* stems from Martin's assumption that being a writer is the centrally defining factor about Kingsley-as-father, even though he might have been every bit as fascinating on that score (and perhaps more usefully conflicting too) if he'd followed his own grandfather into, as it happens, the glass business.

3

It's pointless to speculate on what Kingsley would have made of *Experience*: the form and tone of the book is shaped by his absence. This is also true, in contrasting ways, of *Night Train* and of *Koba the Dread*. However, in *Night Train*, Martin's first work of fiction to appear after his father's death, Kingsley would no doubt have recognised a process of displacement which parallels that of his own genre fiction: a *noir* thriller with an American setting, narrated by a female (if not strikingly feminine) cop who can nevertheless give unexpected voice to her author's thoughts. 'Motive, motive,' grumbles Detective Mike – for that is her name – Hoolihan; 'We never give it a second's thought. We don't care about the why. We say: Fuck the why.'[16] And Kingsley would surely have appreciated the homage paid in *Koba the Dread* to his old friend Robert Conquest's *The Great Terror*, noting that in the end Conquest had indeed supplied a book which would mitigate Martin's lefty foolishness. Martin himself feels that his father would have liked *House of Meetings* (2006).[17] Perhaps he would have done. Almost certainly, family loyalty would have restrained him from agreeing, in public at least, with Tibor Fischer's assessment of his son as 'an atrocity-chaser . . . constantly on the prowl for gravitas-enlargement offers (the Holocaust, serial killers, 9/11, the Gulag, the

Beslan siege) as if writing about really bad things will make him a really great novelist'.[18] He might well have shared Fischer's unease, while resisting the animosity implicit in 'atrocity-chaser'.

By comparison, it's a good deal easier to guess what Kingsley would have thought of *Yellow Dog* (2003), the fourth and surely the last of Martin's substantial low-life London novels – this one, like *Money* and *The Information*, including a transatlantic excursion. The first problem with *Yellow Dog*, and the simplest to deal with, is the extent to which it reheats ingredients which have already become overfamiliar: thugs and crooks, writers and film-makers, set against an excitably incoherent background of pornography and violence. The *Morning Line*, avidly read by John Self, has metamorphosed (via *Money*) into the *Morning Lark*, a paper bearing some resemblance to the *Daily Sport*, which employs a journalist called Clint Smoker and whose readers are routinely referred to as its 'wankers'. Somewhere near the centre of the plot – which I don't entirely follow and which Martin would probably insist is unimportant anyway – there's a convoluted joke involving Joseph Andrews and *Joseph Andrews*. Xan Meo, the more-or-less main character, has published a book of short stories called *Lucozade*: the title story, which is itself a version of Martin's 'State of England', concerns 'a middle-aged bodyguard who, at some earlier period in his career, had plied his trade on the American entertainment circuit. "He had spent a year in Las Vegas, working for Joseph Andrews," it said. And "Lucozade" later mentioned that Joseph Andrews had retired to Los Angeles.'[19] Unfortunately for him, there's an actual Joseph Andrews who has done exactly this and isn't pleased. When Xan – he is talking to Andrews's henchman Mal Bale, whom we may suppose to be Mal from 'State of England' – tries to explain that he'd intended Joseph Andrews as an allusive disguise for the pop singer Tom Jones, it doesn't help much: 'It's just uh, it's just a kind of joke. *Tom Jones, Joseph Andrews*: they're both novels by Henry Fielding . . . You can't say Tom Jones.' To which Mal understandably replies: '. . . Well you can't fucking say Joseph Andrews neither! Either. Jesus.' The joke is compounded by the subsequent revelation that Joseph Andrews is Xan's father – which is precisely the kind of surprise sprung by Fielding in *Joseph Andrews*; or, for that matter, in *Tom Jones*. It's clever and funny, yet far too slight an idea on which to build a novel.

The second problem concerns the one strand which separates

Yellow Dog from the other 'London' novels: an 'alternate world' royal family. Here we find Henry IX, who has a pornographic princess for a daughter and attendants with names such as Bugger and Love to make for comic exchanges ('Oh, Bugger'; 'Coming, Love'). It's all a terrible misjudgement, continually reminding the reader of the immensely more subtle way in which Kingsley develops his similar idea in *The Alteration*. It seems to reveal an impoverished imagination and to offer one explanation for Martin's recourse to the Holocaust and the Gulag as fictional starting-points. Although he has insisted, with some justice, that 'No writer can determine what may appeal to his imagination and it is simply philistine to arraign him for the things he happens to write about best,'[20] it seems worth risking the taint of philistinism to notice some of the things which his Anglo-American fictional world almost entirely excludes. For example: the working life of shops or offices or factories on which novelists of the Alan Sillitoe and David Storey generation so depended; the more formal, dinner-party world which underpins the fiction of, say, Anthony Powell or indeed Elizabeth Jane Howard; landscape, villagescape, townscape, or any sense of place beyond stylised bits of London and various American cities; high culture, especially serious music, opera or ballet; schools, universities and anything to do with education or the intellect; politics, apart from satirical or parodic references . . . And ordinary people. In his revealing and self-contradictory 1985 interview with John Haffenden, he says: 'It is funny that what assails me most strongly when I walk the street is the thought, "Pity the plain", which I say to myself again and again.' By 'plain', he means 'a lack of luck, conspicuous disadvantage'. He continues: 'I have a huge amount of sympathy for them: I think the plain are the real livers of life, the real receivers; they have great vividness.'[21] But his fictional world, oscillating between the glamorous and the grotesque, finds little room to treat 'real lives of life' with the attentive regard which they deserve and the novel demands. What's missing, in fact, in these biggish books is any sense of Dickensian, or for that matter Angus Wilsonian, diversity.

As for the third problem: as I struggled to reread *Yellow Dog*, two sentences from the Amises kept drifting without invitation into my mind. This is the first: 'After a while the reader is physically oppressed by the dishonesty of his prose.'[22] And this is the second: 'It isn't so much that it's a bad book . . . no, [it] goes further than that, in not *seeming to be by a writer*.'[23] One is Martin on Trotsky's *History of the Russian Revolution*; the other is Kingsley on John Wain's *Living in the Present*; and both seem dismayingly applicable to *Yellow Dog*.

4

'Nothing is more inherited than family humour,' says Martin, speaking of his father; 'and if I'd had his dates and he'd had mine, I'd have written something like his body of work and he'd have written mine.' 'I certainly feel there's a continuity,' he adds, describing himself as 'basically a comic writer who has written uncomic books'; Kingsley 'was too, with his sorties into more serious stuff'.[24] But they are far too different, in temperament and in talent, for this to be usefully true. A kind of parallel exists, as we've seen, for their first four novels or so; after that, despite their personal closeness, they really inhabit separate literary planets. And, while this is true of tone and content, it is even more crucially true of style.

Style matters above all else because the business of writers is to write. When people of Martin's and my age were growing up, a common literary debating point – triggered, often, by the kind of sixth-form practical-criticism class he failed to attend – was whether or not it would be possible to write a great fascist poem: Yeats and Pound and Eliot would then be invoked as instances of poets who, at one time or another, held uncomfortably right-wing views but who nevertheless didn't seem to have produced a work that could properly, rather than colloquially, be called 'fascist' (a useful by-product of such discussions was to make us careful about that word, guarding us from appalling coinages such as Kingsley's 'fascist lunches' or Martin's 'fascist mansion' for Lemmons).[25] The weary consensus tended to be that the 'great fascist poem' was possible but improbable: on the whole, writers inclined towards decent liberal views, yet one couldn't be absolutely sure – and it would be neither decent nor liberal to insist. Martin, of course, has become a great insister. On nuclear weapons or Islamist terrorism, on masculinity or the redundancy of religion, he announces his position and declares that anyone who disagrees is moronic or subhuman, a procedure which some might suggest does approach the 'fascist'. On the other hand, literature – and indeed the culture which is a civilised society's common property – operates from the contrary premise: it doesn't matter what you, as a writer, think or believe, as long as you do your job well; nor does it matter whether or not the reader agrees with you, since an intelligent reader can withhold his consent without compromising his appreciation. That is why criticism, in the end, can only ask: 'Is it any good?'

We know where Kingsley got his style from, because we know about his childhood and adolescent reading (even if we didn't, we might work it out). We also know, thanks to his letters to Larkin, whom he most consistently admired among twentieth-century novelists as a writer of prose fiction: Christopher Isherwood. As early as March 1946, he's using Isherwood as a slightly surprising yardstick when he tells his friend that Hilly 'is continually giving evidence of appreciation. She liked Good Berlin, and I wd lend her Mr Trains if I had it.'[26] Six years later, putting together a modern-novel course at Swansea, he laments that his 'ridiculous integrity' has led him to include 'cheerless craps' such as 'Ginny Woolf and Dai Lawrence and Morgy Forster', instead of 'chaps I really go for, you know old Grahame Green and Henry Greene and Christopher Sherwood and Evelyn Hoare and so on'.[27] It was pre-war Isherwood he admired – like many other readers, he was unimpressed by *The World in the Evening* (1954) – and the influence is everywhere. Sometimes it's allusively visible (in *I Like It Here* or the 'Berlin Diary'-style passage in *Memoirs*), but Kingsley also absorbed two more general lessons. One was his instinctive adoption of what Isherwood called 'tea-tabling', the representation of major themes through tiny domestic incidents; and this he does throughout his writing career, from Jim Dixon's hangover in *Lucky Jim* to Clare Morrison's lost-and-found piece of chalcedony in *The Folks that Live on the Hill*. The other is precisely identified by Jane Howard. 'Kingsley's originality with language', she says, 'was his unselfconsciousness: he didn't realise how unusual it was.'[28] Yet this too comes from the ironic, conversational style of Isherwood's Berlin books, surely among the practically beneficial models for any young prose writer. Martin, however, wouldn't agree with this assessment. For him, Gore Vidal's description of Isherwood as 'the best prose writer in English' is 'a meaningless tribute anyway . . . the nervous hets among Vidal's readers will be wondering whether the verdict is really a literary one'.[29] The tone of that sentence speaks for itself.

Martin's style – if such a thing can be identified – is the exact
opposite, veering away as far as possible from an English conversational voice towards a demotic statelessness. His literary mentors
were Saul Bellow and Vladimir Nabokov, 'neither of whom writes
English'. That, of course, is Kingsley, in his uninhibited essay 'Sacred
Cows', from which I've already quoted. He goes on: 'Nabokov, in a
way peculiar to foreigners, never stops showing off his mastery of
the language; his books are jewels a hundred thousand words long.
Bellow is a Ukrainian-Canadian, I believe. It is painful to watch him
trying to pick his way between the unidiomatic on the one hand
and the affected on the other.'[30] What's surely clear, even if we don't
fully endorse Kingsley's estimation, is that Nabokov and Bellow,
both of them teaching lessons exactly opposed to Isherwood's,
are *not* practically beneficial models for a young prose writer. In
Martin's case their dangerous example was compounded by other
factors: the lack of proper childhood reading, the ten-year-old's year
at Princeton trying to be an American, the overimmersion in pop-
song and television culture. The result is that he doesn't write
recognisably literate English; and this applies not only to his novels –
which, as we've already discovered, become increasingly cluttered
with ugliness and incomprehensibility – but also to his critical prose.
Here are two sentences (and they are both *complete* sentences) from
the same article in *The War Against Cliché*. 'Nobody ever accused
Audrey Callaghan, say, of putting out for Frank Sinatra.'[31] 'But we
don't want her sounding like a flake.'[32] This isn't, to my ear, the
language of critical discourse nor even the language of ordinarily
tolerable English prose.

5

If that sounds harsh, it's because I can't help feeling that our
responsibility to our language – and with it something of Eliot's
obligation 'To purify the dialect of the tribe'[33] – must override the
odd bruising of an ego. And, of course, it's perfectly possible that it's
my ear that's at fault.

One quality we might look for or welcome (or even sometimes
aspire to) in a writer is generosity. Kingsley could be abusively rude
in person, scurrilous in his private letters, malicious in his published

Memoirs. He was obstinate too: he formed his literary tastes early on and would seldom admit to changing his mind about them. His running battle with Jane Austen is a case in point. In a letter written as late as 1993, he gleefully tells Paul Fussell that he'd 'concluded that JA was a 2nd-rate pisser while still at school'.[34] Yet when I asked Jane Howard about this, suggesting that after all Kingsley's ironic-comic mode has a good deal in common with Austen's, she attributed his avowed dislike to 'inverted social snobbery' and said that he admired Austen more than he cared to admit. She also pointed out that, however offensive he may have been to people he found intolerable, he never 'pissed on' anyone simply because they didn't know or hadn't read something.[35] He had the teacher's instinct: to inform as kindly as possible. Sargy Mann confirms this. While convalescing at Gardnor House after an eye operation, he went on to Hampstead Heath to draw. 'The eye wept and wept, so I thought, "Fuck it, I'm going to write a poem. How do poems work?"' He decided on a simple rhyme scheme; he wrote the beginning of one poem, then another. He returned to hospital and then again to Gardnor House, where he wrote some more. He wondered 'if Kingsley could bear to look at them' and handed over manuscript sheets. Kingsley typed them up and, over a drink a couple of days later, said, 'Shall we have a look at those poems?' 'He was a wonderful teacher,' says Sargy. 'He started on one of the poems: it was in blank verse, but there was a point in the middle where two lines rhymed for emphasis.' Kingsley wondered whether this was deliberate, warning against accidental rhymes or assonances: 'The reader must not be made to pause without profit,' he told Sargy.[36]

That generosity seems to underlie so much of Kingsley, even at his most ferocious. It's closely related to his self-regenerative ability to bounce back from the worst of times: so many of his finest books – *Lucky Jim, Take a Girl like You, Girl, 20, Jake's Thing, Stanley and the Women, The Folks that Live on the Hill* – share an undercurrent of magnificently cussed stoicism, making the creative best of things. The relationship between his novels continually changes as one reads and re-reads them. I now think, as I wouldn't have done when I began this book, that there's much to be said for A. N. Wilson's assertion that 'the mordant late Amis is even better than the early farces'.[37] Certainly, the period from *Jake's Thing* onwards, which once looked as if it would be poisoned by bitterness and misogyny, can now begin to appear as a steady imaginative reconnection with the 'real livers of life', a reassertion of generosity.

It's difficult to detect anything comparable in Martin: at least, not yet. And the 'yet' is important, because a writer approaching sixty is still, unless he takes Kingsley's or some other route to prematurely induced old age, a young writer (this sounds like a defensive assertion, but it's a true one). He has a saddening tendency to use the sneer as a first rather than as a last resort and to compromise a high moral stance with low attacking strategies. The case of Philip Larkin – with Jane Howard, the literary figure who comes closest to being a partner in the family firm of Amis & Son – is instructive. One piece on Larkin, written immediately after his death in 1985, simply gets him wrong: 'All his values and attitudes were utterly, even fanatically "negative",' says Martin. 'He really was "anti-life" . . .'[38] This is to fall for Larkin's Eeyorish persona and to ignore the gleeful twinkle which delighted most people who knew him even slightly. Nor is Martin, who has little feeling even for his father's poetry, a very perceptive reader of the poems. None of this would matter, if eight years later he hadn't published an indignant (and, I'm afraid, a sneer-first) review of Andrew Motion's *Philip Larkin: A Writer's Life*, the tone of which will be clear enough from one sentence: 'In Andrew Motion's book we have the constant sense that Larkin is somehow falling short of the cloudless emotional health enjoyed by (for instance) Andrew Motion.'[39] And even this wouldn't matter much – or would at least be dismissible as journalistic trivia – if elsewhere in *The War Against Cliché*, indeed as a footnote to the Margaret Thatcher piece already quoted, we didn't find this: 'Larkin was a great poet (see below), but in his personal life he was a clear example of UK toilet-training run amok.'[40] That, needless to say, is a nastier remark than anything in Motion's book or, for that matter, in this one.

6

When Martin left his English agent and fell out with her husband, he claims to have been taken by surprise because he thought (or hoped) it would be possible for Julian Barnes to distinguish between 'church' and 'state', although 'business' and 'pleasure' might be simpler and more accurate. I think it's usually possible to make the same sort of distinction between a writer and his work: I've met and liked several writers whose work seems to me just about worthless, though perhaps fewer where those polarities are reversed – no doubt because there are always far more bad writers around than there are good ones. I've never met Martin Amis. But it seems to me that in his own case he has made this healthy distinction increasingly hard to sustain, by treating himself, and allowing himself to be treated, as a celebrity; and that this is a mistake. Ideally, a writer should be more or less invisible, judged solely by his books; living somewhere inaccessible helps, too, as Larkin well knew when he kept himself hidden in Hull. Martin, it seems, is everywhere; and this has been especially true, as it happens, during the months I've been writing about him – a circumstance I hadn't foreseen and one which hasn't helped me to think straight about his books. When your subject keeps popping up in the newspapers, writing or saying daft things, it's hard not to take notice.

Here, then, in the full consciousness that they might be viewed as ephemeral irritations, are two representative last straws. One is an essay called 'The Age of Horrorism', in the *Observer* of 10 September 2006; the other is a 'You Ask the Questions' feature in the *Independent* of 15 January 2007. My concern with the first isn't to take issue with its analysis of the growth of 'Islamism', but rather to ask how a writer with any feeling for his language could have come up with a coinage as grotesque as 'horrorism' or how any thoughtful person could produce a sentence such as this: 'Today, in the West, there are no good excuses for religious belief – unless we think that ignorance, reaction and sentimentality are good excuses.'[41] This can only mean that all archbishops and bishops, all priests and theologians, to say nothing of all believers, of any creed, are ignorant, reactionary, sentimental, or a combination of all three. And, however staunch an atheist (which is itself a sort of belief) one may be, such a statement is plainly foolish and impertinent. It is also quite strikingly bad-mannered.

So to 'You Ask the Questions', from which I've already cited Martin's reply to the reader who asked how he would have spent 'his working life' if his 'father hadn't been a famous writer'. Another reader, describing 'horrorism' as 'unintentionally hilarious', wondered whether Martin had any more such phrases. 'Yes, I have.

Here's a good one (though I can hardly claim it as my own): the phrase is "fuck off".' A question about his favourite among his own novels prompted him to choose *Yellow Dog*, because it had received some harsh reviews, and to describe one reviewer as 'a creep and a wretch. Oh yeah: and a fat arse.' And to an admittedly odd question which accused him of being a snob, he replied: 'I have described the institution of the monarchy as "a wank" – a phrase free, I think, of exaggerated respect.'[42] The self-satisfied self-quotation compounds the offence.

7

In my Preface I quote Martin's remark that 'the fit reader, the ideal reader, regards a writer's life as just an interesting extra'.[43] I don't linger there over the word 'fit', which he seems to be using in its primary sense of 'suitable' or 'appropriate'. But I wonder whether he doesn't also want an athletic connotation, as it might apply to a tennis (though surely not a darts) player; and this sense of author and reader engaged in a sporting contest is obviously attractive – in his middle-period novels, he's certainly playing games with the reader. Novelists have always done that: not least, Henry Fielding, so often invoked in both Kingsley's work and Martin's. Nevertheless, there are other ways in which reading a novel isn't at all like playing tennis.

It seems to me that someone who can read with pleasure (for instance) Fielding, Jane Austen, Dickens, George Eliot, Henry James, E. M. Forster, Virginia Woolf, Graham Greene, Christopher Isherwood, Iris Murdoch and Kingsley Amis has a pretty good claim to be regarded as a 'fit' reader of English fiction. What, then, is happening when he finds himself ultimately defeated by Martin Amis – though not by Ian McEwan or Alan Hollinghurst or Rose Tremain or Graham Swift? Is his fitness failing him? Or is there indeed something qualitatively different about Martin's fiction, which is a formula intended to leave open the possibility of a distinct (though to this reader elusive) kind of excellence? I don't know. All I can do is to record my painful discovery that the way in which I read English novels begins to falter with Martin's, somewhere in the region of *London Fields*.

I began this book on a dismal November morning, wandering

around South London with a notepad, searching for a catalytic clue to Kingsley's imaginative roots and finding a yellow rose defiantly flowering outside his childhood home. I end it on a sunny May evening in the Waveney valley. A short time ago, I coaxed a toad away from the danger of the garden path and into the safe cover of tall plants, among which he grappled his way like a mountaineer before turning to glance back at me, a bit reproachfully. Now, the recently arrived swifts are wheeling and screeching above my walled garden: 'Which', as Ted Hughes once pointed out, 'means the globe's still working'.[44] I think it's at least arguable that noticing such things may be a healthier, a 'fitter', way of responding to rotten times than obsessively attending to their rottenness. What matters most about the world is still there; and it will still be there when we, unimportantly, are gone.

Acknowledgements

I would like to thank the following for their help in answering questions, lending books and documents, sharing their own insights on the Amises, or contributing in other ways to my work on this book: John Amis, Martin Amis, Antony Bardsley, Julian Barnes, Bernard Bergonzi, Robert Conquest, Brian Cox, Georgina Difford, Roger Eno, Natasha Fairweather, James Fenton, Leah Fritz, John Fuller, Richard Gilmour, Jacqui Graham, Rex Harley, Elizabeth Jane Howard, Alan Hurd, Peter James, Zachary Leader, Ian McEwan, Frances Mann, Sargy Mann, Georgina Morley, Frederic Raphael, Christopher Reid, Michael Schmidt, Peter Scupham, Margaret Steward, Ann Thwaite, Anthony Thwaite, Bruno Vincent, Robert Wells.

I am grateful to the Authors' Foundation and to the Royal Literary Fund for financial assistance while I was planning, researching and writing this book.

A good deal of my reading and preparation for this and other work over the past few years has been done at Mount Pleasant, a writers' retreat in the Surrey Hills: I am greatly indebted to this excellent place and in particular to its housekeeper, Edith Stokes, and secretary, George Crawshay.

Permissions Acknowledgements

For permission to reproduce copyright material the author and publishers wish to make the following acknowledgements:

Extracts from *The Letters of Kingsley Amis* reprinted by permission of HarperCollins Publishers Ltd © The Estate of Kindsley Amis 2000; 'A Bookshop Idyll' from *A Case of Samples*, copyright © Kingsley Amis 1956; 'Lovley', 'Shitty', 'Wasted' and 'Senex' all from *Collected Poems* copyright © Kingsley Amis 1979; 'Untitled' first published in *TLS* copyright © 2004; 'Instead of an Epilogue' and other extracts from *Memoirs*, copyright © Kingsley Amis, 1991. Reprinted by kind permission of Jonathan Clowes Ltd., London, on behalf of the Literary Estate of Kingsley Amis. Extracts from *Experience* by Martin Amis, published by Jonathan Cape. Reprinted by permission of The Random House Group Ltd © Martin Amis, 2000.

All efforts have been made to contact the relevant copyright holders; if any have been inadvertently omitted the publishers will be happy to give full acknowledgement in all future editions.

Notes

1. The Angry Child

1 *Memoirs*, p. 16.

2 *Stanley and the Women*, p. 147.

3 *Letters*, p. 460.

4 *Memoirs*, p. 2.

5 Ibid.

6 *Take a Girl like You*, p. 104.

7 John Amis, *Amiscellany*, p. 19.

8 Ibid., p. 22.

9 John Amis to NP, 23 November 2006.

10 *Memoirs*, p. 4.

11 *The Old Devils*, p. 351.

12 *Memoirs*, p. 5.

13 *What Became of Jane Austen?*, p. 204.

14 Ibid., p. 206.

15 *The Riverside Villas Murder*, p. 18.

16 *Memoirs*, p. 15.

17 John Amis to NP, 23 November 2006.

18 *Memoirs*, p. 16.

19 *Take a Girl like You*, p. 56.

20 John Amis, *Amiscellany*, p. 31.

21 John Amis to NP, 23 November 2006.

22 *Memoirs*, p. 25.

23 *What Became of Jane Austen?*, p. 204.

24 *Experience*, p. 22.

25 *Memoirs*, p. 26.

26 *The Amis Collection*, p. 43.

27 *The Riverside Villas Murder*, p. 10.

28 *You Can't Do Both*, p. 44.

29 Ibid., p. 36.

30 *The Riverside Villas Murder*, p. 31.
31 *The Amis Collection*, p. 43.
32 *The Amis Collection*, pp. 43–4.
33 *Memoirs*, p. 12.
34 Ibid., p. 21.
35 Ibid., p. 27.
36 Ibid., p. 28.
37 Ibid., pp. 28–9.
38 Ibid., p. 22.
39 Eric Jacobs, *Kingsley Amis: A Biography*, p. 41.
40 *Memoirs*, p. 27.
41 *Letters*, p. 523.
42 *Memoirs*, p. 30.
43 Eric Jacobs, *Kingsley Amis: A Biography*, p. 38.
44 *Memoirs*, p. 31.
45 *Rudyard Kipling and His World*, p. 27.
46 *Memoirs*, p. 33.
47 Ibid., p. 36.
48 Graham Greene, *A Sort of Life*, p. 11.
49 *Rudyard Kipling and His World*, p. 19.
50 *The Biographer's Moustache*, p. 88.
51 *What Became of Jane Austen?*, p. 89.

2. THE JAZZ AGE

1 Philip Larkin, *Jill*, pp. 14–15.
2 Andrew Motion, *Philip Larkin: A Writer's Life*, p. 61.
3 *Experience*, p. 238.
4 *Letters*, p. 73.
5 Ibid., p. 513.
6 *Memoirs*, p. 36.
7 Ibid., p. 38.
8 Philip Larkin, *Jill*, p. 16.
9 *Memoirs*, p. 71.
10 Philip Larkin, *Jill*, p. 18.
11 *Memoirs*, p. 65.
12 Philip Larkin, *All What Jazz*, p. 3.
13 *Memoirs*, p. 52.
14 Ibid., p. 65.
15 *Letters*, p. 51.

16 Philip Larkin, *Jill*, p. 17.
17 Philip Larkin, *Jazz Writings*, p. 168.
18 Charles Fox et al., *Jazz on Record*, p. 8.
19 *The Amis Collection*, p. 224.
20 *Memoirs*, p. 53.
21 Ibid., p. 47.
22 Ibid., p. 54.
23 Philip Larkin, *Jill*, p. 12.
24 Ibid., p. 14.
25 *Memoirs*, p. 53.
26 *The Amis Collection*, p. 49.
27 *Memoirs*, p. 101.
28 *Collected Poems*, p. 147.
29 *Memoirs*, p. 54.
30 Ibid., pp. 54–5.
31 John Betjeman, *Letters*, Volume 2, p. 537.
32 *Letters*, pp. 1–5.
33 *You Can't Do Both*, p. 81.
34 Ibid., p. 84.
35 Ibid., p. 92.
36 *Memoirs*, p. 72.
37 Ibid., p. 79.
38 Ibid., p. 78.
39 *My Enemy's Enemy*, p. 53.
40 *Memoirs*, p. 88.
41 *Collected Poems*, p. 16.
42 *Memoirs*, p. 89.
43 Ibid., pp. 92–3.
44 *My Enemy's Enemy*, p. 30.
45 Ibid., p. 33.
46 *Letters*, p. 602.
47 *My Enemy's Enemy*, pp. 75–6.
48 Ibid., p. 96.
49 *Letters*, p. 10.
50 *Collected Poems*, p. 13.
51 *Memoirs*, p. 96.
52 Ibid., p. 46.
53 *Letters*, p. 97.
54 *Memoirs*, p. 73.
55 *Letters*, p. 41.
56 Andrew Motion, *Philip Larkin: A Writer's Life*, p. 116.

57 Philip Larkin, *Early Poems and Juvenilia*, pp. 108–9.

58 Andrew Motion, *Philip Larkin: A Writer's Life*, p. 131.

59 *Letters*, p. 92.

60 Philip Larkin, *Further Requirements*, p. 33.

61 *Letters*, p. 99.

62 Ibid., p. 102.

63 *Letters*, p. 104.

64 Ibid., p. 200.

65 Eric Jacobs, *Kingsley Amis: A Biography*, p. 126.

66 *Letters*, p. 253.

67 Ibid., p. 43.

68 Ibid., p. 45.

69 Ibid., p. 49.

70 Ibid., p. 43.

71 Ibid., p. 45.

72 Eric Jacobs, *Kingsley Amis: A Biography*, p. 109.

73 Humphrey Carpenter, *The Angry Young Men*, p. 12.

74 *Letters*, p. 62.

75 Ibid., p. 70.

76 Ibid., p. 88.

77 Ibid., p. 89.

78 Ibid., p. 91.

79 *Memoirs*, p. 48.

80 *Letters*, p. 935.

81 *You Can't Do Both*, p. 264.

82 *Memoirs*, p. 48.

83 Ibid., p. 103.

84 Ibid., p. 104.

85 *Letters*, p. 145.

86 Ibid., p. 149.

87 Ibid., p. 153.

88 Ibid., p. 154.

89 Ibid., pp. 154–5.

90 Ibid., p. 158.

91 Ibid., p. 159.

92 *You Can't Do Both*, p. 239.

93 Ibid., p. 241.

94 Ibid., p. 261.

95 *Letters*, p. 161.

96 *The Riverside Villas Murder*, p. 18.

97 *Letters*, p. 169.

98 Ibid., p. 193.
99 Ibid., p. 64.
100 Ibid., p. 79.
101 Ibid., p. 183.
102 Ibid., p. 195.
103 Ibid., p. 203.
104 Ibid., p. 207.
105 *Memoirs*, p. 56.
106 *Memoirs*, p. 48.
107 Ibid., p. 49.
108 *Letters*, p. 179.
109 Ibid., p. 180.
110 Ibid., p. 182.
111 Ibid., p. 208.
112 Ibid., p. 209.
113 Ibid., loc. cit.
114 *Memoirs*, p. 49.

3. JIM AND THE 1950s

1 *Letters*, p. 213.
2 *What Became of Jane Austen?*, p. 151.
3 *Memoirs*, p. 120.
4 Dylan Thomas, *Under Milk Wood*, p. 16.
5 *Letters*, p. 227.
6 Ibid., p. 223.
7 *Memoirs*, p. 127.
8 Ibid., p. 128.
9 Ibid., p. 57.
10 *Letters*, p. 231.
11 Ibid., p. 232.
12 Ibid., p. 243.
13 Ibid., p. 254.
14 Ibid., p. 262.
15 Ibid., p. 263.
16 Ibid., p. 273.
17 Ibid., p. 280.
18 Ibid., pp. 281–2.
19 Ibid., p. 288.
20 Ibid., p. 289.

21 Ibid., pp. 291–2.

22 Ibid., p. 297.

23 Ibid., p. 298.

24 Ibid., p. 299.

25 Ibid., p. 303.

26 Ibid., p. 304.

27 Ibid., p. 310.

28 Ibid., pp. 312–13.

29 Eric Jacobs, *Kingsley Amis: A Biography*, p. 155.

30 *Letters*, p. 325.

31 *Letters*, p. 327.

32 Eric Jacobs, *Kingsley Amis: A Biography*, p. 156.

33 *Letters*, p. 321.

34 Ibid., p. 434.

35 *Memoirs*, p. 43.

36 *Letters*, p. 335.

37 Ibid., p. 335.

38 John Wain, *Hurry on Down*, p. 4.

39 *Penguin New Writing*, 40, p. 127.

40 *Letters*, p. 341.

41 Ibid., p. 342.

42 Ibid., p. 361.

43 Ibid., loc. cit.

44 Ibid., p. 360.

45 Ibid., p. 364n.

46 Ibid., p. 366.

47 Ibid., p. 367n.

48 Ibid., p. 374.

49 Ibid., p. 395.

50 Ibid., p. 425.

51 Harry Ritchie, *Success Stories*, p. 72.

52 *Letters*, p. 306.

53 *Lucky Jim*, p. 63.

54 *Letters*, p. 263.

55 *The Amis Collection*, p. 3.

56 Ibid., p. 4.

57 *New Review*, 1:4, p. 22.

58 *Lucky Jim*, pp. 28–9.

59 Ibid., pp. 33–4.

60 Ibid., p. 123.

61 Walter Allen, *Tradition and Dream*, pp. 300–1.

62 *The Amis Collection*, p. 39.

63 Ibid., p. 94.

64 Ibid., p. 92.

65 Ibid., p. 59.

66 Ibid., p. 103.

67 *Letters*, p. 402.

68 *That Uncertain Feeling*, p. 13.

69 *New Review*, 1:4, p. 23.

70 Harry Ritchie, *Success Stories*, p. 69.

71 *That Uncertain Feeling*, p. 238.

72 Ibid., pp. 239–40.

73 *Memoirs*, p. 148.

74 *Letters*, p. 421.

75 *Collected Poems*, p. 80.

76 *Memoirs*, p. 149.

77 *Poems 1951*, pp. 189–98.

78 Robert Conquest to NP, 20 December 2006.

79 *Letters*, pp. 419–20.

80 Robert Conquest (ed.), *New Lines*, p. xii.

81 Ibid., p. xv.

82 Robert Conquest to NP, 20 December 2006.

83 Donald Davie, *The Poet in the Imaginary Museum*, p. 72.

84 Donald Davie, *Purity of Diction in English Verse*, p. 197.

85 *Letters*, pp. 423–4.

86 *Collected Poems*, p. 23.

87 Ibid., p. 65.

88 Ibid., pp. 56–7.

89 Ibid., p. 46.

90 Philip Larkin, *Selected Letters*, p. 244.

91 *Letters*, p. 425.

92 Ibid., p. 425n.

93 Ibid., p. 436.

94 Ibid., p. 430n.

95 Eric Jacobs, *Kingsley Amis: A Biography*, p. 208.

96 *Letters*, p. 431.

97 Ibid., p. 443.

98 Ibid., p. 433.

99 Ibid., p. 435.

100 Ibid., p. 436.

101 Ibid., p. 432.

102 Ibid., p. 439.

103 Ibid., pp. 440–1.

104 Ibid., p. 446.

105 Ibid., pp. 507–8.

106 Ibid., p. 465.

107 *Memoirs*, p. 137.

108 *Letters*, p. 477.

109 Ibid., p. 484.

110 Ibid., p. 487.

111 Ibid., p. 489.

112 Ibid., p. 490.

113 *Memoirs*, p. 169.

114 *Letters*, p. 494.

115 Ibid., p. 495.

116 Ibid., p. 496.

117 *Letters*, p. 505.

118 Ibid., p. 487.

119 *The Amis Collection*, p. 4.

120 *I Like It Here*, p. 7.

121 Christopher Isherwood, *Prater Violet*, p. 7.

122 *I Like It Here*, p. 8.

123 Ibid., p. 11.

124 Ibid., p. 23.

125 Ibid., p. 44.

126 Ibid., pp. 26–7.

127 Ibid., p. 32.

128 *Letters*, p. 521.

129 *I Like It Here*, p. 14.

130 Ibid., p. 69.

131 Ibid., p. 89.

132 Ibid., p. 167.

133 Charles Osborne, *W. H. Auden: The Life of a Poet*, p. 184.

134 *Memoirs*, p. 193.

135 *Letters*, p. 534.

136 Ibid., p. 540.

137 Ibid., p. 541.

138 *Memoirs*, pp. 193–4.

139 Ibid., p. 197.

140 *Letters*, p. 232.

141 *Memoirs*, p. 209.

142 *New Maps of Hell*, pp. 17–18.

143 *Memoirs*, p. 207.

144 Ibid., p. 198.

145 Richard Bradford, *Lucky Him*, p. 201.

146 John Fuller, *W. H. Auden: A Commentary*, pp. 292–3.

147 *Memoirs*, p. 202.

148 Ibid., loc. cit.

149 *Letters*, pp. 558–9.

150 Zachary Leader, *The Life of Kingsley Amis*, p. 397.

151 Ibid., p. 423.

152 Ibid., p. 424.

153 F. Scott Fitzgerald, *The Great Gatsby*, p. 186.

154 *Memoirs*, p. 211.

155 *Letters*, p. 574.

156 *Take a Girl like You*, pp. 68–9.

157 Ibid., pp. 244–5.

158 Ibid., p. 40.

159 Ibid., p. 206.

160 Richard Bradford, *Lucky Him*, p. 189.

161 *The Amis Collection*, p. 7.

162 *Letters*, p. 974.

163 Ibid., p. 1033.

164 Harry Ritchie, *Success Stories*, p. 74.

165 *The Amis Collection*, p. 102.

166 *Letters*, p. 467.

4. The Sea Change

1 Philip Larkin, *Selected Letters*, p. 324.

2 *Letters*, p. 603.

3 *Poetry Nation*, 2, 1974, p. 73.

4 *Memoirs*, p. 137.

5 *That Uncertain Feeling*, p. 143.

6 *Memoirs*, p. 220.

7 *The Old Devils*, p. 360.

8 *Memoirs*, p. 224.

9 *New Review*, 1:4, July 1974, p. 24.

10 *Memoirs*, p. 219.

11 Ibid., loc. cit.

12 Zachary Leader, *The Life of Kingsley Amis*, p. 466.

13 *Memoirs*, p. 217.

14 Donald Davie, *These the Companions*, p. 134.

15 Ibid., p. 136.

16 *Memoirs*, p. 221.

17 See *Letters*, pp. 865, 867.

18 Ibid., p. 403.

19 Ibid., p. 409.

20 Richard Perceval Graves, *Robert Graves and the White Goddess*, p. 351.

21 Miranda Seymour, *Robert Graves: Life on the Edge*, p. 409.

22 *Letters*, p. 606.

23 Eric Jacobs, *Kingsley Amis: A Biography*, p. 226.

24 *One Fat Englishman*, p. 168.

25 Ibid., p. 48.

26 Ibid., p. 68.

27 Ibid., pp. 119–20.

28 Ibid., p. 60.

29 Ibid., p. 145.

30 Ibid., p. 70.

31 Eric Jacobs, *Kingsley Amis: A Biography*, p. 228.

32 *Letters*, p. 603.

33 *Letters*, p. 633.

34 Ibid., p. 639.

35 *One Fat Englishman*, p. 171.

36 Eric Jacobs, *Kingsley Amis: A Biography*, p. 254.

37 Elizabeth Jane Howard, *Slipstream*, p. 338.

38 Eric Jacobs, *Kingsley Amis: A Biography*, p. 255.

39 Elspeth Huxley, *Peter Scott*, pp. 156–7.

40 *The Amis Collection*, p. 89.

41 Elizabeth Jane Howard, *Slipstream*, p. 339.

42 Ibid., pp. 339–40.

43 *Collected Poems*, p. 83.

44 *Letters*, p. 609.

45 Ibid., p. 612.

46 Ibid., p. 613.

47 *Collected Poems*, p. 101.

48 *Letters*, p. 633.

49 Ibid., p. 635.

50 Elizabeth Jane Howard, *Slipstream*, p. 346.

51 *One Fat Englishman*, pp. 135–8.

52 Elizabeth Jane Howard, *After Julius*, pp. 181–4.

53 Elizabeth Jane Howard to NP, 23 May 2007.

54 *Letters*, p. 640.

55 Philip Larkin, *Selected Letters*, p. 348.

56 Elizabeth Jane Howard, *Slipstream*, p. 349.

57 *Letters*, p. 650.

58 David Bailey and Peter Evans, *Goodbye Baby & Amen*, pp. 8–9.

59 Philip Larkin, *Collected Poems*, p. 167.

60 *Letters*, p. 655.

61 *The James Bond Dossier*, p. 9.

62 Ibid., p. 19.

63 Ibid., p. 97n.

64 *Letters*, p. 540.

65 Ibid., pp. 643–4.

66 Ibid., p. 651n.

67 *Memoirs*, p. 35.

68 *Daily Mail*, 8 March 1963.

69 *The Anti-Death League*, p. 11.

70 Ibid., p. 12.

71 Sargy Mann to NP, 17 May 2007.

72 *The Anti-Death League*, p. 46.

73 Ibid., p. 124.

74 Ibid., p. 170.

75 Ibid., p. 265.

76 *The Anti-Death League*, p. 143.

77 Ibid., pp. 97–8.

78 *The Amis Collection*, pp. 86–7.

79 *The Anti-Death League*, p. 212.

80 *Letters*, pp. 663–4.

81 Ibid., p. 677.

82 Ibid., p. 661.

83 Ibid., p. 668.

84 Ibid., p. 669.

85 Ibid., p. 673.

86 *Memoirs*, p. 279.

87 Ibid., p. 285.

88 Elizabeth Jane Howard, *Slipstream*, p. 368.

89 *Memoirs*, p. 283.

90 Elizabeth Jane Howard, *Slipstream*, p. 370.

91 *Letters*, p. 689.

92 *Memoirs*, p. 292.

93 *Letters*, p. 660.

94 *I Want It Now*, p. 29.

95 Ibid., p. 53.

96 Ibid., p. 61.

97 Ibid., p. 188.

98 Ibid., p. 58.

99 Ibid., p. 92.

100 Ibid., p. 101.

101 Ibid., p. 120.

102 Sargy Mann to NP, 17 May 2007.

103 Zachary Leader, *The Life of Kingsley Amis*, p. 606.

104 *Letters*, pp. 714–15.

105 *The Amis Collection*, p. 115.

106 *The Green Man*, p. 7.

107 Ibid., p. 10.

108 Ibid., p. 164.

109 John Amis to NP, 23 November 2006.

110 *The Green Man*, p. 77.

111 *Letters*, p. 886.

112 *On Drink*, p. 19.

113 Ibid., p. 59.

114 Ibid., p. 72.

115 Ibid., p. 12.

116 Zachary Leader, *The Life of Kingsley Amis*, p. 492.

117 Elizabeth Jane Howard, *Slipstream*, p. 376.

118 Zachary Leader, *The Life of Kingsley Amis*, p. 609.

119 *Letters*, p. 682n.

120 Ibid., p. 683.

121 Ibid., p. 706.

122 Ibid., p. 708.

123 *the Review*, 18, 1968, pp. 29–30.

124 *Letters*, p. 709.

125 *What Became of Jane Austen?*, p. 163.

126 Brian Cox to NP, 9 November 2006.

127 *The Amis Collection*, p. 263.

128 Ibid., p. 264.

129 Ibid., p. 6.

130 *New Review*, 4:1, July 1974, p. 27.

131 *Girl, 20*, p. 60.

132 *Letters*, p. 713.

133 *Girl, 20*, p. 112.

134 Ibid., p. 121.

135 Ibid., p. 157.

136 Ibid., p. 137.

137 Ibid., p. 204.

138 Ibid., p. 173.

139 Ibid., p. 90.

140 Sargy Mann to NP, 17 May 2007.

141 Elizabeth Jane Howard to NP, 23 May 2007.

142 Roy Fuller, *The Second Curtain*, pp. 22–4.

143 *Girl, 20*, p. 69.

144 *Collected Poems*, pp. 133–4.

145 Ibid., p. 123.

146 Ibid., p. 122.

147 Ibid., p. 135.

148 Zachary Leader, *The Life of Kingsley Amis*, p. 612.

149 Robert Lowell, *Collected Poems*, pp. 323–4.

150 *Times Literary Supplement*, 14 May 2004, p. 14.

151 *The Riverside Villas Murder*, pp. 222–3.

152 *Collected Poems*, p. 103.

153 *The Riverside Villas Murder*, p. 43.

154 Ibid., p. 20.

155 Ibid., p. 12.

156 Ibid., p. 54.

157 Ibid., p. 74.

158 Ibid., p. 136.

159 Ibid., p. 61.

160 Ibid., pp. 146–7.

161 Ibid., pp. 156–7.

162 *The Riverside Villas Murder*, p. 220.

163 George Orwell, *Collected Essays, Journalism and Letters*, volume 4, p. 126.

164 *Letters*, p. 757.

165 *New Review*, 1:4, July 1974, p. 21.

166 *Letters*, p. 742.

167 Ibid., p. 743.

168 Elizabeth Jane Howard, *Slipstream*, p. 375.

169 *Collected Poems*, pp. 56–7.

170 *Letters*, p. 779.

171 Ibid., p. 754.

172 *New Review*, 1:4, July 1974, p. 21.

173 *Ending Up*, p. 7.

174 Ibid., p. 55.

175 Ibid., p. 13.

176 Ibid., p. 8.

177 Elizabeth Jane Howard to NP, 23 May 2007.

178 *Ending Up*, p. 144.

179 Ibid., p. 128.

180 Ibid., p. 26.

181 *The Crime of the Century*, p. vi.

182 Ibid., p. 4.

183 Ibid., p. 48.

184 Ibid., p. 75.

185 Ibid., p. 104.

186 Ibid., p. 108.

187 *Memoirs*, p. 31.

188 Elizabeth Jane Howard, *Slipstream*, p. 405.

189 *Letters*, p. 801.

190 Ibid., p. 803.

191 Zachary Leader, *The Life of Kingsley Amis*, p. 649.

192 *Memoirs*, pp. 115–16.

193 Ibid., p. 118.

194 *Girl, 20*, p. 121.

195 *New Review*, 1:4, July 1974, p. 28.

196 *The Alteration*, p. 7.

197 *Letters*, p. 772.

198 *The Alteration*, p. 20.

199 Ibid., p. 35.

200 Ibid., p. 179.

201 *Letters*, p. 793.

202 Ibid., pp. 813–14.

203 Ibid., p. 997.

204 Kingsley's version of this epigram is 'Advice to a Story-Teller', *Collected Poems*, p. 149.

205 *Jake's Thing*, pp. 21–2.

206 *Letters*, p. 876.

207 *Jake's Thing*, p. 149.

208 Ibid., p. 94.

209 *Collected Poems*, p. 149.

210 *Jake's Thing*, p. 127.

211 *Letters*, p. 796.

212 *Collected Poems*, pp. 146–7.

213 *Jake's Thing*, p. 190.

214 Ibid., p. 211.

215 Ibid., p. 212.

216 Ibid., p. 235.

217 Ibid., p. 266.

218 Ibid., p. 286.

219 John Baxter, *A Pound of Paper*, p. 164.

220 Elizabeth Jane Howard, *Slipstream*, p. 407.

221 Ibid., p. 417.

222 *Letters*, p. 812.

223 Ibid., p. 822.

224 Ibid., p. 823.

225 Ibid., p. 867.

226 Ibid., p. 834.

227 Elizabeth Jane Howard to NP, 23 May 2007.

228 *Letters*, p. 849.

229 *Collected Poems*, p. 153.

230 *Letters*, p. 855n.

231 John Betjeman, *Letters*, volume 2, p. 538.

232 *Letters*, p. 850.

233 *Russian Hide and Seek*, p. 19.

234 Ibid., p. 180.

235 Ibid., p. 178.

236 Ibid., p. 48.

237 Ibid., p. 183.

238 Ibid., p. 169.

239 Ibid., p. 202.

240 Ibid., p. 138.

241 *Letters*, p. 893.

242 Ibid., p. 891.

243 Elizabeth Jane Howard, *Slipstream*, p. 426.

5. FOLKS THAT LIVE ON THE HILL

1 W. B. Yeats, *Collected Poems*, p. 234.

2 *Letters*, p. 905.

3 Ibid., p. 908.

4 Ibid., p. 905.

5 Ibid., p. 909.

6 Ibid., p. 924.

7 Ibid., pp. 926–7.

8 *Experience*, p. 312.

9 *Letters*, p. 930.

10 Ibid., p. 935.

11 *The Old Devils*, p. 134.

12 Eric Jacobs, *Kingsley Amis: A Biography*, p. 334.
13 Zachary Leader, *The Life of Kingsley Amis*, p. 715.
14 *Daily Telegraph*, 17 October 2005.
15 *Stanley and the Women*, p. 147.
16 Ibid., p. 57.
17 Ibid., pp. 173–4.
18 Ibid., p. 292.
19 *What Became of Jane Austen?*, p. 204.
20 *Stanley and the Women*, pp. 54–5.
21 Ibid., p. 291.
22 Ibid., p. 296.
23 Ibid., p. 299.
24 Ibid., p. 49.
25 Ibid., p. 317.
26 Ibid., p. 248.
27 Ibid., p. 164.
28 Ibid., p. 72.
29 Ibid., p. 305.
30 Ibid., p. 259.
31 Ibid., p. 183.
32 Ibid., p. 162.
33 *Letters*, p. 870.
34 *The Amis Collection*, pp. 246, 247.
35 *Letters*, p. 955.
36 Ibid., p. 980.
37 Zachary Leader, *The Life of Kingsley Amis*, p. 722.
38 *Memoirs*, p. 328.
39 *Letters*, p. 938.
40 Ibid., p. 940.
41 *Memoirs*, pp. 328–36.
42 *Letters*, p. 941.
43 Ibid., p. 943.
44 Ibid., pp. 954–5.
45 Ibid., p. 960.
46 Ibid., p. 994.
47 Ibid., pp. 979–80.
48 Ibid., p. 977.
49 Eric Jacobs, *Kingsley Amis: A Biography*, p. 335.
50 *Letters*, pp. 1001–2.
51 Eric Jacobs, *Kingsley Amis: A Biography*, p. 351.
52 *The Amis Collection*, pp. 15–16.

53 *The Old Devils*, p. 325.

54 Ibid., pp. 232–3.

55 *Letters*, pp. 1013–14.

56 Ibid., p. 1133.

57 Ibid., p. 109.

58 Ibid., p. 255.

59 *Memoirs*, p. 136.

60 *Letters*, p. 998.

61 Ibid., p. 1068.

62 *Memoirs*, p. 133.

63 *Letters*, pp. 939, 941.

64 *The Old Devils*, p. 242.

65 Zachary Leader, *The Life of Kingsley Amis*, p. 741.

66 *The Old Devils*, p. 87.

67 Ibid., p. 319.

68 Ibid., p. 321.

69 Ibid., p. 170.

70 Ibid., p. 384.

71 Zachary Leader, *The Life of Kingsley Amis*, p. 751.

72 Anthony Thwaite to NP, 28 March 2007.

73 *Letters*, p. 1075.

74 *Difficulties with Girls*, p. 168.

75 Ibid., p. 35.

76 Ibid., p. 71.

77 Ibid., p. 91.

78 Ibid., p. 112.

79 Ibid., p. 201.

80 Ibid., p. 256.

81 *Letters*, p. 1079n.

82 *Difficulties with Girls*, pp. 97–9.

83 Ibid., pp. 61, 63.

84 *The Rachel Papers*, p. 97.

85 *Letters*, p. 990.

86 Ibid., p. 1059.

87 Ibid., p. 994n.

88 *The Folks that Live on the Hill*, p. 235.

89 Ibid., p. 137.

90 Ibid., p. 37.

91 Ibid., p. 229.

92 Ibid., p. 230.

93 Zachary Leader, *The Life of Kingsley Amis*, p. 304.

94 *The Folks that Live on the Hill*, p. 28.

95 Ibid., p. 208.

96 *Letters*, p. 1092.

97 Ibid., p. 1042.

98 Ibid., p. 1082.

99 Ibid., p. 1087.

100 Ibid., p. 1102.

101 *Memoirs*, pp. 155–6.

102 *Letters*, p. 1099.

103 *Memoirs*, p. 115.

104 Ibid., p. 338.

105 Ibid., p. 18.

106 Ibid., p. 19.

107 William Cooper, *Scenes from Provincial Life*, p. 54.

108 *Memoirs*, p. 240.

109 *The Russian Girl*, p. 34.

110 Ibid., pp. 3–4.

111 Ibid., p. 53.

112 Ibid., p. 67.

113 Ibid., p. 105.

114 Ibid., p. 107.

115 Ibid., pp. 242–3.

116 Ibid., p. 295.

117 Julian Barnes to NP, 23 February 2007.

118 Zachary Leader, *The Life of Kingsley Amis*, p. 767.

119 Ibid., p. 773.

120 Ibid., p. 776.

121 Ibid., p. 756.

122 *Guardian Review*, 5 March 2005.

123 Ian McEwan to NP, 14 May 2007.

124 Julian Barnes to NP, 23 February 2007.

125 *Letters*, p. 1119.

126 Ibid., p. 1120.

127 Ibid., p. 1120n.

128 *The Amis Collection*, p. 3.

129 *Letters*, p. 156.

130 Ibid., pp. 888–9.

131 *You Can't Do Both*, p. 73.

132 Ibid., p. 160.

133 Philip Larkin, *Collected Poems*, pp. 81–2.

134 Philip Larkin, *Further Requirements*, pp. 31–2.

135 *You Can't Do Both*, p. 27.
136 Ibid., p. 65.
137 Ibid., p. 77.
138 Ibid., p. 115.
139 Ibid., p. 133.
140 Ibid., p. 135.
141 Ibid., p. 140.
142 Ibid., p. 195.
143 Ibid., p. 196.
144 Ibid., p. 261.
145 Ibid., p. 290.
146 *Letters*, p. 1024.
147 Ibid., p. 1041.
148 *The Biographer's Moustache*, p. 268.
149 Ibid., p. 267.
150 Ibid., p. 184.
151 Ibid., p. 165.
152 Ibid., p. 250.
153 Ibid., p. 29
154 Ibid., p. 2.
155 Ibid., p. 42.
156 Ibid., p. 51.
157 Ibid., p. 63.
158 Ibid., p. 250.
159 Ibid., pp. 43–4.
160 Ibid., p. 267.
161 Ibid., p. 253.
162 Ibid., p. 6.
163 Ibid., p. 74.
164 Ibid., p. 81.
165 Ibid., p. 282.
166 *Letters*, p. 1058.
167 Ibid., p. 1075.
168 Zachary Leader, *The Life of Kingsley Amis*, p. 803.
169 *Night Train*, p. 70.
170 Zachary Leader, *The Life of Kingsley Amis*, p. 801.
171 *Letters*, pp. 1133–4.
172 Zachary Leader, *The Life of Kingsley Amis*, p. 802.

6. Martin and the Mods

1 *Einstein's Monsters*, p. 7.

2 *Experience*, p. 44.

3 Ibid., p. 23.

4 *Independent*, 15 January 2007.

5 Zachary Leader, *The Life of Kingsley Amis*, p. 379.

6 *Experience*, p. 242n.

7 Zachary Leader, *The Life of Kingsley Amis*, p. 261.

8 Ibid., p. 379.

9 *Experience*, p. 104.

10 Ibid., p. 105.

11 Ibid., p. 156.

12 Ibid., pp. 157–8.

13 Ibid., p. 221.

14 Ibid., p. 221n.

15 Ibid., p. 148.

16 Zachary Leader, *The Life of Kingsley Amis*, p. 379.

17 *Memoirs*, p. 12.

18 *Experience*, pp. 134–5.

19 Ibid., p. 141.

20 Ibid., p. 61.

21 Ibid., p. 142.

22 Ibid., pp. 136–7.

23 Ibid., pp. 139–40.

24 Thom Gunn, *Collected Poems*, pp. 85–6.

25 *The Moronic Inferno*, p. ix.

26 *Experience*, p. 33.

27 Ibid., p. 59.

28 Ibid., p. 138

29 The tendentious nature of this paragraph, obvious even to its author, prompts my only long (*Experience*-like) note. Three related thoughts are rattling around here: firstly, a genuine puzzlement over whether or not the ritualised adolescent violence which used to be characteristic of boys' schools – especially, for obvious practical reasons, boarding schools – actually constitutes an essential stage of male development; secondly, a recollection of Iris Murdoch's distinction between the 'nice' and the 'good', with its clear implication that an understanding of good and evil must come from experience beyond the range of the nice and the nasty; and thirdly, a recognition that some novelists (I had in mind William

Golding, whose *Free Fall* I'd recently re-read) transform their childhood distress into fiction in ways which others don't begin to attempt.

30 *Experience*, p. 102.

31 Ibid., p. 103.

32 Ibid., p. 105.

33 Ibid., p. 101.

34 Ibid., p. 144.

35 Zachary Leader, *The Life of Kingsley Amis*, p. 531.

36 *Experience*, p. 145.

37 Zachary Leader, *The Life of Kingsley Amis*, p. 532.

38 *Experience*, p. 294.

39 *Visiting Mrs Nabokov*, p. 186.

40 *Experience*, p. 295.

41 Ibid., p. 292.

42 Zachary Leader, *The Life of Kingsley Amis*, p. 534.

43 *Success*, p. 26.

44 *Visiting Mrs Nabokov*, p. 188.

45 Ibid., loc. cit.

46 *Experience*, p. 295.

47 Ibid., p. 13.

48 Elizabeth Jane Howard, *Slipstream*, p. 356.

49 *Experience*, p. 16.

50 Elizabeth Jane Howard, *Slipstream*, p. 357.

51 Ibid., p. 358.

52 Charles Hamblett and Jane Deverson, *Generation X*, pp. 12–13.

53 Ibid., p. 22.

54 *Experience*, p. 292n.

55 Ibid., p. 168.

56 Ibid., p. 97.

57 Ibid., p. 96.

58 Ibid., p. 13.

59 Ibid., loc. cit.

60 Elizabeth Jane Howard, *Slipstream*, p. 358.

61 *Experience*, p. 14.

62 Elizabeth Jane Howard to NP, 23 May 2007.

63 *Experience*, p. 25n.

64 Ibid., pp. 9–11.

65 Ibid., p. 15.

66 Ibid., p. 21.

67 Ibid., p. 20.

68 *Experience*, p. 37.

69 Ibid., p. 55.

70 Ibid., p. 108.

71 Ibid., p. 126.

72 *Letters*, p. 1019.

73 *Experience*, p. 150.

74 Ann Thwaite (ed.), *My Oxford*, p. 211.

75 *Experience*, pp. 86–7.

76 Ann Thwaite (ed.), *My Oxford*, p. 204.

77 *Experience*, p. 39.

78 Ibid., p. 41.

79 Ibid., p. 44.

80 *Koba the Dread*, p. 6.

81 Ann Thwaite (ed.), *My Oxford*, p. 204.

82 Ibid., p. 207.

83 Elizabeth Jane Howard to NP, 23 May 2007.

84 Ann Thwaite (ed.), *My Oxford*, p. 208.

85 *Experience*, p. 26.

86 Ann Thwaite (ed.), *My Oxford*, p. 203.

87 *Experience*, p. 174.

88 Ibid., p. 155.

89 Ann Thwaite (ed.), *My Oxford*, p. 209.

90 *Experience*, p. 173.

91 Kingsley Amis to John Fuller, 20 November 1968.

92 John Fuller to NP, 6 February 2007.

93 Anthony Thwaite to NP, 28 March 2007.

94 Ann Thwaite (ed.), *My Oxford*, pp. 210–11.

95 Ibid., p. 210.

96 *Experience*, p. 193.

97 Ann Thwaite (ed.), *My Oxford*, p. 211.

98 *Experience*, p. 212.

99 Ibid., p. 231n.

100 Ann Thwaite (ed.), *My Oxford*, p. 212.

101 *Experience*, p. 231.

102 Ibid., p. 232.

103 Ibid., pp. 270–1.

104 Ann Thwaite (ed.), *My Oxford*, p. 212.

105 *Collected Poems*, p. 147.

7. RACHEL AND THE 1970s

1 *Experience*, p. 25n.
2 Ibid., pp. 22–3.
3 *The Rachel Papers*, p. 7.
4 *Experience*, p. 15.
5 Ibid., p. 264.
6 *The Rachel Papers*, p. 107.
7 Ibid., p. 9.
8 Ibid., p. 35.
9 Ibid., p. 29.
10 Ibid., p. 92.
11 David Lodge, *The Art of Fiction*, pp. 17–20.
12 *The Rachel Papers*, pp. 93–4.
13 Ibid., p. 97.
14 Ibid., pp. 46–7.
15 Ibid., p. 124.
16 Ibid., p. 163.
17 Ibid., p. 73.
18 Ibid., p. 176.
19 T. S. Eliot, *Collected Poems*, p. 17.
20 *The War Against Cliché*, p. 204.
21 *The Rachel Papers*, p. 211.
22 *Experience*, p. 93.
23 *The Rachel Papers*, p. 41.
24 Ibid., p. 49.
25 Ibid., p. 128.
26 *Experience*, p. 34n.
27 Ibid., p. 35.
28 Ibid., p. 53.
29 Ibid., p. 128.
30 *Dead Babies*, pp. 65–6.
31 Ibid., p. 181.
32 Ibid., p. 53.
33 Ibid., p. 102.
34 Ibid., p. 135.
35 Ibid., p. 137.
36 Ibid., p. 180.
37 *The War Against Cliché*, p. 300.
38 *Experience*, p. 24.

39 *The War Against Cliché*, pp. 84–5.

40 Ibid., p. 87.

41 The name also alludes jokingly to Alexander Grant, dancer and partner of Sir Frederick Ashton.

42 *The War Against Cliché*, p. 75.

43 Ibid., p. 74.

44 Frederic Raphael, *Cuts and Bruises*, p. 202.

45 *Success*, p. 88.

46 Ibid., p. 181.

47 Ibid., p. 50.

48 *Success*, p. 41.

49 Ibid., p. 122.

50 Ibid., p. 34.

51 Ibid., p. 184.

52 Ibid., p. 214.

53 Ibid., p. 53.

54 Ibid., p. 170.

55 Ibid., p. 174.

56 *Experience*, p. 331.

57 Ibid., p. 24n.

58 *Success*, p. 57.

59 *Experience*, p. 24n.

60 *Success*, p. 58.

61 Ibid., p. 147.

62 *Visiting Mrs Nabokov*, p. 187.

63 *Success*, p. 187.

64 Ann Thwaite (ed.), *My Oxford*, p. 211.

65 *Success*, p. 52.

66 *I Like It Here*, p. 32.

67 *Success*, p. 175.

68 *Lucky Jim*, p. 59.

69 *Success*, p. 67.

70 Ibid., p. 17.

71 Ibid., p. 49.

72 Ibid., p. 82.

73 Ibid., p. 25.

74 Ibid., p. 224.

75 Zachary Leader, *The Life of Kingsley Amis*, p. 647.

76 Ian McEwan to NP, 14 May 2007.

77 Craig Raine, *The Onion, Memory*, p. 2.

78 Christopher Reid, *Arcadia*, p. 25.

79 Craig Raine, *The Onion, Memory*, p. 49.

80 *Experience*, p. 250n.

81 *Letters*, p. 871.

82 Ibid., pp. 915–16.

83 *Other People*, p. 15.

84 Ibid., p. 19.

85 Ibid., p. 166.

86 Ibid., p. 27.

87 Ibid., p. 37.

88 Ibid., p. 54.

89 Ibid., p. 121.

90 Ibid., p. 111.

91 *Other People*, p. 88.

92 Ibid., p. 114.

93 Ibid., p. 40.

94 Ibid., p. 52.

95 Ibid., p. 89.

96 Ibid., p. 168.

97 Ibid., p. 160.

98 Ibid., p. 206.

99 Charles Olson, *Call Me Ishmael*, p. 15.

100 *The Moronic Inferno*, p. 1.

101 *Guardian Review*, 6 March 2004.

102 Zachary Leader (ed.), *On Modern British Fiction*, p. 3.

8. THE STATE OF ENGLAND

1 And not only of our generation: Angus Wilson, disinclined to share the same island, moved to France.

2 *The War Against Cliché*, p. 19.

3 Ibid., p. 20.

4 *Visiting Mrs Nabokov*, p. 99.

5 *The War Against Cliché*, p. 21.

6 Ibid., p. 33.

7 Ibid., p. 21.

8 Zachary Leader (ed.), *On Modern British Fiction*, p. 66.

9 Ian McEwan to NP, 14 May 2007.

10 *Granta*, 7, 1983, p. 6.

11 *Guardian Review*, 12 November 2005.

12 Philip Larkin, *Collected Poems*, p. 118.

13 *Granta*, 7, 1983, p. 8.

14 *Money*, p. 9.

15 W. H. Auden, *Collected Poems*, p. 454.

16 *Money*, p. 23. Nick Carraway is the narrator of *The Great Gatsby*; the phrase about Fielding Goodney echoes Larkin's description of 'Professor Lal' as 'My contact and my pal' in 'Naturally the Foundation will Bear the Expenses' (*Collected Poems*, p. 134); while the opacity of John Ashbery's poetry is perfectly caught by P. J. Kavanagh's brilliant index entry, 'Ashbery, John, sleep-inducing difficulty of' (P. J. Kavanagh, *A Kind of Journal*, p. 233).

17 *New Statesman*, 6 February 1976, p. 156.

18 *Experience*, p. 6n.

19 *Money*, pp. 72–3.

20 Ibid., p. 87.

21 *Money*, p. 233.

22 Ibid., p. 168.

23 Ibid., p. 222.

24 *The Moronic Inferno*, p. 84.

25 *Money*, pp. 64–5.

26 Ibid., p. 356.

27 Ibid., p. 362.

28 John Haffenden, *Novelists in Interview*, p. 5.

29 Ibid., p. 8.

30 *The Moronic Inferno*, p. 5.

31 *Money*, p. 235.

32 *The War Against Cliché*, p. 201.

33 *Money*, p. 91.

34 Ibid., p. 147.

35 Ibid., pp. 250–1.

36 Ibid., p. 309.

37 Ibid., p. 55.

38 Ibid., p. 230.

39 Ibid., p. 274.

40 *Experience*, p. 177.

41 *Money*, p. 205.

42 Ibid., p. 310.

43 *Letters*, p. 976.

44 *Experience*, p. 177n.

45 *Letters*, p. 989.

46 *Experience*, p. 99n.

47 *Letters*, pp. 1021–2.

48 *Einstein's Monsters*, p. 11.

49 *Visiting Mrs Nabokov*, p. 99.

50 *Einstein's Monsters*, p. 7.

51 Ibid., p. 8.

52 Ibid., p. 16.

53 Ibid., pp. 17–18.

54 Ibid., p. 21.

55 *Einstein's Monsters*, p. 13.

56 Ibid., p. 31.

57 Ibid., pp. 31–2.

58 Ibid., p. 32.

59 Ibid., p. 48.

60 Ibid., p. 41.

61 Ibid., p. 73.

62 Ibid., p. 75.

63 *Einstein's Monsters*, pp. 83–4.

64 Ibid., pp. 95–6.

65 Ibid., p. 97.

66 See also Adam Mars-Jones, *Venus Envy*; the relevant passages are reprinted in *The Fiction of Martin Amis*, ed. Nicolas Tredell, pp. 84–7.

67 *Einstein's Monsters*, p. 9.

68 John Haffenden, *Novelists in Interview*, p. 1.

69 Ibid., p. 2.

70 Ibid., p. 3.

71 Ibid., p. 2.

72 Sargy Mann to NP, 17 May 2007.

73 *Visiting Mrs Nabokov*, p. 84.

74 Ibid., p. 179.

75 Ibid., p. 154.

76 *The War Against Cliché*, p. 4.

77 Ibid., p. 351.

78 *Visiting Mrs Nabokov*, p. 226.

79 Ibid., pp. 227–8.

80 *London Fields*, p. 302.

81 Ibid., p. 134.

82 Ibid., pp. 134–5.

83 Ibid., p. 78.

84 Ibid., p. 162.

85 Ibid., p. 4.

86 Ibid., p. 15.

87 D. H. Lawrence, *Women in Love*, p. 36.

88 *London Fields*, p. 296.
89 Ibid., p. 16.
90 Ibid., p. 124.
91 Ibid., p. 202.
92 John Haffenden, *Novelists in Interview*, p. 5.
93 *London Fields*, p. 260.
94 Nicolas Tredell (ed.), *The Fiction of Martin Amis*, pp. 97–8.
95 *London Fields*, p. 27.
96 *London fields*, p. 3.
97 David Lodge, *The Art of Fiction*, p. 58.
98 *London Fields*, p. 251.
99 *The War Against Cliché*, p. 5.
100 *London Fields*, p. 360.
101 Ibid., p. 212.
102 Ibid., p. 171.
103 Ibid., p. 189.
104 *London Fields*, p. 187.
105 Ibid., p. 413.
106 Ibid., pp. 437–40.
107 Ibid., p. 26.
108 *Visiting Mrs Nabokov*, p. ix.
109 *Time's Arrow*, p. 14.
110 Ibid., p. 63.
111 Ibid., p. 120.
112 *Experience*, p. 158.
113 Ibid., p. 69.
114 Ibid., pp. 49–50.
115 Ibid., p. 278.
116 Ibid., p. 247.
117 Ibid., p. 249.
118 *The Information*, pp. 38–9.
119 *The War Against Cliché*, p. 113.
120 *The Information*, p. 170.
121 Ibid., p. 127.
122 Ibid., p. 475.
123 Ibid., p. 462.
124 Ibid., p. 171.
125 Ibid., p. 53.
126 Ibid., p. 119.
127 Ibid., pp. 204–5.
128 Ibid., p. 71.

129 Ibid., p. 249.

130 Ibid., p. 399.

131 Ibid., p. 45.

132 Ibid., p. 244.

133 Ibid., p. 357.

134 Ibid., p. 45.

135 Ibid., p. 298.

136 *The Moronic Inferno*, p. 145.

137 *The Information*, p. 136.

9. FATHERS AND SONS

1 *Collected Poems*, pp. 102–3.

2 *What Became of Jane Austen?*, pp. 204–11.

3 *Experience*, p. 7.

4 *Letters*, p. 1066.

5 'Open Book', BBC Radio 4, 19 November 2006.

6 *Experience*, p. 158.

7 Ibid., p. 91.

8 Ibid., p. 92.

9 Ibid., p. 93.

10 Ibid., p. 95.

11 Ibid., p. 112.

12 *Koba the Dread*, p. 20.

13 *Experience*, p. 304.

14 Ibid., p. 305.

15 H. E. Bates, *My Uncle Silas*, p. 141.

16 *Night Train*, p. 107.

17 'Open Book', BBC Radio 4, 19 November 2006.

18 *Sunday Telegraph*, 1 October 2006.

19 *Yellow Dog*, p. 229.

20 *The War Against Cliché*, p. 74.

21 John Haffenden, *Novelists in Interview*, p. 12.

22 *Koba the Dread*, p. 35.

23 *Letters*, p. 434.

24 'Open Book', BBC Radio 4, 19 November 2006.

25 *Koba the Dread*, p. 9.

26 *Letters*, p. 52.

27 Ibid., p. 296.

28 Elizabeth Jane Howard to NP, 23 May 2007.

29 *The Moronic Inferno*, p. 108.

30 *The Amis Collection*, p. 19.

31 *The War Against Cliché*, p. 29.

32 Ibid., p. 31.

33 T. S. Eliot, *Collected Poems*, p. 218.

34 *Letters*, p. 1127.

35 Elizabeth Jane Howard to NP, 23 May 2007.

36 Sargy Mann to NP, 17 May 2007.

37 *Daily Telegraph*, 3 October 2005.

38 *Visiting Mrs Nabokov*, p. 201.

39 *The War Against Cliché*, p. 165.

40 Ibid., p. 20n.

41 *Observer Review*, 10 September 2006.

42 *Independent*, 15 January 2007.

43 *Experience*, p. 117.

44 Ted Hughes, *Season Songs*, p. 27.

Select Bibliography

First editions of works by Kingsley and Martin Amis are used for quotations and references in the text except for those marked with an asterisk.

1. Books by Kingsley Amis

Bright November. Fortune Press: London, 1947.

A Frame of Mind. School of Art, University of Reading: Reading, 1953.

Lucky Jim. Gollancz: London, 1954. *Penguin: Harmondsworth, 1961.

The Fantasy Poets: 22: Kingsley Amis. Fantasy Press: Oxford, 1954.

That Uncertain Feeling. Gollancz: London, 1955.

A Case of Samples: Poems 1946–1956. Gollancz: London, 1957.

I Like It Here. Gollancz: London, 1958. *Penguin: Harmondsworth, 1968.

Take a Girl Like You. Gollancz: London, 1960.

New Maps of Hell. Gollancz: London, 1961.

My Enemy's Enemy. Gollancz: London, 1962. *Penguin: Harmondsworth, 1965.

One Fat Englishman. Gollancz: London, 1963. *Penguin: Harmondsworth, 1966.

The Egyptologists, with Robert Conquest. Cape: London, 1965. *Penguin: Harmondsworth, 1968.

The James Bond Dossier. Cape: London, 1965. *Pan: London, 1966.

The Anti-Death League. Gollancz: London, 1966. *Penguin: Harmondsworth, 1968.

A Look Round the Estate: Poems 1957–1967. Cape: London, 1967.

Colonel Sun, as Robert Markham. Cape: London, 1968. *Pan: London, 1970.

I Want It Now. Cape: London, 1968. *Panther: London, 1969.

The Green Man. Cape: London, 1969. *Vintage: London, 2004.

What Became of Jane Austen? And Other Questions. Cape: London, 1970. *Panther: London, 1972.

Girl, 20. Cape: London, 1971. *Panther: St Albans, 1973.

On Drink. Cape: London, 1972. *Panther: St Albans, 1974.

The Riverside Villas Murder. Cape: London, 1973. *Penguin: Harmondsworth, 1984.

Ending Up. Cape: London, 1974. *Penguin: Harmondsworth, 1987.

Rudyard Kipling and his World. Thames & Hudson: London, 1975.

The Alteration. Cape: London, 1976. *Vintage: London, 2004.

Jake's Thing. Hutchinson: London, 1978. *Penguin: Harmondsworth, 1979.

Collected Poems 1944–1979. Hutchinson: London, 1979.

Collected Short Stories. Hutchinson: London, 1980.

Russian Hide and Seek. Hutchinson: London, 1980. *Penguin: Harmondsworth, 1981.

Every Day Drinking. Hutchinson: London, 1983.

Stanley and the Women. Hutchinson: London, 1984. *Penguin: Harmondsworth, 1985.

How's Your Glass. Weidenfeld & Nicolson: London, 1984.

The Old Devils. Hutchinson: London, 1986. *Vintage: London, 2004.

The Crime of the Century. Dent: London, 1987. *Orion: London, 1993.

Difficulties with Girls. Hutchinson: London, 1988.

The Folks that Live on the Hill. Hutchinson: London, 1990.

The Amis Collection: Selected Non-Fiction 1954–1990. Hutchinson: London, 1990.

Memoirs. Hutchinson: London, 1991.

The Russian Girl. Hutchinson: London, 1992. *Penguin: London, 1993.

Mr Barrett's Secret and Other Stories. Hutchinson: London, 1993.

You Can't Do Both. Hutchinson: London, 1994. *Vintage: London, 2004.

The Biographer's Moustache. Flamingo: London, 1995.

The King's English. HarperCollins: London, 1997.

The Letters of Kingsley Amis, ed. Zachary Leader. HarperCollins: London, 2000.

2. BOOKS EDITED BY KINGSLEY AMIS

Spectrum: A Science Fiction Anthology (5 volumes, with Robert Conquest). Gollancz: London, 1961–5.

G. K. Chesterton: Selected Stories. Faber: London, 1972.

Poet to Poet: Tennyson. Penguin: Harmondsworth, 1973.

The Faber Popular Reciter. Faber: London, 1978.

The New Oxford Book of Light Verse. Oxford University Press: Oxford, 1978.

The Golden Age of Science Fiction. Hutchinson: London, 1981.

The Amis Anthology. Hutchinson: London, 1988.
The Amis Story Anthology. Hutchinson: London, 1992.

3. BOOKS BY MARTIN AMIS

The Rachel Papers. Cape: London, 1973. *Panther: St Albans, 1976.
Dead Babies. Cape: London, 1975. *Triad/Panther: St Albans, 1977.
Success. Cape: London, 1978.
Other People: A Mystery Story. Cape: London, 1981. *Penguin: Harmondsworth, 1982.
Invasion of the Space Invaders. Hutchinson: London, 1982.
Money: A Suicide Note. Cape: London, 1983.
The Moronic Inferno and Other Visits to America. Cape: London, 1986.
Einstein's Monsters. Cape: London, 1987.
London Fields. Cape: London, 1989.
Time's Arrow. Cape: London, 1991. *Penguin: London, 1992.
Visiting Mrs Nabokov and Other Excursions. Cape: London, 1993. *Penguin: London, 1994.
The Information. Flamingo: London, 1995.
Night Train. Cape: London, 1997. *Vintage: London, 1998.
Heavy Water and Other Stories. Cape: London, 1998. *Vintage: London, 1999.
Experience. Cape: London, 2000. *Vintage: London, 2001.
The War Against Cliché. Cape: London, 2001.
Koba the Dread. Cape: London, 2002.
Yellow Dog. Cape: London, 2003.
House of Meetings. Cape: London, 2006.

4. OTHER WORKS CITED IN THE TEXT

Allen, Walter, *Tradition and Dream*. Phoenix House: London, 1964; Pelican: Harmondsworth, 1965.
Amis, John, *Amiscellany*. Faber: London, 1985.
Auden, W. H., *Collected Poems*. Faber: London, 1976.
Bailey, David and Peter Evans, *Goodbye Baby & Amen*. Corgi: London, 1970.
Banks, Lynn Reid, *The L-Shaped Room*. Chatto & Windus: London, 1960.
Barnes, Julian, *Metroland*. Cape: London, 1980.
— *Flaubert's Parrot*. Cape: London, 1984.
Barstow, Stan, *A Kind of Loving*. Michael Joseph: London, 1960.

Bates, H. E., *My Uncle Silas*. Cape: London, 1939; Penguin: Harmondsworth, 1958.

Baxter, John, *A Pound of Paper*. Doubleday: London, 2002.

Betjeman, John, *Letters*, volume 2: *1951 to 1984*, ed. Candida Lycett Green. Methuen: London, 1995.

Bradford, Richard, *Lucky Him*. Peter Owen: London, 2001.

Braine, John, *Room at the Top*. Eyre & Spottiswood: London, 1957.

Burroughs, William, *The Wild Boys*. Calder & Boyars: London, 1972.

Carpenter, Humphrey, *The Angry Young Men*. Allen Lane: London, 2002.

Conquest, Robert (ed.), *New Lines*. Macmillan: London, 1956.

Cooper, William, *Scenes from Provincial Life*. Cape: London, 1950.

Crispin, Edmund, *The Moving Toyshop*. Gollancz: London, 1946.

— *Holy Disorders*. Gollancz: London, 1946.

Davie, Donald, *Purity of Diction in English Verse*. Routledge & Kegan Paul: London, 1967.

— *The Poet in the Imaginary Museum*. Carcanet: Manchester, 1977.

— (ed.) *The New Oxford Book of Christian Verse*. Oxford University Press: Oxford, 1981.

— *These the Companions*. Cambridge University Press: Cambridge, 1982.

Eliot, T. S., *Collected Poems*. Faber: London, 1962.

Fenton, James, *Terminal Moraine*. Secker & Warburg: London, 1972.

Fitzgerald, F. Scott, *The Great Gatsby*. 1926; Penguin: Harmondsworth, 1950.

Forster, E. M., *Collected Short Stories*. Sidgwick & Jackson: London, 1947.

Fox, Charles, Alun Morgan, Peter Gammond and Alexis Korner, *Jazz on Record: A Critical Guide*. Hutchinson: London, 1960.

Fuller, John, *W. H. Auden: A Commentary*. Faber: London, 1998.

Fuller, Roy, *The Second Curtain*. Verschoyle: London, 1953; Penguin: Harmondsworth, 1962.

Golding, William, *The Inheritors*. Faber: London, 1955.

— *Pincher Martin*. Faber: London, 1956.

— *Free Fall*. Faber: London, 1959.

— *The Spire*. Faber: London, 1964.

Graves, Richard Perceval, *Robert Graves and the White Goddess*. Weidenfeld & Nicolson: London, 1995.

Green, Jonathon, *The Dictionary of Contemporary Slang*. Pan: London, 1984.

Greene, Graham, *Brighton Rock*. Heinemann: London, 1938.

— *A Sort of Life*. Bodley Head: London, 1971; Penguin: Harmondsworth, 1972.

Gunn, Thom, *Collected Poems*. Faber: London, 1993.

Haffenden, John, *Novelists in Interview*. Methuen: London, 1985.

Hamblett, Charles, and Jane Deverson, *Generation X*. Tandem: London, 1964.

Howard, Elizabeth Jane, *The Beautiful Visit*. Cape: London, 1950.

— *The Long View*. Cape: London, 1956.

— *The Sea Change*. Cape: London, 1959.

— *After Julius*. Cape: London, 1965; Pan: London, 1995.

— *Something in Disguise*. Cape: London, 1969.

— *Odd Girl Out*. Cape: London, 1972.

— *Getting It Right*. Hamish Hamilton: London, 1982.

— *The Light Years*. Macmillan: London, 1990.

— *Marking Time*. Macmillan: London, 1992.

— *Confusion*. Macmillan: London, 1993.

— *Casting Off*. Macmillan: London, 1995.

— *Slipstream: A Memoir*. Macmillan: London, 2002.

Hughes, Ted, *Season Songs*. Faber: London, 1976.

Huxley, Elspeth, *Peter Scott: Painter and Naturalist*. Faber: London, 1993.

Isherwood, Christopher, *Mr Norris Changes Trains*. Hogarth Press: London, 1935.

— *Goodbye to Berlin*. Hogarth Press: London, 1939.

— *Prater Violet*. Methuen: London, 1946; Penguin: Harmondsworth, 1961.

— *The World in the Evening*. Methuen: London, 1954.

Jacobs, Eric, *Kingsley Amis: A Biography*. Hodder & Stoughton: London, 1995.

Kavanagh, P. J., *A Kind of Journal*. Carcanet: Manchester, 2003.

Larkin, Philip, *Jill*. Fortune Press: London, 1946; Faber: London, 1964.

— *A Girl in Winter*. Faber: London, 1947.

— *All What Jazz*. Faber: London, 1970.

— (ed.) *The Oxford Book of Twentieth-Century Verse*. Oxford University Press: London, 1973.

— *Collected Poems*, ed. Anthony Thwaite. Faber/Marvell Press: London, 1988.

— *Selected Letters*, ed. Anthony Thwaite. Faber: London, 1992.

— *Jazz Writings*, ed. Richard Palmer and John White. Continuum: London, 2001.

— *Further Requirements*, ed. Anthony Thwaite. Faber: London, 2001.

— *Trouble at Willow Gables and Other Fictions*, ed. James Booth. Faber: London, 2002.

— *Early Poems and Juvenilia*, ed. A. T. Tolley. Faber: London, 2005.

Lawrence, D. H., *Women in Love*. Secker: London, 1921; Penguin: Harmondsworth, 1960.

Leader, Zachary (ed.), *On Modern British Fiction*. Oxford University Press: Oxford, 2002.

— *The Life of Kingsley Amis*. Cape: London, 2006.

Lodge, David, *The Art of Fiction*. Secker & Warburg: London, 1992.

Lowell, Robert, *Collected Poems*. Faber: London, 2003.

McDermott, John, *Kingsley Amis: An English Moralist*. Macmillan: London, 1989.

McEwan, Ian, *First Love, Last Rites*. Cape: London, 1975.

MacInnes, Colin, *City of Spades*. MacGibbon & Kee: London, 1957.

— *Absolute Beginners*. MacGibbon & Kee: London, 1959.

— *Mr Love and Justice*. MacGibbon & Kee: London, 1960.

Mars-Jones, Adam, *Venus Envy*. Chatto & Windus: London, 1990.

Motion, Andrew, *The Pleasure Steamers*. Carcanet: Manchester, 1978.

— *Philip Larkin: A Writer's Life*. Faber: London, 1993.

Murdoch, Iris, *Under the Net*. Chatto & Windus: London, 1954.

— *The Flight from the Enchanter*. Chatto & Windus: London, 1955.

— *The Sandcastle*. Chatto & Windus: London, 1956.

— *The Bell*. Chatto & Windus: London, 1958.

— *The Nice and the Good*. Chatto & Windus: London, 1968.

— *The Black Prince*. Chatto & Windus: London, 1973.

— *The Sacred and Profane Love Machine*. Chatto & Windus: London, 1974.

Olson, Charles, *Call Me Ishmael*. Cape: London, 1967.

Orwell, George, *Collected Essays, Journalism and Letters*, volume 4 (Secker & Warburg: London, 1968; Penguin: Harmondsworth, 1970.

Osborne, Charles, *W. H. Auden: The Life of a Poet*. Eyre Methuen: London, 1980.

Powell, Anthony, *Hearing Secret Harmonies*. Heinemann: London, 1975.

Raine, Craig, *The Onion, Memory*. Oxford University Press: Oxford, 1978.

Raphael, Frederic, *Cuts and Bruises*. Carcanet: Manchester, 2006.

Reid, Christopher, *Arcadia*. Oxford University Press: Oxford, 1979.

Ritchie, Harry, *Success Stories*. Faber: London, 1988.

Sallinger, J. D., *The Catcher in the Rye*. Hamish Hamilton: London, 1951.

Salwak, Dale, *Kingsley Amis: Modern Novelist*. Harvester Wheatsheaf: Hemel Hempstead, 1992.

Seymour, Miranda, *Robert Graves: Life on the Edge*. Doubleday: London, 1995.

Sillitoe, Alan, *Saturday Night and Sunday Morning*. W. H. Allen: London, 1958.

— *The Loneliness of the Long-Distance Runner*. London: W. H. Allen, 1959.

Stewart, J. I. M., *A Staircase in Surrey*. Gollancz: London, 1974–8.

Storey, David, *This Sporting Life*. Longmans: London, 1960.

Swift, Graham, *Waterland*. Heinemann: London, 1983.

Thomas, Dylan, *Under Milk Wood*. Dent: London, 1954.

Thwaite, Ann (ed.), *My Oxford*. Robson: London, 1977.

Tredell, Nicolas (ed.), *The Fiction of Martin Amis*. Ikon: Cambridge, 2000.

Wain, John, *Hurry on Down*. Secker & Warburg: London, 1953; Penguin: Harmondsworth, 1979.

— *The Contenders*. Secker & Warburg: London, 1958.

— *Strike the Father Dead*. Macmillan: London, 1962.

— *Letters to Five Artists*. Macmillan: London, 1969.

Waugh, Evelyn, *Brideshead Revisited*. Chapman & Hall: London, 1945.

Wilson, Angus, *Anglo-Saxon Attitudes*. Secker & Warburg: London, 1956.

— *The Old Men at the Zoo*. Secker & Warburg: London, 1961.

— *Late Call*. Secker & Warburg: London, 1964.

— *As If by Magic*. Secker & Warburg: London, 1973.

Yeats, W. B., *Collected Poems*. Macmillan: London, 1950.

Index

Abbado, Claudio 209
Abbey Timbers 51, 54, 55, 62, 63
Abels, Cyrilly 115
Aeron-Thomas, John 102
Aeron-Thomas, Margaret 102
Aldiss, Brian 141
Allen, Henry 'Red' 29, 30
Allen, Walter 87–8
 Tradition and Dream 87
Allison, Drummond 127
Alvarez, A. 79, 95
Amis, Antonia (*née* Phillips) 336, 351, 360
Amis, Gladys *see* Foster, Gladys
Amis, Hilary *see* Kilmarnock, Lady
Amis, Isabel (*née* Fonseca) 352
Amis, J.J. & Co 2, 4
Amis, Jacob 349
Amis, James 3–4
Amis, John 3, 4, 8–9, 27, 166
 Amiscellany 9
Amis, Joseph James ('Dadda') 2–3, 4, 5, 216, 368
Amis, Julia ('Mater') 2–3, 4, 5

AMIS, SIR KINGSLEY WILLIAM 1–256, 257–61, 262, 264, 265–6, 268–9, 270, 271–2, 274–5, 276–9, 280, 283, 284, 286, 287, 289, 292, 293, 295, 300, 301, 304, 309, 310, 311, 313, 314, 318, 320, 322, 323, 325, 326, 336, 337, 345, 349, 352, 353, 354, 358, 359–63, 365, 366, 367, 368, 369, 370, 371–3, 375, 376
LIFE:
 army service 37–44
 birth 7
 childhood 1–22
 death 256, 353, 358

education (school) 1, 9–10, 12, 14, 15–21
education (university) 23–37, 44–5, 54–5
employment 63–6, 80, 126–31
homes 1–2, 21–2, 35, 54, 60–2, 64, 65, 66, 127–8, 162–3, 167, 182–3, 188–9, 211–14, 222–3
honours 209, 229, 235–6
marriages 56–7, 38–62, 105–07, 146, 155, 162–3, 190–1, 201–02
politics 17, 34–5, 41–2, 109, 146–7, 168–9, 220–1, 235, 245
relationships 50–6, 105, 116, 137–46
travels 99–104, 110–17, 132–3, 141–3, 145–6, 155–9, 254–6
WORKS:
 'Against Romanticism' 99
 Alteration, The 173, 191–5, 196, 340, 368
 Amis Collection, The 236, 238
 Anti-Death League, The 94, 147, 150–4, 159, 172, 177, 180, 196, 207, 208, 225, 335
 'Arts Policy, An' 220
 'Attempt at Time-Travel, An' 140–1
 'Belgian Winter' 39, 49
 'Beowulf' 49
 Biographer's Moustache, The 22, 94, 245, 250–4
 'Bobby Bailey' 18, 206
 Book of Bond, The 154
 Bright November 48–9, 205
 Case of Samples, A 98, 104
 Collected Poems 43, 49, 175, 205–06
 Colonel Sun (as Robert Markham) 155
 'Court of Inquiry' 41
 Crime of the Century, The 183, 186–8, 191

AMIS, SIR KINGSLEY WILLIAM (*cont.*)
'Crisis Song' 206
Difficulties with Girls 197, 214,
    229–31, 232, 233
Dixon and Christine 66–72, 74, 293
Ending Up 183–6, 193, 195, 207, 223
Egyptologists, The (with Robert
    Conquest) 147, 148–50
'Evans Country, The' 206
'Farewell Blues' 206
Folks that Live on the Hill, The
    233–5, 253, 324, 370, 372
Frame of Mind, A 75
Girl, 20 171–5, 177, 179, 181, 183,
    191, 200, 210, 252, 253, 310,
    372
Green Man, The 107, 163–6, 179,
    184
'Here is Where' 99
'Hours of Waking' 205
I Like It Here 68, 76, 100, 102, 104,
    107–10, 117, 118, 120, 122,
    301, 318, 370
'I Spy Strangers' 38, 41–2, 44
I Want It Now 77, 155, 159–62, 199,
    217, 252
'In Memoriam W.R.A.' 179, 358
'Instead of an Epilogue' 237–8
Jake's Thing 190, 195–201, 205, 217,
    229, 232, 233, 250, 301, 345,
    360, 372
James Bond Dossier, The 147–8
King's English, The 169, 192, 250
'Kipling at Bateman's' 205
Legacy, The 50, 67, 68, 72, 100
'Letter to Elisabeth' 43, 206
Letters 107, 359
'Lovely' 175
Lucky Jim 34, 59–60, 63, 64, 66–76,
    77, 70–87, 88, 89, 90, 91, 99,
    100, 124, 135, 156, 199, 217,
    282, 293–4, 295, 296, 302, 357,
    370, 372
'Masters' 98
'Memoir of my Father, A' 7, 358
Memoirs 11, 17, 24, 26, 35, 39, 57,
    65, 94, 104, 106, 112, 128, 157,
    203, 221, 224, 225, 236–8, 245,
    262, 359, 370, 372
My Enemy 40
'My Enemy's Enemy' 40–1
'Moral Fibre' 65, 102
New Maps of Hell 95, 113, 126

'Nothing to Fear' 95
'Ode to Me' 174, 206
Old Devils, The 5, 63, 127, 214, 215,
    223–9, 232, 246, 252, 255
On Drink 166–7
One Fat Englishman 133–7, 161, 254
'Pernicious Participation' 169–70
'Point of Logic, A' 140
'Progress' 205
'Radar' 49
'Real and Made-up People' 84, 85,
    171
'Reunion, A' 206
Riverside Villas Murder, The 7, 11,
    12, 18, 29, 153, 177–82, 183,
    186, 191, 216, 245, 248, 271,
    258
Rudyard Kipling and his World 18,
    20, 22
Russian Girl, The 94, 239–42, 332
Russian Hide and Seek 40, 94, 109,
    206–08, 220, 304
'Sacred Cows' 238, 371
'Sacred Rhino of Uganda, The' 10–11,
    193
'Senex' 197, 206
'Shitty' 175, 206
Socialism and the Intellectuals 108–09
'Something Nasty in the Bookshop'
    98, 183
'Sonnet from Orpheus' 205
Stanley and the Women 2, 215–20,
    221, 222, 223, 229, 232, 233,
    300, 332, 336, 345, 360, 372
Take a Girl like You 3, 21, 52, 64, 65,
    88, 97, 104, 117–22, 123, 124,
    133, 162, 193, 223, 228,
    229–30, 231, 241, 252, 297
That Uncertain Feeling 5, 40, 63, 64,
    65, 75, 90–4, 97, 100, 107, 123,
    134, 223, 224, 301, 326
'Their Oxford' 33, 198–9, 206
'Things tell less and less . . .' 176–7,
    196
'Voice of Authority, The' 98
'Wasted' 175–6, 206
What Became of Jane Austen? 236
'Who Else Is Rank' 42–3
'Why Lucky Jim Turned Right' 168
'Words' 205
You Can't Do Both 9, 11, 28, 35–6,
    57, 181, 216, 245–50, 271, 297,
    358

Amis, Leslie 3, 4–5, 6
Amis, Louis 336, 349

AMIS, MARTIN LOUIS 11, 24, 49, 61,
    62, 65, 107, 115, 145, 146, 162,
    182, 187, 190, 198, 205, 211, 212,
    215, 220, 222, 234, 238, 244, 251,
    255, 257–363, 366–75
LIFE:
  birth 61, 257, 337
  childhood 257–71
  education (school) 265–7, 271–2, 274
  education (university) 286–92
  employment 285, 301–02
  homes 259, 269–1, 268–9, 271–3,
      279–84, 301, 341, 349
  marriages 336, 349, 351, 352, 360
  relationships 289–92
WORKS:
  'Bujak and the Strong Force' 338–9
  'Career Move' 330
  Dead Babies 281, 292, 303–08, 309,
      312, 317, 318, 320–324, 340,
      351, 356
  Einstein's Monsters 337–41
  Experience 263, 265, 266–7, 272,
      280, 282, 285, 290, 293, 300,
      310, 314, 320, 335, 351, 353,
      358, 359, 366
  House of Meetings 362, 366
  Information, The 251, 313, 328, 341,
      348, 362, 353–7, 367
  'Introduction: Thinkability' 337–8,
      339
  Invasion of the Space Invaders 342
  Koba the Dread 361, 362, 366
  'Little Puppy That Could, The' 340–1
  London Fields 310, 313, 328, 338,
      341, 343–9, 355, 375
  Money 310, 313, 328–36, 341, 342,
      348, 349, 367
  Moronic Inferno, The 264, 324
  Night Train 255, 362, 366
  Other People 320–3, 330
  'Problem City' 329–30
  Rachel Papers, The 274, 280,
      293–301, 302, 303, 304, 311,
      312, 317, 318, 324, 356
  'State of England' 294, 313, 355
  Success 272, 280, 302, 312–17, 318,
      320, 328, 355
  'Time Disease, The' 339–40
  Time's Arrow 350–1, 362

  Visiting Mrs Nabokov 349
  War Against Cliché, The 326, 371,
      373
  Yellow Dog 335, 348, 359, 367–9,
      375

Amis, Philip Nicol 61, 62, 65, 107, 115,
    145, 146, 162, 211, 234, 257, 258,
    261, 262, 265, 268, 269–71, 275,
    277, 278, 280, 301, 342
Amis, Rosa Annie ('Peggy') 5, 6–7, 9, 10,
    13, 22, 57, 107, 249, 258
Amis, Sally Myfanwy 79, 102, 107, 146,
    182, 234–5, 256, 259, 261, 271,
    272, 273, 301, 316
Amis, William Robert 1, 3, 4, 5, 6–8, 10,
    12, 13, 15, 43, 115–16, 143,
    178–9, 216, 247–8, 249, 258, 358
Angry Young Men 88, 97, 115, 122, 123
Ardagh, Mr 279–82
Armstrong, Louis 28, 44, 78
Ashley, Mr 10
Attenborough, Richard 149
Auden, W.H. 11, 14, 18, 24, 28, 34, 36,
    80, 110–11, 114–15, 127, 281, 329
  Poems 11
  'September 1, 1939' 115
  'Shield of Achilles, The' 329
Austen, Jane 91, 113, 166, 307, 308,
    319, 321, 355, 372, 375
  Emma 91
  Mansfield Park 397, 315
  Pride and Prejudice 279
Ayer, A.J. 171

Bach, J.S. 288–9
Bailey, David Shackleton 146, 213
Balcon, Jill 182
Banks, Billy 29, 30, 180
Banks, Lynn Reid 124
  The L-Shaped Room 124
Bardwell, Hilary see Kilmarnock, Lady
Bardwell, Leonard 51, 58–9, 63, 66, 71,
    82, 86, 191, 217, 149, 258, 259,
    284
Bardwell, Margaret see Partington,
    Margaret
Bardwell, Margery 51, 249, 258
Bardwell, William 59, 117
Barker, Pat 327
Barley, J.C. ('Billy') 102–03
Barnes, Julian 163, 220, 243–4, 309,
    318, 327, 342, 352–3, 373

Barnes, Julian (*cont.*)
   Flaubert's Parrot 253, 244
   Metroland 309
Barr, Miss 10
Barstow, Stan 124, 125
   Kind of Loving, A 124
Bartley, James ('Jo') 64, 190
Basie, William ('Count') 29, 224
Basil, Connie 213
Bates, H.E. 363
Bateson, F.W. 54–5
Baxter, John 201
BBC Radio Three 232
BBC Third Programme 16, 73
Beatles 172, 231, 286, 288, 297, 304
   'Day in the Life, A' 298
   'Hey, Jude' 285
   'Lovely Rita' 298
   Sergeant Pepper's Lonely Hearts Club Band 231, 297
   'When I'm Sixty-Four' 298
Bechet, Sidney 29
Bellow, Saul 238, 324, 333, 371
Benchley, Robert 255
Benn, Anthony Wedgwood 192
Bennett, Arnold 40, 230, 326
Beowulf 169
Berigan, Bunny 53
Berkhamsted 21–2, 24, 54, 58, 107, 214
Bertolelli's 189, 318
Bethell, Mr 284
Betjeman, John 34, 198, 206, 222
Bill, The 232
Bishopgore Grammar School 265
Black Papers on Education 169–70, 266
Blackmur, R.P. 112, 113, 116
Blackstone, Bernard 63
Blair, Tony 338
Blunden, Edmund 289
Blunden, George 36, 277
Bly, Robert 347
Bone, Gavin 32
Booker, Hylan 336
Borges, Jorge Luis 309
Bottrall, Ronald 69
Bowen, Elizabeth 115
Bowman, Ruth 52, 60
Boyars, Arthur 60, 79
Boyd, Jaime 212, 302
Boyd, William 222, 327
Bradbury, Malcolm 59
   Eating People Is Wrong 59
Bradford, Richard 26, 114

Lucky Him 26
Bragg, Melvyn 225
Braine, John 65, 77, 88, 90, 124, 150, 189, 192, 194, 237, 258
   Room at the Top 77, 88, 124
Bridge, Ann 15
Britten, Benjamin 165–6
   Peter Grimes 115
Brown, Cleo 29, 51
Brown, Mervyn 26, 44
Brown, Philip 26
Buford, Bill 327, 342
   Among the Thugs 342
Burgess, Anthony 354
Burney, Fanny 315
Burns, Dolly 155
Burroughs, William 115, 307–08, 309, 359
   Wild Boys, The 307
Bursa Kebab House 190, 318
Burton, Sybil 272
Butterfield, Herbert 126

Camberwell School of Art 162, 280
Cambridge 21, 126–31, 133, 136, 140, 142, 143, 144, 147, 165, 168, 185, 190, 265–9
   Churchill College 128, 131
   Darwin College 126
   Gonville and Caius College 129, 131
   Peterhouse 126, 127, 128, 130, 140, 143, 265
   Queens' College 130
   St Catharine's College 21
Cambridgeshire High School for Boys 266–7
Cape, Jonathan 140, 149, 154, 155, 159, 205, 293
Carey, John 283
Carmichael, Hoagy 52
Carpenter, Humphrey 52
Carroll, Lewis 37, 323, 330
   Through the Looking-Glass 202
Case, Virgil A. 115–16
Caton, R.A. 47–9, 152
Causley, Charles 79
Cecil, Lord David 33, 54–5, 67, 197
Charteris, Hugo 79
Chekov, Anton 319
Cheltenham Literary Festival 137–8, 139
Chesterton, G.K. 12, 13
   Man Who Was Thursday, The 12, 13
   Napoleon of Notting Hill, The 12

Christie, Agatha 188
Churchill, Sir Winston 314
City of London School 1, 4, 14, 15–21, 25, 178, 271
Clough, Corporal 40
Clowes, Jonathan 205, 236, 250
Cobb, John 190–1
Coburn, James 273
Coburn, Lisa 273
Cohen, Richard 250
Coleridge, Samuel Taylor 24, 176
    'Frost at Midnight' 176
Coles, E. Frank 42, 54, 55
Collins, Alan 115
Colman's Mustard 1, 3
Connolly, Cyril 54, 114
Conquest, Robert 9, 35, 69, 79, 94–5, 96, 101, 105, 109, 132, 140, 143, 147, 158, 169, 171, 189, 190, 195, 198, 201, 205, 211, 214, 221, 222, 223, 229, 232, 234, 237, 250, 254, 271, 301, 320, 327, 336, 363, 366
    Egyptologists, The (with Kingsley Amis) 147, 148–50
    Great Terror, The 366
    Reflections on Landscapes 95
Cooper, William 74, 90, 123, 239, 296
    Scenes from Married Life 90
    Scenes from Provincial Life 74, 88, 90, 239, 296
Corke, Hilary 79
Coronation Street 232
Cox, C.B. 169
Crabbe, George 114–15, 315
Craig, Tessa 182
Crewe, Quentin 145
Crispin, Edmund see also Montgomery, Bruce 27, 45–6
    Case of the Gilded Fly, The 45
    Holy Disorders 46
    Moving Toyshop, The 46
Critical Quarterly 169
Critical Survey 169
Cronin, A.J. 108
Crosland, Anthony 121, 134, 156
Czechoslovakia 155, 156

Daily Express 104, 142–3, 145, 221
Daily Mirror 222
Daily Sport 367
Daily Telegraph 30, 192
Daily Telegraph Magazine 166
Dale, F.R. 16, 21

Davenport, John 101
Davie, Donald 9, 18, 21, 79, 80, 96, 127, 129–31, 169, 203, 204, 213
    Purity of Diction in English Verse 96–7
    These the Companions 130, 131
    'Varsity Match, The' 127
Davie, Doreen 131
Davies, Andrew 230
Davies, Laing and Dick 274, 294
Davis, Miles 31
Day-Lewis, Cecil 48, 163, 182–3, 184
    'At Lemmons' 182
Day-Lewis, Daniel 182, 189
Day-Lewis, Tamasin 182
de la Mare, Walter 175
Deeping, Warwick 50
Deighton, Len 154, 158
de Palma, Brian 331
Deller, Keith 343
Deverson, Jane 276
Dickens, Charles 252, 314, 321, 346–7, 368, 375
    Bleak House 252
    Great Expectations 252
Dodds, Johnny 78
Donne, John 76, 283
Doubleday 74
Douglas-Henry, Jim 138, 144, 146
Douglas-Home, Sir Alec 146–7
Douglas-Smith, A.E. 17
Drake, Charlie 305
Dryden, John 147
du Cann, Edward 26, 29, 34
Dumas, Alexandre (père et fils) 257
Duncan, Edgar 157
Duncan, Ivar-Lou 157
Durham, Jim 190, 192, 361
Durham, Nita 192
Dylan, Bob 336
Dyment, Clifford 68
Dyson, A.E. 169

East Anglia, University of 126
Eliot, George 375
    Middlemarch 281
Eliot, T.S. 80, 369, 371
    'The Love Song of J. Alfred Prufrock' 299
Ellingham, Reverend C.J. 14, 19, 20
Ellington, Edward Kennedy ('Duke') 8, 29, 224
Empson, William 14, 76, 80

Encounter 79, 168, 169, 279, 308
Enright, D.J. 95, 96
Esquire 114, 337, 308
Essex, University of 169, 213
Evans, Gil 224
Evans, J.R. 73
Evans, Peter 146
Ewart, Gavin 48, 235
Exeter, University of 283
Eynsham 60–2, 142

Faber Popular Reciter, The 203
Fairlie, Henry 105–06, 107, 173
Fame, Georgie 277
Faulkner, William 148
Feldman, Gene 115
Feldman, Victor 31
Felton, Anton 163
Fenton, James 187, 309, 318
    Terminal Moraine 309
Fielding, Henry 110, 118, 148, 184, 194,
        329, 367, 375
    Joseph Andrews 367
    Tom Jones 367
First Reading 73, 75, 78
Fischer, Tibor 366–7
Fitzgerald, F. Scott 329
    Great Gatsby, The 116
Fleming, Ian 148, 158
Fletcher, Iain 79
Fonseca, Isabel *see* Amis, Isabel
Forster, E.M. 123, 158, 324, 339, 348,
        375
    Howards End 123
    'Machine Stops, The' 339
Fortune Anthology 48
Fortune Press 47–9, 68
Foster, Bobbie 5
Foster, Gladys (*née* Amis) 5, 115
Foster, Ralph 5, 115
Foster, Rosemary 5
Fowles, John 327
Fraser, G.S. 78, 79
Fraser, Russell 156, 158
Friends' School, Saffron Walden 266,
        271, 274
Frost, Robert 238
Frostrup, Mariella 360
Fulham Road 146, 271–3, 274, 316
Fuller, John 127, 257, 289
Fuller, Roy 38, 39, 48, 68, 69, 174, 239,
        252, 257, 289

Second Curtain, The 174
Fussell, Paul 372

Gale, George 104, 105, 109, 126, 31,
        143, 145, 222, 270, 272
Garcia, Eva 259, 261, 268–9
Garcia, Joe 259, 261, 268
Gardnor House, Hampstead 189, 202,
        209, 211, 212, 213, 372
Garrick Club 190, 201, 209, 211, 220,
        232, 236, 243, 244, 256
Gartenberg, Max 115
Gary, Romain 137
Gee, Maggie 345
Generation X 276–7
Gibbs, Mrs 279
Gilbert and Sullivan 8
Gillan, Patricia 190–1, 196
Gillespie, John Birks ('Dizzy') 31
Ginsberg, Allen 115
Golding, William 79, 120, 124, 125, 150,
        158, 309
    Free Fall 124
    Inheritors, The 124
    Pincher Martin 124
    Spire, The 150
Gollancz, Diana 45, 72
Gollancz, Livia 154
Gollancz, Victor 12, 45, 50, 72, 73–4,
        75, 91, 98, 107, 109, 117, 125,
        143, 149, 154, 159, 252, 352
Graham, W.S. 79
Granta 308, 327, 328
Graves, Richard Perceval 132
Graves, Robert 130, 132–3, 140, 145,
        147, 266, 285
Greece 155, 170, 286
Green, Jonathon 330
Greene, Graham 21–2, 67, 108, 149,
        158, 163, 264, 375
    Brighton Rock 163
    Heart of the Matter, The 281
Guardian 243
Gunn, Thom 78, 79, 96, 97, 99, 127, 264
    'Corridor, The' 264
    'Elvis Presley' 78
    'On the Move' 99

Hadley Common *see* Lemmons
Haffenden, John 341, 368
Haley, Bill 123
Hall, Julian 34, 47, 49
    Senior Commoner, The 34, 47, 49

Hamblett, Charles 276
Hamilton, Charles 11
Hamilton, Ian 127, 168
HarperCollins 250, 254, 353
Harrison, Harry 141
Hartley, Anthony 80
Harwell *see* Abbey Timbers
Hawkey, Raymond 154
Haydn, Joseph 8
Hayes, John 359
Healey, Denis 290
Healey, Tim 290
Heath, Edward 168
Heinz, Drue 227
Heller, Joseph 137
Henderson, Rob 278, 279, 285–6, 292, 295, 301
Hersey, John 345
Hesse, Hermann 309, 347
Hewer, Rosalind 289–91
Hinde, Thomas 79
Hines, Earl 78
Hitchcock, Alfred 270
Hitchens, Christopher 171, 301, 318
Hoff, Harry *see* Cooper, William
Holbourne, David 276
Holiday, Billie 29
Hollinghurst, Alan 375
Holloway, John 80, 95–6, 130
Homer 16
Hood, Christopher 223
  Other Side of the Mountain, The 223
Hough, Graham 126
Housman, A.E. 14, 236
Howard, Anthony 220
Howard, Colin 142, 144, 145, 153, 155, 165, 174, 182, 183, 189, 272, 273, 274, 278, 280, 284, 286, 302
Howard, David 138
Howard, Elizabeth Jane 137–46, 153, 154, 155, 156–7, 159, 162–3, 167, 171, 172, 174, 181, 182, 182, 184, 185, 189, 192, 198, 202, 205, 213–14, 216, 217, 220, 221, 227–8, 230, 234, 237, 266, 269, 270, 272, 273, 274–5, 278, 279, 280, 286, 287, 292, 307, 310, 313, 314, 360, 368, 370, 372, 373
  After Julius 139, 142
  Beautiful Visit, The 138
  Casting Off 214
  Confusion 214
  Getting It Right 183, 205, 221
  Light Years, The 214
  Long View, The 138
  Marking Time 214
  Odd Girl Out 183
  Sea Change, The 138
  Slipstream 203
Howard, Katharine (*née* Somervell) 138, 182, 184
Hughes, Noel 25
Hughes, Ted 376
Hutchinson 205, 250
Huxley, Aldous 11, 13–14
  Point Counter Point 13
Huxley, Elspeth 138

Iles, Norman 23, 25–6, 32
Independent 374
Isherwood, Christopher 24, 34, 36, 39, 67, 100, 107, 110, 158, 296, 370, 375
  'Berlin Diary' 39, 370
  Prater Violet 107
  World in the Evening, The 370
Ishiguro, Kazuo 327

Jacobs, Eric 9, 20, 52, 95, 136, 222, 244–5, 256
James, Clive 85, 171, 182, 190, 220, 301, 318
James, Henry 13, 110, 112–13, 148, 375
  Ambassadors, The 110
  'Aspern Papers, The' 112
  Bostonians, The 113
James, Norah C. 15
Jastrow, Robert 338
Jazz on Record 30
Jefferies, Richard 340
  After London: Wild England 340
Jennings, Elizabeth 79, 96, 124
John o'London's 13
Johnson, Paul 168
Jones, Monica 59, 71, 86, 126
Joseph, Michael 68
Joyce, James 50, 311
  Ulysses 311

Kafka, Franz 281
  Trial, The 281
Kavanagh, Pat 243–4, 293, 352–3
Keats, John 64, 147
Keeler, Christine 146
Keeley, Mary 155, 159
Keeley, Mike 155, 159, 176

Kempston, Murray 112
Kennedy, John F. 145, 270
Kentish Town 214, 222
Kermode, Frank 221
Kerouac, Jack 115, 309
Kettle, Arnold 122
Keyes, Sidney 127
Kilmarnock, Alastair Boyd, Lord 212–13,
    222, 243
Kilmarnock, Hilary, Lady (formerly
    Hilary Amis née Bardwell) 50–4,
    55–7, 58–9, 60–2, 64–6, 78, 91,
    99, 105–07, 114, 116, 119, 122,
    125, 133, 137–8, 140, 141, 143,
    144, 145, 146, 153, 176, 212–13,
    219, 222, 233, 243, 255, 257–61,
    264, 268, 269–70, 271–2, 274,
    278, 287, 294, 302, 303, 352
Kilmartin, Terence 190, 220
King, Francis 79
King-Hall, Stephen 109
    Defence in the Nuclear Age 109
Kinks, The 277
Kinsley, James 80, 105, 117
Kintisch, Erik 50
Kipling, Rudyard 18, 22
Kirkup, James 79
Köchel, Ludwig 193

Lane, Homer 36
Lang, Eddie 52
Larkin at Sixty 237
Larkin, Philip 2, 9, 14, 18, 23–34, 37,
    43, 44, 46–8, 49, 51, 52, 55, 56–7,
    59–60, 61, 66–71, 72–3, 75, 77,
    78, 79, 80, 82, 84, 86, 91, 96, 99,
    100, 102, 105, 106, 107, 108, 111,
    116, 117, 124, 125, 126, 127, 129,
    132, 136, 143, 144, 146, 162–3,
    166, 167, 169, 174, 177, 182–3,
    190, 197, 198, 201, 203–04, 205,
    206, 211, 212, 220, 221, 222,
    223–4, 229, 233, 234, 237, 242,
    244, 246–7, 258, 287, 302, 322,
    325, 328, 329, 336, 353, 370, 372,
    374
    All What Jazz 28, 224
    'Annus Mirabilis' 117, 146
    'Born Yesterday' 80
    'Church Going' 99
    'Dockery and Son' 27, 224
    Early Poems and Juvenilia 45
    Girl in Winter, A 34, 47, 66

    'I Remember, I Remember' 246–7
    Jill 23, 26, 47, 66, 287
    Michaelmas Term at St Bride's 34
    North Ship, The 47, 49
    'Old Fools, The' 166, 224
    'Self's the Man' 328
    Trouble at Willow Gables 34, 45
    'View, The' 174
Lawrence, D.H. 11, 13, 28, 84, 158,
    245–7, 281
    Lady Chatterley's Lover 13
    Sons and Lovers 246–7
    Women in Love 344
Lawrence, T.E. 14
    Seven Pillars of Wisdom 14
Leader, Zachary 95, 116, 159, 176, 190,
    220, 234, 258, 273
    Life of Kingsley Amis, The 95
Leavis, F.R. 126, 347
Le Carré, John 158
Lee, Laurie 101, 104
    Rose for Winter, A 101
Lehmann, John 69, 73, 74, 79
Leishman, J.B. 60
Lemmons, Hadley Common 162–3, 167,
    172, 182, 184, 188–9, 202, 209,
    286, 302, 313, 369
Lenin, Vladimir Ilyich 35
Lerner, Laurence 95–6
Levi, Primo 360
    If This Is a Man 360
Levin, Bernard 189
Lewis, C.S. 33, 64
Lichtenstein, Gene 114
Lindsay, Derek 79
Listener 203, 308
Lloyd, John Russell 35
Lodge, David 296, 346
    Art of Fiction, The 296
London Magazine 79, 279, 308
Longman, Mark 50
Longmans, Green 50
Lorre, Peter 178
Lowell, Robert 176
    'Old Flame, The' 176
Lucas, Dora 6
Lucas, George (father) 5–6
Lucas, George (son) 6
Lucas, Jemima (née Sweetland) 5–6
Lyttelton, Humphrey 106

McAndrew, Jean 116
McAndrew, John 116

McAndrew, Megan 116
McCullers, Carson 137
McDermott, John 195, 236
    Kingsley Amis: An English Moralist
        236
Macdonald, Dwight 113
McEwan, Ian 222, 244, 309, 318–19,
        317, 375
    First Love, Last Rites 309
McIlvanney, Hugh 220
MacInnes, Colin 123
    Absolute Beginners 123
    City of Spades 123
    Mr Love and Justice 123
MacInnes, Mairi 79, 95
Mackendrick, Alexander 273
    High Wind in Jamaica, A 273–4
Mackness, Arthur 6
MacLachlan, Donald 137
Maclean, Alan 97
Maclaren-Ross, Julian 82
McLuhan, Marshall 113
Macmillan 96, 97
Macmillan, Harold 146
Macnaughton-Smith, Michael 26
McNeil, Helen 345
Magnet 11, 14
Mahler, Gustave 188, 232
Maida Vale 143, 144, 145, 155, 162,
        171, 172, 273, 274, 280
Mailer, Norman 238
Majorca 130, 132–3, 141, 142, 145–6,
        149, 266, 269, 274, 285
Mandrake 60
Mann, Frances 162
Mann, Sargy 151, 162, 173–4, 182, 183,
        189, 280, 286, 342, 372
Marlborough College 19–20, 27, 35, 99,
        341
Márquez, Gabriel García 309
Mars-Jones, Adam 327
Marsh, Mr 14
Marston, Doreen 50, 67
Martial 195
Martians 289, 309, 319–20
Marx, Karl 35
Maschler, Tom 140, 149, 154, 159, 163,
        205, 293, 352
Maugham, W. Somerset 5, 11, 82–3, 85,
        99, 101, 302, 303
Maxwell, Robert 38, 192, 222
Mayne, Peter 101
    Narrow Smile, The 101

Melville, Herman 324
    Moby-Dick 324
Menippus 305
Michie, James 60, 86
Mingo, Billy 18, 35
Milton, John 169
Mods and Rockers 268, 275–7, 282, 287,
        297, 298, 305
Monk, Theolonious 31
Monroe, Marilyn 265
Montagu, Ashley 113, 115
Montgomery, Bruce *see also* Crispin,
        Edmund 27–8, 37, 45–7, 72, 167,
        180, 237, 258
Moody Blues 277
Moore, Henry 114
Moore, W.G. 46
Moreschi, Alessandro 191
Morris, Hilary 52
Morris, Jean 79
Morrison, Blake 220
Motion, Andrew 23, 46, 309, 373
    Philip Larkin: A Writer's Life 373
    Pleasure Steamers, The 309
Movement, The 76, 78–9, 06, 97, 112,
        115, 122, 130, 309
Mozart, Wolfgang Amadeus 8, 84–5,
        174, 179, 192, 209
Murdoch, Iris 34, 79, 88–9, 90, 92, 120,
        124, 125, 139, 150, 158, 240, 307,
        309–10, 375
    Bell, The 124
    Black Prince, The 310
    Flight from the Enchanter, The 124,
        240
    Italian Girl, The 240
    Sacred and Profane Love Machine, The
        310
    Sandcastle, The 92, 124
    Under the Net 88–9, 124, 150
Murdoch, Rupert 254
Murphy, Patsy 99
My Oxford 198, 285, 288, 290, 300

Nabokov, Vladimir 238, 336, 371
Nashville 155–9, 161, 176, 204, 280, 283
New Lines 9, 79, 80, 95–9, 104, 130,
        327
*New Oxford Book of Christian Verse,
    The* 204
New Oxford Book of Light Verse, The
        198, 203, 204
New Poems 1952 68–9

New Review 308, 319
New Soundings 73
New Statesman 78, 87, 91, 168, 187, 190, 308, 311, 318, 354
New York Post 115
Nichols, Red 51
Nicholson, Geoff 105, 220, 235
Nicholson, Mavis 105, 235, 272
Norbury 1–2, 3, 9, 18, 139, 148, 202, 215–16, 243–3, 360
Norbury College 10, 12

Oakes, Philip 95
Oakeshott, Michael 126
O'Brien, Flann 34, 50
    At Swim-Two-Birds 50, 100
Observer 159, 190, 220, 307, 333, 336, 342, 343, 374
O'Connor, William Van 16
Olivier, Laurence 157, 279
Olson, Charles 324
    Call Me Ishmael 324
Orwell, George 181, 335
    Animal Farm 330
    'Decline of the English Murder' 181
Osborne, John 88
Owen, Peter 97
Owen, Wilfred 306
Oxford 21, 23–37, 38, 44–6, 50–7, 58, 64, 72, 75, 86, 87, 118, 127, 129, 132, 140, 162, 165, 168, 190, 192, 195, 197–9, 217, 224, 239, 277, 280, 281, 282, 283–4, 286–92, 293, 294, 296, 300, 309, 316
    Balliol College 25, 290
    Christ Church 37, 129
    Corpus Christi College 54
    Exeter College 161, 283
    Magdalen College 37
    Merton College 72
    New College 54–5
    Ruskin School of Drawing and Fine Art 51
    St Hilda's College 291
    St John's College 21, 23–8, 29, 32, 34, 40, 44, 46, 54, 283
Oxford Book of Twentieth-Century Verse 203
Oxford Poetry 60
Oxford University Press 203

Packard, Vance 113
Parker, Charlie 31

Parkes, Graham 26, 27, 29, 44
Partington, David 262–3, 303, 345
Partington, Lucy 262, 303, 345, 351–2
Partington, Margaret (*née* Bardwell) 262–3, 303, 345
Partington, Marian 262, 316, 345
Partington, Mark 262, 345
Partington, Roger 61, 262
Pears, Peter 165
Penguin New Writing 76
Phillips, Antonia *see* Amis, Antonia
Plekhanov, Georgiy Valentinovich 35
PN Review 308
Poets of the 1950s 95
Pope, Alexander 33
Porter, Peter 190
Portugal 99, 100, 102–04, 108, 109, 133, 324
Postgate, John 60
Pound, Ezra 281, 369
Powell, Anthony 34, 67, 117, 158, 162, 189, 190, 252, 289, 310, 368
    Hearing Secret Harmonies 310
Powell, Dulcie (*née* Lloyd) 364
Powell, Enoch 168
Powell, Jim 358, 363–6
Powell, Violet 117, 162
Presley, Elvis 78, 123, 265
Price, Hugh 55, 57
Primrose Hill 222, 232, 233, 256, 362
Prince, Jack 255
Prince Philip, Duke of Edinburgh 221
Princeton 95, 111–17, 121, 126, 133, 136, 155, 156, 158, 264–5, 295, 371
Profumo, John 146
Protest 115
Punch 107, 132
Pym, Barbara 311

Queen 188
Queen Elizabeth II 79
Quennell, Peter 233
Quinn, Anthony 273

Radio Caroline 268, 277
Radio London 277
Raine, Craig 309, 318, 319–20
    Onion, Memory, The 309
    'Return Ticket' 319
Raphael, Frederic 311
Raybould, Jane 189
Raybould, Terry 189

Raymond, John 79
Read, Piers Paul 318
Records and Recording 191
Rees, Goronwy 168
Reid, Christopher 289, 309, 318, 319
    Arcadia 309
Reid, Sergeant-Major 37
Render, Helen 303
Review, the 168
Reynolds, Mack 159
Richard, Ivor 156
Richards, Frank *see* Hamilton, Charles
Richardson, Samuel 118
Richenberg, Leonard 17, 19, 20, 217
Ritchie, Harry 83, 92
    Success Stories 83
Robson, W.W. 79
Rollins, Sonny 114
Ronda 213, 302–03
Rose, Mark 116
Rose, Saul 20
Ross, Alan 27–8, 46, 69
Rubinstein, Hilary 72, 73–4, 91, 98, 99,
    109, 149
Rukeyser, William 136, 143, 147
Rush, Michael 255
Rush, Virginia 255
Rushdie, Salman 327
Russel, Nick 26, 55, 56–7
Russell, Charles Ellsworth ('Pee Wee') 29,
    30, 31

St Hilda's School 9–10
Saki (H.H. Munro) 135
Salinger, J.D. 238, 296
    Catcher in the Rye, The 296
Salwak, Dale 183, 245
Sartre, Jean-Paul 192
Saucy, Tupper 161, 295
Scott, George 79
Scott, J.D. 74, 78, 80
Scott, Nicola 145, 189
Scott, Paul 79
Scott, Peter 138
Scott-Kilvert, Iain 79
Schubert, Franz 8
Seale, Delilah 352
Seale, Lamorna 352
Seven, The 27
Shakespeare, William 17, 144, 149, 192,
    321, 351
    Antony and Cleopatra 149, 244
    Hamlet 282, 299–300, 358

    Merchant of Venice, The 10, 194
    Othello 335
    Romeo and Juliet 207
    Tempest, The 144
Shearing, George 31
Shilton 291–2, 304
Show 132
Sibelius, Jean 8
Sillitoe, Alan 65, 77, 88, 90, 124, 125,
    368
    *Loneliness of the Long-Distance
        Runner, The* 124
    Saturday Night and Sunday Morning
        65, 77, 124
Simpson, Elisabeth 43, 51
Sims, David 64, 65, 102, 190
Sinatra, Frank 108
Sinclair, Andrew 131
Sinclair, Clive 222
Sir Gawain and the Green Knight 186
Sir Walter St John's School, Battersea
    271–2, 274
Sitwell, Edith 80–2
Sleight, Richard 79
Small Faces 277
Smith, David Nicol 33
Smith, Sydney Goodsir 79
Smythe, Willie 64
Snow, C.P. 74, 311
Soames, Christopher 314
Soames, Emma 314
Somervell, Sir Arthur 138
Soref, Harold 171
South Wales Echo 260
Spectator 74, 78, 80–1, 89, 104, 105,
    109, 124, 279, 308, 354
Spectrum 95, 147
Spender, Stephen 79, 123, 127
Spenser, Edmund 169
Stallworthy, Jon 203
Steele, Tommy 123
Steiner, George 131, 185, 190
Sterne, Lawrence 100
    Tristram Shandy 100
Stewart, Desmond 79
Stewart, J.I.M. 163, 198
    Staircase in Surrey, A 198
Storey, David 124, 125, 150, 368
    This Sporting Life 65, 124
Sullivan, Walter 157, 237
Summer, Montagu 68
Sunday Telegraph 137, 168
Sunday Times 82, 183

Sussex Tutors 162, 279–82, 284
Sutton, James Ballard 28, 47
Swansea 5, 60, 63–6, 75, 80, 100, 102,
    103, 105, 107, 113, 116, 117, 127,
    128, 130, 140, 142, 158, 176, 190,
    193, 201, 224, 232, 255, 257, 259,
    265, 271, 294, 303
Swift, Graham 222, 327, 375
    Waterland 327
Swift, Jonathan 33, 317
Swinburne, Algernon Charles 135
Symons, Julian 48
Szamuely, Tibor 361

Taylor, Elizabeth 139
Tennyson, Alfred, Lord 31, 129
Thatcher, Margaret, Lady 209, 220, 315,
    325–6, 333, 349, 373
Thomas, Dylan 48, 66, 92, 224–5, 226,
    237, 246
    Adventures in the Skin Trade 225
    'Story, A' 225
    Under Milk Wood 64, 225
Thomas, Eve 201, 223, 255
Thomas, Stuart 201, 223, 225, 255, 271
Thomas, W.D. 64, 80, 86
Thwaite, Ann 198, 290
Thwaite, Anthony 229, 237, 289–90,
    311, 360
Time and Tide 13
Times Literary Supplement 76, 122, 279,
    293, 301–02
Times, The 168
Today 245
Tolkien, J.R.R. 33
Tomalin, Claire 311
Tosswill, Christopher 53, 55, 119
Toynbee, Philip 237
Traherne, Thomas 129
Trelford, Donald 220, 336
Tremain, Rose 327, 375
Tremlett, George 224
Trotsky, Leon 369
    History of the Russian Revolution 369
Truth 79
Tuohy, Frank 79
Tyrrell, Harold 103

'Uncle Tommy' 13
Uniacke, Lily 167, 182, 209, 211

Vanderbilt University *see* Nashville
Vaughan Williams, Ralph 8

Vaughan Williams, Ursula 209
Venuti, Joe 52
Vidal, Gore 370
Vogue 74

Wain, John 33, 37, 44–5, 54, 65, 68, 73,
    75, 79, 88, 95, 96, 115, 124, 127,
    258, 293, 369
    'Ambiguous Gifts' 76
    Contenders, The 124
    Hurry On Down 75, 76–8, 88, 123
    Living in the Present 75, 124, 369
    Mixed Feelings 75
    'Music on the Water' 45
    Strike the Father Dead 45
Waley, Arthur 34
Waller, Mr ('Big') 10, 12
Waller, Mr ('Little') 10
Waller, Thomas ('Fats') 29, 30
Walton, William 8
Watkins, Alan 202
Waugh, Evelyn 67, 90, 158, 291, 296
    Brideshead Revisited 32, 44, 90, 292,
        300
    Decline and Fall 158
Wechsler, James 115
Wells, Alexandra 291–2
Wells, H.G. 12
    War of the Worlds, The 12
West, David 26
West, Fred 303–04, 351
West Norwood 4, 8
Westcott, Isabel 64
Wharton, Gordon 95
Whitehouse, Mary 325
Whittome, Anthony 205
Who, The 277
Widdowson, Wally 26
Wilde, Oscar 64
Williams, David 26
Williams, Gillian 29, 51, 55
Williamson, T B. 16
Wilson, A.N. 215, 327, 372
Wilson, Angus 89, 90, 126, 150, 305,
    310, 310–11, 368
    Anglo-Saxon Attitudes 89
    As If By Magic 310–11
    Bit off the Map and Other Stories, A
        89
    Late Call 150
    No Laughing Matter 150
    Old Men at the Zoo, The 150
Wilson, Colin 90

Wilson, Harold 147
Windsor, Duchess of 43
Winters, Yvor 97
Wizard 11, 14
Woolf, Virginia 90, 113, 158, 375
Wordsworth, Jonathan 283, 289, 294
Wordsworth, William 24, 169, 358, 359
    Prelude, The 359
Wormald, Brian 126

Worsthorne, Peregrine 171
Wylie, Andrew 352–3

Yeats, W.B. 151, 211, 369
Yevtushenko, Yevgeny 168, 239
Young, Hugo 325
    Iron Lady, The 325

Zeegan, Ronald 256

Visit **www.panmacmillan.com** to read more about all our books and to buy them. You will also find features, author interviews and news of any author events, and you can sign up for e-newsletters so that you're always first to hear about our new releases.